Constitutional Ambiguity and the Interpretation of Presidential Power

SUNY series in American Constitutionalism

Robert J. Spitzer, editor

SUNY series on the Presidency: Contemporary Issues

Robert P. Watson, editor

Constitutional Ambiguity and the Interpretation of Presidential Power

RICHARD W. WATERMAN

SUNY
PRESS

Published by State University of New York Press, Albany

For information, contact State University of New York Press, Albany, NY
www.sunypress.edu

Library of Congress Cataloging-in-Publication Data

Name: Waterman, Richard W. author.
Title: Constitutional ambiguity and the interpretation of presidential
    power / Richard W. Waterman.
Description: Albany : State University of New York Press, [2025] | Series:
    SUNY series in American Constitutionalism | Includes bibliographical
    references and index.
Identifiers: LCCN 2024033997 | ISBN 9798855801200 (hardcover : alk. paper) |
    ISBN 9798855801187 (ebook) | ISBN 9798855801194 (pbk. : alk. paper)
Subjects: LCSH: Executive power—United States—Interpretation and
    construction. | Constitutional law—United States. | Constitutional
    history—United States.
Classification: LCC KF5053 .W38 2025 | DDC 342.73/062—dc23/eng/20241018
LC record available at https://lccn.loc.gov/2024033997

*This book is dedicated to two political scientists
who played a primary role in my career:
Woodrow Jones and Joseph Stewart*

Undefined powers are discretionary powers, limited only by the object for which they were given.

—Alexander Hamilton

Contents

Introduction   1

Chapter 1 Constitutional Ambiguity and Presidential Power   5

Chapter 2 Writing a New Constitution   23

Chapter 3 Constitutional Ambiguity   57

Chapter 4 Obstacles to the Interpretation of the Constitution
           in Early America   81

Chapter 5 The Sovereign Power and Constitutional Interpretation 115

Chapter 6 A Strict Interpretation of the Constitution   161

Chapter 7 A Living Constitution   203

Chapter 8 The Unitary Executive Theory   219

Chapter 9 The Constitution and the Supreme Practical Test   257

Notes   269

References   273

Index   313

Introduction

There are people who would curtail the duties our Chief Executive because they think that the President has too much power. And there are people who do not trust the President on specific issues, while others want to tie his hands for personal reasons, or for the benefit of certain groups. What the Presidency needs is a continuing study and a broader understanding of its powers and duties.

—Harry Truman, *Mr. Citizen*, 171

The main theme of this book is that constitutional ambiguity provides the foremost opportunity for presidents to the expand their power. Presidents interpret the Constitution's silences, as well as its various nebulous nooks and crannies, to discover new powers that are not clearly enumerated. Though many scholars recognize the existence and role of constitutional ambiguity, a detailed analysis of this concept is required, for at this time in our nation's history legal experts and presidential scholars are concerned with the vast expansion of presidential power without a counterbalancing method of accountability, leading to the rise of autocracy (e.g., Hetherington and Weiler 2009; Matheson 2009; Posner and Vermeule 2010; Levitsky and Ziblatt 2018; Mounk 2018; McConnell 2020; Prakash 2020; Yoo 2020). A key question then is whether America is on the verge of establishing a strongman or autocratic presidency and whether constitutional ambiguity is contributing to this development (Howell and Moe 2023). To explore this issue, I examine books, pamphlets, and other writings from various observers of the American presidency and the Constitution from the Founding to the present day, creating what Alexander Bickel (1962) described as a "continuing colloquy" on the meaning of the US Constitution, in this case in its relationship to presidential power.

Many individuals observed presidential power in the eighteenth, nineteenth, and early twentieth centuries (i.e., before the advent of the *modern* or *imperial presidency*, which are the primary focus of much contemporary work). The observers I cite often provide a different viewpoint on presidential power. It is important to rediscover their insights, particularly since much of the material I cite has been unobserved by presidential and constitutional scholars for far more than a century. I also examine three primary methods of interpreting the Constitution. The first, a strict constructionist approach, has been criticized for establishing a presidency that is too weak and ineffectual. The second, the idea that the Constitution is organic, flexible, and living, provides the basis for the accretion of presidential power but does not set limits upon it. The third, the unitary executive theory is of recent derivation and is specifically designed to promote a stronger presidency. Each of these theoretical frameworks find support in different interpretations of the Constitution, with the latter two benefiting considerably from constitutional ambiguity.

My Approach

> It is not immediately clear . . . whether the insights from the rich theoretical and empirical literature rooted in the study of the modern presidency transfer to the study of presidents who served in earlier years and who were likely to have quite different incentive structures. Enhancing our knowledge about how earlier presidents affected the nation's policy making is consequential not simply because our understanding of the historical presidency is not as richly detailed as it could be.
>
> —Jon Rogowski, "The Historical Presidency," 797

To examine these important issues, I include references from an eclectic assemblage of observers of the presidency: the Framers and others from the Founding generation, judges (in their written opinions and other writings), presidents, members of Congress, experts in both constitutional law and theory, historians, political scientists, public administrators, journalists, economists, military practitioners, teachers, religious figures, literary scholars, poets, composers, ordinary citizens, and overseas commentators. In addition to the Constitution's words, the notes from the Constitutional Convention, the Framers' writings, *The Federalist Papers* and *Anti-Federalist*

Papers, the debates from the ratifying conventions, laws passed by Congress, judicial decisions, and presidential statements/directives, I examine memoirs, biographies, speeches, diaries, letters, newspapers, pamphlets, and government documents. To ensure generalizability, I include observations from each decade from the Founding to the present time. Rather than summarize this material, such as simply listing several publications that reflect one specific point of view, I permit the constitutional observers to speak for themselves, sometimes at considerable length, for which I ask the reader's forbearance. I do not mean to test your patience, but rather to reflect the frank viewpoints of these observers as accurately as possible.

Why is it important to examine the perspective of copious observers of the presidency in a variety of different fields? After all, most studies of presidential power are written by constitutional lawyers, historians, and political scientists. While each discipline offers a diversity of viewpoints, there also are significant divisions of opinion across them. For example, Morton Horwitz (1992, 9) wrote, "The separation between law and politics has always been a central aspiration of American legal scholars." And eminent legal scholar Richard Posner (2016, 35) explained, "While the topic of presidential leadership has fascinated political scientists and historians for decades, legal scholars have ignored it. Legal scholars rarely discuss 'leadership'—of the president or anyone else. They are concerned with the legal constraints on the presidency, not the opportunities that the office supplies to its occupant." Meanwhile, Louis Fisher (2014, 4) opined, "Legal analysts, when narrowly applied, can become hypertechnical and divorced from important principles. The framers were not primarily theoreticians. Those who drafted the Constitution and fought for its ratification had served in public life and wanted a government that would function effectively."

As for the perspective that historians bring to the table, C. A. Woody (1886, 4), a principal from the public schools of LaPort City, Iowa, advised, "What can or should be more interesting to the young American than the recital of his nation's history,—the grandest chronicled in the thousands of years of the world's existence—a history replete with the exploits of heroism; romantic in its characters of patriotism and love of liberty; rich in its examples of eloquence, with and logic; unprecedented in mental and moral development, in inventions, increase in population, and progress in every particular. The teacher who can not make United States History interesting has surely missed his calling." In the most laudatory terms possible, Meade Minnigerode (1924, 51) described the politics of the 1840s: "Heaven, and historians, alone know, now, what it was all about." That may be true, but as James McGregor Burns (1965, 95) stated, "American historiography has changed a good deal since the last century, especially in its greater concern with economic, intellectual, social, and other forces. Yet this shift has taken place with little apparent diminution in the belief in the central and critical role of the President in influencing history and bringing about change and progress." Julian Zelizer (2012, 19) also identified a "presidential-centered history with an emphasis on the expanding power of the office." Stephen Skowronek (2015, 14) advised that it is important to understand both the individual presidents and the office they occupy: "How the history of the institution is narrated depends a lot on how the contributions of individual incumbents are interpreted, and how the contributions of individual incumbents depends a lot on how we understand the institution and its place in the larger governing scheme. Nonetheless, each pole anchors a distinct set of concerns." As to the broad sweep of history, Martin Fausold (1991, 246) commented, "Most historians believe that tensions in the American constitutional system are to be expected. . . . Historians, however, are not inclined to see that the tensions or attendant problems can be significantly lessened by new constitutional arrangements."

As for the viewpoint of political scientists, Charles Thach (1923, ix) wrote, "An eminent political scientist has been heard to remark that, while all political scientists necessarily know some history, there are but few historians who know political science." Meanwhile, Alan Shank (1991, 247) advised, "Using historical precedents, the political scientists agree there is an evolutionary constitutional development of the presidency. But they no longer find heroes in the White House. . . . Political scientists find recurring patterns of constitutional conflict in the Cold War (1945–1989) and in domestic policy stagnation (at least since Johnson's Great Society)." Regarding the differences between political science and legal studies, Frank Goodnow (1904, 40), then the president of the American Political Science Association, commented, "Unless we conceive of all law as a part of Political Science, it becomes necessary then to differentiate Political Science from legal science. Strictly speaking, of course all law which does not affect the relations of the State and its officers is to be assigned to legal rather than to Political Science." Most books on the president's constitutional authority provide but one disciplinary viewpoint. I examine different perspectives across time to develop a more generalizable and reliable focus on the changing nature and scope of presidential power.

Chapter 1

Constitutional Ambiguity and Presidential Power

The real danger to the Constitution lies in the gradual erosion of its principles, as from time to time, in the excesses of party strife, some one of these principles is so ignored that it ceases to be of vital force. . . . Unhappily a written form of government is not a Gibraltar that can resist the waves, but a sandy beach, which, while it seems to beat back the devouring waters, is always losing in the struggle. Each decade sees some principle of the Constitution either weakened or nullified, and the difficulty is that the people are only sensible of their peril after the principle is destroyed, and when it is too late to restore it.

—James Beck, *The Vanishing Rights of the States*

Presently, America is at a crossroads in its history, as exemplified by the insurrection of January 6, 2021, and the presidency of Donald John Trump. The supreme practical test of any constitution is whether it can prevail in times of conflict and stress. While our nation faces an uncertain future, we have confronted this supreme practical test before. In a November 26, 1860, letter to his brother, William Tecumseh Sherman (Thorndike 1894, 86) wrote, "If by a successful revolution [the Southern states] can go out of the Union, they establish a principle that will break up the government into fragments. Some local disaffection or temporary excitement will lead one State after another out of the Union. . . . If so, shall the government resist? If so, then comes a fearful subject for Americans to think of."

5

Herman Belz (1969, 1) wrote, "The American Civil War, itself the product of constitutional disagreement, created a constitutional crisis as difficult and significant as any ever faced by the American people." Presidents, judges, lawyers, scholars, and politicians were confronted with more-than-theoretical questions regarding the Constitution's meaning—among these questions, the scope of presidential power and a new concept: the war power. Consequently, the Civil War and Reconstruction represented a period of rejuvenated interest in the Constitution. As Alfred Conkling (1866, 3) wrote after the war, "One of the consequences of the Rebellion has been to awaken public attention more strongly than it had yet been, to a great problem of constitutional law; a problem of transcendent importance, and demanding the earnest and dispassionate consideration of the American people."

Today there likewise is a rejuvenated interest in the Constitution as we confront a substantial accretion of presidential power. Simply stated, presidential power has been transformed entirely since the Framers wrote the Constitution in 1787, and yet not one word of Article II, which identifies the president's powers and duties, has been changed. How and why then has the power of the presidency expanded? While the Constitution is an amazing document, it includes copious examples of undefined power. For example, one of the lawyers who worked in Abraham Lincoln's War Department, Timothy Farrar (1867, 430, 438), addressed the definitional issues with the executive vesting clause:

> By Article II., "The executive power shall be vested in a President of the United States." This declares the essential and perfect unity of the executive department. . . . In this sentence, the nature of the power is not otherwise defined than by its name; but it is obvious from that only, that the "executive power" can be nothing but the executive power of the government, which must mean the power to execute the Constitution and all the laws made under it.

Early in the twentieth century, Clarence Berdahl (1921, 11) described the Article II vesting clause: "The lack of such express limitations in the article dealing with the Executive has led to some difference of opinion as to whether the executive power vested in the President by the Constitution is defined and limited by the following specified powers, or whether it includes other powers not enumerated but naturally executive in character." Why then were the president's constitutional powers undefined? Carl Swisher (1951, 334) asserted, "The Constitution was vague about the character and scope of executive power not because of poor draftsmanship but because of uncertainty in the thinking of the framers and their inability to reach agreement." The Constitution's undefined nature led eminent constitutional scholar Edward Corwin (1957 edition, 2, 4) to ask a fundamental question about the executive vesting clause: "Do these words comprise a grant of power or are they merely a designation of office? . . . If the former, then how are we to explain the more specific clauses of grant in the ensuing sections of the same article?" More recently, Akhil Amar (2006, 186) answered, "The opening language of Article II gave the president a supple textual mandate to act in various situations that might be impossible to define in advance . . . without a companion catalogue of concrete powers and limitations, the open-ended words at the outset of Article II would have been dangerously indeterminant, failing to exemplify the general sort of executive power America envisioned and to qualify this power in key ways" (see also Mortenson 2019, 2020; Natelson 2009). Consequently, William Howell and David Brent (2013, 63–64) inquired, "What does it mean . . . to vest the president with the 'executive power'; and then to require the president to 'take care' that the laws of the United States are 'duly and faithfully executed'? This question, of course, implies other ancillary ones." Hence, Judson Landon (1889, 129), a preeminent legal scholar of the nineteenth century, advised that the president "has the undefined power to take care that the laws shall be faithfully executed," and Michael Herz (1993, 252–53) advised, "The use of the passive voice in the Take Care Clause indicates that the President will not necessarily be executing the laws directly, but only overseeing others to ensure their 'faithful' execution." On this point, James Monroe's attorney general William Wirt (McConnell 2020, 345) advised, "The constitution assigns to Congress the power of designating the duties of particular officers: the President is only required to take care that they execute them faithfully" (see also Garvey 2014; Mader 2022). Regarding the clause's meaning, Jack Goldsmith and John Manning (2016, 1838) wrote, "The Court treats the meaning of the clause as obvious when it is anything but that. The Court's decisions rely heavily on the Take Care Clause but almost never interpret it, at least not in any conventional way."

Questions have been raised about other Article II clauses, such as the recess appointment and the meaning of the word adjournment. And John Fairlie (1905, 4) noted, "What class of positions come within the term 'inferior officers' has never been carefully defined, and probably cannot be determined with exactness." A dozen years later, Westel Willoughby (1917, 489) stated, "The Constitution does not define the term 'inferior officers,' but it would appear that in this class are included all officers subordinate or inferior to those officers; in whom other appointments may be vested." And three years later Everett Kimball (1920, 183) stated, "The term 'inferior officer' is not defined by the Constitution, but would seem to mean those in whom the power of appointment may not be vested; that is, persons other than heads of departments, or judges, or the president himself." The courts then grappled with this definitional issue in such cases as *Ex Parte Siebold*, 100 U.S. 371, 373 (1879), and *United States v. Mouat*, 124 U.S. 303 8 S. Ct. 505 31 L. Ed. 463 (1888).

According to B. A. Hinsdale (1895, 272), the treaty power similarly is undefined: "The character and scope of the treaty-making power . . . is not defined, and could not well be defined, in the Constitution, and we must go to the Law of Nations for such a definition." And no power is more important to the presidency today than the office of commander-in-chief. And yet, as President James K. Polk noted in his "Special Message to Congress" on January 2, 1849: "The manner of conducting the war is not defined by the Constitution." During World War II, Louis Koenig (1944, 42) advised, "The office of commander-in-chief is a source of considerable and undefined power." Controversy continued into the postwar era. Samuel Huntington (1985 edition, 178) professed, "The [commander-in-chief] clause is unique in the Constitution in that it grants authority in the form of an office rather than in the form of a *function*. . . . This difference in form is of considerable importance. By defining the presidential power as an office, the Framers left undefined its specific powers and functions." With America on the cusp of war in Vietnam, Rowland Eggers (1963, 105) stated, "If the Constitution creates dilemmas in foreign-policy processes as a result of the vagueness and ambiguity with which it allocates authority for the conduct of international relations, the dilemmas created by the war-powers provisions are equally profound." At the end of the Vietnam War, Gerald Jenkins (1974, 142) wrote, "The struggle has its origins in the ambiguities of the Constitution" (see Bimbilovsky 2009). The following decade, Henry Cox (1984, 1) queried, "Why did presidents engage in military commitments without congressional authorization? Which controls over warmaking were reserved for Congress? By what criteria were delegations of discretionary authority made to the president? Why did Congress either willingly—or not so willingly—forfeit this authority?

What attempts did legislators make to dominate the course of foreign relations, and why?"

In the last decade of the twentieth century, Michael Glennon (1990, 71–72) noted, "The scope of the President's plenary power to make war has been the subject of sustained controversy." Attention to ambiguity has continued into the twenty-first century. Carl Cooper Jr. (2005, 6) of the Defense Technical Information Center advised, "The debate on where the Constitutional authority to make war resides is older than the Constitution itself," and Ingrid Wuerth (2007, 62) stated, "The Commander in Chief Clause is widely understood as a particularly difficult arc of constitutional interpretation." Finally, Gary Lawson (2008, 381) wrote, "The evident import of the clause is to establish a chain of command rather than to define the scope of the Commander-in-Chief s power."

These are but a select few citations from scholars regarding the undefined nature of the president's Article II powers. What is of interest, however, is the vast nature of questions raised by scholars and legal experts across the broad scope of American history. While some level of disagreement is to be expected, the fact that the courts were forced to address so many of these issues reflects the presence of ambiguities in the meaning of Article II's provisions. Yet, although the literature is rife with references to constitutional ambiguity there is no single volume dedicated to an examination of this topic and its impact on presidential power. Why then is such a volume warranted?

Presidential Power is Dangerous

America to-day is in a somber, soul-questioning mood. We are in a period of clamor, of bewilderment, of an almost tremendous unrest. We are hastily revising our social conceptions. We are hastily testing all our political ideals. . . . Today, more than ever before in American history, dire prophesies gain credence. Some foretell the dissolution of the Republic and the rise under democratic forms of an absolutist empire. . . . Grave men hope or fear a sudden destructive cataclysm, in which the ponderous pillars of our society will fall upon a blind and wretched people. Revolutionary and reactionary agitators are alike disillusioned. They no longer place their faith upon our traditional democracy.

—Walter Weyl, *The New Democracy*, 1912

Long before the insurrection of January 6, 2021, which for the first time in American history threatened the peaceful transfer of presidential power, there were deep concerns with the prospect of increasing presidential power. In an early work on American government, Augustus Woodward (1809, 12) wrote,

> The first shock which our government must sustain, endangering its existence, or menacing its stability, must be derived from the executive department. It is here the storm will arise; and in this quarter may we expect the first blow to our union. It is here the mind of the patriot must dwell, with an anxious solicitude; and watch, with an unceasing vigilance. Happy will it be for America, if, foreseeing, with her usual prudence, her dangers at a distance, she neglects not her protection from the violence of the tempest, until her exertions can no longer be availing! The existing construction of the executive department of the government of the United States of America is perhaps not perfectly adapted to the tranquil and steady administration of the affairs of this growing and stupendous republic. Gradually must it become less so, as its population advances; and as its interests multiply.

Then, in what may very well be the first book ever published exclusively about the American presidency, Woodward (1825, 53) wrote, "Two evils might attach to the relationship between the legislative and the executive power. First, the legislative power might be under the influence of the executive power. Secondly, the legislative might control the executive power—in the exercise of its exclusive and legitimate functions. Too unfortunately, both these evils exist in our government."

Other observers of the presidency likewise expressed their concerns with power in general. In the late nineteenth century, Albert Stickney (1879, 61) commented, "There never has been a government on the face of the earth where the men have not used the power that the law gave them. There never will be one." Or as Bertrand Russell ([1938] 1996, 3) affirmed, "Of the infinite desires of man, the chief are the desires for power and glory." One of the Framers of the Constitution, George Mason (Farrand 1913, 578) similarly stated, "From the nature of man we may be sure, that those who have power in their hands . . . will always . . . increase it." Henceforth, the Framers established a constitution with a labyrinth of checks and balances and separations of powers to ensure that neither of the three branches could encroach upon the power of the others. And yet even Madison's political patron had his reservations about the new Constitution. As Peter Henriques (2006, 109) found, "Jefferson . . . had been extremely critical of the Constitution's failure to limit the number of terms an individual could be president, for he feared it would lead to monarchy, and, if there was anything that Jefferson opposed, it was monarchy." He was not alone. Bruce Ackerman (2005, 5) noted, "When [the Framers] looked at the presidency, the Convention feared a demagogue, and it designed the electoral college to reduce the chances that a political opportunist could ascend to power. But the onset of party competition undermined its basic premises." Meanwhile, Stephen Knott (2019, 1) contended, "The American founders, especially those who considered themselves Federalists, understood that moderation and stability have their place and that constant upheaval is not healthy for a political order. . . . The American founders also understood something many twentieth-century presidents did not: that the more you expand the roles of responsibilities of the presidency, the more you diminish it."

Concerns regarding presidential power appeared as soon as the Constitution was published, such as in an *Independent Chronicle* article published in December 1787 in response to Benjamin Franklin's endorsement of the Constitution: "Does not every man know, that nothing is more liable to be abused than power. Power, without a check, in any hands, is tyranny; and such powers, in the hands of even *good men*, so infatuating is the nature of it, will probably be wantonly, if not tyrannically exercised. The world has had experience enough of this, in every stage of it" (Bailyn 1993, 1:6). In *The Federalist Papers no. 67*, Alexander Hamilton defended the presidency against such charges: "The writers against the Constitution seem to have taken pains to signalize their talent of misrepresentation. Calculating upon the aversion of the people to monarchy, they have endeavored to enlist all their jealousies and apprehensions in opposition to the intended President of the United States; not merely as the embryo, but as the full-grown progeny, of that detested parent. To establish the pretended affinity, they have not scrupled to draw resources even from the regions of fiction."

Hamilton favored a strong presidency, but other contemporaries were more concerned with the potential abuse of presidential power and the lack of accountability to control such power. At the Virginia Ratifying Convention, Anti-Federalist William Grayson noted (Elliot 1900, 3:491),

"If you give the executive extensive powers for so long a time as this government is organized, it would be dangerous to trust the President with such powers. How will you punish him if he abuses his power? Will you call him before the Senate? They are his counsellors and partners in crime. Where are your checks? We ought to be extremely cautious in this country. If ever the government be changed, it will probably be into a despotism." Writing in 1798 during the presidency of John Adams, William Manning (Kammen 1987, xxiii) stated, "The Federal Constitution by a fair construction is a good one prinsapaly, but I have no dout but that the Convention who made it intended to destroy our free governments by it, or they neaver would have spent 4 Months in making such an inexpliset thing. As one said at the time of its adoption, it is made like a Fiddle, with but few Strings, but so that the ruling Majority could play any tune upon it they please."[1]

Such concerns were expressed throughout American history. For example, during the Civil War, Sidney George Fisher (1862, 266) wrote, "It is thus clear that the proper organization of Executive power is a problem yet to be solved." And shortly after the war, Louis Jennings (1868, 35–37) commented, "It has been often represented that the Executive Department of the United States government is the most powerful and the least under control known to any country. Although there were bounds prescribed in the Constitution beyond which the President could not pass, yet those bounds seemed too elastic for the public safety, and the most accomplished American statesmen and constitutional writers have expressed misgivings lest one day the liberties of the people should be invaded."

Concerns continued well into the twentieth century. In his memoirs written shortly after he left office, former president Herbert Hoover (1952, 104) expressed his concerns: "I had felt deeply that no President should undermine the independence of the legislative and judicial branches by seeking to discredit them. The constitutional division of powers is the bastion of our liberties and was not designed as a battleground to display the prowess of Presidents. They just have to work with the material that God—and the voters—have given them." Still, the Great Depression, which wreaked havoc on Hoover's presidency, was the very kind of emergency that generates presidential power. Thus, during Franklin Roosevelt's first term, Irving Brant (1936, 19) stated, "The cry against concentration of power in America is older than the Constitution. It rang through colonial halls in the period of parturition and was heard in the accouchement chamber where the Federal Union was born. Today, and in all the todays that aggregate our national history, it is and has been the loudest, most piercing sound in the ears of the American people." During Roosevelt's second term, former US solicitor general James Beck (1939, 373) argued, "If history teaches us anything, it has had one consistent lesson, and that is that one man power is fatal to liberty. We cannot safely ignore the significance of this change in the *ethos* of the people. It has disturbed the equilibrium of government, against which Washington so eloquently warned in his Farewell Address." And the same year, John Foster Dulles (1939, 33) inscribed,

> No nation of large population and complex economy can claim to have found a method of assuring a political system which will perfectly perform its intended function. . . . Sooner or later failure is inevitable as a result of misjudging the weight of conflicting desires, or misjudging the means of satisfying those that predominate. It is equally inevitable that when failure occurs there will be an effort to change the "authority." Therefore, if civil war is to be avoided, there must be provided a peaceful means for periodically changing the nature and personnel of the "authority."

Apprehensions with presidential power continued during World War II. Louis Koenig (1944, 17) advised, "The danger of executive powers in crisis, even from the standpoint of the Presidency, may lurk in abundance. With a plentitude of power at his command, the President may undertake too much." After the war, William Munro (1946, 186) commented, "The framers of the Constitution faced a difficult problem in determining what powers should be given to the President . . . it seemed . . . important to place limits upon these presidential powers lest they be utilized to create an executive absolutism. In short, the problem was to create an executive sufficiently strong to ensure the faithful execution of the laws and yet not so strong as to open the door for a presidential dictatorship."

The next decade, Edward Corwin and Louis Koenig (1956, vii) asked, "Should one man have available the immense powers that are today the President's for the asking—indeed, for the taking?" Controversies continued during the 1960s and 1970s with the Vietnam War. As a result, during the presidency of Lyndon Johnson, Carl Friedrich (1967, 19) opined, "A primary consideration in working out the presidency was to prevent it from becoming a despotic or tyrannical office in the sense of concentrating arbitrary power in the hands of the man occupying it. However the actual separation is worked out . . . there is always present the notion that power must not be concentrated." That same year, in testimony before the Senate Foreign Relations Committee, Ruhl Bartlett declared (Goldsmith 1980, 5), "It is the greatest danger of democracy in the United States and to the freedom of its people and their welfare—as far as foreign affairs are concerned—is the erosion of legislative authority and oversight and the growth of a vast pyramid of centralized power in the Executive Branch of the Government."

During the Watergate scandal with Richard Nixon in the Oval Office, Charles Hardin (1974, 1) concluded, "In 1973 America was gripped by its gravest political crisis since the Civil War. The president all too often was out of control . . . the heritage of Washington, Jefferson, and Lincoln—so long miraculously intact—was crumbling to dust." Additionally, Arthur Schlesinger Jr. (2004a edition, 9) wrote, "The belief of the Nixon Administration in its own mandate and in its own virtue, compounded by its conviction that the republic has been in mortal danger from internal enemies, has produced an unprecedented concentration of power in the White House and an unprecedented attempt to transform the presidency of the Constitution into a plebiscitary presidency."

By the presidency of George W. Bush, Stephen Graubard (2004, xii) averred, "An America that rebelled against the mother country, imagining it would have no further truck with kings, courtiers, or warriors, has since the beginning of the twentieth century known all, rarely so identified, but unmistakably as such." And following Donald Trump's presidency, William Howell and Terry Moe (2023, 145) advised, "Donald Trump exposed the fragility of American democracy. He did it by simply exercising his powers as president and pushing them to the hilt." The authors concluded that we face the real danger of a "strongman presidency" (see also Hennessey and Wittes 2020). With autocracy on the rise around the world, and with the potential for an autocratic presidency, in recent years various scholars (e.g., Matheson 2009; Posner and Vermeule 2011; McConnell 2020; Prakash 2015; 2020; Yoo 2020) have advocated either a stronger or more accountable presidency. The key question, then, is this: Are we on the precipice of such a radical development that would fundamentally alter the Constitution's carefully constructed checks and balances? And if so, how is it possible that the Constitution can be interpreted to allow for such an expansion of presidential power?

Regarding the first question, not everyone agrees that presidential power is dangerous. Harry Truman told Merle Miller (1974, 375), "There's always a lot of talk about how we have to fear the man on horseback, have to be afraid of the . . . strong man, but so far, if I read my American history right, it isn't the strong men that have caused us most of the trouble, it's the ones who were weak. It's the ones who just sat on their asses and twiddled their thumbs when they were President." There was, in fact, a long tradition of such sentiment. Saikrishna Prakash (2015) cited an impressive array of viewpoints from the ratification debates demonstrating that many observers advocated an even stronger presidency than the Constitution promised. Meanwhile, "John Adams had definite convictions concerning the role of the executive and legislative branches in a democracy, and he refused to minimize the executive's responsibilities" (Brown 1975, 210). Adams argued in his *Defence of the Constitutions of Government of the United States*, "If there is one certain truth to be collected from the history of all ages, it is this: that the people's rights and liberties, and the democratic mixture in a constitution, can never be preserved without a strong executive, or, in other words without separating the executive power from the legislature." As Gordon Wood (2017, 177, 185, 190) revealed, "No American was more infatuated with the English Constitution" than Adams. "The English Constitution that Adams admired in 1779 was the one interpreted by the Swiss jurist Jean Louis De Lolme in his *La Constitution de l'Angleterre* first published in French at Amsterdam in 1771." It was "De Lombe's new understanding of the English constitution as a struggle between aristocracy and democracy that took on a heightened meaning for Adams." At the commencement of the French Revolution, Adams wrote a series of essays under the title "Discourses on Davila." However, two men responsible for the Declaration of Independence, Adams and Thomas Jefferson, disagreed on the nature and extent of presidential power. In a December 6, 1787, exchange of letters with Jefferson, Adams noted, "You are afraid of one [the president]—I, of the few [e.g., the Senate]. We agree perfectly that the man should have a full fair and perfect Representation.—You are Apprehensive about Monarchy; I, of Aristocracy. I would therefore have given more Power to the President and less to the Senate" (Adams 2016, 63).

The debate over the appropriate extent of presidential power therefore precedes the Constitution and continues to this very day. Furthermore, the concern with presidential power is no longer simply a theoretical issue. The insurrection of January 6 threatened the very foundation of a democratic government: the idea of free and fair elections. In its executive summary of the events precipitating this event, the House Select Committee in 2022 recommended former president Donald Trump be charged with series of offenses against the government that he then led including four criminal charges. The summary also identified specific violations of the US Constitution including the oath of office, the take care clause, and the commander-in-chief power.

Consequently, presidential power may be the very threat that many of the Founders feared, at least when power falls into the wrong hands. And the threat has not ended. Whether Donald Trump is reelected or not, he provided a roadmap for how to expand presidential power far beyond the Framers' intent. His model of expansive presidential power is there for any future president, Republican or Democrat, to seize (Bauer and Goldsmith 2020). How then can America avoid a decline into an autocratic or strongman presidency? The answer would be easy if we were able to identify a priori the types of presidents who expanded presidential power. But that, in turn, raises another difficulty.

Who Are the Dictators and Demagogues?

> I believe that the constitution, if reverently preserved, obeyed, and acted out in practice, will insure the stability and continuance of the Government, and the liberty and prosperity of the people. And I believe, as confidently, that, if the constitution be, habitually, broken and despised, by men in office, the Government will lose all hold upon the affection and respect of the people, and will become weak, irregular and arbitrary, fluctuating, from day to day, with the changing passions of men and factions.
>
> —Edward Bates, *The Diary of Edward Bates 1859–1866*

One of the first textbooks to examine the potential for abuse of power was published in 1796: Elhanan Winchester's "plain political catechism" for the students of Pennsylvania. Winchester (1796, 56–57) asked, "Is there any real danger of our government degenerating into tyranny?" His answer, "It is impossible, while an equal and free election continues, and the constitution remains even what it is now." Winchester's optimism masked a basic problem that he could not have foreseen. Abuse of power could be rectified if it was merely a matter of identifying demonstrably dangerous presidents. Yet, as former senator George Hoar (1903, 1:214) commented in his autobiography, "We should be deaf and blind to all the lessons of history, if we were to declare it to be safe that men trusted with Executive or even with Legislative power should act on that [moral, constitutional] principle. Unfortunately, humanity is so constituted that the benevolent despot is likely to work more mischief even than a malevolent despot." Furthermore, as Augustus Woodward (1809, 12–13) wrote, "The President of the United States, during the term for which he is elected, is invested with the prerogatives of a monarch. These powers are almost too great to be exercised, with undeviating correctness, by any individual mind; however energetic, and however enlightened."

Who then might these benevolent despots be? Frederic Stimson (1907, 511) argued,

England always lost her liberties under her most popular kings; and the rights and safety of the people are never so much in danger as when they themselves are willing to subordinate their liberty birthrights to the passion for equality or other immediate ends. It was under Elizabeth, Henry VIII, George III, that the English constitution was most at stake. So ours has been strained to its breaking-point, not by Andrew Johnson or Franklin Pierce, but by Jefferson, Lincoln and [Theodore] Roosevelt.

Many observers of the presidency likewise noted the growth of presidential power during Lincoln's presidency, though they did so with considerable admiration. Adolphe de Chambrun (1874, 256) commented, "Within a period of four years, a vigorous executive, wielding formidable powers, came forth from the confusion and anarchy into which the country had been thrown in the beginning of 1861. Under the control of unprecedented circumstances these powers, step by step, attained such proportions that President Lincoln, with a stroke of the pen, broke the fetters of 4,000,000 slaves. Nothing could then longer resist his will." Meanwhile, Englishman James Lothrop Motley (1889, 170) wrote, "I venerate Abraham Lincoln exactly because he is the true honest type of American Democracy. There is nothing of the shabby genteel, the would-be-but-couldn't-be fine gentleman; he is the great American Demos, honest, shrewd, homely, wise, humorous, cheerful, brave, blundering occasionally, but through blunders struggling onward towards what he believes the right."

Yet Lincoln greatly expanded presidential power, establishing important precedents for his successors. As Caleb Patterson (1947, 66) wrote, "On the floor of Congress Lincoln was repeatedly called 'tyrant,' 'usurper,' 'despot,' 'absolute as the Czar of Russia,' 'monarch,' and instigator of 'an absolute irresponsible, uncontrollable government, a perfect military despotism.'" Lincoln was not the only president to be described as a dictator. Clinton Rossiter ([1948] 2011, 3) recognized the existence of a "constitutional dictatorship" during the presidency of Abraham Lincoln, as well as the presidencies of Woodrow Wilson and Franklin Roosevelt. On the eve of America's entry into World War I, Hannis Taylor (1916, 2) wrote, "I have been forced to conclude that no man who ever filled the Presidential office was so opposed to the basic principles for which the Democratic party stands as Mr. Wilson. . . . To use an epithet he once employed in stigmatizing Jefferson, Mr. Wilson is 'a philosophical radical,' intent upon transforming the Presidency of the United States into a Political Dictatorship with himself as its head." As such, Wilson's governing style represented "the new tyranny."

Other scholars argued that FDR's active presidential leadership saved the nation during a period of intense crisis. Talbot Odell (1942, 3) noted, "President Roosevelt, in the crisis of 1933, assumed the leadership which Congress, by its very nature and size, was incapable of furnishing. Many Americans profess to fear that the dictatorship which a state of war or emergency imposes upon the President will spell the end of democracy in this country, yet history clearly demonstrates that democracy flourishes when the Executive is strong and languishes when it is weak." And one of Roosevelt's former aides, Rexford Tugwell (1969, 11) posited that without FDR's leadership, America might well have become a dictatorship, while Lincoln prevented the nation from breaking into two separate countries.

While there was a defense for the expansion of presidential power, there were also concerns. As Wilfred Binkley (1947, 294) identified, "A President who considers himself a tribune of the people, when possessed with an excellent radio voice and a fearless personality will inevitably start powerful interests demanding that Congress resume its 'proper' function of legislation and cease being a 'rubber stamp.' The 'dictator' has been violently condemned in the case of every President of the type under consideration." Such concerns were prominent in the post–World War II years, and by the end of the twentieth century Martin Sheffer (1999, x) wrote, "In times of declared war, the President acts as a 'constitutional dictatorship.' The Constitution is, as Chief Justice Hughes once said, a 'fighting Constitution.' There is a tacit understanding that nothing, literally nothing, will be permitted to block winning the war. What is necessary, as determined by the chief executive, is done. The President's duty is to ensure the national survival. Legal niceties are given little attention." And George W. Bush's first head of the Office of Legal Counsel, John Yoo (2009a, xi; see 2009b), advised, "Certainly, the fear that a President might abuse power for personal gain or to maintain his or her position has haunted America from her birth." What Yoo did not acknowledge was that once presidents invoked emergency powers, they set precedents for future presidents. As such, even if Lincoln, Wilson, and Franklin Roosevelt acted in the best interests of the nation at a time of crisis, they also planted the seeds for future presidents to expand their authority, even in periods where an emergency did not exist.

Emergencies and Presidential Power

Almost all scholars agree that emergencies require strong presidential leadership. Hence, we remember Lincoln for his leadership skills, while denouncing the presidency of his predecessor, James Buchanan, as weak and ineffectual in the face of an existential constitutional crisis. Wilson is venerated for his leadership during World War I, while FDR is honored for his leadership through the Great Depression and World War II. And George W. Bush is credited with his initial strong response to the 9/11 attacks on the World Trade Center in New York and the Pentagon in Washington, DC. Still, precedents were set by these presidents. Is it therefore possible to limit the power presidents have derived from past emergencies? Apparently not. In his memoirs, Herbert Hoover (1952, 357), wrote of the New Deal, "Every collectivist revolution rides in on a Trojan Horse of 'Emergency.' It was a tactic of Lenin, Hitler, and Mussolini. In the collectivist sweep over a dozen minor countries of Europe, it was the cry of the men striving to get on horseback. And 'Emergency' became the justification of the subsequent steps. This technique of creating emergency is the greatest achievement that demagoguery attains. The invasion of the New Deal Collectivism was introduced by this same Trojan Horse."

Claudius Johnson, Daniel Ogden Jr., H. Paul Castleberry, and Thor Swanson (1970, 47) added, "Emergencies, crises, and the many modern functions of government that require executive action have also contributed immeasurably to make [the president] the key figure in government." And the *Final Report of the Special Committee on National Emergencies and Delegated Emergency Power* (US Congress 1976, 1) noted,

> For more than forty years, emergency authority intended for use in crisis situations has been available to the Executive. The President has had extraordinary powers—powers to seize property and commodities, seize control of transportation and communications, organize and control the means of production, assign military forces abroad, and restrict travel. This dangerous state of affairs is a direct result of Congress' failure to establish effective means for the handling of emergencies and its willingness to defer to Executive branch leadership.

Meanwhile, Arthur Schlesinger Jr. ([1973] 2004a, 266) decried, "The theory of the Presidency [Richard Nixon] embodied and propagated meant that the President of the United States, on his own personal and secret finding of emergency, had the right to nullify the Constitution and the law. No President had ever made such a claim before." Schlesinger continued (320–21), "On the whole, Presidents had used these powers with discretion. Still the situation was a mess. There were no standards by which to define national emergencies, nor was there any prescribed procedure by which to invoke, review or end them." And Louis Henkin (1996, 53) wrote, "The Constitution recognizes no 'emergency powers,' whether for the President, or for other branches of the federal government."

The enactment of the National Emergencies Act of 1974 closed many of the existing loopholes created by previous legislation. Still, Donald Trump was able to declare emergency power as a justification for reappropriating money to build a wall between the US and Mexico. He also stated that he possessed extensive emergency power that nobody even knows the presidency has. As Elizabeth Gotein and Andrew Boyle of the *New York Times* reported,[2] "The president is right. Some of the most potent emergency powers at his disposal are likely ones we *can't* know about, because they are not contained in any publicly available laws."

Further raising concerns, E. Pendleton Herring (1940, 16) noted, "Presidential powers in times of emergency really rest upon the imperative of events. Legal considerations have little meaning." Thus, crisis presidents and their successors can use emergencies to permanently extend their authority with the result, as Bruce Ackerman (2010, 4) noted, that "the *very same features* that have made the presidency into the platform for credible tribunes of the People, like Abraham Lincoln or Franklin Roosevelt, are also conspiring, under different conditions, to make it into a vehicle for demagogic populism and lawlessness in the century ahead."

Each of these individuals was concerned with the power of the presidency, a point made frighteningly palpable by polling following the insurrection of January 6, 2021. In May 2021, "Sixty-six percent of voters who identified as Republican in a Quinnipiac Poll . . . said they think [President] Biden's victory was not legitimate."[3] Furthermore, a national survey in 2021 by pollster John Zogby found that "a plurality of Americans (46%) believed a future civil war was likely, 43% felt it was unlikely, and 11% were not sure."[4] The possibility of such extreme violence was then exponentially increased on July 13, 2024 as a result of an attempted assassination of candidate Donald Trump in Butler, Pennsylvania. As Stephen Collinson wrote, "The attempted assassination of Donald Trump, which opens a dark new chapter in America's cursed story of political violence, shook a nation already deeply estranged during one of the most tense periods of its modern history."[5]

Given these serious concerns, understanding the nature of presidential power is not merely an academic question. It has significant implications for our nation's future. As I will demonstrate, a copious citation of the constitutional and presidential literature across American history demonstrates a consistent concern with ambiguity, and it provides the rocket fuel for the accretion of presidential power. I therefore examine how the Constitution was written and how much attention the Framers dedicated to a discussion of the president's powers and duties, as well as various methods of constitutional interpretation.

Chapter 2

Writing a New Constitution

Analysis of the US Constitution first occurred in the various writings of the Framers, at the state ratifying conventions, and in sundry pamphlets. There also was much discussion of the Constitution through an exchange of letters between two Founders who were far from Philadelphia in 1787 and one who played a principal role at the convention. These remarkable letters reveal the inner thoughts of these key players in the development of the presidency as well as disclosing their concerns about the Constitution. The exchange demonstrates that even at a distance, Adams and Jefferson had a direct impact on the theory and substance of the new Constitution. As such, it is worth examining them in some detail.

These communications occurred slowly across the Atlantic Ocean. The first exchange occurred between James Madison and Thomas Jefferson (June 6, 1787), and it involved the impact of John Adams's book *The Defence of the Constitutions of Government of the United States* on convention delegates and the broader public. Though he admitted that there was some merit to Adams's musings, Madison was largely critical of Adams's book and hoped that it would not be taken seriously by either other delegates or the public. In response, on June 28, Jefferson expressed his own ideas for a new government (Smith 1995, 1:480):

> The idea of separating the executive business of the confederacy from Congress, as the judiciary is already to some degree, is just and necessary. I had frequently pressed on the members individually, while in Congress, the doing this by a resolution of Congress for appointing an Executive committee to act during

the sessions of Congress, as the Committee of the states was to act during their vacations. But the referring to this Committee all executive business as it should present itself, would require a more persevering self-denial that I supposed Congress to possess. It will be much better to make that separation by a federal act. The negative proposed to be given them on all the acts of the several state legislatures is now for the first time suggested to my mind. Primâ facie I do not like it.

On July 18, Madison provided Jefferson with inside information on the convention's activities (Smith 1995, 1:483–84), while expressing dissatisfaction with the secrecy of its activities, a viewpoint Jefferson ardently shared: "I have taken lengthy notes of every thing that has yet passed, and mean to go on with the drudgery, if no indisposition obliges me to discontinue it. It is not possible to form any judgment of the future duration of the Session." On September 6, Madison next provided Jefferson with an update on the convention's progress (1:490–91): "A Government will probably be submitted to the *people* of the *states* consisting of a President *cloathed* with *executive power*; a *Senate chosen* by the Legislatures, and another *house chosen* by the *people* of the *states* jointly *possessing* the *legislative power* and a regular *judiciary* establishment. The mode of constituting the *executive* is among the few points not yet fully settled." On September 28, 1787, Jefferson expressed his ideas on good government in a letter to John Adams (Cappon 1987, 199): "The first principle of a good government is certainly the distribution of its powers into executive, judicial, and legislative, and a subdivision of the latter into two or three branches." On October 24 and November 1, Madison sent Jefferson a copy of the new Constitution, along with his opinions of it (Smith 1995, 1:496): "The first of these objections as it respects the Executive, was peculiarly embarrassing. On the question whether it should consist of a single person, or a plurality of co-ordinate members, on the mode of appointment, on the duration of office, on the degree of power, on the re-eligibility, tedious and reiterated discussions took place. The plurality of co-ordinate members had finally but few advocates." He also discussed presidential power:

The questions concerning the degree of power turned chiefly on the appointment to offices, and the controul on the Legislature. An *absolute* appointment to all offices—to some offices—to no offices, formed the scale of opinions on the first point. On the second, some contended for an absolute negative, as the only possible means of reducing to practice, the theory of a free government which forbids a mixture of Legislative and Executive powers. Others would be content with a revisionary power to be overruled by three fourths of both Houses.

Meanwhile, Adams responded to Jefferson on November 10, 1787 (Cappon 1987, 210). He too had finally received a copy of the new Constitution: "They have adopted the Idea of the Congress at Albany in 1754, of a President to nominate officers and a Council to Consent: but thank heaven they have adopted a third Branch, which that Congress did not. I think that Senates and Assemblies should have nothing to do with executive Power." On December 9, Madison informed Jefferson of the public's fervent interest in the Constitution (Smith 1995, 1:508): "The Constitution proposed by the late Convention engrosses almost the whole political attention of America. All the Legislatures except that of R. Island, which have assembled have agreed in submitting it to State Conventions. Virginia has set the example of opening a door for amendments, if the Convention there should chuse to propose them." And on December 20, Jefferson reflected his opinions in a letter to Madison in words eerily predictive of Franklin Roosevelt's four electoral victories and Donald Trump's attempt to hold onto power following his loss in the 2020 election (Smith 1995, 1:513):

The second feature I dislike, and greatly dislike, is the abandonment of the necessity of rotation of office, and most particularly in the case of the President. Experience concurs with reason in concluding that the first magistrate will always be re-elected if the constitution permits it. He is then an officer for life. . . . If once elected, and at a second or third election outvoted by one or two votes, he will pretend false votes, foul play, hold possession of the reins of government, be supported by the states voting for him, especially if they are the central ones lying in a compact body themselves and separating their opponents; and they will be aided by one nation of Europe, while the majority are aided by another. The election of a President of America some years hence will be much more interesting to certain nations of Europe than ever the election of a king of Poland was.

As the discussion continued, a letter from Jefferson to Adams dated February 28, 1796, referenced the American presidency and the French Revolution (Cappon 1987, 259):

> I fear the oligarchical executive of the French will not do. We have always seen a small council get into cabals and quarrels, the more bitter and relentless the fewer they are. We saw this in our committee of the states; and that they were from their bad passions, incapable of doing the business of their country. I think that for the prompt, clear and consistent action so necessary in an Executive, unity of person is necessary as with us. I am aware of the objection to this, that the office becoming more important may bring on serious discord in elections. In our country I think it will be long first; not within our day; and we may safely trust to the wisdom of our successors the remedies of the evil to arise in theirs.

As these letters indicate, the Constitution did not satisfy everyone, or as Luther Martin noted on January 29, 1788 (Bailyn 1993, 1:651), "There was a great diversity of sentiments." In 1811, Alexander Grayson reflected on the politics of Pennsylvania (Hart 1898, 73), "Where the source of power has been diligently explored and discovered, like that of the Nile, and universal suffrage with the right to pull down and build up again, thence recognized as a fundamental, may well puzzle the learned advocates for strong executives, independent judiciaries, and in the end, perhaps, turn all their fine-spun theories into lumber, little better than nonsense."

Given such divergent viewpoints, the final document agreed upon in 1787 was a compromise. And yet, as W. A. Peffer (1900, 247) estimated, "It is, probably, safe to say that, of the whole population of the country, when the Constitution was put into effect, the number that had no part in the work of establishing the National Government, either for or against it, although they were subject to its rule, constituted at least twenty-five per cent." Benjamin Fletcher Wright (1958, 58) announced in his Gaspar Bacon Lecture, "The Constitution, when it was finally signed, was not completely satisfactory to anyone. It embodied no individual's—and no group's—dream of perfection. The fact that both Franklin and Hamilton were willing to sign it reflects not only the degree to which it was a compromise—'a bundle of compromises' if you like—but also the extent of mutual confidence which made compromise possible and acceptable."

This chapter examines the Constitutional Convention and the events that led up to it. Of principal interest is the attention Framers dedicated to the issue of presidential power. On this point, James Bryce (1893 edition, 38) asked this pertinent question: "Why was it thought necessary to have a President at all?" Contrarily, Mary Bilder (2015, 42–43) wrote, "The strength needed to govern an extensive and expansive country like the United States was thought to require the authority of an executive analogous to a monarch. . . . The unease about monarchy and permanent division would shadow the Convention." Despite their distaste for monarchy, then, the Framers were aware of the requisite need for an executive with some sort of power. How then did they arrive at the creation of the presidency? It began with a legislative government without an executive.[1]

The Articles of Confederation

This simple arrangement, a confederation of sovereign states, performing certain functions through a body of delegates, proved in the course of a short time so inadequate that it is easy to pass these Articles by with an amused smile at their utter unfitness for the work at hand. As a matter of fact, they were in many respects models of what articles of confederation ought to be, an advance on previous instruments of like kind in the world's history. Their inadequacy arose from the fact that a mere confederacy of sovereign states was not adapted to the social, political, and industrial needs of the time.

—Andrew McLaughlin, The Confederation
and the Constitution, 1783–1789

In his *Child's History of the United States*, Charles Morris (1900, 145) informed his young students about the form of government Americans created after they declared independence from Great Britain:

They had thrown overboard the old government of kings. They had to make a new government of the people. I hope you do not think this was an easy task. If an architect or builder is shown a house and told to build another like that, he finds it very easy to do. But if he is shown a heap of stone and bricks and wood and told to build out of them a good strong house unlike any he has ever seen, he will find his task a very hard one, and may spoil the house in his building. That was what our people had to do. They could have built a king's government easily enough. They had plenty of patterns to follow for that. But they had no pattern for a people's government, and, like the architect and his house, they might spoil it in the making. The fact is, this is just what they did. Their first government was spoiled in the making, and they had to take it down and build it over again.

Not only was this new metaphorical house unfamiliar in form or function, but the political times during which it was established were decidedly turbulent. In 1787, Benjamin Rush (1886, 147) recalled, "The confederation, together with most of our State constitutions, were formed under very unfavorable circumstances. We had just emerged from a corrupted monarchy. Although we understood perfectly the principles of liberty, yet most of us were ignorant of the forms and combinations of power in republics." In a letter to James Duane (September 3, 1780), Alexander Hamilton (2001, 70–71, 73, 75, 77–78, 82) identified the defects of the Articles of Confederation: "The fundamental defect is a want of power in Congress. . . . It may be pleaded, that Congress had never any definitive powers granted them and of course could exercise none—could do nothing more than recommend . . . the confederation itself is defective and requires to be altered; it is neither fit for war, nor peace. . . . Another defect in our system is want of method and energy in administration." Hamilton's criticisms (98, 101–2) were published in July and August 1781, under the pseudonym The Continentalist. Creating a new government required learning and experience. The Articles, for all their faults, provided this necessary basis and the groundwork for a more comprehensive and powerful national government. Hence, in *The Continentalist No. III*, Hamilton warned, "Political societies, in close neighborhood, must either be strongly united under one government, or there will infallibly exist emulations and quarrels. This is in human nature; and we have no reason to think ourselves wiser, or better, than other men." Consequently, in 1783 Alexander Hamilton explained his *Reasons for a New Constitution* (Hart 1898, 177–78):

In confounding legislative and executive powers in a *single* body; as that of determining on the number and quantity of force, land and naval, to be employed for the common defence, and of directing their operations when raised and equipped; with that of ascertaining and making requisitions for the necessary sums or quantities of money to be paid by the respective states into the common treasury, contrary to the most approved and well-founded maxims of free government, which require that the *LEGISLATIVE*, EXECUTIVE, and *JUDICIAL* authorities be deposited in *distinct and separate hands*.

Given Hamilton's criticisms, it is unsurprising that former senator Albert Beveridge (1916, 304) described the Articles of Confederation as "a very masterpiece of weakness. The so-called Federal Government was like a horse with thirteen bridle reins, each held in the hands of separate drivers who usually pulled the confused and powerless beast in different directions." Hence, it quickly became apparent that if the Articles were not revised, the thirteen states would not remain united. As Benson Lossing (1868, 20) advised, "The League now assumed a national attitude, and the powers of the Confederacy were speedily tested. The bright visions of material prosperity that gladdened the hearts of the Americans at the close of the war soon faded, and others more sombre appeared when the financial and commercial condition of the forming republic was contemplated with candor." Likewise, Thomas Bailey (1956, 136) noted, "Economic storm clouds continued to hang low in the mid-1780's." Such concerns became apparent in international affairs, as well, when Congress considered the treaty with Great Britain ending the war. As John Alexander Jameson (1902, 82–83) wrote,

The long struggle [of war with Great Britain] had given time for careful consideration of the Articles. Maryland's persistent criticism had prepared men to find defects in them. Conventions of New England States, pamphlets, and private correspondence had found flaws in the new plan of government; but a public trial of it was a necessary preliminary to getting rid of it. The efforts of the individual States to maintain the war, the disposition of each State to magnify its own share in the result, the popular jealousy of a superior power, transferred now from parliament to the central government, and inflamed by the politicians who saw their quickest road to dignity in the State governments, were enough to ensure the Articles some lease of life. A real national government had to be extorted through the "grinding necessities of a reluctant people." Congress and its committees had already begun to declare that it was impossible to carry on a government efficiently under the Articles.

Opposition was not merely political. It was palpably expressed by soldiers who physically threatened the new government. As Jonathan Elliot (1907, 5:93) noted, as Congress deliberated "mutinous soldiers presented themselves, drawn up in the street before the state-house, where Congress had assembled." In his correspondence to Congress, General George Washington (1931, 27:32–33) denounced the mutiny, while also upholding the honor of the American soldiers:

> While I suffer the most poignant distress in observing that a [handful of Men contemptable in numbers, and equally so in point of Service] should disgrace themselves as the Pennsylvania Mutineers have done, by insulting the Sovereign Authority [of the United States, and that of their own]; I feel an [in]expressible satisfaction, that even this behavior cannot stain the name of the American Soldiery. . . . I cannot sufficiently express my surprise and indignation, at the arrogance, the folly and wickedness of the Mutineers.

Therefore, even before Shays's Rebellion in Massachusetts, the fragile government grappled with internal security issues. As Samuel Eliot Morison and Henry Steele Commager (1962, 274) wrote,

> While it would be too much to say that the Confederation was falling apart in 1786, there was enough evidence of growing disunion to alarm thinking men. George Washington, Robert Morris, John Adams, Roger Sherman, the Rutledges, and others of the generation who had won independence, had come to the conclusion that the Union of the States could not endure without a major operation on the government. All attempts to give it a limited taxing power by amendment had failed, owing to the selfishness of one state or another.

As was often the case, Thomas Jefferson disagreed, as Albert Beveridge (1916, 315–16) stated, "He did not think badly of the weakness of the

Articles of Confederation which so aroused the disgust, anger, and despair of Washington, Madison, Jay, and other men of their way of thinking, who were on the ground. 'With all the imperfections of our present government,' wrote Jefferson in Paris, in 1787, 'it is without comparison the best existing or that ever did exist.' "

Few others agreed with Jefferson, and on January 16, 1788, Edward Rutledge stated the "confederation [was] so weak, so very inadequate to the purposes of the union, that unless it was materially altered, the Sun of American Independence would indeed soon set—never to rise again" (Bailyn 1993: 22, V 2). Justice Joseph Story (1858, 1:184) acknowledged, "Whatever may be thought as to some of these enumerated defects, whether they were radical deficiencies or not, there cannot be a doubt, that others of them went to the very marrow and essence of government." And Alexander Johnston (1880, 8) wrote, "A human society bound together by no stronger ties than those provided by the Articles of Confederation must tend naturally to anarchy." The Founders concluded that a new constitution was required. This was a remarkable development, with the nation establishing not only a new government but one with an executive who has considerable power.

The State Constitutions

When the framers of the Constitution met in 1787 many of them were not novices in the science of constitution-making. On May 10, 1776, Congress had "recommended to the respective assemblies and conventions of the United Colonies, where no government sufficient to the exigencies of their affairs" had "been hitherto established, to adopt such government as" should, "in the opinion of the representatives of the people, best conduce to the happiness and safety of their constituents in particular, and America in general." Eleven of the states acting upon this recommendation had adopted new constitutions before 1781. The experience of these four years so prolific of new constitutions could not fail to be beneficial to the members of the Federal Convention, and particularly so from the fact that many of them had been members of the constitutional conventions in their respective states.

—Thomas Moran, *The Rise and Development
of the Bicameral System in America*

When they arrived in Philadelphia, it was apparent that the Articles needed more than revision—the country required a new constitution and one with an executive officer of some sort. This was not an easy decision, however, for the Framers were aware of the dangers of a hereditary monarchy, an idea reinforced by a statement from King George III of England (November 10, 1782) acknowledging, "I cannot conclude without mentioning how sensibly I feel the dismemberment of America from this empire, and that I should be miserable indeed if I did not feel that no blame on that account can be laid at my door" (Bancroft 1889, 1:292). Jefferson's Declaration of Independence six years earlier had indicted the British king for numerous offenses. And once the convention met in Philadelphia, wild rumors spread among the populace that it was about to create a new American monarchy: "This wild talk, which ought not to have imposed upon a village clown, was fervently believed. The post-bags came filled with letters to the delegates, reproaching them for their wickedness, or begging to know if it were true. To these one answer was invariably given. 'While we cannot affirmatively tell you what we are doing, we can negatively tell you what we are not doing; we never once thought of a King'" (McMaster 1885, 437).

But if not a king, what then was this new executive to be? There were few if any examples for an acceptable executive. This included the colonial governors. As Michael McConnell (2020, 20) insightfully reminds us, "While the king sparked colonial ire, it was the colonial governors who solidified discontent with broad prerogative power. The governors' prerogative powers *vis-à-vis* colonial legislatures were significantly more formidable than those of the king *vis-à-vis* Parliament, and they had frequently abused those powers in their own self-interest. . . . This made the colonial governors deeply unpopular figures, hardly an attractive model for a republican executive." Nor were the state governorships established after the revolution a fit model: "Correcting for the overreach of these colonial executives, state constitutions after Independence made their governors pitiably weak. Madison called them 'little more than Ciphers.' Most had short terms, were saddled with councils, lacked the veto or the power of appointment, and were elected by—and therefore dependent on—the legislature" (20–21).[2]

Furthermore, Forrest McDonald (1994, 130) noted, "All the states designed features to prevent executive abuse in [the] future." Except for New York, only the Massachusetts and South Carolina governors had a veto power, only Maryland's governor had an appointment power that carried with it any real influence, and only the governors of Delaware and North Carolina had pardon and reprieve powers. Virginia's governor could issue reprieves but not pardons. Of all the state governors, only New York's was granted any real authority. The New York governor was elected by the people and had the power to serve multiple terms, a veto through a council on revision, the ability to call the legislature into session and issue a periodic report on the state of the state, to grant pardons and reprieves except in cases of treason and murder, to execute the laws, correspond with the Continental Congress, and command the armed forces (McDonald 1994, 133–34). It is generally remarked that the presidency was based on the model of New York's chief executive. In a series of lectures, former president Benjamin Harrison (Harrison and Harrison 1901, 178) stated, "In New York the first constitution provided that the supreme executive power and authority should be vest in a governor, who was to be chosen at a popular election and to hold office for three years." McConnell (2020, 21), however, did not share this opinion:

> Because of the similarity to the final version of the presidency produced by the Philadelphia Convention, it has long been thought that the New York governorship served as a more or less direct model. But note that the Philadelphia Convention voted against the direct election by the people, voted against the Council of Revision idea, never seriously considered a Council of Appointments, rejected any executive power to prorogue the legislature, made the President commander of the militia only in limited circumstances, and made presidential pardons final. . . . To the extent that New York was a model at all, it was inexact and indirect. Certainly, no delegate referred to New York as a model, in the way George Mason proposed the Virginia Declaration of Rights as a model for a federal Bill of Rights.

If not New York, then which other state or states served as a model? According to Thomas Moran (1904, 220), "The president in the Constitution is a copy of the executive officer in the early State constitutions and colonial charters, and is derived very remotely from the king of England. In fact, the chief magistrate in Pennsylvania, Delaware, and New Hampshire was styled the 'President.' It was this official who was reproduced with some modifications in the Federal Constitution."

The states were revolutionary in another manner. As Akhil Reed Amar (2021, 155) wrote, "In 1776, STATE AFTER STATE, building on each other in self-conscious conversational fashion, introduced the world to an entirely different constitutional model." Their innovation was a written constitution. Although we speak of a British constitution, nowhere is it a written document. Rather, it contains a miasma of common law, judicial decisions, parliamentary laws, and monarchical edicts. On the other hand, a written constitution was accessible to all, published widely in newspapers across the new nation. A layperson could consult a written constitution, whereas the British constitution required specialized skills to understand even some of its most basic rights and privileges. But for it to be easily interpretable, a written constitution also required brevity and clarity, two qualities often at war with each other. If terms were left undefined, then once again it would be left to lawyers and those with specialized skills to interpret the document. Since state constitutions were relatively brief, they had erred on the side of general applications rather than specific delineations of executive power. As we shall see, this also was a limitation of our present constitution.

Still, a written constitution offered vast informational benefits to the public, and constitutions were hardly of recent origin. As James Schouler (1908, 114) found, "Written constitutions, as we know them in America, should not be deemed a pure innovation the product of creative genius but rather the fruition of methods to which these English-speaking colonists had long been habituated by their royal charters." William Morey (1891, 554) similarly noted, "The growth of written constitutions under proprietary grants may be illustrated from the history of Maryland, the first colony to be erected under such a grant. The basis of all political power and privilege in the colony was, of course, the royal charter granted to Lord Baltimore in 1632." Meanwhile, Charles Borgeaud (1892, 614; see also Borgeaud 1895) noted, "The Agreement of the People, drawn up by Cromwell's soldiers (1647), the Instrument of Government of the Protectorate (1653), and farther back, before the Puritan revolution, the Fundamental Orders of Connecticut (1639), together with the well-known Plantation Covenants, subscribed by the early non-conformists as they settled on American soil, are the documents to which may be traced the origin of written constitutions."

Although these constitutions were written, the enumerated powers were not necessarily fixed. As Hannis Taylor (1906, 213) noted, reflecting the views of a *living constitution*, even written constitutions were elastic, meaning that their powers could vary over time: "Nothing has been more remarkable in the history of our Federal Constitution than the ease with which it has adapted itself, by the aid of judicial interpretation, to the ever-increasing wants of a rapidly swelling population, continually organizing new systems of local government beyond our original limits." Three decades later, D. W. Brogan (1933, 117) wrote, "The growth in power and prestige of the presidency is an example of the unforeseen possibilities of a written constitution, for, in normal times, the President's powers as set out in the Constitution, would not account for his immense prestige, and for his great potency for good and evil." Consequently, there is more to a constitution than its mere written words.

Meanwhile, Massachusetts introduced a second important innovation. After the voters rejected the first iteration of a state constitution, a second document was drafted, not by the legislative body but by a special convention established specifically for that purpose (Amar 2021, 159). As the document stated (Munro, Evans, and Hoar 1917, 21),

> The mode of ratification adopted by the Convention was peculiar. Profiting by the experience of 1778, it did not submit the Constitution as a whole to popular vote. Instead, it asked the adult freemen to convene in their town meetings to consider and debate the Constitution clause by clause, to point out objections, if any, to particular articles, and to send in their returns to the secretary of the Convention, with the yeas and nays on every question. The people were then asked to empower the Convention at an adjourned session on June 5 to ratify and declare the Constitution in force if two-thirds of the voters were in favor of it, or, if not, to alter it in accordance) with the popular will as expressed in the returns, and ratify it; as thus amended. It was now almost four years since the machinery of constitution making had been set in motion. About 16,000 people out of a total population of 363,000 voted on the Constitution. This was a larger vote than was cast for Governor during the next six years.

The state constitutions thus provided various building blocks and the ratification method proved vital to the eventual acceptance of the new constitution.

A New Constitution

> The Convention that made our Constitution were obliged to invent an Executive department, a machine, so to speak, by which the Executive authority, essential to every Government, could be applied. In this as in all other things, the English Constitution was necessarily the model. They could have no other, for the customs and ways of thinking of England was theirs also.
>
> —Sidney George Fisher, *Trial of the Constitution*

The establishment of an executive office was fraught with potential dangers. As Mark Peterson (2007, 95) wrote, "The framers, while rejecting the infirmities of the Articles of Confederation, nonetheless retained a deep fear of concentrated government power, the 'mischief of faction,' and the potential imprudence of an impassioned public." That they created a president at all is somewhat of a miracle, so intensely did they distrust the power of the existing executives. In this regard, as Wilfred Binkley (1947, 284) noted, "When the time came to establish the government under the Constitution it was extremely fortunate for the Federalists that they had within their group the leader to whom all turned as the one man for the presidency. George Washington was a national hero endeared to the masses as the savior of his country. He was fitted by character, inherent ability, and positive training for the office of Chief Executive."

American history might have been quite different had Washington not been in Philadelphia in 1787, and this was a distinct possibility as the date for the convention loomed. Washington initially declined the invitation to attend the Constitutional Convention in Philadelphia. He already had declined an invitation to come to Philadelphia in May 1787 to attend a meeting of the Society of Cincinnatus and had declined to be its president for another term. But the Virginia legislature was determined to name him as a delegate to the convention. As historian Ron Chernow (2010, 522) explained, "Washington confessed his fear that the Constitutional Convention might fail, much as he had been haunted by fear of failure when named commander in chief in 1775. . . . On the other hand, this might be a last opportunity to salvage a deteriorating nation. Any failure, he said, could be construed 'as an unequivocal proof that the states are not likely to agree in any general measure . . . and consequently that there is an end put to the federal government.'" Meanwhile, Jared Sparks (1839, 399) commented,

> Some of his friends in various parts of the country expressed themselves doubtingly in their letters, as to the propriety of his going to the convention, and some advised against it. Many thought the scheme illegal, since there was no provision in the articles of the confederation for such a mode of revision, and it had not been proposed by Congress. It was feared, therefore, that the doings of the convention would end in a failure, and perhaps in the disgrace of the delegates.

The Virginia legislature, however, declined to accept his refusal. In his biography of Washington, Chief Justice John Marshall (2000, 319) noted,

> The Governor of Virginia, who was himself elected a member of the convention, transmitted to him the act and the vote of the assembly in a letter, pressing most earnestly on him all those motives for yielding to the general wish, which were furnished by the importance of the crisis, and the gloomy state of American affairs. He was urged, at all events, not to decide positively against it, but to leave himself at the liberty to be determined by future events.

Chernow (2010, 523) concluded, "In retrospect, it seems foreordained that Washington, with his unerring sense of duty, would go to Philadelphia. He was a casualty of his own greatness, which dictated a path in life from which he couldn't deviate. Had he turned down the call of duty, he would have felt something incomplete in his grand mission to found the country, but he patently had to convince himself and the world of his purely disinterested motives. Now he could proceed as if summoned from self-imposed retirement by popular acclaim."

Washington's decision to attend was a game changer, providing the convention and its secret deliberations with a respectability it likely would have lacked had he declined the invitation. Still, as he prepared to attend, Alexander Hamilton (2001, 166) wrote to Washington: "The prevailing apprehension among thinking men is that the Convention, from a fear of shocking the public opinion, will not go far enough. They seem to be convinced that a strong well mounted government will better suit the popular palate than one of a different complexion. Men in office are indeed taking all possible pains to give an unfavorable impression of the Convention; but the current seems to be running strongly the other way." To Hamilton (2001, 168) Washington's presence was of critical importance, for if "the government be adopted, it is probable general Washington will be the President of the United States. This will insure a wise choice of men to administer the government and a good administration." The alternative: "A reunion with Great Britain, from a universal disgust at the state of commotion, is not impossible, though not much to be feared. The most plausible shape of such a business would be the establishment of a son of the present monarch in the supreme government of this country with a family compact."

Washington, always concerned with his public image, worried that his attendance at the convention would signal his interest in leading the country. As Douglas Southall Freeman (1954, 117) noted of Washington's opinion at the convention's end, "Personally, the comments on the Constitution that most disturbed Washington were predictions that he would be chosen without opposition as the first President of the United States; but he told himself it was neither necessary nor modest to think of an unfilled office in a government not yet created, and he gave his thought to the reception of the document by the people rather than to its possible interruption of his retired way of living." Washington once again was the one "indispensable man." Without him, the Constitution likely would not have been written or ratified, nor would the presidency exist in its current form. And had he not served as our first chief magistrate, it is likely the presidency would not have survived.

Still, Hamilton's viewpoint of Washington's importance was prescient as the Framers met in Philadelphia with representatives from eleven states to discuss, debate, and decide on a new Constitution. A total of seventy-four delegates were appointed, though nineteen did not attend, and only thirty-nine signed the final document after four months of debate. The New Hampshire delegates did not arrive until July 23 "after the Convention had decided some of its most difficulty problems. Hence, most of the conspicuously troublesome questions were therefore passed upon by delegations of the eleven states" (McLaughlin 1935, 148). Among the most important of these were determining the parameters of the new federal institutions.

The Framers' Intent

> When the delegates to the Constitutional Convention met in the summer of 1787, the only thing that made them more uncomfortable than heat was the topic of the executive.
>
> —John Yoo, *Crisis and Command*

Few of the delegates to the Constitutional Convention had anything but vague ideas about the office they were about to establish. This is particularly the case with the so-called Father of the Constitution. As Charles Thach (2017 edition, 70) wrote, "The truth is that Madison's views on executive power were extremely vague when he came to Philadelphia in 1787." In 1786 he wrote, "I have made up no final opinion whether the first magistrate should be chosen by the Legislature or the people at large or whether the power should be vested in one man assisted by a council of which the President shall be only primus inter pares" (Thach 2017, 70–71). On April 16, 1787, Madison (1999, 81–83) wrote to Washington: "I have scarcely ventured as yet to form my own opinion either of the manner in which [the executive] ought to be constituted or of the authorities with which it ought to be cloathed." In the same letter, however, Madison declared, "A negative in *all cases whatsoever* on the legislative acts of the States, as heretofore exercised by the Kingly prerogative, appears to me to be absolutely necessary, and to be the least possible encroachment on the State jurisdictions. Without this defensive power, every positive power that can be given on paper will be evaded & defeated." Madison did not specify that this "Kingly prerogative" should be vested in an executive, however. It might instead have been placed in a privy council.

Meanwhile, Washington was concerned with the specter of monarchy. As Saikrishna Prakash (2015, 16) wrote, "George Washington, the man whom many supposed could be king if he desired . . . was amazed 'that even respectable characters speak of a monarchical form of government without horror.'" Washington wrote to Madison,

> I am fully of opinion that those who lean to a Monarchical government have either not consulted the public mind, or that they live in a region where the leveling principles in which they were bred, being entirely irradicated, is much

> more productive of Monarchical ideas than are to be found
> in the Southern states . . . I also am clear that even admitting
> the utility; nay, necessity of the form—yet that period is not
> arrived for adopting the change without shaking the Peace of
> this Country to its foundations.

Given these concerns, it is unsurprising that at the convention the "construction of a national executive was attended with great diversity of opinion" (Curtis 1884, 240). As Richard Frothingham (1872, 592) explained, "This determination to frame a new government brought face to face in the Convention the antagonisms of American society; the errors of opinion and rooted prejudices; the local interests, jealousies, and ambitions of the people of the several States." Still, as Justice Joseph Story (1858, 2:315) confirmed, "In the convention, there does not seem to have been any objection to the establishment of a national executive." And according to eminent historian George Bancroft (1889, 2:89), when it came to the issue of power, the most "delicate" question was how to distribute "powers between the general government and the states" rather than the president and Congress. Bancroft's use of the word *delicate* is interesting. The word was used repeatedly by Joseph Story (1873, 328, 369) regarding the powers of the presidency, as in, (1) "Considering the delicacy and extent of the power, it is too much to expect that a free people would confide to a single magistrate, however respectable, the sole authority to act conclusively, as well as exclusively, upon the subject of treaties"; and (2) "The power to receive ambassadors and ministers is always an important, and sometimes very delicate function." As I will demonstrate, our earliest presidents often used *delicate* to refer to the various Article II powers conferred upon them by the US Constitution. They also referred to the delicacy of acting under the enumerated powers of the presidential office. Given its prominence in early statements by both scholars and presidents, What does this largely overlooked word in constitutional interpretation mean?

Textualists remind us that we should look to the contemporary meaning of words, as expressed in the dictionaries of the time. According to the 1818 and 1855 versions of Samuel Johnson's Dictionary, the word *delicate* is defined as "nice, dainty, polite, pure, fine." Another way of thinking about this word is that if something is dainty, then it needs to be handled with care. By inference, then, the Constitution and the president's powers under Article II must be handled with care. One can also infer that if one does not handle something delicate with care, it can be broken. Delicacy therefore required a careful balancing act, ensuring direct fealty, as best as possible, to the Constitution's intent. And yet, due to constitutional ambiguity, "the construction of the executive department was fraught with bewildering difficulties, of which a new set rose up as fast as the old ones were overcome" (Bancroft 1891, 271).

Surprisingly then, though little noticed by historians, the first proposal to create an executive under the new Constitution contained a vast array of enumerated executive power. Resolution 7 of the Virginia Plan would have vested in the presidency all "Executive rights" that had been "vested in Congress under the Articles of Confederation," as well as providing the executive with "a general authority to execute the National laws." As Michael McConnell (2020, 24) noted, "The first half of the provision transferred to the new executive a suite of powers listed in Article IX of the Articles of Confederation: determining on peace and war, sending and receiving ambassadors, entering into treaties and alliances, regulating captures and prizes, granting letters of marque and reprisal. . . . These powers were not new to the federal government, but the Virginia Plan transferred them from the legislative to the executive branch. All were prerogatives of the British monarch."

In the end, the Framers delegated most of these powers to the legislative branch. Nevertheless, they did believe that the executive had to be strong enough to check the power of Congress, though not strong enough to be the equivalent of the British king. Still, as Saikrishna Prakash (2015, chap. 1) convincingly argued, the American presidency, even at its creation, was more powerful than many other European monarchies. And as John Bassett Moore (1912, 36–37) commented, "No less remarkable is the executive power vested by the Constitution in the President of the United States; for, owing to their reprobation of the absolute power then exercised by the monarchs of Europe, and their special abhorrence of the arbitrary course of George the III of England, the American people felt a peculiar jealousy of executive authority." Consequently, Patrick Henry observed, the "Constitution is said to have beautiful features; but when I come to examine these features, sir, they appear to me horribly frightful. Among other deformities, it has an awful squinting; it squints towards monarchy" (Prakash 2015, 20).

For this and other reasons, Henry opposed the new constitution. Nevertheless, as Caleb Patterson (1929, 228–29) wrote in a positive missive on presidential power, "From an institution that smacked of monarchy and was one of the chief objects of criticism by the opponents of the

Constitution, the Presidency has become the champion of the welfare of the nation and the most admired feature of the work of the Convention of 1787." But did this development owe its lineage solely to the Constitution? According to Patterson, "The Presidency in this newer and more comprehensive sense is an institution superimposed by the unwritten constitution as a means of overcoming the mechanics of our governmental system" (e.g., the difficulties inherent in the separation of powers).

Why then did the Framers provide the new executive with the potential for extraordinary power? One common theme was that the presidency should be imbued with sufficient *energy*. In *Federalist no. 70*, Alexander Hamilton noted, "Energy in the executive is a leading character in the definition of good government." At the Virginia Ratifying Convention, William Grayson said, "By having such a President, we should have more independence and energy in the executive, and not be encumbered with the expense, &c., of a court and an hereditary prince and family" (Elliot 1900, 3:279). Justice Story (1858, 2:318, 320) wrote that the office promoted "decision, activity, secrecy, and dispatch," which "generally characterize the proceedings of one man in a much more eminent degree than the proceedings of a greater number; and in proportion as the number is increased, these qualities will be diminished. . . . In the legislature promptitude of decision is not of great importance. It is more often an evil, than a benefit." Energy consequently was a necessity for both the presidency and good government. As Israel Andrews (1900, 167) advised, "There is no difference of opinion at the present time in regard to the importance of unity in the executive. All are agreed that this power must be lodged in the hands of one man. To divide responsibility is to introduce feebleness."

Energy suggests an active presidency, but it does little to define that activity. In the introduction to one of the several editions of Charles Thach's *The Creation of the Presidency*, Herbert Storing (Thach [1923] 1969, vii) wrote, "While . . . two developments combined in a rather general opinion by 1787 in favor of a vigorous and independent executive, some significant differences remained, and it was by no means clear how they would be resolved." Given conflicting imperatives, the Framers anticipated that Congress would have the most power in the newly formed government. Yet, as William Munro (1930, 127) noted,

> In general . . . the three outstanding powers of the nation's chief executive were given in a strictly limited form. The predominance of authority was intended to be lodged with

Congress. But if the framers of the new Constitution expected it to remain there, if they counted upon Congress to be the dominant factor in the directing of public policy, they made one serious omission. They provided Congress with no channel into which its powers could be concentrated and made conclusive. They provided it with no prime minister or other authoritative leader who could prefigure the will and power of Congress to the public imagination.

How Much Power?

The first man, put at the helm will be a good one. No body knows what sort may come afterwards. The Executive will be always increasing here, as elsewhere, till it ends in a monarchy.

—Benjamin Franklin, *The Men Who Made the Constitution*, 84

Power was very much on the minds of the Framers of the US Constitution. Yet "the main debate at the Constitutional Convention concerned the distribution of power between the national government and the states rather than the distribution of power between the two branches of the national government" (DiPaolo 2010, 6). Charles and Mary Beard (1921, 146) identified nine issues debated at the convention. Interestingly, although the state legislatures were mentioned, the presidency was nowhere included in this list. Despite its potential for abuse, presidential power did not seem to be an immediate concern for the Framers. Still, as David Saffell (1973, 28) commented, "Concerning general presidential powers, the Framers were surprisingly generous. Despite the fact that they were operating in a period marked by a decided bias in favor of strong legislative authority, due primarily to antagonism toward King George and most of the colonial governors, the supporters of a strong presidency were able to win decisive battles in Philadelphia. This stands in marked contrast to the early state constitutions which granted governors only minimal authority."

One primary reason for this generosity was, once again, the convention's presiding officer—George Washington. One member of the Maryland legislature stated, "By your [Washington's] letter you have taught us how to value, preserve, and improve that liberty which your services under the smiles of Providence have secured" (Bancroft 1889, 1:128). And following the convention, Pierce Butler wrote to his son, "Entre nous, I do [not] believe they [the executive powers] would have been so great had not many of the members cast their eyes toward General Washington as President: and shaped their Ideas of the Powers to be given a President, by their opinions of his Virtue" (Thach 2017 edition, 153). James Bryce (1917, 1:23) later acknowledged,

> Even while the debates were proceeding, every one must have thought of him as the proper person to preside over the Union as he was then presiding over the Convention. The creation of the office would seem justified by the existence of a person exactly fitted to fill it, one whose established influence and ripe judgment would repair the faults then supposed to be characteristic of democracy, its impulsiveness, its want of respect for authority, its incapacity for pursuing a consistent line of action.

Akhil Amar (2021, 212–13) agreed: "The federal Constitution's single most distinctive feature—its biggest and most obvious break with all thirteen state regimes then in place—was its breathtakingly strong executive, by American Revolutionary standards. This distinctive feature owed more to Washington alone than to all the other delegates combined." These Framers understood that once in office, Washington would delineate what the Framers left undefined. Still, as Glenn Phelps (1987, 345) noted, "When George Washington took the oath of office in 1789 . . . there remained great doubts . . . as to just what this presidency was. . . . Ambiguity reigned . . . regarding the political character of the presidency. The cryptic words of Article II . . . offered little guidance to the first occupant of the office."

While Washington feared monarchy, as Prakash (2015) demonstrated, some would have favored placing even greater power in the president's hands. For example, at the Pennsylvania Ratifying Convention, James Wilson declared (Elliot 1888, 2:510, 512–13), "The objection against the powers of the President is not that they are too many or too great; but, to state it in the gentlemen's own language, they are so trifling, that the President is no more than the tool of the Senate." Still, given the potential for executive abuse of power and the countervailing enormous respect for the presiding officer, one might assume that the power of the presidency was a central focus of debate at the Constitutional Convention. Instead, as late as June 1787, as McConnell (2020, 48) noted,

The presidential office . . . had no generalized "executive" power, no "federative" powers, no express authority to receive additional delegated powers from Congress, and only the three enumerated powers of law execution, some appointments, and veto. The president had no power with respect to foreign affairs; he was not even given the power to command military forces. . . . The executive was unitary but weak. . . . The result was a mere shadow of the "energetic" executive that some delegates had spoken of.

Rather than an extensive debate about presidential power, considerations were related to two basic questions: (1) Should the nation adopt a plural or single executive? (2) How should the executive be elected? The decision to establish a unitary executive settled the first matter, but consideration of the second issue was more troublesome, with the Framers unable to specify a method of electing the president. "As the deadlock about the election of the executive continued, delegates grew loath to clothe the office with serious powers" (McDonald 2007, xiii). Hence, "during the month of August, when so much time was spent devising the electoral scheme, there was little attention given to the question of presidential powers" (Robinson 1987, 89). Furthermore "as late as August 31, the method of election of the chief magistrate, the question of eligibility to reelection, the degree of participation by the Senate and President respectively in control of foreign affairs and the naming of judges, the method of impeachment, succession in case of vacancies, and the matter of a council were all yet unsettled" (Thach 2007 edition, 116, 121).

The task of enumerating the powers of the presidency was finally assigned to the Committee of Detail, which did much of the actual work of creating the presidential office. It met for ten days, during which time its members debated and added the following powers: to command the army, navy, and militia (when called into active service); demand or request opinions of department heads in writing; grant pardons and reprieves; make appointments and treaties with the advice and consent of the Senate; and a qualified veto (see Ewald 2012). Still, the committee spent no time discussing the "subject of [presidential] control of foreign policy" (Thach [1923] 1969). And as George Tickner Curtis (1889, 1:576) described, "What those powers were to be had not been fully settled when the first draft of the Constitution came from the committee of detail."

The Committee on Postponed Matters, also known as the Committee of Eleven, next shifted "the powers to appoint judges, to appoint ambassadors, and to make treaties" from the Senate to the president (McConnell 2020, 80). On September 8 the Committee on Style and Arrangement was assigned the responsibility of establishing a final draft of the Constitution. According to the Abel Upshur (1863, 104), "It is manifest that this committee had no power to change the meaning of anything which had been adopted, but were authorized merely to 'revise the style,' and arrange the matter in proper order." The whole convention then "voted to transfer authority to appoint the Treasurer from Congress to the President. Second, they lowered the number of votes needed for Congress to override a veto from three-fourths to two-thirds." As McConnell (2020, 85–86) noted, "These two final changes in presidential power had opposite valence. The former strengthened the president's hand, giving him control over the disbursement of funds. The latter weakened the President by making it easier (though scarcely easy) for Congress to enact legislation over his opposition." Accordingly, there was no uniform attempt to increase the power of the presidency. Rather the changes fortified the Constitution's checks and balances.

Why didn't the Framers spend more time debating the new executive's powers? As John Fiske (1898, 310) stated, "Now in the earlier part of the work of the Federal Convention, in dealing with the legislative department, the delegates were on firm ground, because they were dealing with things of which they knew something by experience." Because it was familiar ground, Donald Morrill (1903, 66) wrote, "The powers conferred upon Congress are for the most part enumerated in Section 8 of Article I of the Constitution, and so concise and explicit is the language employed that it is difficult to find a single superfluous word in the entire section." But as Max Farrand (1921, 133–34) remarked, "No such office as that of President of the United States was then in existence. It was a new position which they were creating. We have become so accustomed to it that it is difficult for us to hark back to the time when there was no such officer and to realize the difficulties and the fears of the men who were responsible for creating that office." Therefore, as Thach (1922, 132) noted in his dissertation,

> Manifestly it was [the Committee on Style and Arrangement]
> that organized the executive, as it was the committee of detail
> that enumerated its powers. If it could work out a compromise,

it was a foregone conclusion that the Convention would accept it. . . . There was . . . no real chance to upset the foundations of the compromise. The fact that the Convention stood at the threshold of freedom was the strongest defense the new plan could have. By accepting it, the way was cleared for final action—the putting of the instrument into its final form and ratification.

In the end, the Framers dedicated little time to an examination or explication of presidential power. As Daniel Farber (2021, 21) wrote, "The discussion of the presidency at the Constitutional Convention was primarily focused on structural issues: whether to have a single head of the executive branch or divided control by several leaders; and if the former, how and by whom the president would be chosen and how the president could be removed. The convention's perplexity over these issues can be seen in the number of inconclusive discussions and votes before delegates finally came to a resolution. More time was spent on these matters than on precisely delineating the powers of the office." Consequently, as McDonald (2017, xiv) noted, it took but three days for the Framers to consider these issues. Madison's notes provide few other details regarding the debate on issues relevant to the presidency and the Committee on Style and Arrangement's document (Farrand 1913, 608, 626–28).

Again, why didn't the Framers dedicate more time to debate the new executive powers? Sadly, the most often cited reason is that the convention was nearing its end and the delegates were tired, cranky, and eager to go home. Consequently, Article II, was "put together in slipshod fashion," as Forrest McDonald (2017, xiv), an expert on this era in presidential history, advised. The rush to devise and approve the powers in Article II offers a first explanation for the rampant ambiguities in its language.

The Ratification Debates

By a resolution of the convention, it was recommended that assemblies should be called, in the different states, to discuss the merits of the constitution, and either accept or reject it; and that, as soon as nine states should have ratified it, it should be carried into operation by congress. To decide the interesting question, respecting the adoption or rejection of the new constitution, the best talents of the several states were assembled in their respective conventions. The fate of the constitution could, for a time, be scarcely conjectured, so equally were the parties balanced. But, at length, the conventions of eleven states assented to, and ratified the constitution.

—Charles Goodrich, *A History of the United States of America*[3]

The method chosen for the ratification debates was designed to increase the probability of ratification. According to Edward Mead Earle (1937, viii–ix),

It would have been a counsel of perfection to consign the tender mercies of the legislatures of each and all of the thirteen States. Experience clearly indicated that ratification then would have had the same chance as the Scriptural camel passing through the eye of a needle. It was therefore determined to recommend to Congress that the new Constitution be submitted to conventions in the several States especially elected to pass upon it and that, furthermore, the new government should go into effect if and when it should be ratified by nine of the thirteen States actually ratifying. This was an act of revolutionary *coup d'état*.

As social choice theory teaches us, the rules of the game are an important determinant of any outcome. The method the Framers established is a perfect example of this point. Still, even if the new Constitution was to be debated in ratifying conventions rather than state legislatures, ratification was by no means a certainty. New York and Virginia were vital, and with only eleven states participating—North Carolina and Rhode Island would join the union later—ratification really required nine of eleven states. And while there was a fair amount of discussion about the proposed presidential office, it was not the centerpiece of the ratification debates. The potential "aristocratic" power of the Senate was a far greater concern.

Several presidential powers were the subject of debate. In Massachusetts, the "towns questioned provisions that allowed 'matters of great Importanc' to be decided by the president and two-thirds of the Senate—the ratification of treaties, which became the supreme law of the land—with no participation by the House of Representatives, which would reflect the people's will most directly. One town added that 'the Ligilsative power is blended with the Executive, the President being vested with both & having no other Council than the Senate'" (Maier 2010, 151). There also were concerns with the president's pardon power. Abraham White claimed that "the president had the power of deciding life and death, and without the use of a jury." Samuel Adams responded that "the president could only pardon a criminal or '*put him to his Jury for trial*.' After a few inconclusive exchanges over whether an act of Congress or a treaty approved only by the president and the Senate could oblige the militia to engage in conflicts outside the United States, the convention moved on to Article III and the judiciary" (Maier 2010, 189–90). Rather than the presidency, the primary focus of the Massachusetts Ratifying Convention was the legislative branch. Of the convention, Pauline Maier (2010, 192) noted, "The convention's pace quickened once it left Article I behind. That made some sense, since everyone assumed that the powers of Congress would define those of the new government. The president would execute Congress's decisions—to impose new taxes, for example, or declare war—and the judiciary would try violates of the law, so Article I of the Constitution, which defined the structure and powers of Congress, was the most important."

Likewise in Pennsylvania, when it was proposed that the convention move on to a discussion of Article II, John Smilie complained that the convention "had not yet got over the first six words of the Preamble." On December 4, 1787, instead of focusing on the presidency, Robert Whitehill "immediately went back to attacking the powers and structure of Congress in Article I" (Maier 2010, 107, 111). The South Carolina Convention was more thorough, spending "three days on Article I, roughly two on Article II" (250). The New Hampshire Convention dedicated a full day to Congress's Article I, Section 8 powers, but "Article II, on the executive, got less than a morning" (220). In New York, after spending considerable time debating Article I, Section 8, Paragraph 7 on post offices and post roads, the committee of the whole moved onto to Article II "with little or no debate." Two days later, on July 4, 1788, the convention considered an "amendment that would create an executive council to assist the president in making appointments, taking that responsibility from the Senate, and defining the qualifications for council members." Anti-Federalist delegates also "proposed to confine the president to a single, seven-year, nonrenewable term . . . and to prevent him from commanding the army, militia, or navy in person or granting pardons for treason without Congress's consent." Yet the "delegates were making up for lost time, moving rapidly through Article II on Saturday, July 5" (370–71).

When North Carolina later ratified the constitution, as they turned their attention to Article II, Section 1, "the majority of members again held their tongues." James Iredell, a future Supreme Court justice, warned, "It would be a great defect in forming a Constitution for the United States, if it was so constructed that by any accident an improper person could have a chance to obtain that office," though he concluded that "every contingency is provided for" to ensure "the choice will always fall upon a man of experienced abilities and fidelity." As to the idea that the president should have a council, Iredell noted that England had a similar system and asked "whether that system ought to be imitated by us." Iredell defended the president's pardon power: "Suppose we were involved in a war. It would be then necessary to know the designs of the enemy. This kind of knowledge cannot always be procured, but by means of spies, a set of wretches whom all nations despise, but whom all employ . . . a principle of self defense would urge and justify the use of them on our part." To do so, a presidential pardon would be a strong incentive (Bailyn 1993, 2:870–72, 876). After James Iredell defended these provisions, the "delegates then zipped through the rest of Article II with only one speech by Archibald Maclaine, who answered objections nobody had made" (Maier 2010, 416–17). Meanwhile, the Resolutions of Maryland recommended that "the President shall not command the army, in person, without the consent of Congress" (Bailyn 1993, 2:556).

The most rigorous debate occurred in Virginia, where the prospects for ratification were not promising. A draft of the Harrisburg Conference of September 3, 1788, read (Gallatin 1879, 1:1),

> We, &c . . . are united in opinion that a federal government is the only one that can preserve the liberties and secure the happiness of the inhabitants of such an extensive empire as the United States, and experience having taught us that the ties of our Union, under the Articles of Confederation were so weak as to deprive us of some of the greatest advantages we had a right to expect from such a government, therefore are fully convinced that a more efficient one is absolutely necessary. But at the same time we must declare that although the constitution proposed for the United States is likely to obviate most of the inconveniences we labored under, yet several parts of it appear to be exceptionable to us that nothing but the fullest confidence of obtaining a revision of them by a general convention and our reluctance to enter into any dangerous measures could prevail on us to acquiesce in its organization in this State.

Albert Beveridge (1916, 321) concluded, "So a decided majority of the people of Virginia were against the proposed fundamental law; for, as in other parts of the country, few of Virginia's masses wanted anything stronger than the weak and ineffective Government of the State and as little even of that as possible." Primary opposition to the Constitution was led by Patrick Henry. In the debates, Henry and William Grayson "raised one objection after another. The president's term was too long and, given the lack of term limits, he could be re-elected indefinitely. An executive council should advise the president in place of the Senate, whose advisory function violated the separation of powers between the executive and legislative branches and added to the already excessive powers of the Senate." Along with criticizing the method of selecting the president, Grayson complained that the Constitution provided the president too much power, which could lead to foreign intervention in presidential elections (Maier 2010, 286). Patrick Henry declared (McConnell 2020, 87, 205),

> If your American chief, be a man of ambition, and abilities, how easy it is for him to render himself absolute! The army is in his hands, and if he be a man of address, it will be attached to him; and it will be the subject of long meditation with him to seize the first auspicious moment to accomplish his design. . . . The President, in the field, at the head of his army, can prescribe the terms on which he shall reign master, so far that it will puzzle any American ever to get his neck from under the galling yoke.

In the end, Virginia ratified the Constitution, but in so doing left a relatively sparse record endorsing the new presidential office.

A more spirited discussion occurred contemporaneously in pamphlets published by various interested parties. As Pauline Maier (2010, ix) wrote, "Debate over the Constitution raged in newspapers, taverns, coffeehouses, and over dinner tables as well as in the Confederation Congress, state legislatures, and state ratifying conventions. People who never left their home towns were and were little known except to their neighbors studied the document, knew it well, and on some memorable occasions made their views known." Earle (1937, ix) referred to this debate as a "veritable war . . . and once more Americans showed themselves masters of pamphleteering and other forms of political controversy."

Surprisingly, given that the new nation had just rejected the yoke of monarchy, "there was a fair amount of sympathy for a strong (even, under some circumstances, a hereditary) executive to resist the aristocratic tendencies of the legislature; and some of the Anti-Federalists objected that the President would be too weak to stand up to the Senate and would become a mere tool of aristocratic domination" (Storing 1981b, 49). For example, an individual writing under the pseudonym Cincinnatus lamented the "absurd division" of the executive power between the president and senate, which "must be productive of constant contentions for the lead, must clog the executive of government to a mischievous, and sometimes to a disgraceful degree" (Yoo 2009a, 37).

Other pamphleteers argued that the presidency would be too powerful, with arguments in favor of "a plural executive or an executive council. . . . Many objected that with his veto, his powers as commander-in-chief, his powers of appointment, and his general authority to see that the laws are faithfully executed, the 'President-General' . . . could find justification for almost anything he might wish to do" (Storing 1981b, 49). A critic writing as Cato warned that the new office might degenerate into monarchy: "Wherein does this president, invested with his powers and prerogatives, essentially differ from the King of Great Britain?" (Yoo 2009a, 38). And an "Old Whig" maintained that the president, in reality, is to be "as much a king as the King of Great-Britain, and a King too of the worst kind; an elective King" (38). In a letter to his constituents, John Williams wrote, "The powers given to the president are very great" (Bailyn 1993, 2:119). Among the recurrent criticisms was that the president and the Senate could, with but two-thirds of its members, make treaties. There was concern about the provision that the president could call forth the militia of the several states. Another frequent criticism was the division of power between the executive and legislative branches, which could either fuel factions or prove ineffective in controlling the powers of the federal government—a result of the legislature's influence over the president through the electoral process.

Some pamphleteers responded to these criticisms. John Stevens Jr. (Bailyn 1993 2:119), writing as Americanus, directly addressed the charge that the president would be another king: "On this side of the Atlantic, all apprehensions arising from this source are visionary. Why then should we tie up our own hands [by making a president ineligible for reelection], and deprive ourselves of the services of a man, with whose conduct we are perfectly satisfied?" Stevens also favored granting "solely to the President, and the subordinate ones to the heads of departments," the power of appointment. As for the pardon power, he asked, where else "would we place it with greater safety and propriety?" (Bailyn 1993, 2:59–60).

Of these various debates, Michael Riccards (1987, 46) commented, "Although these and other polemical debates were vigorously carried out in the newspapers and through pamphlets, they generally lacked vigor and depth." Contrary to much other opinion, Riccards noted, "Again, systematic discussions of the proposed Constitution took place at the state ratifying conventions, where Federalist and Anti-Federalist factions went through the new document section by section. . . . And it was at these conventions that the presidency was being discussed at some length and often in passionate and fearful terms." Yet, as Michael McConnell (2020, 87) noted, "Five state ratifying conventions proposed more than fifty amendments, but the only proposals related to the powers of the presidency were to bar pardons in treason cases and to forbid the commander in chief from leading troops in battle." Furthermore, there "wasn't much discussion about what the various provisions bearing on executive power meant."

Controversy and Conflict

> There is no doubt that the founders were men of ideas, were, in fact, the leading intellectuals of their day. But they were as well the political leaders of their day, politicians who competed for power, lost and won elections, served in their colonial state legislatures or in Congress, became governors, judges, and even presidents.
>
> —Gordon Wood, *Revolutionary Characters*

What then was the Framers' own verdict regarding the work they accomplished in Philadelphia? Dennis Rasmussen (2021, 2–3) wrote, "Most of the founders who lived into the nineteenth century—or even to the dawn of the new century, like Washington—came to feel deep anxiety, disappointment, and even despair about the government and the nation that they had helped to create." That the Constitution has endured would seem miraculous to many of the Framers. Henceforth, an originalist interpretation of the Constitution should identify that many of the Framers, as well as other leaders of the Founding generation, had reservations regarding the results of the work of the Constitutional Convention. Several did not see the document as a finished work. Some thought it a failure; others, but a temporary bridge until a better constitution could be provided. And far from sharing one idea of original intent, Paul Heike (2014, 198) noted, the idea is a myth that "symbolizes cooperation and interdependence by toning down internal conflicts among those actors and by erasing the contingency of their plans and actions, their local and regional (rather than national) interests, and all sorts of major and minor disagreements." And when it came to the presidency, as Sidney Warren (1964, 4) maintained, "James Wilson, one of the delegates, reflecting on it later, called the construction of the presidency the 'most difficult part of this system.' This is not surprising that this should have been true. The delegates divided sharply on the vital question of executive power."

Certainly, developing an enduring constitution with an executive acceptable to the citizens of 1787 was an enormous and highly controversial undertaking, though as John Adams wrote to John Jay (December 16, 1787), "The public mind cannot be occupied about a nobler object than the proposed plan of government. It appears to be admirably calculated to cement all America in affection and interest as one great nation." Yet Adams too had reservations: "A result of accommodation and compromise, cannot be supposed perfectly to coincide with any one's ideas of perfection. But, as all the great principles necessary to order, liberty and safety, are respected in it, and provision is made for corrections and amendments as they may be found necessary, I confess I hope to hear of its adoption by all the States" (Diplomatic Correspondence 1833, 356).

Even with multiple compromises, or perhaps because of them, as James McCabe (1874, 571) noted, "The new constitution was not entirely satisfactory to any party, and represented the sacrifices made by all to achieve the great end of a central government, strong enough to carry out the objects of the Union. It was a document of compromises." Hence, as Adolphe de Chambrun (1874, 278) noted, "Contemporary documents prove that the framers of the Constitution were not assured of its duration; for we seldom find in the journals and writings of the day, an expression of unalloyed satisfaction. . . . A feeling of doubt and uncertainty continued up to the close of that century. Even after the presidency of Washington many Americans had serious misgivings about the future of the Republic." As to the presidency's position in the governmental hierarchy, Chambrun (1874, 282, 284) surmised, "Then the question would at once arise whether the legislative or executive branch of the government would take ascendancy. Now, whatever, may be the apparent strength of the first, it does not require a prophet's eye to foresee the ultimate triumph of the second. . . . An active and energetic foreign policy necessarily implies that the executive who directs it is permanent and clothed with powers in proportion to his vigor or action." And Justice Joseph Story (1858, 1:191) advised, "Let it not . . . be supposed, that a constitution, which is now looked upon with such general favor and affection by the people, had no difficulties to encounter at its birth. The history of those times is full of melancholy instruction on this subject, at once to admonish us of past dangers, and to awaken us to a lively sense of the necessity of future vigilance."

Conclusion

In sum, then, the Constitution left much unsaid. We therefore can conclude that the Framers spent little time debating or delineating the powers of the new presidential office, the result was a series of compromises, and the powers and duties of the presidency were largely left undefined. This provided the basis for compromise, but it also established ambiguity regarding the meaning of the various presidential powers. Additionally, the Framers were skeptical that the Constitution would survive and many were disappointed in the results. Finally, there was considerable opposition to the Constitution among the public, as well as among the Framers themselves. Original intent was therefore clouded in controversy and disagreement from the very creation of the Constitution.

In fact, ambiguity was an important component of original intent. As one of the most eminent constitutional scholars of his age, Judge Thomas Cooley (1889, 207–8) commented that diverse interpretations of the Constitution appeared from the very beginning: "The Constitution was a compromise between sharply conflicting views. It is possible, that some things were purposely left uncertain, because no agreement could be reached on words, which would have removed the obscurity." At the end of the Civil War, Thomas D'Arcy (1865, 34) wrote, "The Constitution of the United States was a compromise between state jealousy and the strong sentiment of self-preservation; between the science and scholarship of such men as the authors of the *Federalist*, and the wild theories of the demagogues of the day. It betrays, therefore, very naturally, both in its strengths and its weaknesses, in its provisions and omissions, the unmistakable marks of this twofold parentage." There were repercussions to this compromise document. Writing one hundred years after the Constitution went into effect, Judge Judson Landon (1889, 304) noted, "The possession of power is too often followed by its abuse. This abuse must result in the abasement of the people, or their resistance to the government itself, unless, indeed, the people possess the power to reform the government, and intelligence and unity enough to exercise such power aright."

Chapter 3

Constitutional Ambiguity

A Historical Time Series

"Constitutions," the great Napoleon once remarked, "should be short and obscure."

> —William Emerson, "Franklin Roosevelt as
> Commander in Chief in World War II"

Chapter 2 demonstrated that the Framers of the Constitution and the subsequent ratifying conventions dedicated precious little time to an examination of presidential power. Without a clear reference to power in these debates, we are left with the concept of presidential power unmoored to a specific definition. Instead, across time, the US Constitution provides sufficient ambiguity for the redefinition of the presidency's constitutional powers. As William Howell and David Brent (2013) described, these range across the spectrum, from "a strong to a weak presidency." Consequently, disagreements about the extent and nature of presidential power continues to the present day and it involves vastly different interpretations of Article II, some of which provide an "open-ended grant of power." For example, not only did Donald Trump expand presidential power in dangerous ways, but his 2024 campaign promises an even greater expansion if he is elected again. In 2023, the Heritage Foundation conducted a multi-million-dollar study, *Project 2025*, specifically designed to promote a radical expansion of presidential power. It would provide presidents with virtually unlimited control over the executive branch, including tens of thousands of civil service positions. Given this radical proposal, we need to consider these pertinent questions posed by Akhil Reed Amar (2021, xiii): "The Constitution was a set of words. . . . What did these words mean and how should they be read and made real? Would these words continue to work as the Revolutionaries who drafted and ratified them passed from the scene and gave way to a new generation of conversationalists?" We also need to examine the attitudes of the Framers. Regarding their views, Lee Strang (2019, 13) commented, "At the Philadelphia Convention, the Framers took great care to craft the Constitution's structure, text, grammar, and even punctuation; they did so to communicate as clearly as possible the meaning they wished to convey to the Ratifiers, government officials, and Americans generally. For example, the Framers extensively debated whether the text that became Article I, Section 8, cl.10, should include the words 'punishment,' 'declare,' and 'felonies,' in the grant to Congress of power over admiralty and international law."

The Framers had clear ideas about Congress' Article I powers because they were familiar with legislative institutions: Parliament in England, the colonial state assemblies, and the Congress under the Articles of Confederation. But the Framers had no acceptable preexisting model for an executive office. They knew what they did not want, such as a king or a colonial governor, but they were far less certain about what they did want. As such, they spent far less time debating the words included in Article II than those in Article I. Henceforth, we are left to delve into the questions of the Framers' incentives and original intent in creating the presidency without a clear guide to their thinking.

There is little doubt that these men ably met the challenge of creating an entirely new executive institution. Yet, as Robert Hirschfield (1976, 292) commented, "The power of the Presidency is a complex phenomenon. It cannot be determined simply by reference to the Constitution; nor does it become fully evident by reviewing the history of what Presidents have done or gotten away with. The reason for this elusiveness is that presidential power varies, and that its reality at any given time is the product of a number of factors." Or as Michael Genovese ([2011] 2017, 2) reminded us, "Presidential power is . . . dynamic, not static." And Jeremy Bailey (2019, 3) stated that "during difficulty," particularly crisis situations, the "president's extraconstitutional power seems to be related to the ebb and flow of the president's constitutional power." Hence, in addition to the power fluctuations that occur during the regular patterns of a four- or eight-year term of office, there are longitudinal effects of power as it fluctuates across historical time and ambiguity has played a central role in this development. In this chapter I demonstrate that constitutional ambiguity has been a subject of continuing concern as well as a mainstream idea in the realm of constitutional interpretation. To address this point, I employ a historical time series of the viewpoints of observers of the presidency across American history.

Finding Power in the Constitution's Nooks and Crannies

There can be little question that the original conception of the American presidency was worked out by the makers of the American Constitution as a republican substitute to the hereditary monarch of English eighteenth-century constitutionalism especially as represented by colonial governors, but with the image of George Washington in their minds as the kind of man who could and would occupy the office. Yet, he was definitely to be more restrained than a king . . . it has been argued in recent years that much of his apparent power is deceptive, and that his responsibilities greatly exceed his resources for fulfilling them. This argument is only one part of an ongoing debate as to the "real" position of the American president in twentieth-century America.

—Carl Friedrich, *The Impact of
American Constitutionalism Abroad*

As Erwin Hargrove and Roy Hoopes (1975, 5) wrote, "The primary sources of presidential power can be found in Article II of the Constitution. . . . It is a surprisingly short Article, consisting of four sections of approximately 920 words. Despite, the brevity, it was one of the most intensely debated articles at the Constitutional Convention." While I disagree with the last part of their statement, interpreting the president's Article II powers is of central concern. Yet the Article's very brevity has created considerable diversity of opinion regarding the proper mode of interpreting its 920 or so words, only a fraction of which are related to an enumeration of presidential power. Consequently, multiple methods of interpretation exist. Some textualists examine only Article II's words, using dictionary definitions from the eighteenth century as a guide. Others examine each clause separately. Others, such as Saikrishna Prakash (2015, 4) argue, "If we do not pay attention to all the Article II pieces and how they fit together, we will fail to appreciate that the Constitution established a complete mosaic and that its presidency is more than just the sum of a few narrow clauses." But how do these pieces fit together? As eminent constitutional scholar Edward Corwin (1941, 122) wrote, "It is a common allegation that the terms in which the President's powers are granted are the loosest and most unguarded of any part of the Constitution, and this is true when Article II is read by itself. But what warrant is there for reading it thus, rather than in its context, the Constitution as a whole? When it is read in this way the net impression left is quite different." The problem, however, as Corwin continued, is as follows:

> In short, the Constitution itself reflects not one but two conceptions of executive power: the conception that it exists for the most part to serve the legislative power, wherein resides the will of society, and the conception that it ought to be within generous limits autonomous and self-directory. The source of this dualism was the eighteenth-century notion of a balanced constitution; its consequence has been a constantly renewed struggle for power between the political branches. Nor has the struggle ceased to this day, although its total result has been, especially within recent years, the vast aggrandizement of the presidency.

While this dualism beckoned Corwin's (1940) "invitation to struggle," it was complicated by yet another factor. Dualism further encouraged ambiguity. As historian James Sterling Young (1966, 351) noted, "In defining this position as such (as head, indeed, of the executive branch), the constitution . . . falls somewhat below its customary level of clarity." Therefore, it is difficult to develop a satisfactory definition of presidential power. As Ken Gormley (2020, 2) identified, "Article II, Section 1, vest the 'executive Power' in the president, but does nothing to define the powers that lie at the heart of the chief executive's office." But what is the historical basis for constitutional ambiguity? Has it developed as we move further away from the Founding, and therefore is it merely a manifestation of the concept of a living constitution or the increasing power of the presidency over time? Or is it a fundamental idea that can be traced across American history? To examine these questions, I employ a historical time series representing the views of various observers of the Constitution and the American presidency, to examine their perceptions of constitutional ambiguity versus clarity throughout American history.

A Historical Time Series

Some scholars argue that the Framers' intent to give the Congress a leading role in government is evident in the fact that Article I of the Constitution grants many explicit powers to the Congress in comparison to the ambiguity and vagueness of the President's powers outlined in Article II. Indeed, a survey of the historical record reveals that, over time, Presidents have successfully exploited the ambiguity of their formal powers to increase the power of the Presidency vis-à-vis the Congress.

—Marybeth Ulrich, "National Security Powers:
Are the Checks in Balance?"

We can find evidence of constitutional ambiguity in the writings of the Framers. In *Federalist no. 37*, James Madison identified the difficulties of eliminating imprecision without writing a prolix of encyclopedic language, and the Anti-Federalist Cato (1788) (Ketcham 1986, 317) noted, "I endeavored to prove that the language of the article relative to the establishment of the executive of this new government was vague and inexplicit, that the great power of the President, connected with his duration in office would lead to oppression and ruin." Writing during the first year of James Madison's presidency, Augustus Woodward (1809, 13) advised, "The propriety of increasing the stability of the executive department of our government, and of rendering it, as far as human nature will admit, exempt from the mutations incident to individual statesmen, or temporary party, is a subject by no means unworthy of the intelligent mind of America." During the John Quicy Adams presidency, Woodward (1825, 29, 65) then noted that the power of the presidency already had transitioned beyond its constitutional mandate: "It is a great evil, in the Cabinet system, when the legitimate powers of the Presidential office are detorted from the hands in which the Constitution has placed them." He continued, "It ought, lastly, to be a sufficient, a conclusive, and a fatal objection to the present cabinet system, that it is not sanctioned or recognised by the Constitution or by the laws." Woodward (1825, 55) also observed, "A solemn and written Constitution should be deemed so sacred, that even when proceedings are recommended by evident and obvious utility, and the want of sanction is rather to be ascribed to neglect than prohibition, care should be taken, at as early a period as practicable, to legitimate the deviation."

While Woodward wrote about the presidency as early as 1809, scholarly interest in the Constitution didn't emerge consistently until the 1820s. During that decade the first book on the Constitution was written by Thomas Sergeant (1822, preface) who noted, "The author of the following treatise believes [the Constitution's] object and plan to be novel. He has met with no work, whence he could derive assistance. He does not doubt, that many imperfections may be found in it, which he has himself been unable to detect or remedy. The learned and candid reader will appreciate the difficulties attending the undertaking, and make every reasonable allowance." The next year, John Taylor (1823, 163) noted a fundamental disagreement regarding whether the Constitution established a national government or a compact of the states. As I examine in chapter 5, as the nation struggled with its very identity, the debate about a national government versus a compact of states raged until the Civil War, with constitutional scholars, as well as politicians, offering entirely different interpretations of the Constitution's meaning. New York Justice James Kent (1826, 236–37) also observed ambiguity in the relationship of the powers of the government: "No constitution can contain accurate detail of all the subdivisions of its powers, and of all the means by which they might be carried into execution. It would render it too prolix. Its nature requires only the great outlines should be marked, and its important objects designated, and all the minor ingredients left to be deduced from the nature of those objects."

Concern with constitutional ambiguity continued into the 1830s. Writing during the presidency of Andrew Jackson, Nathaniel Chipman (1833, 255–56) noted, "The powers delegated by the constitution are for the most part expressed in general terms." Also in the 1830s, Supreme Court Justice Joseph Story (1858, 1:284–86) explained,

> There may be obscurity, as to the meaning, from the doubtful character of words used, from other clauses in the same instrument, or from an incongruity or repugnancy between the words, and the apparent intention derived from the whole structure of the instrument, or its avowed object. In all such cases interpretation becomes indispensable. . . . Interpretation also may be strict or large; though we do not always mean the same thing, when we speak of a strict or large interpretation . . . perhaps the safest rule of interpretation after all will be found to be to look to the nature and objects of the particular powers, duties, and rights, with all the lights and aids of contemporary history; and to give to the words of each

just such operation and force, consistent with their legitimate meaning, as may fairly secure and attain the ends proposed.

In the following decade with Martin Van Buren as president, Abel Upshur (1863, 116) addressed the constitutional ambiguity inherent in Article II:

> The most defective part of the Constitution beyond all question, is that which relates to the Executive Department. It is impossible to read this instrument, without being struck with the loose and unguarded terms in which the powers and duties of the President are pointed out . . . it is a reproach to the Constitution, that the executive trust is so ill-defined, as to leave any plausible pretence, even to the insane zeal of party devotion, for attributing to the President of the United States the powers of a despot; powers which are wholly unknown in any limited monarchy in the world.

And with James Buchanan as president, William Duer (1858, 83) wrote,

> A vigour of action duly proportioned to the exigencies which arise must be imparted to the executive power. But for this purpose, the proportion of power vested to the occasions that may be expected to require its exercise should be as exact as possible; for if the power fall short, the evils already adverted to will ensue; and if it exceed its true proportion, the liberties of the people would be endangered. It is difficult, however, in a written Constitution, to adopt general expressions precisely, descriptive of the proper extent and limitation of this power.

Prior to the Civil War, scholarly interest in the Constitution was limited, with much of it targeted at the issues of state's rights, sovereignty, and slavery. The Civil War and the apparent failure of the Constitution, however, renewed interest in the nation's fundamental document. Afterward there was a steady focus on what the document meant and how it should be interpreted, particularly as the idea of a living constitution became a dominant theoretical paradigm. Among those writing about constitutional ambiguity during the Civil War and Reconstruction were Sidney Fisher (1862, 20) and Theodore Dwight (1867, 257), while Alfred

Conkling (1866, 4–5), during the presidency of Andrew Johnson, wrote specifically about the executive:

> It has . . . been briefly treated by our writers on constitutional jurisprudence; and, with regard to some of its elements, subjected also to judicial scrutiny. And yet, now, under all the lights thus shed upon it, after the lapse of three-quarters of a century, it not only remains practically unsolved, but presents itself under new and alarming phases. I hardly need to say that I refer to the SCOPE [of] EXECUTIVE POWER in our national system of government, and, incidentally, to the line which separates it from the legislative power.

The later decades of the nineteenth century witnessed broader interest in constitutional construction. In the 1870s, George Washington Paschal (1870, ix) and Adolphe de Chambrun (1874, 151–52) remarked on the Constitution's ambiguity. In the 1880s with Grover Cleveland serving as president, John McMaster (1885, 1:460–61) wrote, "The form . . . of a republican government was guaranteed to each by express words; but any one who would read the instrument [i.e., the Constitution] carefully, and not suffer his understanding to be clouded with a multitude of fine phrases, could see that it was the form, and not the substance, that was promised." Later that decade, James Bryce (1917, 274) wrote, "We see . . . that several salient features of the present American government, such as the popular election of the President, the influence of senators and congressmen over patronage, the immense power of the Speaker, the Spoils System, are due to usages which have sprung up around the Constitution and profoundly affected its working, but which are not parts of the Constitution, nor necessarily attributable to any specific provision which it contains." Meanwhile, Woodrow Wilson ([1885] 1901, 8–9) even considered the Constitution's brevity a strength:

> For it to go beyond elementary provisions would be to lose elasticity and adaptability. The growth of the nation and the consequent development of the governmental system would snap asunder a constitution which could not adapt itself to the new conditions of an advancing society. If it could not stretch itself to the measure of the times, it must be thrown off and left behind, as a by-gone device; and there can, therefore, be

no question that our Constitution has proved lasting because of its simplicity. It is a corner-stone, not a complete building; or, rather, to return to the old figure, it is a root, not a perfect vine.

Meanwhile, other scholars commenting on constitutional ambiguity from the late nineteenth century included eminent scholars Judson Landon (1889, 16), Christopher Tiedeman (1890, 137), and Albert Bushnell Hart (1893, 128).

By the turn of the century there was increased interest in the presidential office. As Hugh Heclo (1977, 8) stated, "During most of the 19th century, scholars gave only passing attention to the Presidency as a small part of the more general study of American government. Slowly at the turn of the century, however, and more quickly after 1930, the Presidency emerged as a specialized area for research and interpretation." These authors again noted the Constitution's ambiguity. For instance, Nelson Case (1904, 231) stated, "The constitutional limitation on the right of the President to participate in legislation has never been clearly defined." With William Howard Taft as president, William Draper Lewis (1909, 93–94) argued, "We must admit, that though the skill with which the constitution was drawn makes it one of the really great achievements of our race, it is not equally perfect in all its parts. Brevity and the statement of general principles not only may but do, in parts of the constitution, degenerate into intolerable uncertainty as to the real principle intended to be enunciated." Future president Woodrow Wilson (1908, 193), who was now a proponent of a stronger presidency, and Van Vechten Veeder (1903, 1:293) also expressed concerns with the Constitution's ambiguity.

The next decade, Charles Beard ([1910] 1914, 187) stated, "The functions of the President are prescribed by the Constitution, but his real achievements are not set by the letter of the law." Former president William Howard Taft (1916, 2–3) likewise noted the Constitution's ambiguities, as did Thomas Reed Powell (1912, 215), Max Farrand (1913, 201), Andrew McLaughlin with Albert Bushnell Hart (1914, 2), and future Supreme Court justice George Sutherland (1919, 16). After World War I, Everett Kimball (1920, 168) noted, "The most important power of the president comes not from the Constitution but from the political system which the Constitution made necessary," while during the presidency of William Howard Taft, William MacDonald (1921, 54) wrote, "The actual powers of the President, as everyone knows, far transcend [Article II's] comparatively simple and obvious limits." Writing in 1923 on the creation of the presidency, Charles Thach (2017, 124) concluded,

> The completion of Article II of the Constitution seems, at first sight, a logical place for an evaluation of the work of the Convention and an interpretation of the executive established by it. A closer view reveals the fact that such an evaluation and interpretation is hardly possible. Rushed through in the last days of the Convention's being, as much of it was, the executive article fairly bristles with contentious matter, and, until it is seen what decision was given to these contentions, it is impossible to say just what the national executive meant.

Other notables from this period agreed. Former secretary of war Newton Diehl Baker (1925, 6) and Edward Corwin (1925, 290–92) referenced the Constitution's vague language.

By the 1930s, with the nation mired in the Great Depression and Herbert Hoover in the White House, William Munro (1930, 1–2) reminded us,

> The written Constitution of the United States is a document that occupies five pages of print in the World Almanac and can be read in half an hour. But alongside it, and based upon it, there has developed during the past hundred and forty years an unwritten constitution of vastly greater dimension. It fills the statutes-at-large, the law reports, the printed laws of the individual commonwealths, and constitutional treaties to the extent of a million or more pages. This unwritten constitution is made up of federal and state enactments, judicial decisions, usages, doctrines, precedents, official opinion, and points of view which have profoundly altered the implications of the original instrument. It has made the government of the United States a different affair from that which the framers of the written constitution intended it to be. So great has this divergence become at the present day that no one can now obtain even a silhouette of the American political system if he confines his study to the nation's fundamental law as it left the hands of its architects in 1787.

Later that decade, with Franklin Roosevelt as president, Wilfred Binkley (1937, 15–16) asked, "What did the terms 'legislative power,' 'executive power,' 'judicial power' mean? To modern Americans these expressions represent quite definite concepts, clarified as they have been, by a century and a half of experience and judicial definition. To the men who made our earliest constitutions the content of these terms was inchoate." Other authors from this decade included Charles and William Beard (1930, 22), Charles Howard McIlwain (1932, 15), and Thurmond Arnold (1937, 29).

At the commencement of the next decade, E. Pendleton Herring (1940, 2–3) wrote, "We have created a position of great power but have made the full realization of that power dependent upon influence rather than legal authority," a statement highly reminiscent of Richard Neustadt's thesis. And with Harry Truman as president, Clinton Rossiter ([1948] 2011, 217–18) added, "It must follow that a serious crisis will result invariably in an increase in the prestige and competence of the President. This is made doubly certain by the broad and flexible grants of power to the President found in the Constitution." And Louis Brownlow (1949, 15), of the eponymous committee that recommended the establishment of what became the Executive Office of the President, advised,

> The Constitution assigns so many roles to the President that it is difficult to arrive at a single, simple, all-inclusive definition of his powers, duties and obligations. Yet for all the difficulty which besets any effort to define the nature of the Presidency or a President as a political entity in itself, the undertaking becomes incredibly complicated when the definition is attempted in terms of the separation of powers between the Executive, Legislative, and Judicial Branches of Government set up by the Constitution.

Other scholars from this period included Carl Swisher (1943, 1017) and George Milton (1945, 322), as well as Ford Hall, Pressly Sikes, John Stoner, and Francis Wormuth (1949, 106).

In a book originally published in the 1950s, former president Harry Truman (1960, 172) wrote, "When the founding fathers outlined the Presidency in Article II of the Constitution, they left a great many details vague. I think they relied on the experience of the nation to fill in the outlines." And with Dwight Eisenhower in the White House, Edward

Corwin (1957, 1–2) once again noted, "Article II is the most loosely drawn chapter of the Constitution. To those who think that a constitution ought to settle everything beforehand, it should be a nightmare." Robert Carr (1951, 979) and Charles Pritchett (1959, vii) also referenced the Constitution's ambiguity. Writing during John Kennedy's presidency, Bernard Schwartz (1963, 2–3) advised, "The provisions of Article II are among the most skeletonlike in the entire basic document. . . . One who reads Article II cannot help but be struck by the fact that its key provisions are imprecise and indefinite by comparison with the articles defining the other branches. The relative vagueness of Article II has more than once been the subject of animadversion." And with Lyndon Johnson as president, James Sterling Young (1966, 158) opined that the president's powers were "as bare as Mother Hubbard's kitchen." He was joined in this opinion by Theodore White (1961, 367), John Roche and Leonard Levy (1964), David Haight and Larry Johnston (1965, 2), and Marilyn Prolman (1969, 28). Meanwhile, Walter Travis (1967, 1) noted, "In the writing of the Constitution the framers conceived an executive office that was to be independent from the newly proposed national legislature. But in doing so, they never clearly defined the relationship that ought to exist between the two branches of government. . . . This omission has created a problem in executive-legislative relationships that has confronted every president and every Congress since 1789."

Statements regarding constitutionally vague language were evident in the 1970s, such as the following from Richard Haynes (1973, 3), who was writing in the tumultuous scandal plagued days of Richard Nixon's presidency: "This awesome power of the presidency is predicated upon one brief clause of the Constitution: 'The President shall be Commander in Chief.' This vaguely worded sentence provides the power resources of the presidency." And during Jimmy Carter's first year as president, a former member of Franklin Roosevelt's administration, Rexford Tugwell (1977, 18) noted, "Interpretations of the Constitution, it should be said, differ; they differ because of its sometimes ambiguous language and also because certain of its provisions have become irrelevant or insufficient." Other scholars writing during this decade included Louis Fisher (1974, 258), Grant McConnell (1976, 7–8), and Stephen Wayne (1978, 5), as well as Raymond Tatalovich and Byron Daynes (1979, 428). Meanwhile, as Ronald Reagan ascended to the presidential office, Louis Koenig (1981, 41) advised: "If the power and presence of the chief executive in foreign affairs are subject to fluctuation, it is because the framers intended they be. In drafting the Constitution, they granted, after careful deliberation, substantial powers to both the legislative and executive branches. For the most part, the framers defined those powers vaguely and left the inevitable doubts and conflicts for struggle and resolution between the branches." And as novelist E. L. Doctorow (2014, 57–58) observed in 1987, "Not including the amendments, it is approximately 5,000 words long—about the length of a short story. It is an enigmatically dry, unemotional piece of work, tolling off in its monotone the structures and functions of government, the conditions and obligations of office, the limitations of powers, the means for redressing crimes and conducting commerce. . . . It is no more scintillating reading than I remember it to have been in Mrs. Brundage's seventh-grade civics class."

In the 1980s, William Goldsmith (1980, 1–2, 11; 1984, 13), Nelson Polsby (1986), Christopher Deering (1988, 137), and Richard Hodder-Williams (1987, 12) referenced constitutional vagueness, as did Thomas Cronin (1989, 180): "The Constitutional Convention of 1787 successfully invented the American Presidency, yet its outline of executive powers in Article II was loosely drawn." This basic theme was repeated in the 1990s during the presidency of George Herbert Walker Bush. Richard Pious (1991, 197) commented, "These grants of power are ambiguous, undefined, or incomplete. They do not cover the entire field of war powers, and their loose construction virtually invites the president and Congress into boundary disputes." Richard Nathan (1991, 197), who served in the Nixon administration added, "Article II created a relatively weak executive branch in terms of the president's relationships with the Congress." With Bill Clinton as president, David Currie (1997, 28–29) wrote, "Apart from prescribing the exact terms of the oath the President was to take before entering upon his duties . . . Article II said very little about how the President was to perform his functions. It also said very little about the officers with whose assistance he was to perform them." Forrest McDonald (1994, 2) referred to Article II as "imprecise, even muddled." Norman Thomas, Joseph Pika, and Thomas Watson (1993, 12) posited, "The powers of the presidency are so vast and vague that incumbents have tremendous latitude in shaping the office to their particular desires." Other scholars who noted ambiguity from this decade included Jack Rakove (1990, 193) and Joan Biskupic and Elder Witt (1997, 169).

The twenty-first century has witnessed continuing interest in the impact of constitutional ambiguity. Writing during George Walker Bush's presidency, Daniel Farber (2003, 127) stated, "The text and history of Article

II fail to offer decisive guidance regarding presidential power (even for those who are inclined to take it.)." Alan Brinkley and Davis Dyer (2004, ix) opined, "Article II of the United States Constitution provides a spare, even skeletal description of the role of the president of the United States." Robert Remini (2006, 27), one of Andrew Jackson's primary biographers added, "The relation between the executive and the legislative branches had not been made clear in the Constitution." Harold Krent (2005, 1) noted, "Article II itself is quite vague, never defining the 'executive' power with specificity." During the first year of Barack Obama's presidency, Fred Greenstein (2009, 96) commented, "The Constitution of the United States has been said to have an 'unfinished character.' This is particularly true of its sparse worded second article, which devotes more than a thousand words to its characterization of the presidency and only 146 words . . . to the specific responsibilities of the chief executive." Even John Yoo (2009a, 1), who served with George W. Bush and has advocated a stronger presidency, argued, "The Framers thought long and hard about the question of executive power. In the words of Jack Rakove, creating the presidency was 'their most creative act.' It was also their most ambiguous. Details of this new Presidency were left open, sparking controversy from the beginning."

In the next decade Roger Davidson (2011, 254) posited, "In contrast to Article I's precise listing of powers, Article II—the executive article—is quite loosely drawn. (However experienced the Founders were in legislative affairs, they had no clear models for the republican chief executive they were creating)." Harold Bruff (2015, 20) agreed, "Article II spells out detailed procedures for electing presidents but lapses into generalities when identifying the powers of the office. Plainly, the framers were more comfortable specifying processes than substance." Fergus Bordewich (2016, 59) wrote of the work of the first US Congress, "The vast undefined space that remained instantly became a battleground. . . . The [removal] debate that ensued marked the first collision between broad interpreters of the Constitution, Madison among them, and those who insisted that if the Constitution didn't stipulate a power, that power simply didn't exist." And during the presidency of Donald Trump, Roger Davidson, Walter Oleszek, Frances Lee, and Eric Schickler (2018, 293) advised, "Understanding the chief executive's relations with Congress is no easy task. The Founders did not clearly define the legislative-executive relationship and it remains a work in progress."

Among others writing about constitutional ambiguity and the presidency from the twenty-first century are Gary Lawson (2008, 375),

Eric Posner and Adrian Vermeule (2010, 184), Irwin Morris (2010, 61), Robert Spitzer (2011, 61), Curtis Bradley and Trevor Morrison (2013, 1098), Justin Vaughn and José Villalobos (2015, 23), Aditya Bamzai (2017, 931), Lisa Maneheim and Kathryn Watts (2018, 19), Daphna Renan (2018, 2189–90), Ken Gormley (2020, 1–2, 3), and William Howell (2023, 44). Commenting on the present attempt to interpret presidential power, with Joseph Biden in the White House, Stephen Skowronek, John Dearborn, and Desmond King (2021, 201) noted, "There is, in fact, something oddly contrived about today's belated push for constitutional clarity, as if only now, suddenly, the meaning of the framers' handiwork has become clear and dispositive. Stranger still is the idea that the Constitution locks us into a strong state design with all administrative power under the president's command and control."

This historical time series covers over two hundred years of insights on the US Constitution, with observers writing from the presidency of James Madison to Joseph Biden. Still, any time series, even a historical one, must deal with the issue of *autocorrelation*—that is, in this case, the idea that various scholars are simply mimicking what others before them said. While some scholars may have done so, it is unlikely that the idea would be repeated for more than two centuries without substantial countervailing evidence. And yet, constitutional ambiguity was referenced by presidents, judges, cabinet secretaries, and other administration officials, as well as constitutional law scholars, political scientists, experts in public administration, and historians—a wide range of constitutional observers. Furthermore, I found few references to the language of the Constitution as being clearly expressed. One publication from the 1820s noted its brevity in a different context (Hallowell 1826, 5):

> The perspicuous brevity of the Constitution has left but little room for misinterpretation. But if at any time ardent or timid minds have exceeded or fallen short of its intentions; if the precision of human language has, in the formation of this instrument, been inadequate to the expression of the exact ideas meant to be conveyed by its framers; if from the vehemence of party spirit, it has been warped by individuals, so as to incline it either too much towards monarchy or towards an unmodified democracy; let us console ourselves with the reflection, that however these aberrations may have transiently prevailed, the essential principles of the Representative System of government

have been well preserved by the clearsighted common sense of the people; and that our affections all concentrate in one great object, which is the improvement and glory of our country.

Within three decades "the clearsighted common sense of the people" devolved into Civil War. Meanwhile, several observers noted the Constitution's clarity, including Francis Lieber (1853, 299), who was writing before his tenure in Abraham Lincoln's War Department. Corporate lawyer Grosvenor Lowrey (1863, 11, 12) noted the Constitution's clarity, though he also made an exception related to the commander-in-chief clause when he wrote, "These powers it is impossible to declare in advance; such as they are, they inhere in the eternal frame of things." Jabez Curry (1889, 18–19), a Southern opponent of Lincoln and emancipation, scholars Rossiter Johnson (1910, 227) and Nicholas Butler (1917, 36), and an official from Woodrow Wilson's administration, George Creel (1920, 15–16), also found clarity in the Constitution. There may be others of which I am unaware, but it is apparent that the preponderance of opinion throughout American history has identified a lack of specificity at the heart of our Constitution; that is, the great majority of opinion expressed by multiple observers is that in the Constitution, Article II includes vague and ambiguous language, and that this vague language has contributed to an expansion of presidential power.

Key Questions

How then does constitutional ambiguity influence presidential power? What are its specific effects? On this issue there are different theoretical points of view. According to Richard Neustadt (1960 [1990]), formal powers are not how presidents acquire power. They do so via persuasion and bargaining with others, primarily Congress, because they lack constitutional or legal command authority. And yet Carl Swisher (1953a, 249–50) posited, "Turning more specifically to the constitutional aspects of the problems of the executive branch, we find that branch at present perhaps more alive to the changing tasks of government than either of the other two." Steven Calabresi and Christopher Yoo (1997) proposed, "No one can doubt the President's constitutional power to control the entire executive branch (including the Treasury Department) and the actions of all of his subordinates." And William Howell (2003) demonstrated that presidents can develop "power without persuasion." So, is the presidency an office of limited formal and command authority, as Neustadt argued, or does the Constitution's ambiguity provide the basis for the development of broader executive power? Alternatively, does ambiguity limit presidential power, particularly among presidents who adopt a strict construction- ist interpretation? As "An American Citizen" wrote in the *Independent Gazetteer* of Philadelphia on September 26, 1787, "From such a servant with powers so limited and transitory, there can be no danger, especially when we consider the solid foundations on which our national liberties are immovably fixed by the other provisions of this excellent constitution" (Bailyn 1993, 1:24). But as Saikrishna Prakash (2020, 1, 4) argued, "Our Founding Fathers certainly did not fashion a Constitution that authorized presidents to amend and expand their constitutional office. . . . If presidents can unilaterally alter the Constitution, they can circumvent the document that spells out and limits their authority." Consequently, as Supreme Court Justice Robert Jackson advised in *Youngstown Sheet & Tube Co. v. Sawyer*, 343 U.S. 579 (1952), "That comprehensive and undefined presidential powers hold both practical advantages and grave dangers for the country will impress anyone who has served as legal adviser to a President in time of transition and public anxiety."

If presidential power is undefined, it similarly raises questions about the application of a literal, originalist, or textualist interpretation. On this point, two legal scholars, Eric Posner and Adrian Vermeule (2010, 11) commented, "Although the Constitution read literally, gives the president few express unilateral powers, he enjoys (and agencies enjoy) a mass of delegated powers, whose breadth and ambiguity mean that there is usually some statute or other in the picture to which the president or an agency can plausibly appeal." Prakash (2020, 1, 8) argued that we have a living presidency and "a president with kingly powers." Yet "modern presidents have advanced [power] on all fronts, pushing the boundaries of their constitutional office outward," creating "a creeping constitutional coup."

Is the development of presidential power evidence of a "constitutional coup," and if so, did the Framers intentionally introduce ambiguity? Michael Mezey (1989, 41) suggested the Framers' "vagueness about the presidency" likely reflected their own "desire for a much stronger presidency than the country at large would have been prepared to accept," a point of view shared by Thomas Cronin, Michael Genovese, and Meena Bose (2018, 2):

The constitutional founders purposely left the presidency impre-
cisely defined. This was due in part to fears of both monarchy
and the masses, and in part to hopes that future presidents
would create a more powerful office than the framers were able
to win ratification for at the time. . . . Thus the paradox of the
invention of the presidency: To get the presidency approved in
1787 and 1788 the framers had to leave silences and ambiguities
for fear of portraying the office as overly powerful.

Still, William Howell and David Brent (2013, 66) countered,

As an explanation of the Framers' intentions regarding the
presidency . . . intentional ambiguity can take us only so far.
While rigidity is to be avoided in any Constitution, the clarity
of Article I (which lays out Congress's formal structure and
powers) and Article III (which defines the judiciary's) stands in
stark relief to Article II. Moreover, there are plenty of constitutions in other countries that contain far more specific language
about the formal powers of the executive. Indeed, the U.S.
Constitution, coming in at 4,602 words in its original form, is
roughly a third of the size of the international average of 13,368
words, and a tiny fraction of the world's longest constitution
(India's, established in 1949) of 74,971 words.

In "other contested domains the Framers eschewed ambiguity in favor
of painstaking detail," such as the delineation of the Electoral College
process (Howell and Brent 2013, 68, 70). They also were far more explicit
in their identification of Congress' authority. Hence, the Constitution is
a combination of the more detailed explication of power to Congress in
Article I and the ambiguous language in Article II. On this point, Howell
and Brent added,

If the origins of this ambiguity are themselves unclear . . . other
matters are not: the ambiguity of Article II in the U.S. Constitution was not a foregone conclusion. The Framers of the
U.S. Constitution could have specified with a great deal more
exactitude what they meant by the executive power and the
take care clause. Moreover, their failure to do so had stark
consequences for the future development of the office of the

presidency, which produced clear winners and losers in the initial debate over presidential power. Though it took some time, champions of a strong presidency eventually won out.

Given this "paradox of the invention of the presidency," what can we learn from the actual words and provisions of Article II? Are they indeed ambiguous? Do they invite the potential for increased presidential power, or do they limit it? To answer these questions, we must first consider another question.

What Is Presidential Power?

Authority is not confined to government. It applies to the whole field of industry, labor and finance. There are many more people in positions of authority in private life than in government service. All organized life, private and public, depends upon the authority of some over others and the fineness and durability of that life depend upon the integrity with which authority is exercised.

—Franklin Roosevelt, *On Our Way*, 262

Raymond Tatalovich and Byron Daynes (1984, 28) remind us that "presidential power is a complex, elusive phenomenon, not amenable to simple explanation." And yet, as Richard Fallon ([2004] 2014, 184) described, "the Constitution establishes one president, vested with the whole 'executive power.'" And this power is expanding, though not at a constant pace, according to two advocates of the unitary executive theory, Steven Calabresi and Christopher Yoo (2003, 699): "Presidential power ebbed and flowed several times during the second fifty years under the Constitution. Congress reasserted itself and remained ascendant in the years following Andrew Jackson's presidency until the crisis of the Civil War, which led the country to look to the president for leadership once again." Yoo, Calabresi, and Nee (2004, 109) added, "The period between 1889 and 1945 saw a tremendous growth in presidential power, as strong Presidents like the two Roosevelts and Wilson . . . helped remake the institution of the presidency into the primary institution for mobilizing and implementing political will. Their administrations set the stage for the imperial presidency that would dominate modern times." And George Herring (2008,

336) indicated, "[Theodore] Roosevelt believed that America's new role required a strong executive. . . . Building on precedents set by McKinley, he established a firm basis for what would later be called the imperial presidency."

These observers noted that presidential power is expanding, though not necessarily consistently. Hence, it is important to address a fundamental question: What is presidential power? Defining that term was a task Justice Robert Jackson assumed in *Youngstown Sheet & Tube Co. v. Sawyer*. As Jeffrey Frank (2020, 328) noted of President Truman's "concept of executive authority—the 'inherent powers' of his office—were unusually broad, even farfetched." Justice Jackson agreed, and in his famous schema he identified three different categories of presidential power:

1. When the President acts pursuant to an express or implied authorization of Congress, his authority is at its maximum, for it includes all that he possesses in his own right plus all that Congress can delegate. In these circumstances, and in these only, may he be said (for what it may be worth) to personify the federal sovereignty. If his act is held unconstitutional under these circumstances, it usually means that the Federal Government as an undivided whole lacks power. A seizure executed by the President pursuant to an Act of Congress would be supported by the strongest of presumptions and the widest latitude of judicial interpretation, and the burden of persuasion would rest heavily upon any who might attack it.

2. When the President acts in absence of either a congressional grant or denial of authority, he can only rely upon his own independent powers, but there is a zone of twilight in which he and Congress may have concurrent authority, or in which its distribution is uncertain. Therefore, congressional inertia, indifference or quiescence may sometimes, at least as a practical matter, enable, if not invite, measures on independent presidential responsibility. In this area, any actual test of power is likely to depend on the imperatives of events and contemporary imponderables rather than on abstract theories of law.

3. When the President takes measures incompatible with the expressed or implied will of Congress, his power is at its lowest ebb, for then he can rely only upon his own constitutional

powers minus any constitutional powers of Congress over the matter.

While he developed broad parameters for understanding presidential power, interestingly, Jackson also noted,

> Loose and irresponsible use of adjectives colors all non-legal and much legal discussion of presidential powers. "Inherent" powers, "plenary" powers, "war" powers, and "emergency" powers are used, often interchangeably and without fixed or ascertainable meanings. The vagueness and generality of the clauses that set forth presidential powers afford a plausible basis for pressures within and without the administration for presidential action beyond that supported by those whose responsibility it is to defend his actions in court. The claim of inherent and unrestricted presidential powers has long been a persuasive dialectical weapon in political controversy.

Despite Jackson's schema, defining presidential power is a difficult task. This point was raised by Justice Felix Frankfurter's concurring opinion in *Youngstown*:

> The issue before us can be met, and therefore should be, without attempting to define the President's powers comprehensively. I shall not attempt to delineate what belongs to him by virtue of his office beyond the power even of Congress to contract; what authority belongs to him until Congress acts; what kind of problems may be dealt with either by Congress or by the President or by the President or by both; what power must be exercised by the Congress and cannot be delegated to the President.

The dissenting opinion issued by Justices Frederick Vinson, Stanley Reed, and Sherman Minton did little to clarify this question:

> The comprehensive grant of the executive power to a single person was bestowed soon after the country had thrown the yoke of monarchy. . . . It is thus apparent that the Presidency was deliberately fashioned as an office of power and independence. Of course, the Framers created no autocrat capable of

arrogating any power unto himself at any time. But neither did they create an automaton impotent to exercise the powers of Government at a time when the survival of the Republic may be at stake.

What then were the boundaries between an autocrat and an automaton? Other than the reference to the government's power at a time when the Republic's survival was at stake, which clearly was not the case during the Korean War, we are left with a broad understanding of the meaning of Article II. As David Currie (1965, 367–68) wrote,

> If Vinson meant to embrace the Solicitor General's argument that the President's powers were not like those of Congress and the courts, limited by the enumeration that followed, Jackson had an answer for him. "If that be true, it is difficult to see why the forefathers bothered to add several specific items, including some trifling ones." Although the text of article II is not as explicit on this point as are articles I and III, Jackson was aided by evidence of the Framers' purposes in concluding that the vesting of "executive power" in the President was not "a grant in bulk of all conceivable executive power," but rather "an allocation of the presidential office of the generic powers thereafter stated."

And as Henry Monaghan (1993, 271) wrote,

> The Court has yet to validate explicitly the Presidency's expansive accumulation of power. . . . The Court, however, affirmatively contributed to the enlarged presidential powers: the Presidency has been a major beneficiary of the legitimation of the vast, open-ended delegation of legislative power, and the Court has employed broad language to describe presidential authority in foreign affairs. . . . If ever forced to take a stand, it seems unlikely that the Court would act to constrain the powers of the Presidency in any significant way.

Further contributing to controversy, over time the courts altered the interpretive framework used to examine presidential power. As Louis Fisher (2017, 2) noted,

Initially, the Court interpreted constitutional disputes between the elected branches without favoring presidential power over Congress. In *Little v. Barreme* (1804), it recognized that when a presidential proclamation in time of war conflicts with congressional policy expressed in a statute, the legislative position establishes national policy. Opinions from that time to the *Curtiss-Wright* decision in 1936 were generally careful in analyzing the relative powers of the President and Congress. For more than eight decades, however, the Supreme Court has used its decisions—including erroneous and misleading dicta—to promote presidential authority.

The Supreme Court has mostly affirmed presidential power (Driesen 2021). The Supreme Court's decision in *Trump v. United States*, decided on July 1, 2024, added further confusion. In a 6–3 decision, the court provided presidents with virtually exclusive immunity for all "official acts" committed by a president during their term of office. Such official acts derived from the president's constitutional powers. As we have seen, however, those powers are undefined and Article II's provisions are vague. Therefore, the decision provides presidents with an extraordinary opportunity to expand their power by employing the vesting, commander in chief, and other clauses to justify a broad range of activities. As such, it may very well have opened Parndora's box, inviting all sorts of presidential abuses of power.

Conclusion

President Roosevelt, in the crisis of 1933, assumed the leadership which Congress, by its very nature and size, was incapable of furnishing. Many Americans profess to fear that the dictatorship which a state of war or emergency imposes upon the President will spell the end of democracy in this country, yet history clearly demonstrates that democracy flourishes when the Executive is strong and languishes when it is weak.

—Talbot Odell, *War Powers of the President*, 3

Presidents who seek power, and may not find explicit justification for it in the constitutional text, can use the wiggle room provided by constitutional ambiguity to redefine their powers. So long as the constitutional text remains ambiguous, presidents can do this by interpreting the Constitution in a manner amenable to their desired outcome. Constitutional ambiguity also creates the need for interpretation. But as I discuss in chapter 4, a series of impediments inhibited constitutional interpretation in early America. A shortage of law schools, poor methods of instruction in the few existing law schools, and a lack of authoritative constitutional documentation were obstacles. At the same time, few states offered instruction on the Constitution to their citizens, and even in the late nineteenth and early twentieth centuries civics classes promoted citizenship rather than knowledge of government or the Constitution. Consequently, at a time when there was a great need to understand the Constitution, when students of government needed to understand the Framers' original intent, there were severe barriers to doing so.

Chapter 4

Obstacles to the Interpretation of the Constitution in Early America

If every President and every Congress can go behind the uniform construction given to the Constitution by the courts, and by the practice of the government, we are at sea indeed, on the billows of change, and the law of the land ceases to be a "rule of conduct," but becomes merely the arbitrary decree of any party that happens for the time to be uppermost.

—Sidney George Fisher and Charles Edward,
Kansas and the Constitution

The Constitution consisted of myriad compromises, as well as the use of undefined powers. But there were other factors beyond the Constitution's few words that promoted constitutional ambiguity during the nineteenth century. As a result, Arthur Holcombe (1958, viii) wrote,

In the course of the Constitution's comparatively long life the opinion of it, formed by those it was designed to serve, has undergone great changes. In the beginning it was accepted reluctantly and with misgiving. A generation passed before there was general confidence in its suitability for the purposes of a people who looked forward to an extraordinary growth in numbers, wealth, and power. A century passed before the whole body of the people gave their definitive consent to the political system which had been established under its authority. There has never been a time when the Government of the Union was not challenged by some problem which tested its structure and powers.

This was particularly the case during the early years of the Republic. Under Chief Justice John Marshall's leadership, the Supreme Court was reinvigorated and the process of defining the Constitution's provisions began. And in "An Address Delivered before the Members of the Suffolk Bar [. . .]," Justice Joseph Story (1829, 1) extolled, "In comparing the present state of jurisprudence with that of former times, we have much reason for congratulation." Still scholars paid little attention to the Constitution until the 1820s, more than thirty years after the Constitutional Convention. For example, as Nathan Dane (1823, 1:iii) opined in the first of an eight-volume collection of legal documents,

> He early found there was in the United States nothing like *one collected body of American Law, or one system of American Politics*; but all was found in scattered fragments. Scarcely any native American Law was in print, but the colony statutes, charters, and some of the constitutions. No judicial decisions, made in America, of any importance, had been published, and but very few forms. The law enacted here was found separately published in many States, in Colony, Province, and State statutes.

Why was so little attention dedicated to the Constitution? One answer is that during America's first decades the state of constitutional scholarship was hampered by a lack of quality law schools and available legal documentation. Hence, the first comprehensive constitutional law books were not published until the works of Thomas Sergeant (1822), John Taylor (1823), and James Kent (1826). In 1824, in his second address to the "Associate Members of the Bar of Philadelphia," William Rawle (1824) described "the first book devoted exclusively to the Constitution in which historical background, political philosophy, and the actual articles of the document were systematically discussed" (Kammen 1987, 77). Rawle (1829, 30) believed, "The principles of this constitution to be thoroughly understood should be frequently contemplated. The composition of such a government presents a novel and sublime spectacle in political history." But it was only in 1829, when Dane published a ninth volume of his *General*

Abridgment and Digest of American Law, that he focused his attention mainly on the US Constitution.

The key work of this era then was Supreme Court Justice Joseph Story's *Commentaries on the Constitution of the United States*. With the support of Chief Justice John Marshall, Story's work was designed to educate lawyers and laypeople on the nature of constitutional law. As a positive reflection of democracy in America, it became the most influential of the early works of constitutional interpretation. In 1840, Story added another text designed purely for a non-legal audience: *A Familiar Exposition of the Constitution of the United States*. Reflecting the current state of power in the United States government, the book included two chapters on the presidency but more than ten chapters on Congress. Though several important works of constitutional scholarship were written during this period, there still were significant gaps, as Harold Hyman (1973, 370) determined: "Before 1865 very little relevant scholarship existed about states' constitutional institutions, while counties and cities were virtually ignored. Prewar giants among American legal commentators, including Kent, Marshall, and Story had concentrated so completely on national-state relationships that in 1865 intrastate configurations were opaque. In the 1860's when majorities in state constitutional conventions and legislatures claimed limitless powers as a factor of numbers, no effective denial to the claim was available from law and jurisprudence."

While scholarship was limited, so too was the quantity and quality of law schools, and few of the nation's authoritative documents were available for the perusal of judges, lawyers, or ordinary citizens. The state of public education regarding the Constitution similarly was a disgrace. These impediments made it exceedingly difficult for scholars to address constitutional issues, such as the state of presidential power, prior to the Civil War. This chapter addresses each of these impediments to constitutional interpretation, which further provided a ripe environment for constitutional ambiguity.

The Development of Legal Education

> Every American lawyer must feel the utility of reducing to system, the principles and practice of our National Jurisprudence, of tracing them up to their constitutional source, and of exhibiting, in a succinct manner, the general origin, and uniform harmony, of the whole.
>
> —Thomas Sergeant, *Constitutional Law*

The term *the law* is reflected in different applications. According to Reverend Francis Wharton (1884, 2–3), "The term 'law' is frequently applied not only to the principles of human government, but to the order of nature and to the processes of the human mind. This large use of the term has been productive of many ambiguities." In America the study of law occurred at an incremental pace beginning with the Colonial Era. Lawrence Friedman (2019, 1) noted, "The colonial period is, for most lawyers and laymen, the dark ages of American law. . . . Until well after independence, there were no handy and accessible collections of colonial cases and statutes. Even now, only scattered collections of colonial cases have ever been published. Many colonial statutes survive only in ancient or rare editions." And as G. Edward White (2012, 46) observed, "There were no law schools in the colonies. . . . Most lawyers, well into the nineteenth century, were self-trained part-time professionals. The primary way to acquire legal training in America was to 'read' for the bar, which typically meant attaching oneself to a law office, performing clerical duties, and studying practical treaties." Without law schools, for early Americans, the primary legal resource was the 1769 publication of William Blackstone's *Commentaries on the Law of England*, which sold 1,557 copies at sixteen dollars for a the four-volume set. As White (2012, 47) continued, "The demand in America for copies of Blackstone's treaties testified to the fact that most aspiring lawyers were self-taught."

Given the sparsity of law schools, the reputation of lawyers in colonial America was hardly inspiring. Charles Warren (1908, 3–4), the assistant attorney general of the United States, commented, "In all the Colonies, he was a character of disrepute. In many of them, persons acting as attorneys were forbidden to receive any fee; in some, all paid attorneys were barred from the courts; in all, they were subjected to the most rigid restrictions as to fees and procedure." This attitude was not as harsh as William Shakespeare's suggestion from Henry VI, part 2, act IV, scene 2, "The first thing we do, let's kill all the lawyers." Still, despite these restrictions, "being a professionally 'trained' lawyer—a member of the bar—was a status that Americans aspired after, guarded against interlopers, and used as a basis for entry into political life" (White 2012, 47). Consequently, the development of law schools was necessary to train a new cohort of attorneys. These schools were, however, a novel phenomenon in America, as Warren (1908, 1) described,

> The Harvard Law School, the first collegiate school of law now
> in existence, was founded in Massachusetts in 1817. The first

private school of law, the Litchfield Law School, was opened in Connecticut thirty-three years earlier, in 1784. The first American professorship of law was established at the College of William and Mary in Virginia in 1779. For one hundred and fifty years prior to 1779, lawyers were obliged to rely upon their own exertions for a legal education. The early lawyers were few in number, lacking in education, and weak in influence. It was sixty-six years from the landing of the Pilgrims and fifty years from the foundation of Harvard College before Harvard sent out, in the Class of 1686, her first graduate destined to be trained for the bar, Benjamin Lynde. It was one hundred and ten years after the establishment of Massachusetts Bay Colony before a lawyer sat in her General Court as a legislator—John Read, in 1738. It was one hundred and thirty-five years before a regular Bar Association existed in the Province of Massachusetts. Harvard College was one hundred and forty-eight years old before she admitted a lawyer to her councils as a member of the Corporation—John Lowell, in 1784.

John Langbein (2004, 17) wrote of another early American law school: "The origins of the Yale Law School trace to the earliest days of the nineteenth century, when there was as yet no university legal education. Law was learned mostly by clerking as an apprentice in a lawyer's office. The first law schools, including the New Haven school that became Yale, developed from the apprenticeship system." Meanwhile, William Rawles (1904, 9) noted of the University of Indiana, "The importance of the College, the growth of the State, and the need for instruction in the professions of law and medicine induced the General Assembly in 1838 to enlarge the scope of the institution and to transform it into a university. By an act of February 25, 1838, Indiana College Act establishing became the Indiana University, with authority to grant additional degrees in law and medicine."

Because there were few law schools in early America, the quality of legal education was of questionable value. In a series of lectures delivered annually at Columbia College in New York (now Columbia University), its former president William Alexander Duer (1858, 20) recalled, "Until lately, it was a reproach to our college that it sent forth its graduates more familiar with the constitution of the Roman Republic, and the principles of the Grecian confederacies, than with the fundamental laws of their own country. To remedy this evil, it was proposed to ingraft this new branch of study upon the general course pursued in this institution." With a dearth of law schools, constitutional interpretation was left to a diminutive elite. One of these lawyers was James Kent, who in the 1820s wrote one of the most influential books on the Constitution. In a short essay, Kent (1872, 383) described his legal education:

> When the College was broken up & dispersed in July 1779 by the British, I retired to a country village & finding Blackstone's com[mentaries] I read the 4th volume, parts of the work struck my taste, & the work inspired me at the age of 16 with awe, and I fondly determined to be a lawyer. In November 1781 I was placed by my father with Mr. (now called Judge) Benson, who was then attorney general at Poughkeepsie on the banks of the Hudson, & in my native County of Dutchess. There I entered on law, & was the most modest, steady, industrious student that such a place ever saw.

Kent was not alone in this form of legal training. Of John Marshall, Allan B. Magruder (1890, 8) wrote, "He began the study of law at the age of eighteen; but the impending struggle with Great Britain so absorbed his mind as to interrupt his studies before he had obtained a license to practice. He joined a company of volunteers, and by precept and example stimulated the spirit of resistance to British oppression. . . . In 1780–81 Marshall was admitted to the bar and entered on the practice of law in Fauquier County." It was at the age of eighteen that Marshall read a book that transformed his life, the same book as Kent. As former senator Albert Beveridge (1916, 1:56) wrote in a highly influential biography of Marshall, "A book was placed in the hands of John Marshall, at this time, that influenced his mind even more than his reading of Pope's poetry when a small boy. Blackstone's 'Commentaries' was published in America in 1772 and one of the original subscribers was 'Captain Thomas Marshall, Clerk of Dunmore County, Virginia.' The youthful backwoodsman read Blackstone with delight; for this legal classic is the poetry of law, just as Pope is logic in poetry." Marshall did have a short, formal education in the law: "William and Mary College, 'the only public seminary of learning in the State,' was only twelve miles from Yorktown; and there the young officer attended the law lectures of George Wythe for perhaps six weeks—a time so short that, in the opinion of the students, 'those who finish this Study in a few months, either have strong natural parts or else they know little about it'" (Beveridge 1916, 1:154, 157–58). As for Mr. Wythe, Beveridge continued,

> Mr. Wythe, the professor of law, was the life of the little institution in this ebbing period of wartime. He established "a Moot Court, held monthly or oftener . . . Mr. Wythe & the other professors sit as Judges. Our Audience consists of the most respectable of the Citizens, before whom we plead our Causes, given out by Mr. Wythe Lawyer like I assure you." The law professor also "form'd us into a Legislative Body, Consisting of about 40 members." Wythe constituted himself Speaker of these seedling lawmakers and took "all possible pains to instruct us in the Rules of Parliament." These nascent Solons of old William and Mary drew original bills, revised existing laws, debated, amended, and went through all the performances of a legislative body.

As for Marshall, Beveridge (1916, 1:161) commented,

> He would begin his professional career at once and make ready for the supreme event that filled all his thoughts. So while in Richmond he secured a license to practice law. Jefferson was then Governor, and it was he who signed the license to the youth who was to become his greatest antagonist. Marshall then went to Fauquier County, and there, on August 28, 1780, was admitted to the bar. "John Marshall, Gent., produced a license from his Excellency the Governor to practice law and took the oaths prescribed by act of Assembly," runs the entry in the record.

In a more recent biography of Marshall, Richard Brookhiser (2018, 27, 28) wrote, "The law in Virginia, and in the United States generally, was in a fluid state. A remark of James Kent, a New York judge, about his prerevolutionary legal education applied to the profession through the thirteen colonies: 'We had no law of our own, and no one knew what it was.'"

> Day-to-day decisions in Virginia were issued by county courts, run by justices of the peace, and served by lawyers who

were their cronies. These local officials often knew little of the law, nor did they care so as long as the interests of their patrons and friends were safeguarded. In a letter to a fellow veteran-turned-lawyer, Marshall called them "the county court establishment." Its lawyers, he wrote, feared "that they do not possess abilities or knowledge sufficient to enable them to stand before [real] judges of law."

Kent and Marshall were not alone in their less than formal education. Even the so-called Father of the Constitution and the Bill of Rights, James Madison, after receiving a degree from the College of New Jersey (Princeton University), studied the law by borrowing books from Thomas Jefferson's library. Mary Bilder (2015, 36, 37) stated, "In 1783, Madison was considering law as a possible profession. . . . In notes taken during his law reading, Madison seemed particularly drawn to the way in which the law wrestled with the inherent ambiguities in language." As such, though he never pursued membership in the bar, his studies were due preparation for his later political career, for ambiguity was at the center of the law, as well as the writing of constitutions. Likewise, Joseph Story, after he received a degree from Harvard University, studied law in the traditional manner of the time (Hillard 1868, 4). Henceforth, a man who can be credibly described as the most important interpreter of the Constitution in American history, James Madison, and certainly its most significant chief justice of the United States, John Marshall, and two of the early American jurists to write commentaries on the Constitution, James Kent and Joseph Story, all had meager formal legal educations. Most lawyers followed their example. They read *Blackstone's Commentaries* or Coke's works and then joined a law firm to learn the basics of the law. As a result, in early America there was a severe dearth of qualified lawyers and even fewer who were masters of constitutional law, a pattern that continued until the Civil War. Consequently, writing of legal reform in an address to the graduating class of the University of Albany Law School on March 23, 1855, David Dudley Field (1855, 6–7, 30) advised both caution and hope for the legal profession:

Let us first consider the profession. Its present condition we all know. We see and regret its failure, as a body, to fulfil the whole of that high trust which is reposed in it, and to satisfy all the expectations which it might justly raise. Far be it from me, in saying this, to assent to those terms of obloquy with which some delight to assail it, or even to include all its members in the censure to which, as a profession, I fear we must submit ourselves. But, every candid person must admit that its condition, at the present, is not such as he would wish it to be.

Field recommended the following:

We have now arrived at that stage in our progress, when a code becomes a want; and however much its consummation may be retarded by the betrayal of seeming friends or the resistance of open enemies, it will certainly, sooner or later, be accomplished. The age is ripe for a code of the whole of our American law. The materials are about us in abundance, derived from many ages and nations; and we must now have a system of our own, symmetrical, eclectic, filmed on purpose.

While the availability of law schools was still limited, everything changed with the onset of the Civil War. As a commentator from 1861 noted, "The apparatus for studying our Constitution has improved more rapidly since the integrity of the Union was threatened than at any preceding period" (Hyman 1973, 33). After Chief Justice Roger B. Taney challenged President Abraham Lincoln in *Ex Parte Merryman* (1861), "lawyers and judges formed the group most necessary to reach in order to counter Taney-ish stances. In Perry Miller's apt phrase lawyers were the 'pontiffs of this society.' Enjoying a swift rise in popular esteem, lawyers were increasing in number among states' legislators and congressmen. The recruitment into political life of lawmakers who were law-trained created problems as well as opportunities for the effective conduct of the war" (Hyman 1973, 128). Still, as the secretary of the Constitutional Centennial Committee, Hampton L. Carson (1889, 1:1–2), noted in 1889,

The political debates of the present generation leave a painful impression of the neglect of constitutional study. A failure to apprehend the reasons upon which constitutional provisions were founded has too frequently led astray the public judgment. In this neglect numerous theories of construction have found their source, which in turn have led to additional debate, until the public records of discussion on constitutional questions have become a massive collection, which obscures, far more than it enlightens, the popular mind. In politics, as in religion, the commentaries have superseded the authority, as they have darkened the simplicity, of the original text. It has become a duty of patriotism to awaken the spirit of constitutional inquiry, emancipated from the prejudices of party.

Obstacles to a legal education therefore persisted after the war, such as the classroom methods for instruction. According to Anthony Chase (1979, 336–37) in his "The Birth of the Modern Law School," "The lecture method of legal instruction, which frequently amounted to little more than a professor standing before a class reading one or two chapters from a legal treatise and which, even in the hands of a brilliant scholar, often left the majority of students in dazed incomprehension, was the standard mode of teaching in the Harvard Law School in 1869." And as Oliver Wendell Holmes (1892, 124) noted, the reputation of lawyers hardly improved:

> The lawyers are a picked lot, "first scholars" and the like, but their business is as unsympathetic as Jack Ketch's.[1] There is nothing humanizing in their relations with their fellow-creatures. They go for the side that retains them. They defend the man they know to be a rogue, and not very rarely throw suspicion on the man they know to be innocent. Mind you, I am not finding fault with them; every side of a case has a right to the best statement it admits of; but I say it does not tend to make them sympathetic.

In a later lecture, Holmes (1896, 34–35) added, "We will not be contented to send forth students with nothing but a rag-bag full of general principles,—a throng of glittering generalities, like a swarm of little bodiless cherubs fluttering at the top of one of Correggio's pictures." Likewise, the president of Harvard University, Charles Eliot, argued in the *Annual Report for 1874–1875* (Chase 1979, 337, 342), "It should be the aim of a University's Law School to train young men of good preliminary education and average ability, taken by the hundred, for the higher walks of the profession." But as Anthony Chase continued,

> Since most law school instruction actually takes place outside the library (casebooks originally having appeared because of the

limited number of copies of case reports in the library) it was actually the case method classroom which Eliot presented as the appropriate analogue to the hospital in medical education. It was the case method which Eliot perceived to be clinical education in law. Early critics of the case method argued that to learn substantive law through the study of individual cases was a hopelessly time consuming exercise. Professor Christopher Tiedeman [the Dean of the University of Buffalo Law School] suggested that "in order to learn the law in relation to the requirements of the statute of frauds, one would have to read not a few cases, but thousands of cases."

A stronger legal curriculum was of vital importance to the development of legal education and constitutional interpretation, for as Supreme Court Justice Harlan Fiske later mused, "I could not say that one who seeks to apply the Constitution today can dispense with an extensive technical training. The gloss which has been placed on the Constitution by a century of decisions and interpretation certainly has produced a labyrinth through which the judge would find great difficulty in threading his path, and at the same time keep his balance, unless he had an extensive legal knowledge of the forestry and what lawyers think it all means" (Kammen 1986, 12). And as J. I. Clark Hare (1889, 1:2) of the District Court of the City and County of Philadelphia explained to a new cohort of lawyers, this also required the establishment of an effective bar association to oversee the legal profession. One was first established on August 21, 1878. On this subject, David McAdam, Henry Bischoff Jr., Richard Clarke, Jackson Dykman, Joshua Van Cott, and George Reynolds (1897, 2:1) wrote, "In every free country the Bar constitutes, and necessarily must, an order of unusual importance. Its function in peace is similar to that of the army in war, viz: to defend society and to guard the general welfare. Whether special privileges are, or are not, conceded in terms of such a body of men, enlightened opinion must realize its value and rely upon its services. It is the natural organ by which outraged law protests against tyranny."

Despite such advances, overall, lawyers, judges, and the American Bar Association continued to be the subject of criticism during the late nineteenth and early twentieth century. Professor William Reynolds Vance likewise stated (Storey 1911, 5–6), "Bluntly put, the American lawyer has proved a failure. In no other free and civilized country are the laws so ill-administered as in these United States." Meanwhile Thomas Cooley (1889,

206) wrote, "The best judges are far from being infallible. And when they go outside of the necessities of a case before them, and seek to determine the gravest political and party questions, they should expect to find their opinions treated with contempt by all opponents. The utmost which can be claimed is, that the decisions in such cases should be respected until changed, and that only constitutional means should be used to effect a change." Additionally, in the "Preliminary Report on the Efficiency in the Administration of Justice," several renowned legal scholars and educators, Charles Eliot, Louis Brandeis, Moorfield Storey, Adolph Rodenbeck, and Roscoe Pound, wrote (1915, 612) that the bar was indeed deficient in organization:

> Until recently there were no serious requirements for admission to the bar outside of a few states. Many states today, some of them old and intelligent, are substantially without such require-ments. . . . Of late there has been a steady growth of sentiment within and without the bar which has produced more adequate requirements of preliminary study and preliminary general education in a majority of the states. But this improvement is the work of a few years, is still in progress in many states, and has much farther to go everywhere.

Henry Upson Sims (1917, 612), a president of the American Bar Association, added, "By no means the least important subdivision of the problem of reforming judicial administration in America is the re-organization of the American Bar." A decade later, in the first Cutler Foundation Lecture at William and Mary College, Calvin Coolidge's solicitor general, James Beck (1927, 9), bemoaned,

> The bar was originally the child of the Church and has never wholly escaped from the spirit of sacerdotalism. Lawyers were originally ecclesiastics and at a time when the subtlety of the scholiast most prevailed. We lawyers are too apt to regard the doctrines of the law as final truths, having their sanction in some judicial ipse dixit or political document. Religion, which rests its justification in supernatural revelation, may well believe in final and indisputable truths, but human laws, whether they are ordinary statutes or fundamental constitutions, have no such authority.

Relatedly, Michael Kammen (1986, 230) cited a 1927 statement by the chairman of the American Bar Association's Committee on American Citizenship: "The law schools are turning out thousands of lawyers every year who know nothing of the Constitution, and the boards of examiners require little, if any, examination of the subject, with the result that when civic organizations, like chambers of commerce, Rotary clubs, etc., seek among lawyers for speakers on the Constitution, it is very difficult to find a lawyer qualified to talk about it."

Perhaps the most scathing analysis was by Fred Rodell (1939, 4): "In TRIBAL TIMES, there were medicine-men. In the Middle Ages, there were the priests. Today there are the lawyers." Not everyone agreed with this sentiment, however. James Bradley Thayer's (1908, 367–68, 371) posthumously published *Legal Essays* noted,

> We, in America, have carried legal education much farther than it has gone in England. There the systematic teaching of law in schools is but faintly developed. Here it is elaborate, widely favored, rapidly extending. . . . On this side of the water, while the training of our profession continued for a long time to be the old one of office apprenticeship and reading, the new conception—new as regards English law—of systematic study at the Universities, has had continuous life, and has borne abundant fruit. If it has sometimes languished, and here and there been intermittent, it has always lived and thrived somewhere; and at last it has so commended itself that there is no longer much occasion to argue its merits. Few now come openly forward to deny or doubt them.

The days of learning the law without a degree were waning. With a greater commitment to a university education, the practices of constitutional law and theory came of age just as questions about the Constitution's meaning were much on the minds of constitutional scholars. These scholars also had access to a wide range of authoritative documents that were not available to scholars during the nineteenth century.

A Lack of Authoritative Documents

Like law schools in early American history, the authoritative documents necessary to understand the Framers' intent were hard, and often impossible, to find. Without access to these documents, even lawyers trained in law schools were at a distinct disadvantage in their attempts to interpret the Constitution. After the Founding, only limited documentation was widely available to scholars, lawyers, politicians, and the public. Prominent among these were *The Federalist Papers*. As Henry Cabot Lodge (1888, xliii) wrote,

> The "Federalist" . . . was the first authoritative interpretation of the Constitution, and was mainly written by the two principal authors of that instrument. It was the first exposition of the Constitution and the first step in the long process of development which has given life, meaning, and importance to the clauses agreed upon at Philadelphia. It has acquired all the weight and sanction of a judicial decision, and has been constantly used as an authority in the settlement of constitutional questions.

In writing of this source, Judge Joseph Story (1858, 1:vii) noted, "From two great sources . . . I have drawn by far the greatest part of my valuable materials. These are, The Federalist, an incomparable commentary of three of the greatest statesmen of their age; and the extraordinary Judgments of Mr. Chief Justice Marshall upon constitutional law." Still, even Story, who released the first edition of his commentaries in the 1830s, did not have access to the notes on the Constitutional Convention. *The Federalist*, and Marshall, who played a significant role in the Virginian ratification debates, would have to suffice.

According to Lodge (1888, xxxvi–xlii), *The Federalist Papers* essays were widely disseminated in newspapers across the nation, as well as through several editions: "The first edition was that of 1788, published by J. and A. McLean of New York." The first volume appeared on March 22, 1788 and and so on through 24 editions leading up to Lodge's 1888 edition. *The Federalist Papers* were written with a specific purpose in mind, however: to convince the participants of the New York Ratification Convention to adopt the new Constitution. Interestingly, according to Edward Mead Earle (1937, x and xi), 'Although *The Federalist* was frankly a campaign document, it is doubtful whether it had much influence in determining the issue of ratification of the Constitution. It holds an important place, of course, as the classic contemporary exposition and defense of the Constitution.'" Earle continued, "*The Federalist* . . . is not without faults. It was avowedly a piece of special pleading, offered in the rough-and-tumble of partisan politics; its inherent worth, therefore, is all the more astonishing. . . . It is not always frank; Hamilton, for example, would have preferred a national to a federal government, and he was contemptuous of popular opinion." Hence, *The Federalist* needs to be understood in different contexts. It explains and analyzes the Constitution, but it was designed to promote ratification of the Constitution in the state of New York. It therefore is a blend of constitutional interpretation and "special pleading," and it does not necessarily reflect the actual views of its authors.

While *The Federalist Papers* was widely disseminated, the same was not true of the *Anti-Federalist Papers*, originally published as essays in newspapers and pamphlets. Written under such pseudonyms as Brutus, Cato, and Caesar, these essays still resonate today, with insights that are relevant to our own time, particularly the concerns with the power of the presidency and its potential for tyranny. As Ralph Ketcham (1986, 16) stated,

> The anti-federalists were at once skeptical and disheartened. They saw in federalist hopes for commercial growth and international prestige only the lust of ambitious men for a "splendid empire" where, in the time-honored way, the people would be burdened with taxes, conscription, and campaigns. . . . Uncertain that any government over so vast a domain as the United States could be controlled by the people, the anti-federalists saw in the enlarged powers of the central government only the familiar threats to the rights and liberties of the people. . . . The broad power to lay and collect taxes, the president's role as commander-in-chief, Congress' authority to pass any laws "necessary and proper" to carry out its enumerated powers, and the "supreme law" and treaty-making powers, all seemed unbounded and at least potentially tyrannical.

Many of these essays are still relevant over two hundred years later. However, after the ratification debates, unlike *The Federalist*, the *Anti-Federalist Papers* was not widely available to scholars, constitutional experts, politicians, or the public. Some essays were reprinted during the nineteenth century. Jonathan Elliot's (1836) expurgated record of the Ratification process—*Debates on the Adoption of the Federal Constitution in the Convention held at Philadelphia in 1787 with a Diary of the Debates of the Congress on the Confederation*—included the insights of some of the authors of the

Anti-Federalist Papers. In 1892, Paul Leicester Ford's *Essays on the Constitution of the United States Published During Its Discussion by the People 1787–1788* was introduced. The publication of the complete views of the Anti-Federalists is a belated contribution to constitutional scholarship. They can be found in the multivolume (with one issue published each year since 1976) *The Documentary History of the Ratification of the Constitution* published by the Wisconsin Historical Society. A comprehensive compilation, however, was not completed until Herbert J. Storing (1981a) published *The Complete Anti-Federalist,* though one reviewer, James Hutson (1983), referred to it as *The Incomplete Antifederalist.*

A similar lacuna existed for many documents related to the national political institutions. A record of the congressional debates, which included important discussions of the Constitution and its meaning (e.g., the removal power and the Decision of 1789) were not initially published in any systematic form. The earliest publication occurred in 1825 with the *Register of Debates Annals of Congress,* followed by *The Annals of Congress* (also known as *The Debates and Proceedings in the Congress of the United States 1789–1824*), which Kammen (1987, 84) noted was not published until 1834. The *Congressional Globe* (1833–1873), and finally the *Congressional Record* were later publications. Meanwhile, as historian Harold Hyman (1973, 538) identified, "In 1873, codifiers achieved the noncoercive, inexpensive, unbureaucratic kind of reform that had become dear to the heart of reformers. A *Revised Statutes of the United States* replaced the haphazard *Statutes at Large.* For the first time in the nation's history its statutes were grouped reasonably by functional categories." Hence, documents related to Congress were published in various forms, in several different venues, some of dubious quality.

The papers of some presidents were published in multivolume editions, such as Jared Sparks (1855) writings of George Washington. Meanwhile, a systematic collection of presidential documents was not published until James Richardson's (1897, v, vi) *A Compilation of the Messages and Paper of the Presidents.* In the prefatory note, Richardson wrote, "It is believed that legislators and other public men, students of our national history, and many others will hail with satisfaction the compilation and publication of these messages and proclamations in such compact form as will render them easily accessible and of ready reference. . . . The Government has never heretofore authorized a like publication." Richardson added, "The compilation has not been brought even to its present stage without much labor and close application, and the end is far from view, but if it shall prove satisfactory to Congress and the country, I will feel compensated for my time and effort." Meanwhile, presidential proclamations and executive orders, as well as federal regulations, were not published in a comprehensive fashion until 1936 with the first issue of the *Federal Register*. Today, we can access these papers through the American Presidency Project, but for more than a century, until Richardson's work was first published, presidential scholarship was at a severe disadvantage.

Each of these precious documents provide valuable information necessary for the interpretation of the US Constitution. Nevertheless, our earliest judges, lawyers, congressmembers, presidents, constitutional scholars, historians, political scientists, journalists, and citizens interpreted the Constitution without access to many of these documents. As a result, while constitutional interpretation has evolved over time, so too has the availability of the nation's authoritative documents. Meanwhile, the piecemeal publication of these documents promoted confusion regarding the Constitution's meaning, as Kammen (1987, 103) attests: "Constitutional confusion was everywhere evident after 1855, verging upon chaos once the Dred Scott decision had been announced." One newspaper editor summed up the situation succinctly in 1856: "The Constitution threatens to be a subject of infinite sects, like the Bible." And as Hyman (1973, 7; includes previous citation) added, such confusion had serious implications: "The United States was not only a political democracy. It was also a federal system in which functional arenas of the states and the federal governments were ill-defined and in flux. Contention was the order on such matters as the fugitive slave law and Congress's power to regulate slavery in national territories because the outcome of constitutional theorizing would become political policy."

Presidents' access to information was constrained in yet another way. While William Wirt (1849, 2:60) introduced the publication of the attorney general's opinions, as of April 1866 Attorney General James Speed complained, "The entire legal labor of this Office, which is growing to be immense . . . devolves upon two persons" (Hyman 1973, 478). Hyman added, "The accumulated defects of the nation's chief legal office evidenced themselves. They ranged from the fact that it lacked almost all professional reference books. . . . Despite the 1861 increase of the Attorney General's nominal authority, district attorneys remained unruly. . . . Some district attorneys did not know how to conduct the simplest courtroom proceeding. Faced with responsibility to plead a Civil Rights law action, such spoilsmen floundered foolishly" (479). Hyman provided examples:

"In November 1865 the Attorney General had loaned to Horace Greeley the only complete text of South Carolina's black code in possession of the government, and had to wait until the publisher printed it before again enjoying possession of the entire text. Two years after Michigan passed an anti-adulteration statute for illuminants, the text was unavailable in Washington, although derivative litigation involving national interests was well under way" (see also Frank 1966). The Department of Justice was not established until 1870. Consequently, presidential understanding of the laws and the Constitution was limited by a lack of vital resources.

Incredibly, it was only on July 23, 1866, that the US Congress enacted legislation relieving Supreme Court justices of the arduous and time-consuming duty of "circuit-riding" (Hyman 1973, 497–98). Likewise, only slowly was the nation's judicial system coming of age. Michael Kammen (1986, 176) noted that "the half century following 1880" witnessed "the emergence of constitutional history as a major field of scholarship in the United States." However, there were serious obstacles to research, as Kammen (1986, 178) continued,

> The National Archives did not yet exist; clerks at the State Department library declared any materials they could not locate to be "lost," probably confiscated by the British during the Revolutionary War. Obtaining precise texts of crucial documents was highly problematic; and criteria for "authentic" reprinting and editing simply did not yet exist. In 1911, when workmen moved Supreme Court records from the Capitol to the new Senate Office Building, the working papers for *McCulloh v. Maryland* (1819) were "found in a very bad state of decomposition" along with original records for such landmarks as the Dartmouth College case, *Chisholm v. Georgia*, and the Dred Scott decision. Previously, according to one newspaper account, "the records were first bound and then carried to a dusty little room near the staircase leading to the dome, placed upon shelves, and allowed to remain there and accumulate dust. Some of the records are almost unintelligible, though those filed in later years are readable, but are yellow with age. . . . These records are of naturally great importance to this nation, and the work of taking care of them is one that should have commenced several years ago."

Notes on Madison's Notes

Did you know that there exists in MS. the ablest work of this kind ever yet executed, of the debates of the Constitutional convention of Philadelphia in 1788? The whole of everything said and done there was taken down by Mr. Madison, with a labor and exactness beyond comprehension.

—Thomas Jefferson, letter to John Adams, August 10, 1815

Most important of all the documents for understanding the Constitution was the unavailability of Madison's *Notes on the Constitutional Convention*. Madison's notes represent the most authoritative source for the meaning of the Constitution, though more than ten Framers left some record of the convention. These other writings were incomplete, such as William Jackson's formal journal of the proceedings. This first official journal of the convention was published in 1819. Also, among the first to be published was Anti-Federalist Robert Yates's *Secret Proceedings and Debates of the Convention Assembled in Philadelphia in the Year 1787*, published in 1821, which according to John Hutson (1987, 412) "suffered the editorial depredations of a political partisan." As Hutson discovered,

> Two pages of Lansing's manuscript copy of Yates's notes have recently been discovered in [Citizen Edmond] Genet's papers at the Library of Congress. When compared to the printed version of the notes, the manuscript demonstrated that Genet deleted half of its contents when arranging them for publication. He changed sentence after sentence, and when the opportunity to belittle Madison presented itself he manipulated the text to stress the Virginian's apostasy from true Jeffersonianism . . . Yates's notes, called by Max Farrand, are thoroughly unreliable.

Still, John Taylor (1823, 11) of Caroline, Virginia, after consulting Yates's notes, advised, "Had the journal of the convention which framed the constitution of the United States, though obscure and incomplete, been published immediately after its ratification, it would have furnished lights towards a true construction, sufficiently clear to have prevented several trespasses upon its principles, and tendencies towards its subversion.

Perhaps it may not be yet too late to lay before the publick the important evidence it furnishes." While Madison consulted Yates's notes, he did not release his own version of the constitutional debate for two more decades. As Clinton Rossiter (1966, 330–32) noted,

> So long as he served in public life, Madison withstood all pressures and temptations to publish his precious notes (about which, indeed, not more than a few friends had any information), and not until several years after his death did men learn most of the things we know about the debates and maneuvers in Philadelphia. . . . Not until 1836, when his will was opened and read, did his friends learn for certain that he desired publication of "the report as by me"; and not until 1840, after Congress had paid his widow a handsome sum for his papers, did the notes finally see the light of day. It is, surely one of the intriguing facts of American constitutional history that the people in whose name and by whose power the great charter of 1787 was proclaimed should have had to wait more than half a century to learn how it came to be written.

To put this matter in context, by the time Madison's notes were published, the eighth president of the United States, Martin Van Buren, was in the last full year of his administration. What then do the notes reveal? According to James Brown Scott (1918, 1), "The notes of debates in the Federal Convention, held in the city of Philadelphia in the State of Pennsylvania, from the 25th day of May to the record 17th day of September, in the year of our Lord of a one thousand seven hundred eighty-seven, are notes which James Madison of Virginia, an eye witness and active participant, made from day to day, from hour to hour, and from minute to minute, of the proceedings of that gathering." As such, they provide an invaluable resource for understanding the arguments, theories, compromises, and intent of the Framers. But the notes were not written at one time; they were rewritten by Madison from the date of the convention until late in his life. In 1911, Max Farrand (1966 1:vii) identified a significant issue with Madison's *Notes*:

> It has been found that most printed texts of the more important records cannot be accepted implicitly because of the liberties that have been taken with the manuscripts in preparing them

for publication. Furthermore, in the case of the most important record of all, Madison's Debates, it is easily proved that, over thirty years after the Convention, the author revised the manuscript and made many changes upon insufficient data, which seriously impaired the value of his notes. This is also true of other records. It has accordingly become the first purpose of the editor in this work to present the records of the Federal Convention in the most trustworthy form possible. Mistakes and inaccuracies are unavoidable, but no effort has been spared to reduce these to a minimum.

A decade later, Gaillard Hunt and James Brown Scott (1920, xxi–xxii) provided more detail on Madison's penchant for rewriting his notes: "The chief source of Madison's corrections was the official *Journal* of the Convention which was printed in 1819 and Yate's *Secret Proceedings and Debates of the Federal Convention* which appeared in 1821. Whenever Madison thought either of these records more correct than his he changed or added to his; but he noted more frequently errors in the official *Journal* itself." Keller and Pierson (1930) described Madison's *Debates* as "defective" (see also Hutson 1986; 1987), while William Crosskey (1953) alleged that Madison fabricated notes as his views on such issues as nationalism changed later in life to a states' rights position. As Hutson (1987, 414) argued,

> What gives Crosskey's charges an appearance of plausibility is that we know that Madison tinkered with his notes for at least thirty years after the convention adjourned. He made alterations as early as 1789 and as late as 1821. His motives have generally been considered—when they have been considered at all—as innocuous and commendable, arising from a desire to improve the accuracy of the notes by incorporating portions of the official journal and Yates's notes, as they became available . . . Crosskey offered no proof of his charges against Madison.

Meanwhile Irving Brant (1954, 449–50) wrote,

> Perhaps the best commentary on all this was furnished by Madison himself when Jonathan Elliott sent him in 1827 the proof sheets of his book containing the debates in the Virginia convention and asked him to correct his speeches. Replying that

he found passages which were defective, obscure, unintelligible or erroneous, probably due in part to a "feebleness of voice caused by an imperfect recovery from a fit of illness," Madison told the editor that "it might not be safe nor deemed fair" to correct them after so many years. "If I did not confound subsequent ideas and varied expressions with the real ones, I might be supposed to do so."

From this statement, Brant concluded, "This does not sound like the utterance of a man who would falsify the record of the framing of the Constitution in order to invalidate its true meaning." Still, Philip Bobbitt (1984 [1982], 12) referred to *Debates* as "fragmentary," indicating "little more than highly particular or highly general positions that can be said to have been endorsed by the adoption of specific language for which the position had been used as support. . . . It is rare that the debate surrounding the adoption of particular language can provide a decisive historical argument for a provision being construed in a particular way." Mary Bilder (2015, 68) remarked that Madison also accentuated passages that were of relevance to his home state of Virginia or of personal interest, such as his commitment to forming a national government. Finally, regarding Madison's coverage of the presidency, Bilder noted,

> In fact, positions taken by Madison were omitted from the Notes. On the controversial matter of the single executive, King and Pierce recorded Madison's advocacy: "The best plan will be a single Executive of long duration" (King); "an Executive formed one man" (Pierce). Madison, however, included no such comment by himself. Even the explanation of Virginia's vote favoring the single executive diminished Madison's responsibility. The vote within the delegation was 3–2, with Madison the apparent tie-breaker (Randolph and Blair had voted against; Madison, McClurg, and Washington had voted yes). Madison did not explain his own vote but tried to create legitimacy for the affirmative vote by claiming that George Wythe, who had left the Convention, favored the single executive. The Notes obscured Madison's own support for the single executive.

What then is the importance of Madison's *Notes* in relationship to the presidency? According to Richard Ellis (1999, xi), *Notes* provides little information. He calculated that "less than a quarter of those 1,300 pages of debate relate to the presidency" and most of those deal with the issues of a single versus a plural presidency and the method of selection. Relatively little attention was dedicated to the powers of the presidential office. And as the reporter for the House of Representatives, Frederic Irland, speculated in 1905, "Madison copied no more than one-tenth of all that was said" (Bilder 2015, 4, 5). In a detailed examination of how Madison compiled his notes, Bilder argued that "the Notes indicate the impossibility of the delegates fully comprehending that the final text of the Constitution in its entirety in September 1787 and the degree to which the understandings of the significance of the Constitution, apart even from its multiple meanings, developed in the years after 1787." As to the reliability of statements in *Notes*, Bilder stated, "Was Hamilton serious about his suggestions concerning an executive on good behavior? The Notes hint that Hamilton's speech was, in significant part, a political strategy to make the Virginia plan appear moderate." If Bilder is correct, then Madison's *Notes* should be read with some caution.

Basic Civics Textbooks for Citizens

> Sir: For good citizenship men and women must not only have good will, but an abiding interest in the welfare of the community. They must also have a working knowledge of social agencies, good judgment as to methods of social activities, and a more or less comprehensive understanding of fundamental principles of social life and progress. Much can be done in childhood and in the elementary grades of the school to create interest and give a certain amount of concrete knowledge of particular social activities and agencies, but not until boys and girls have reached the years of adolescence, the high-school age, can they begin to gain any very full understanding of abstract principles of social, civic, and governmental life.
>
> —P. P. Clayton, secretary of the interior,
> *The Teaching of Community Civics*

Writing in the 1830s, Alexis De Tocqueville (2004, 1:186) believed the Constitution was "the most perfect of all known constitutions," but with an important caveat: "When one looks at the Constitution of the United States, the most perfect of all known constitutions, it is frightening to discover the range of diverse knowledge and discernment that it assumes in the people it is supposed to govern. The government of the Union rests almost entirely on legal fictions. The Union is an ideal nation that exists only in the mind, as it were, and whose extent and limits can be discovered only through an effort at intelligence." This was a significant insight, for as John Dearborn (2021, 27) wrote, "In forming the Constitution, the framers assumed that an educated populace would be needed to make the government established work in practice." William Hickey (1853, xxiii–xxiv) recommended, "It was deemed important to the preservation of British liberty, in the earlier and better days of that country, that *Magna Carta* should be authoritatively promulgated and read to the people—it is no less important to the preservation of American liberty, that every intelligent citizen should, *by his own will and authority*, aided by the liberality of the Government, possess a copy of this *great charter of American liberty.*" Unfortunately, Americans had but a limited understanding or access to this basic document. As George Washington Paschal (1868, vii–viii) wrote in his annotated constitutional text,

> And now, although the sacred instrument has been published in every revision of laws in the United States, in the Manuals of Congress, and by tens of thousands in that excellent *vademecum* by Mr. Hickey, we hazard nothing in saying that the Constitution is not conveniently accessible to one in one hundred of the people whose duty it is to read it. It is not even a book in all our public libraries; it is not in one house in fifty; it is nowhere on the catalogue of school-books; and it is not taught in one school in a thousand.

As Paschal wrote these words, the United States was on the cusp of a major demographic revolution, which included the general extension of the suffrage. However if the suffrage was to expand, how would these new voters have a proper understanding of American government and its Constitution? To remedy this defect, Hampton Carson (1889, 1:1–2), the secretary of the Constitutional Centennial Committee, advised, "Unfortunately for the general public, they are too voluminous or too expensive for the attainment of a wide circulation among the people. The Constitutional Centennial Commission, therefore, have thought it wise to add to their work commemorating the great anniversary a condensed history of that instrument, which even the busy American people may find time to read."

Despite its importance, the movement to require the teaching of the Constitution occurred incrementally. This was due in part to a lack of federal support for education. As Charles Walcott (1901, 1) noted, "Many of our wisest and best statesmen and jurists believe that the General Government has no power, under the Constitution, to appropriate money for educational purposes, that important function having been left to the States." However, there was a vast difference in expenditures at the state level. Laws forbade the education of slaves, and women had but a limited ability to receive even a basic education. Despite the Declaration of Independence's affirmation that "all men are created equal," educational opportunities were far from equal.

Even when textbooks were available, education continued to be deficient. We can see this in the limited number of books on the Constitution published prior to the Civil War. Even afterward, many texts barely examined the Constitution. George S. Williams (1872) provided a book on the US Constitution. Blackburn and McDonald's (1880) book on government and politics did include a chapter on the "Formation of the Constitution, and Washington's Administration." Blackburn and McDonald (1871) also introduced a book for grammar school children that included a shorter, three-page chapter. As the suffrage mounted, however, various teachers, such as Henry Holt (1901, v), expressed a pressing need for improved civics education for the ordinary citizen, even while ignoring the Constitution. Of his own textbook, Holt wrote, "This book was written in the hope of doing a little something to develop in young people the character of mind which is proof against political quackery—especially the quackery which proposes immediate cures by legislation for abiding the ills resulting from human weakness and ignorance." Nevertheless, the book made few specific references to the US Constitution. His work was not alone. James Thompson McCleary (1908, 9) noted,

> At the very beginning of our study, two questions naturally present themselves: First. What is government? Second. Why do we have such a thing? These questions are much easier to ask than to answer. The wisest men of the ages have pondered upon them, and their answers have varied widely. Yet we need not despair. Even boys and girls can work out moderately good answers, if they will approach the questions seriously and with a determination to get as near the root of the matter as possible.

But did this determination include a more substantial knowledge of the Constitution?

Two years later, Henry Talkington (1908, preface), of Idaho's Lewiston State Normal School, commented, "In the United States, from the school district to the nation government, sovereignty is vested in the individual citizen, yet he has often received far too little practical education and training to fit him properly to exercise his sovereign power." Talkington's book includes no chapters on the Constitution and there is no mention of it in the book's index. Mabel Hill, an instructor in social science at the Dana Hall School of Wellesley, Massachusetts, and Philip Davis (1922, 1; originally published in 1915), formerly of the Civic Service House and the Boston editor of *Immigration and Americanization*, offered, "To you, the sons and daughters of many lands, this country gives you a royal welcome." Their book did, not, however, offer information on the Constitution, preferring instead to promote civic values. This point led Charles Beard and Mary Ritter Beard (1918, vi) to advise,

> An examination of the extensive collection of texts in the Library of Congress, which embraces all of the most recent books on civics, shows that they fall into two groups: those which are formal and legal, and those which are 'sociological,' in character. The authors of the first group err, in our opinion, in treating government as a multitude of rules already well settled which, when committed to memory, are calculated to make good and wise citizens. The authors of the second group, it seems to us, in their revolt against the mechanistic theory of government, err just as much in minimizing those concrete political and administrative processes by which social work of a public character is accomplished and in emphasizing in civics private activities which are remoted from official operations.

Still, when Charles Beard and William Bagley (1920, v–vi) wrote a book for "the elementary pupil" that provided ten topics of instruction, it did not identify knowledge of the Constitution as one of its objectives. Instead, as in most books designed for students, education was driven by the need to (1) educate America's youth regarding civic involvement and (2) Americanize the many new immigrants entering the country. With a massive influx of new citizens in the last decades of the nineteenth and the first decades of the twentieth century, it was of vital importance to provide a suitable education. As Alton B. Parker (1922, 732), a judge on the New York Supreme Court and the losing candidate in the 1904 presidential election, wrote,

> Never in the history of this country were there here so many descendants of non-English speaking peoples, brought up to hate the governments of which they were subject, and who are wholly without knowledge of the principles upon which our government was so wisely builded. If their children are made to understand, by careful instruction, the aims of the Fathers, the principles which actuated them and the wisdom which inspired their governmental building, they will come in time to be a helpful addition to our vast population. But if they are not thus educated, it is quite likely that great numbers of them will be led by the Anarchists, the I. W. W's, the Russian Reds, and others of like character to join the forces to openly seek the overthrow of our Government that they may fatten upon the fruits of the people's labors.

Civic education was required but remarkably did not include knowledge of the US Constitution. These books emphasized American values rather than knowledge of the Constitution. Instead, Anna Alida Plass (1912, 63), a teacher of English to foreigners in day and evening schools in Rochester, New York, offered but a one-page description of the Constitution, concluding, "So was founded the United States. So has it become one of the great nations of the world." Charles McCarthy, the legislative reference librarian at Madison, Wisconsin; Flora Swan, the director of practice at the public schools of Indianapolis; and Jennie McMullin (1916), the legislative reference librarian at Madison provided little discussion of the Constitution in their book. The same year, David Excelmons Cloyd (1916, 5, 35), the dean of the School of Education at Des Moines College, offered a book that promised, "The purpose of this monograph is to emphasize the importance of instruction in citizenship in the elementary schools." Yet the monograph contained no chapters on the Constitution.

Again, the primary objective of these works was to promote good citizenship, not knowledge of the Constitution. As Jessie Field, formerly the superintendent of the school in Page County, Iowa, and Scott Nearing (1917, v), a professor of social science at Toledo University, wrote,

Schools are the laboratory for our democracy. People have a right to expect that our public schools should train their children for good citizenship. To be a good citizen means, first of all, to be willing and able to take part intelligently in the affairs of one's own community. To train such citizens, civics must be taught to children in the terms of their own lives. It must be real. It must connect with the affairs with which they are familiar in their town or neighborhood.

Several books did, however, provide valuable information on the Constitution. William Giffin (1888, 118) provided "a full and clear explanation of the important clauses of our Constitution." Likewise, C. W. Bardeen (1903, 47), the editor of the *School Bulletin*, in a book titled *Regents Questions in Civics*, included chapters on the national Constitution, as well as one page dedicated to the powers of the president. Ralph Richard Upton (1907)—a principal at Streator Township High School—provided a civics handbook that was more progressive, offering a chapter on the Constitutional Convention as well as one chapter each on the legislatures' and president's powers, though he disposed of the latter in a perfunctory two pages. Oliver Perry Cornman and Oscar Gerson (1907), with an original copyright date of 1901, included chapters on "the adoption of a new form of government" and "the establishment of the new government." And James McCleary (1908; first published in 1888), a teacher of civics and history in the state normal school of Mankato, Minnesota, offered chapters on the origin of the Constitution, the preamble, the structure of the legislative branch, the powers of Congress, the executive and judicial branches, and the modes of amending the Constitution. The following decade, Eleanor Clark (1910) published *Outlines of Civil Government with Suggestion for Civic Training by Original Work*. It included multiple sections on both the president and Congress. *The Citizenship Syllabus* (Committee for Immigrants in America 1916, 28) offered the following curriculum for "Advanced Civics for Immigrants": "Brief study of the Constitution; what it is and what it contains." And Charles Edgar Finch (1921), the director of junior high school grades and citizenship for Rochester, New York, offered a detailed analysis of the Constitution.

Despite such contributions, as Michael Kammen (1987, 81, 181, 208) discovered in his cultural history of the Constitution, "From 1789 until 1860 only one state, California, required that the Constitution be taught." California did not join the union until 1850. Hence, no state required that the Constitution be taught between 1789 and at least 1850, a period of more than sixty years. It was not until 1862 that there was "a marked increase . . . in the number of states that legally required some sort of instruction concerning the Constitution—a requirement that spread rapidly after 1900." Still, Kammen continued, "There is abundant evidence that constitutionalism continued to be neglected in the curricula of many schools; and that where instruction did occur, the quality was not high. As the authors of one report put it in 1916, 'studying many books about a Constitution which is not read is a common practice, but one that cannot be defended.'"

According to the *American Standard*, writing on Constitution Day in 1925, "Thirty-five States Require Schools to Teach Constitution" (Kammen 1986, 222, 232). Kammen added,

> At first glance, the campaign [to teach the Constitution] seems to have been exceedingly successful. By 1923, legislation requiring constitutional instruction had been passed in twenty-three states; by 1931, forty-three states required it. Some private universities even ruled that no student should be awarded a degree who had not completed at least a one-year course on the U. S. Constitution "with specific reference to the spirit of the founders of the republic and the interpretations of the Constitution by the highest courts of the land." During the mid-1920s annual lectureships devoted to the Constitution were endowed at various colleges and universities, including William and Mary, Virginia, Rochester, and Boston University.

Furthermore, various books were published such as one edited by an individual identified only as E. in 1925: *Little Blue Book No. 687. U. S. Constitution: Declaration of Independence and the Monroe Doctrine.* Even short plays were written to educate those seeking US citizenship (Leighton 1920, 34–37). However, the problem was that many teachers were not interested in teaching the Constitution at all. As Kammen (1986, 232–33, 235) noted, "Educational administrators did not like to be told that their districts were obliged to cover certain topics. And according to the ABA's Committee on Citizenship, 'the teaching profession, generally, is loath to engage in a new subject with which they are not familiar.'"

By the 1920s, scholars and laypeople complained about the public's lack of knowledge of the Constitution and the dangers that ignorance of it entailed. While calling for a "constitutional revival," F. W. Phelps (1920, 10) urged citizens to acquire greater knowledge of the Constitution:

> A study of the Constitution at this time seems to be peculiarly appropriate; we are asked to make changes in our form of government which would involve changes in the Constitution, and, obviously, we cannot either intelligently accept or **intelligently reject** these proposals unless we know something of the document we are urged to change. These proposed changes are of the most intimate concern of every American citizen, native or naturalized, and an evening or two spent in reading the Constitution may prove of value.

In *A Common Sense of the Constitution of the United States*, A. T. Southworth (1924, iii), head of the history department at English High School in Boston, noted,

> The average citizen has rather hazy ideas about the Constitution. Many people have never seen a copy; or if they have, it was so long ago that they have forgotten how it looks. They do not know whether it covers two pages or two hundred. Most of them think it long and involved, when as a matter of fact it is one of the simplest and clearest documents ever written, and is far easier to grasp than ninety per cent of the legal papers of to-day. We cannot understand United States history unless we keep the Constitution clearly in mind. Nor can we read the news columns of the daily paper intelligently without this knowledge, to say nothing of the editorial page.

The following decade, S. McKee Rosen (1935, 3), of Commission on the Social Studies of the American Historical Association, documented,

> In 1929, there was appointed from among educators in the United States a Commission on the Social Studies in the Schools. After five years of investigation accompanied by the publication of particular studies from time to time, the final conclusions of the Commission appeared in June, 1934. Charged with making recommendations concerning education in social sciences, the Commission reported: "The emerging age is particularly

an age of transition. It is marked by numerous and severe tensions arising out of the conflict between the actual trend toward integrated economy and society, on the other side, and the traditional practices, dispositions, ideas, and institutional arrangements, on the other. . . . The Commission deems possible and desirable the attainment and spread of the accurate knowledge and informed opinion among the masses of the American people both concerning the realities, tensions, and problems of the emerging era and concerning ideals, traditions, and experience of other ages and other peoples in order that all choices may be made with reason, with understanding, and with due regard to the moral and cultural, as well as their narrowly economic, implications."

S. McKee Rosen (1935, 3–4) also identified, "In a somewhat similar vein, the Report of the President's Research Committee on Social Trends (1933), viewing the need for social thinking, warns us that: 'Nothing short of the combined intelligence of the nation can cope with the predicaments here mentioned.'" Such warnings were most frightening in an age when depression and war blighted everyday life. In other words, Americans needed to understand basic terminology to build an interconnected spirit of patriotism and commitment to the nation's republican values. Consequently, various texts were prepared specifically for the new citizen. Books such as H. Arnold Bennett's *The Constitution in School and College* (1935) provided teachers with instruction on how to teach the Constitution. In the *Public Affairs Pamphlet*, Robert Cushman (1940, 1) argued,

The average citizen has a very wholesome respect for the Constitution of the United States. His respect does not usually come from any clear or accurate knowledge of the document itself, but grows out of the belief that the Constitution sanctions those policies which he approves and forbids those which seem to him dangerous or oppressive. His reaction to the Supreme Court is similarly direct and forthright; its decisions are sound if he likes them and unsound if he does not.

Among the best books written during this period was an excellent text by Walter Faulkner (1936). The *Child's History and Interpretation of the Constitution of the United States* provided copious detail and drew praise from an array of legal scholars. In an advertisement promoting the book, which was priced "On Sale" at "$3.50 Per Copy," Faulkner received testimonials from Grafton Green, the chief justice of the Supreme Court of Tennessee, and Owen Roberts and Harlan Stone, associate justices of the US Supreme Court. Louis D. Brandeis, associate justice of the Supreme Court, wrote, "Your book . . . bears evidence that it was a labor of love." D. W. DeHaven, an associate justice of the Supreme Court of Tennessee, wrote, "I think your book . . . is a splendid contribution to our literature. You have treated your subject in a way that will make the study of the constitution easy and attractive to the youth of the land. In this you have rendered a real service." Nevertheless, Faulkner's book was published by a small Tennessee press, and the availability of such texts continued to be a problem.

As John Patrick, Richard Remy, and Mary Jane Turner (1986, 9) wrote a half century later, "The depth and extent of the school's responsibilities for teaching about the Constitution are shaped in part by societal expectations. In our democratic system of education, the curriculum of public schools ultimately reflects societal judgments about what should and should not be taught. However, 'society' is not monolithic and various individuals and groups within society may want quite different things from the schools at the same time." Balancing societal expectations and school curriculum, however, creates a wide berth for ideas about the Constitution. By 1987, only forty-three states mandated "instruction about the Constitution in secondary schools." As John Patrick (1987, 2), director of the Social Studies Development Center at Indiana University, writing in the *ERIC Administrative Bulletin*, noted, the problems of teaching the Constitution "have to do with confused curriculum priorities, inadequate treatment in widely-used textbooks, and serious deficiencies in students' knowledge . . . they are deeply rooted in our educational history." As the last decade of the twentieth century dawned, Patrick (1991, 3) again noted, "Most shortcomings in textbook treatments of the Constitution are associated with limitation of the textbook as a medium of instruction." Hence, teaching the Constitution in secondary schools still confronts challenges of censorship and obfuscation. It is no wonder that most Americans know so little about their Constitution. Even the 1993 American Bar Association's Special Committee on Youth Education for Citizenship provided little guidance. It released a book on how to teach teachers to teach the law, and although it included several interesting essays, no essay was dedicated to a study of the US Constitution.

And more recently,

> Respondents of the annual Constitution Day Civics Survey by the Annenberg Public Policy Center of the University of Pennsylvania were asked whether arresting people who entered the Capitol to disrupt the certification of the presidential election violated the Constitution. The sobering results: 49 percent said that arresting insurrectionists violated the Constitution because the insurrectionists were only exercising their constitutional right to petition the government for redress of grievances. The breakdown who agreed with this statement: 53 percent of self-identified conservatives, 51 percent of self-identified moderates and 42 percent of self-described liberals.[2]

Knowledge of the Constitution, therefore, continues to be a troubling issue.

As America today confronts a potential constitutional crisis, knowledge of the Constitution is especially significant. Yet there is little evidence that the public is knowledgeable about our fundamental document.[3] Only 66 percent of those surveyed could identify all three branches of the government, with 17 percent unable to identify even one. If ignorance of the law is no excuse, then there can be no excuse for our ignorance of our fundamental document—the Constitution.

Chapter 5

The Sovereign Power and Constitutional Interpretation

The sovereignty of the nation has its institution in the powers in which the government is constituted. The will of the organic people, in its normal action, works through different members, to which are attached different functions. The nature of these powers and these functions is implicit in the nation in its organism,—their manifestation is in the process of freedom and of rights.

—Elisha Mulford, *The Nation*

The theme of this book is that constitutional ambiguity provides the basis for different interpretations of presidential power, which in turn provides an opportunity for presidents to expand their authority. In this chapter I examine a case study of how ambiguity impacted both the powers of the presidency and the nation's perception of itself. In this instance, ambiguity affected many of the words of the Constitution, including its first three: "We the People." According to Francis Lieber (1861, 27–28), "This Constitution begins with the words: 'We, the people of the United States,'—to me, the most magnificent words I know of in all history. They seem like an entrance, full of grandeur and simplicity, into a wide temple." Historian James Garfield Randall (1929, 13–14) identified, "The phrase 'We the people of the United States' means the people of the States, for the 'United States' is not a distinct people, but a union of several peoples. . . . Supreme law is exercised by the government, but paramount authority resides with the people." And one of the preeminent constitutional scholars of the late nineteenth century, Thomas Cooley (1889, 32), advised, "The theory on which all government in America is constructed, is that sovereignty is in the people. This is not theory merely, for its acceptance makes it the most important and vital fact in government."

Yet despite their grandeur and apparent simplicity, these three words represent a prime example of how ambiguity provide different constitutional interpretations, in this case involving the issue of where the Constitution vests the sovereign power. Did it reside with the people? Not according to Alexander Stephens (1868, 172–73, 192), who served as vice president of the Confederacy. He claimed, "It clearly appears that it was the intention of those who framed what follows [after the preamble], that it was to be a Constitution for States, or, in other words, a Compact between States." Alternatively, was sovereignty vested in the national government? In an early work on the Constitution, Nathaniel Chipman (1833, 239) wrote,

> The power by which the constitution of the United States was ratified, and from which is derived all the authority of the national government thereby instituted . . . is fully expressed in the declaratory clause prefixed to that instrument. "We the people of the United States, in order to form a more perfect union, establish justice, insure domestic tranquility, provide for the common defence, promote the general welfare, and secure the blessings of liberty to ourselves and our posterity, do ordain and establish this constitution for the United States of America."

The question of where sovereignty resided was more than a theoretical curiosity. In England, the King was sovereign, but as Catherine Drinker Bowen (1966, 223) remarked, "The Convention was establishing not a monarchy but a republic; the President would be no sovereign." If not the president, then who was sovereign—the people, the states, or the national government? In time, the debate on this issue involved several presidents and led to a constitutional crisis and civil war. Meanwhile, the debate also had direct applications to the presidency. According to Reverend Charles Ellis Stevens (1894, 147–49),

> Popular feeling among Americans at the close of the Revolu-
> tion was opposed to kingship,—an opposition largely due to
> the fact that the struggle had been forced upon them by their

sovereign in person. The sense of loyalty which previously had so real an existence was forgotten in this new antipathy. One of the gravest difficulties, therefore, which confronted the framers of the Constitution, was the question of how to fill the vacant place in the fabric of government occupied in colonial times by the sovereign, and in such a way as to secure headship for the nation and efficiency in executive functions. It was admitted in debate during the Convention, that the people would not endure the setting up of a king. Yet, as by irresistible instinct, they put much of the royal power back again in its place at the apex of government, in the form of a colonial governor or president made national.

Lori Han and Diane Heith (2018, 34) added, "Nothing was more critical to the development of an American presidency than the distinction between general and limited executive authority, which arose from contemporary interpretations of sovereignty." For example, as Charles Henry Butler (1902, 1:3) wrote, "The treaty-making power of the United States as vested in the Central Government, is derived not only from the powers expressly conferred by the Constitution, but that it is also possessed by the Government as an attribute of sovereignty, and that it extends to every subject which can be the basis of negotiation and contract between any of the sovereign powers of the world." Consequently "this power exists in, and can be exercised by, the National Government, whenever foreign relations of any kind are established with any other sovereign power." Likewise, the president's authority to receive ambassadors and her power as commander in chief derive from the "law of nations." As such, sovereignty is decidedly relevant to the powers of the American presidency. I begin with an examination of three prevalent models of sovereignty and their impact on the development of presidential power, with presidential power strongest under a doctrine of national sovereignty and weakest under the concept of state sovereignty.

Three Models of the Sovereign Power

The term sovereignty in its full sense imports the supreme, absolute, and uncontrollable power by which any independent state is governed. From what has already been said it appears that, although the States were called sovereign and independent in the Declaration of Independence, they were never in their individual character strictly so, because they were always, in respect to some of the higher powers of sovereignty, subject to the control of some common authority, and were never separately recognized or known as members of the family of nations. This common authority was, *first*, the Crown and Parliament of Great Britain; *second*, the Revolutionary Congress; *third*, the Congress of the Confederation; and at length the government formed under the Constitution. The powers of these differed greatly, but in one most important particular there was uniformity: each had control of affairs of war for all the Colonies or States, and of all intercourse with foreign nations.

—Thomas Cooley, *General Principles of Constitutional Law in the United States of America*

The preamble to the US Constitution has been interpreted in different ways and its relationship to sovereignty has been a constant theme in American constitutional and political dialogue. As political scientist Louis Hartz (1955, 44) wrote, "A philosopher, it is true, might look askance at the theory of power the American's developed. It was not a model of lucid exposition. The trouble lay with their treatment of sovereignty. Instead of boldly rejecting the concept, as [Benjamin] Franklin was once on the verge of doing when he said that it made him 'quite sick,' they accepted the concept and tried to qualify it out of existence. The result was a chaotic series of forays and retreats."

Most of the members of the Constitutional Convention favored a stronger national government than the Articles of Confederation. Hence, as historian Gordon Wood (2021, 77) noted, "It was a loaded convention. Nearly everyone present was a nationalist and suspicious of state-based democracy. When two of the delegates from New York, Robert Yates and John Lansing, who were not nationalists, came to appreciate the direction the Convention was taking, they bailed out and left the New York delegation without a quorum and unable to record a vote." One of the earliest books examining American constitutional law cited Yates's notes from the constitutional convention and argued that the Framers intentionally obfuscated their intentions (Taylor 1823, 13):

It is very remarkable, that the Congress of 1787 introduced the word national into the resolve recommending a convention. It expressed an opinion 'that a convention was the most probable means of establishing in these states a firm national government.' So far it unequivocally advocated the exchange of a federal for a national form of government; but an intimation so plain and positive, that the state governments ought to be destroyed, might not have been received with applause, and might have obstructed the removal of the defects of the existing federal union. The expedient of complexity was therefore practised to flatter the opinion of the states, and yet to supply a text for the advocates of a national government.

Hence, the US Constitution was more complex than the Articles of Confederation. As Rufus King explained on June 19, 1787, in his speech related to foreign affairs, including war,[1]

The import of the term "states," "sovereignty," "national," "federal," had been often used and applied in the discussions inaccurately and delusively. The States were not "sovereigns" in the sense contended for by some. They did not possess the peculiar features of sovereignty—they could not make war, nor peace, nor alliances, nor treaties. Considering them as political beings, they were dumb, for they could not speak to any foreign sovereign whatever. They were deaf, for they could not hear any proposition from such sovereign. They had not even the organs or faculties of defence or offence, for they could not of themselves raise troops, or equip vessels, for war. On the other side, if the union of the States comprises the idea of a confederation, it comprises that also of consolidation. A union of the States is a union of the men composing them, from whence a national character results to the whole. Congress can act alone without the States, they can act (and their acts will be binding) against the instructions of the States. If they declare war, war is de jure declared; captures made in pursuance of it are lawful; no acts of the States can vary the situation, or prevent the judicial consequences. If the States, therefore, retained some portion of their sovereignty, they had certainly divested themselves of essential portions of it.

James Madison responded,

> Some gentlemen are afraid that the plan is not sufficiently national, while others apprehend that it is too much so. If this point of representation was once well fixed, we should come nearer to one another in sentiment. The necessity would then be discovered of circumscribing more effectually the State governments, and enlarging more effectually the bounds of the general government. Some contend that the States are sovereign, when in fact they are only political societies. The States never possessed the essential rights of sovereignty. They were always vested in Congress. Their voting as States in Congress is no evidence of their sovereignty. The State of Maryland voted by counties. Did this make the counties sovereign? The States, at present, are only great corporations, having the power of making by-laws, and these are effectual only if they are not contradictory to the general confederation.

If Madison is correct, then under the Articles of Confederation Congress was sovereign though it had no real power, and without power, how could it be sovereign?—a conundrum to be sure. Rather, power, if it existed at all, resided with the individual states, though they were not sovereign—a fascinating contradiction. To be sovereign without power, however, suggests a failed state or in the case of the Articles, a failed Constitution. It could not long survive in such a paradoxical form. Hence, a new Constitution was required. Consequently, as Mary Bilder (2015, 35) wrote, *Notes* "recorded Madison's development of four strategic goals and a series of recommendations for a new government. The national government was to have due supremacy; the states were to have subordinate utility. To prove the necessity of minimizing state power, Madison prepared an outline of problems facing the nation—his famous 'Vices of the Political System' manuscript." At the Virginia Ratifying Convention, Madison made another observation related to foreign policy: "Let us observe . . . that the powers in the general government are those which will be exercised mostly in time of war, while those of the state governments will be exercised in time of peace" (Elliot 1900, 3:259). According to historian Irving Brant (1936, 30–31), "Madison in 1787 saw nothing sacred in the state sovereignty, nothing essential to the freedom of the American people. The states were mere administrative conveniences. He desired, he said, 'that form of government will most approximate the states to the condition of counties.'" Meanwhile, Richard Ellis (2015, 148) argued, "Both Madison and Washington interpreted the [Connecticut] compromise as a devastating defeat, because the principle of state sovereignty had been qualified but not killed." Yet Edward Corwin (1911, 295–96) noted that James Madison's views on this key issue changed and then changed again:

> In the Federalist . . . Madison had accepted the notion that the decision in controversies respecting the boundary line between State and national power would devolve upon the Supreme Court, whose power he described as ultimate, and that, moreover, in a paragraph in which he speaks of the States as possessing "a residuary and inviolable sovereignty." The same twelve-month, however, in which Madison wrote the passage above referred to, he had begun to see new light upon the subject of judicial review. . . . Throughout the ensuing decade Madison came more and more under the influence both of Jefferson's democracy and of his State Sovereignty ideas, with the result that in 1798 he was ready to pen the famous protest of that year against the alien and sedition laws which are known as the Virginia Resolutions.

Madison thus wrote,

> Resolved * * * that this assembly doth explicitly and peremptorily declare that it views the powers of the federal government as resulting from the compact to which the States are parties * * * that in case of a deliberate, palpable, and dangerous exercise of other powers not granted by the said compact, the States who are parties thereto, have the right and are in duty bound to interpose for arresting the progress of the evil and for maintaining within their respective limits the authorities, rights, and liberties appertaining to them.

The key word here is *compact*. According to Samuel Johnson's *Dictionary of the English Language in Miniature* (1818) the word signified "a contract, mutual agreement" and "firm, close, solid, exact." *Dr. Webster's Complete Dictionary of the English Language* (1864) noted, "The law of nations depends on mutual compacts, treaties, leagues, &c. Blackstone." The word *compact* is important because it became a key issue employed in the interpretation of the US Constitution. If the Constitution was a mere compact, it could be broken. If not, then the union was inviolable. Hence, as the nation moved toward Civil War, the debate was whether the Constitution created a compact or a union. As such, the first three words of the Constitution, and the issue of sovereignty, were paramount in the political debates of the age. And on this point the views of various partisans changed over time, often in inconsistent ways. As Corwin (1911, 296–97) wrote, "Years later Madison was at great pains to insist that the purport of this language was ambiguous, but the word 'respectively' taken with the context, indicates, if language means anything, that the original intention was to assert a constitutional prerogative on the part of the individual States to judge for themselves of the scope of the national powers. And indeed it was so understood at the time." And yet, as Corwin noted, Madison's views changed yet again:

> It is true that as early as 1800 Madison and his following had begun to reconsider the extreme position taken in the resolutions of 1798 and to seek retreat from it. In his Report to the Virginia legislature in 1800, Madison begins by reiterating the view set forth in the resolutions: the States are sovereign, any decision of the federal judiciary, therefore, while possibly ultimate in relation to the authorities of the other departments of the Federal Government, can not possibly be so "in relation to the rights of the parties to the constitutional compact, from which the judicial as well as the other departments hold their delegated trusts." Fifty pages farther along, however, Madison's audacity has oozed entirely away. "It has been said," he writes, restating the issue, "that it belongs to the judiciary of the United States, and not the State Legislatures, to declare the meaning of the Federal Constitution." But, he urges, in a far different tone to the one with which he set out, 'a declaration that proceedings of the Federal Government are not warranted by the Constitution is a novelty neither among the citizens nor among the Legislatures of the States * * * nor can the declarations of either, whether affirming or denying the constitutionality of measures of the Federal Government, * * * be deemed, in any point of view, an assumption of the office of the judge. The declarations in such cases are expressions of opinion, unaccompanied with any other effect than what they may produce on opinion by exciting reflection. The expositions

of the judiciary, on the other hand, are carried into immediate effect by force."

Why was the issue of sovereignty so difficult for Madison? He simply may have reconsidered the matter over time, but there is another possibility. Madison was both a constitutional theorist and a practical politician. As such, his views at one point in time conflicted with his interests at another. As such, the so-called Father of the Constitution's ideas about sovereignty changed over time. The complication for the Framers was that while they rejected the sovereignty of the British government, both the Parliament and the King, they were less certain regarding what sovereignty entailed in a new government. Instructive then is President James Monroe's detailed history of sovereignty in America. In his inaugural address (March 4, 1817), Monroe referred to "the States, respectively protected by the National Government under a mild, parental system against foreign dangers, and enjoying within their separate spheres, by a wide partition of power, a just portion of sovereignty."[2] It was, however, in Monroe's May 4, 1822, *Special Message to the House of Representatives Containing the Views of the President of the United States on the Subject of Internal Improvements* where he provided the most detailed analysis of sovereignty by any president. The forty-four-page (single space, 12 pt) message included the words "sovereign" or "sovereignty" twenty-seven times, Constitution or unconstitutional ninety-eight times, and the associated words (powers, empower) over 350 times. Monroe's message examined the period from the Declaration of Independence to the foundations of constitutional sovereignty. Sovereignty in the people extended only to the limited choice of representatives, while the Constitution protected against "any tumult or disorder incident to the exercise of that power by the people"—essentially code words for the Framers' fear of democracy as mob rule. As for the Articles of Confederation, Monroe noted they were

> soon found to be utterly incompetent to the purposes intended by it. It was defective in its powers; it was defective also in the means of executing the powers actually granted by it. Being a league of sovereign and independent States, its acts, like those of all other leagues, required the interposition of the States composing it to give them effect within their respective jurisdictions. The acts of Congress without the aid of State laws to enforce them were altogether nugatory.

It was for this reason that a new Constitution was formed. Monroe noted,

> In the institution of the Government of the United States by
> the citizens of every State a compact was formed between
> the whole American people which has the same force and
> partakes of all the qualities to the extent of its powers as a
> compact between the citizens of a State in the formation of
> their own constitution. It can not be altered except by those
> who formed it or in the mode prescribed by the parties to the
> compact itself. . . . The Government of the United States relies
> on its own means for the execution of its powers, as the State
> governments do for the execution of theirs, both governments
> having a common origin or sovereign, the people—the State
> governments the people of each State, the National Government,
> the people of every State—and being amenable to the power
> which created it. It is by executing its functions as a Govern-
> ment thus originating and thus acting that the Constitution
> of the United States holds the States together and performs
> the office of a league.

While he notes that the people are sovereign in the states and the
national government, Monroe does not mention the limitation on the
people's voting rights in the national government—directly electing only
the members of the House of Representatives. Furthermore, he does not
explain what is meant by "the office of a league." Is it one government or
a league of governments? As Monroe continued,

> There were two separate and independent governments estab-
> lished over our Union, one for local purposes over each State
> by the people of the State, the other for national purposes over
> all the States by the people of the United States. The whole
> power of the people, on the representative principle, is divided
> between them. . . . Had the sovereignty passed to the aggre-
> gate, consequences might have ensued, admitting the success
> of our Revolution, which might even yet seriously affect our
> system. By passing to the people of each colony the opposition
> to Great Britain, the prosecution of the war, the Declaration of
> Independence, the adoption of the Confederation and of this
> Constitution are all imputable to them.

Monroe used various circumlocutions to argue that sovereignty resided in the people, but not to the people in the aggregate, thus referencing their rights as individuals. Rather, sovereignty devolved to the people of the thirteen states, with the states and the national government having their own distinct functions. As such, Monroe attempted to define the precise boundaries of all three theoretical sovereigns in the American republic: the people, the states, and the national government. Yet he did not explain how sovereignty could exist in the individual, but not in the aggregate, especially if it was the aggregate that would decide who was elected to the House or the state legislatures. And if sovereignty resided with the people, what sovereignty existed for the states and the national government? Was that merely a matter of jurisdictional functions? To clarify, Monroe noted,

> A State, also, may contest the right, and then the controversy assumes another character. Government might contend against government, for to a certain extent both the Governments are sovereign and independent of each other, and in that form it is possible, though not probable, that opposition might be made. To each limitations are prescribed, and should a contest rise between them respecting their rights and the people sustain it with anything like an equal division of numbers the worst consequences might ensue.

Monroe therefore recognized the contradictions inherent in existing theories of sovereignty.

Reconciling three theories of sovereignty indeed was difficult. Consequently, Monroe's formulation was hardly conclusive. Sovereignty resided with the people—as individuals but not in the aggregate. Both the national and state governments likewise were sovereign entities, and furthermore, to some extent at least, they were independent of each other. Monroe's dissertation on sovereignty raises as many questions as it settles. The delineation of boundaries of sovereignty between the three principals therefore would become a continuing controversy in American politics. To provide a sounder theoretical basis, a year later, in one of the first books published on the Constitution, John Taylor (1823, 176) introduced the idea of "dual sovereignty." If both the states and the national government held power, then how would these powers be distributed? Three years later, New York State Justice James Kent (1826, 363) delineated the powers of the state and federal government, while discussing the concept of *concurrent powers*:

> The question how far the state governments have concurrent powers, either legislative or judicial, over cases within their jurisdiction of the government of the United States, has been much discussed. . . . It was observed in the Federalist, that the state governments would clearly retain all those rights of sovereignty which they had before the adoption of the constitution of the United States, and which were not by that constitution exclusively delegated to the union. The alienation of state power or sovereignty would only exist in three cases: Where the constitution in express terms granted an exclusive authority to the union; where it granted in one instance an authority to the union; and in another prohibited the states from exercising the like authority; and where it granted an authority to the union, to which a similar authority in the states would be absolutely and totally contradictory and repugnant.

Kent's classification scheme provided the states with considerable latitude, while also noting the need to surrender some authority to the federal government. By establishing a new Constitution in 1787 that represented the "supreme law of the land," the thirteen states ceded some authority, though certain rights were reserved to the states or to the people by the tenth amendment. How much sovereignty they retained, however, continued to be a matter of uncertainty, an issue that had been reflected as early as George Washington's letter of transmittal to Congress on September 17, 1787, accompanying the newly written constitution (*Bacon's Guide* 1863, 351):

> It is obviously impracticable in the federal government of these states, to secure all rights of independent sovereignty to each, and yet provide for the interests and safety of all. Individuals entering into society must give up a share of liberty to preserve the rest. The magnitude of the sacrifice must depend, as well on situation and circumstance as on the object to be obtained. It is at all times difficult to draw with precision the line between those rights which must be surrendered and those which may be reserved; and, on the present occasion, this difficulty was

increased by a difference among the several states as to their situation, extent, habits, and particular interests. . . . That it will meet the full and entire approbation of every state is not perhaps to be expected; but each will doubtless consider that had her interest been alone consulted, the consequences might have been particularly disagreeable or injurious to others; that it is liable to as few exceptions as could reasonably have been expected, we hope and believe; that it may promote the lasting welfare of that country so dear to us all, and secure her freedom and happiness, is our most ardent wish.

Washington noted, "It is obviously impracticable," and the idea that the several states must surrender some sovereignty to the new national government is "obvious." Likewise, "Individuals entering into society must give up a share of liberty to preserve the rest." What liberty did they surrender? Washington did not refer to the Bill of Rights, since those amendments were not yet added. Apparently, it depends: "The magnitude of the sacrifice must depend, as well on situation and circumstance as on the object to be obtained." Hence, in circumstances such as war or a national crisis, individuals (or states?) can expect to surrender more liberty to the federal government than at other times. But what are those situations and circumstances? Washington's answer: "It is at all times difficult to draw with precision the line between those rights which must be surrendered and those which may be reserved; and, on the present occasion, this difficulty was increased by a difference among the several states as to their situation, extent, habits, and particular interests." So, does it depend on the "situation, extent, habits, and particular interests" of each state or is there a uniform concession of some undefined quantity of liberty? And why did Washington use the word *individuals*, rather than states? Was he referring exclusively to the states or to the people who would participate in the state ratifying conventions?

The letter of transmittal obscured each of these issues and demonstrated the inherent difficulties in dividing sovereignty between three different principals. Interpretation therefore continued to be a complex process, subject to debate and ardent disagreement. Consequently, during the Civil War, Joel Parker (1862, 6) commented, "Many persons feared that the powers proposed to be granted were too great, and that there was danger that the new government would swallow up the State organizations, the very thing of all others which it was not designed to accomplish. It underwent a most searching and critical analysis." Of the many questions posited at the time, how could the Constitution guarantee independence if the states ceded power to the new federal government? One answer is provided by the word *federal*. John Taylor (1823, 6) defined the term as follows: " 'Federal,' also adopted into our political phraseology, is a national construction of the terms used in forming our system of government, comprising a definite expression of publick opinion, that state sovereignties really exist. It implies a league between sovereign nations, has been so used by all classes of people from the commencement of our political existence down to this day, and is inapplicable to a nation consolidated under one sovereignty." Again, the word *league* is used to describe the nation. However, that term was not defined, according to historian Daniel Boorstin (1989, 106),

> In those days "federal" meant something different from what it means today. It was still commonly spelled "foederal," because it came from the Latin word foedus, which means "treaty." A treaty was, of course, an agreement made by a sovereign state (or nation). And a "federal" union then, would be a kind of international association held together by fully sovereign states that had made treaties with one another. . . . A "national" union would not be merely a collection of different states, each with its own government. It would be something much stronger. . . . To make that possible each of the "sovereign" state would have to give up some of its "sovereign" powers.

As such, we can extrapolate that a federal system would establish a league. Still, such definitional issues contributed to different interpretations of the word sovereignty until the Civil War and even afterward.

The Sovereign Power and Ambiguity

> The attempt of such an incongruous mixture, as that of the principal of popular suffrage, with that of state sovereignty, in the election of a President and Vice-President of the United States; however laudable the views, in which it may have originated; reflects, perhaps, little ultimate credit on our political sagacity, and soundness of judgment.
>
> —Augustus Woodward, *The Presidency of the United States*

Constitutional ambiguity not only played an important role in different interpretations of the Constitution, it also was a foremost reason leading the nation toward civil war. In the first Gaspar Bacon (1928, 35) lecture on the US Constitution, Scott Wilson noted, "The *first* cornerstone of the Constitution is the principle of constitutional limitations upon the powers of the government. The sovereign people of the United States, fearing the usurpation or abuse of power, carefully limited their different governmental agencies in the exercise thereof." Or as United States District Judge Leon Yankwich (1950, 30) pronounced, "The doctrine of limited sovereignty or the limited state maintains that government is bound by the law of the land and not above it." Yet while they separated power, the Framers, as with so much else, did not clearly define the relationship between the people, the states, and the national government or the boundaries between a federal and a national government. Their intent was not to provide an encyclopedic prolix of all such matters, but rather to identify the basic structure of a new government. Consequently, the question of who has the sovereign power is yet another matter of constitutional interpretation and one that involves issues of presidential power and constitutional ambiguity.

Regarding this issue, in the ninth volume of his *General Abridgement and Digest of American Law*, Nathan Dane (1829, 32–33) wrote, "States' rights and State sovereignty are expressions coined for party purposes, often by minorities, who happen to be dissatisfied with the measures of the General Government." And Jabez Curry (1901, 242–44), for whom the Curry School of Education was christened at the University of Virginia, stated that both the politics of the time and a strict construction of the Constitution were involved with the interpretation of sovereignty: "It can now clearly be seen why the South, being a minority section, with agriculture as the chief occupation, and with the peculiar institution of African slavery fastened on her by Old England and New England, adhered to the State rights, or Jeffersonian, school of politics. Those doctrines contain the only principles or policy truly conservative of the Constitution. Apart from them checks and limitations are of little avail, and the Federal Government can increase its powers indefinitely." According to Curry, only one interpretation of the Constitution was the correct interpretation! Those who disagreed were "enemies." Such incendiary language was far from novel. During the presidency of John Adams, after Congress enacted the Sedition Acts, Vice President Thomas Jefferson respond anonymously in 1798 with the *Kentucky Resolutions*. In his draft, Jefferson (1984, 449) wrote,

Resolved, That the several States composing the United States of America, are not united on the principle of unlimited submission to their General Government; but that, by a compact under the style and title of a Constitution for the United States, and of amendments thereto, they constituted a General Government for special purposes,—delegated to that government certain definite powers, reserving, each State to itself, the residuary mass of right to their own self-government; and that whensoever the General Government assumes undelegated powers, its acts are unauthoritative, void, and of no force; that to this compact each State acceded as a State, and is an integral party, its co-States forming, as to itself, the other party: that the government created by this compact was not made the exclusive and final judge of the extent of the powers delegated to itself; since that would have made its discretion, and not the Constitution, the measure of its powers; but that, as in all other cases of compact among powers having no common judge, each party has an equal right to judge for itself, as well of infractions as of the mode and measure of redress.

Note that Jefferson repeatedly referred to a "compact." Also note that while Jefferson discussed the limits of the federal government at this time, he apparently placed national over state interests when he supported the embargo of 1807. As such, Jefferson's ideas about where the sovereign power resided appear to have been flexible. Regarding the Virginia and Kentucky Resolutions, Francis Thorpe (1901, 2:346–47) wrote:

The Kentucky and Virginia resolutions put the idea of State sovereignty before the country in a practicable form. Copies were promptly sent to all the State legislatures, of which seven immediately formulated replies. . . . Not one State replied in approval of the Kentucky and Virginia resolutions. . . . The jealousy of the States for their sovereignty of which Randolph had spoken in the Federal Convention had become a fixed part of the political creed of most of the American people.

So, was the government of the United States founded upon the idea of a compact? Why did the Founders begin the Constitution with "We the

People" and not "We the States?" The implications of these questions were critical to the nation's very existence, for if one can agree to join a compact, one also can secede from it.

Is the Constitution a Compact?

Along with the question of sovereignty, this is another question that has critical implications for presidential power. If states could secede, presidential power over the union was constricted. So, was the Constitution a compact? In his child's history book of the Constitution, Elhanan Winchester (1796, 11) answered, "Yes, and it is the first trial of the kind, upon a large scale, that has ever been made since the origin of society; and its fate will determine the important question, Whether men are worthy of liberty, or not?"

In 1825, William Rawle's views held contradictory portents for America's future. As Joel Parker (1862, 8) commented,

> It is to be noted that in his final chapter, entitled, "Of the Permanence of the Union," the author, regarding the Constitution as a mere compact,—and without sufficient reference to the circumstancing showing that, if it were regarded as a compact, it was indissoluble, constituting a government which was to be permanent,—distinctly admits the right of the people of a State to secede from the Union, and says that "secessions may reduce the number to the smallest integer admitting combination." But he impairs somewhat the force and effect of his own positions in this respect, when in the same chapter. . . . "In every aspect . . . which this great subject presents, we feel the deepest impression of a sacred obligation to preserve the union of our country."

On this point, Supreme Court Justice Joseph Story (1858, 1:206) asked, "In the first place, what is the true nature and import of the instrument? Is it a treaty, a convention, a league, a contract, or a compact?" Story's answer (1833, 117) was straightforward and differed from Rawle's viewpoint: "There is nowhere found upon the face of the Constitution, any clause, intimating it to be a compact, or in anywise providing for its interpretation, as such." Story's mentor, John Marshall, shared the same viewpoint.

Despite such disagreements, language invoking a compact was common among our early presidents. James Madison referred to a compact in his July 24, 1813, *Proclamation: Recommending a Day of Prayer.* There he referred to our national compact as a "political Constitution." James Monroe in his inaugural address (March 4, 1817) noted that our Constitution created

> the happy Government under which we live—a Government adequate to every purpose for which the social compact is formed; a Government elective in all its branches, under which every citizen may by his merit obtain the highest trust recognized by the Constitution; which contains within it no cause of discord, none to put at variance one portion of the community with another; a Government which protects every citizen in the full enjoyment of his rights, and is able to protect the nation against injustice from foreign powers.

In his inaugural address (March 4, 1825), John Quincy Adams referred to the constitution as a "social compact" as well as a "national covenant." These references to a compact were designed to promote social harmony in the early republic. In contrast, John C. Calhoun, who served as a vice president under two different presidents, J. Q. Adams and Andrew Jackson, and later as a senator from South Carolina, advanced a more dangerous interpretation of the term. In his *Discourse on the Constitution of the United States*, Calhoun (1992, 81, 95) postulated,

> Ours is a system of governments, compounded of the separate governments of the several States composing the Union, and of one common government of all its members, called the Government of the United States. The former preceded the latter, which was created by their agency. Each was framed by written constitutions; those of the several States by the people of each, acting separately, and in their sovereign character; and that of the United States, by the same, acting in the same character—but jointly instead of separately. All were formed on the same model. They all divide the powers of government into legislative, executive, and judicial; and are founded on the great principle of the responsibility of the rulers to the ruled. . . . Each, within its appropriate sphere, possesses all

the attributes, and performs all the functions of government. Neither is perfect without the other. The two combined, form one entire and perfect government.

Importantly, however, Calhoun drew a distinction between the "national government" and the "federal government," declaring that the former was explicitly rejected at the constitutional convention. He noted that Article VII of the Constitution reads, "The Ratification of the Conventions of nine States, shall be sufficient for the Establishment of this Constitution *between* the States so ratifying the Same." Calhoun noted that the Article's reference to "between the States" not "over the States" was significant. As such, he concluded,

> I have now shown, conclusively, by arguments drawn from the act of ratification, and the constitution itself, that the several States of the Union, acting in their confederated character, ordained and established the constitution; that they ordained and established it for themselves, in the same character; that they ordained and established it as a compact *between* them, and not as a constitution *over* them; and that, as a compact, they are parties to it, in the same character. I have thus established, conclusively, that these States, in ratifying the constitution, did not lose the confederated character which they possessed when they ratified it, as well as in all the preceding stages of their existence; but, on the contrary, still retained it to the full.

A critic from South America, Benjamin Romaine (1832, 5), warned of the dangers of Calhoun's rhetoric:

> Your very laboured publications to sustain an existing "paramount" Sovereignty in our several States, since the adoption of the present Constitution of the United States, has occasioned a general surprise, and much painful regret. Your Station, the time, manner, and perplexing matter of your address, has made it a subject of the highest importance, not to us only, but very specially to the Republics of South America,—who had adopted our model, and now held in a confused struggle of formation, from this impracticable doctrine, sought to be sustained among us. Of this anti-federal germ you now stand

forth the unequaled advocate, although we have a deep experience, and certain knowledge of, its distructive tendencies.

And according to Edward Corwin (1914, 82–83), "Even Calhoun admitted,
what indeed would have been undeniable by the hardiest theorizer, that
the government of the United States is a government over individuals. Yet
he contended that this government did not rest upon the consent of these
individuals, but was foisted upon them by the several States." Andrew Jackson, a devout critic of Calhoun's political philosophy, expressed a contrary
viewpoint when he issued *Proclamation 43: Regarding the Nullifying Laws
of South Carolina*, on December 10, 1832:

> This right to secede is deduced from the nature of the Consti-
> tution, which, they say, is a compact between sovereign States
> who have preserved their whole sovereignty and therefore are
> subject to no superior; that because they made the compact
> they can break it when in their opinion it has been departed
> from by the other States. . . . The people of the United States
> formed the Constitution, acting through the State legislatures
> in making the compact, to meet and discuss its provisions,
> and acting in separate conventions when they ratified those
> provisions; but the terms used in its construction show it to be
> a Government in which the people of all the States, collectively,
> are represented. We are one people in the choice of President
> and Vice-President.

In his farewell address on March 4, 1837, Jackson likewise advocated
sovereignty in the people:

> It is to yourselves that you must look for safety and the means
> of guarding and perpetuating your free institutions. In your
> hands is rightfully placed the sovereignty of the country, and
> to you everyone placed in authority is ultimately responsible.
> It is always in your power to see that the wishes of the people
> are carried into faithful execution, and their will, when once
> made known, must sooner or later be obeyed; and while the
> people remain, as I trust they ever will, uncorrupted and incor-
> ruptible, and continue watchful and jealous of their rights, the

Government is safe, and the cause of freedom will continue to triumph over all its enemies.

The problem for Jackson was that at times he referred to sovereignty as residing in the people and at other times in the states or the nation. Often, the dividing line in these opinions was the issue under consideration and political expediency. For instance, when it came to secession, there was no room for state sovereignty. When it came to issues such as slavery, sovereignty resided with the states. When it came to presidential elections and presidential power, sovereignty resided with the people. When it came to the displacement of the Cherokee nation from Georgia, it once again became a state matter.

Furthermore, Jackson referred to the Constitution as a compact, as did the president of the Confederacy Jefferson Davis (1881, 49). Davis rejected the idea of "We the People" as the receptacles of sovereignty: "In the first place, it is clear that the delegates to the Convention of 1787 represented, not the people of the United States in mass, as has been most absurdly contended by some political writers, but the people of the several States, as States." He continued, "It is evident from the term 'Federal Constitution, or its equivalent, Constitution of the Federal Government,' was freely and familiarly applied to the system of government established by the Articles of Confederation—undeniably a league or compact between States expressly retaining their sovereignty and independence—as to that amended system which was substituted for it by the Constitution that superseded those articles." As such, Davis located in the Articles of Confederation legitimacy for the states' rights position, the idea that the states (not the people) ratified the new Constitution, the idea that the amendment process requires consent of the states, and the idea that the Constitution created a league or compact. Finally, he suggested that the Framers exceeded their authority in establishing a new Constitution.

The key word again was *compact*. Did the Constitution establish a compact? In a speech delivered before the US Senate on February 16, 1833, Daniel Webster argued,

> Whether the Constitution be a compact between States in their sovereign capacities, is a question which must be mainly argued from what is contained in the instrument itself. . . . What the Constitution says of itself, therefore, is as conclusive as what

it says on any other point. Does it call itself a "compact"? Certainly not. It uses the word compact but once, and that is when it declares that the States shall enter into no compact. Does it call itself a "league," a "confederacy," a "subsisting treaty between the States?" Certainly not. There is not a particle of such language in all its pages.

Debate on the issue continued, however. In a July 1851 speech, Francis Pickens (1851, 4), a supporter of Calhoun, noted,

> But if the people of the State, with all the interests of the State, be united and we move with judgment and firmness—standing upon our chartered rights as fixed in the compact and deducible from the history of the Confederacy—we can do any thing that a sovereign people dare do—we can save ourselves by joint co-operation with our sister States of the South, if possible to be obtained by prudence and conciliation—but if all hope of co-operation be left and we should be driven to the last sad alternative, if we are cordially united at home, we can save ourselves alone.

Another opinion was offered by Francis Lieber (1861, 5–6), who served in Lincoln's War Department. He noted that most opinion was not based on the Constitution's actual words:

> At no time has the very character and essence of our Constitution been so much discussed as in ours. Never before have measures of such importance been so made to depend, in appearance, upon the fundamental character of the document called the Constitution of the United States, while never before have those in high authority attended less to its genesis, its contents, and its various provisions, in order to justify actions affecting our entire polity. Never before, either in our own, or in, the history of our race, have whole communities seemed to make acts of elementary and national consequence depend upon a single term; upon the question whether the Constitution is a mere contract, or whether the word, derived as it is from *constituere*, must be understood in the sense in which Cicero takes it, when he speaks of *constituere republican*—that

is, organizing the common weal, putting it in order and connecting all the parts in mutual organic dependence upon one another. I have used the words apparently and seemingly, because it admits of little doubt, if of any, that those among the leaders in the present disturbances who make a world of consequences depend upon the solitary question, Is or is not the Constitution of the United States a contract argue on a foregone conclusion. Or is there a man living who believes that they would give up their pursuit of disunion, if it would be proved, by evidence ever so fair, substantial, and free from embittering passion, that the Constitution is not a compact, or is not a mere contract?

Lieber concluded that the idea of the Constitution as a compact was self-serving. It was necessary if one were to argue that the states had certain rights, such as secession. Edward Everett (1861, 8), an avid opponent of slavery, agreed with Lieber:

This assumed right of secession rests upon the doctrine that the Union is a compact between independent states, from which any one of them may withdraw at pleasure in virtue of its sovereignty. This imaginary right has been the subject of discussion for more than thirty years, having been originally suggested, though not at first much dwelt upon, in connection with the kindred claim of a right, on the part of an individual state, to "nullify" an act of Congress.

A compact was therefore a mere "imaginary right." Writing the next year, Joel Parker (1862, 15) noted, "It is not proper to call the Constitution a compact. Its terms, its nature and the powers granted by it, show it to be something more than a compact." After the Civil War, eminent constitutional scholar Thomas Cooley (1891, 26) introduced a section of one chapter entitled "Not a mere Compact." And writing a few years later, Roger Foster (1895, 78–79) advised,

The whole phraseology of the Constitution is in conflict with the one theory as much as with the other. In contradistinction with the preceding instrument of union, it does not call itself a league, nor a compact, nor articles of confederation; but a

Constitution,! which is ordained and established,! which vests powers in a government; and which shall be the supreme law of the land, by which the judges in every State shall be bound, anything in the Constitution or laws of any State to the contrary notwithstanding. The Constitution is founded upon compact, but is not itself a compact.

So the Constitution was founded upon a compact, but it was not a compact. Or was it more than a compact? For many constitutional observers of the time, political expediency was at the heart of the issue. Those who favored secession believed it was a compact, while those who opposed secession found no support for the term in the Constitution's text.

The Impending Crisis

The great novelty of this Constitution—the association of the principle of State sovereignty with a common government of delegated powers acting on individuals under specifications of authority, and thus, therefore not merely a Federal league . . . the Federal principle, contained in itself an element ultimately fatal to its form of government. . . . In the North there never was any lack of rhetorical fervour for the Union. . . . In the North, the doctrine of State Rights was generally rejected for the prevalent notion that America was a single democracy. . . . In the South the Union was differently regarded. State Rights was the most marked peculiarity of the politics of the Southern people; and it was this doctrine that gave the Union its *moral* dignity, and was the only really possible source of sentimental attachment to it.

—Edward Alfred Pollard, *The Lost Cause*

What was the basis for constitutional interpretation in the pre–Civil War period? According to Allan Nevins (1953, 97–98),

At no time in our national history have questions of constitutional law played so large a part in public discussion and in political contests as during the twelve years between 1848 and 1860; between the treaty of peace with Mexico, and the election of Lincoln. Indeed, a question of constitutional interpretation became the central issue between the two leading parties of the country, and in great degree between the North and South. Debate after debate in Congress raged upon this question. Newspapers were filled with it. In every Presidential campaign the leading statesmen of the nation discussed it with fiery conviction. Every voter was supposed to hold a firm opinion on the subject, and by the time of the Dred Scott decision in 1857 most of them did. Never in our history has the vagueness or the ambiguity of the Constitution upon a particular subject, its liability to conflicting constructions, had such momentous consequences in these years; for the Constitutional quarrel was certainly one of the elements in the complex situation which resulted in the Civil War.

And as former assistant secretary of state David Jayne Hill (1916, 49) advised, "The severest test which the American conception of the State has ever been called upon to endure was occasioned by circumstances connected with the Civil War, but it did not involve a denial of the fundamental principles upon which American constitutionalism is based. It consisted, on the contrary, merely in a difference of documentary interpretation. Had the Federal Constitution produced a nation, or only a confederation? That was the question upon which the North and the South disagreed."

Was the Civil War simply the result of a difference of constitutional interpretations? Most scholars and laypeople argue correctly that slavery was the cause of the Civil War. As American industrialist and later historian James Ford Rhodes ([1896] 1920, 1:16–17) wrote, "To the effort to form a more perfect union of the States, slavery was a constant obstacle. It was the subject of two [constitutional] compromises, although the words 'slavery,' and 'slave-trade' do not occur in the Constitution; for an adroit circumlocution was employed to avoid offending delegates who objected to the use of those terms." Rhodes (18) continued, "A defense of the work of our constitutional fathers, including the slavery compromises, is hardly necessary. Their choice lay between achieving a union of the States with those provisions, and failing to accomplish any union at all." Yet even slavery was a matter of constitutional interpretation. Though the word did not appear in the Constitution, some found support for it there, while others did not. Therefore, different constitutional interpretations were at the heart of the debate over slavery and the impending crisis leading up to the Civil War. So, were these constitutional interpretations based on expediency, rather than an actual citation of the Constitution's provisions? Did people see in the Constitution what they wanted to see rather than what actually was written?

What is clear is that the genesis for the Civil War can be found in the Constitution. As Catherine Drinker Bowen (1966, 201) wrote, "The question before the [Constitutional] Convention was not, Shall slavery be abolished? It was rather, Who shall have the power to control it—the states or the national government?" On this point, two Supreme Court decisions appeared to be decisive. In *Swift v. Tyson*, 41 U.S. 1 (1842), the court decided in favor of the federal over the state courts, while in *Prigg v. Pennsylvania*, 41 U.S. 439 (1842), it ruled against a Pennsylvania law. Still, the controversy continued unabated in a series of pamphlets. One of the earliest was from William Goodell's 1834 *The Constitution of the United States versus Slavery*, where he concluded that the Constitution sanctioned slavery. In another pamphlet, *No Treason: The Constitution of No Authority*, Lysander Spooner (1870, 65) wrote, "The Constitution not only binds nobody now, but it never did bind anybody. It never bound anybody, because it was never agreed to by any body in such a manner as to make it, on general principles of law and reason, binding upon him. It is a general principal of law and reason, that a written instrument binds no one until he has signed it." Spooner (v) also wrote, "On the part of the North, the war was carried on, not to liberate the slaves, but by a government that had always perverted the Constitution, to keep the slaves in bondage; and was still willing to do so, if the slaveholders could be thereby induced to stay in the Union." Abolitionist William Lloyd Garrison (1862, 46) avowed, "I adopted the language of the prophet Isaiah, and pronounced the Constitution, in these particulars, to be 'a covenant with death, and an agreement with hell.'" Meanwhile, in a speech before the Scottish Anti-Slavery Society in 1860, Frederick Douglass proclaimed,[3]

> 1st, Does the United States Constitution guarantee to any class or description of people in that country the right to enslave, or hold as property, any other class or description of people in that country? 2nd, Is the dissolution of the union between the slave and free States required by fidelity to the slaves, or by the just demands of conscience? Or, in other words, is the refusal to exercise the elective franchise, and to hold office in America, the surest, wisest, and best way to abolish slavery in

America? To these questions the Garrisonians say Yes. They hold the Constitution to be a slaveholding instrument, and will not cast a vote or hold office, and denounce all who vote or hold office, no matter how faithfully such persons labour to promote the abolition of slavery. I, on the other hand, deny that the Constitution guarantees the right to hold property in man, and believe that the way to abolish slavery in America is to vote such men into power as well use their powers for the abolition of slavery.

Different interpretations of the Constitution existed, not only between sections of the country but within the abolitionist movement itself. However, abolitionists found greater consensus when they focused on the concept of national sovereignty, while supporters of slavery's expansion favored state sovereignty. Both sides did so, however, only when it was convenient. For example, when a stronger fugitive state law was enacted as part of the Compromise of 1850, southern and northern adherents of states' rights suddenly found comfort in the expansion of national power. Hence, Chief Justice Roger Taney, a strong supporter of slavery, found authority in the national government. In 1855, responding to the Wisconsin Supreme Court's decision to release a prisoner found guilty under federal law, Taney wrote (Tyler 1872, 395),

Although the State of Wisconsin is sovereign within its territorial limits to a certain extent, yet that sovereignty is limited and restricted by the Constitution of the United States. And the powers of the general Government and of the State, although both exist and are exercised within the same territorial limits, are yet separate and distinct sovereignties, acting separately and independently of each other within their respective spheres. And the sphere of action appropriated to the United States is as far beyond the reach of the judicial process issued by a State Judge or a State Court, as if the line of division was traced by landmarks and monuments visible to the eye. And the State of Wisconsin had no more power to authorize these proceedings of its Judges and Courts than it would have had if the prisoner had been confined in Michigan, or in any other State of the Union, for an offence against the laws of the State in which he was imprisoned.

As to the Fugitive Slave Law, Harold Hyman (1973, 14) advised, "A very few southerners deplored the fact that by pressing for enactment and enforcement of the 1850 fugitive slave law, they were tacitly admitting Congress's adequacy under certain circumstances to act within states, at least through the national courts. But these protesters went unheeded. In political terms the South demanded the full measure of what the Constitution permitted, in paradoxical contradiction to the coexisting state-rights interpretation of what the Constitution forbade." So if slavery and secession were at stake, how would the nation deal with dueling interpretations of sovereignty? That question was raised by an 1854 act that introduced another new concept into the debate: *popular sovereignty*. It also enervated public discussion of the slavery issue, while destroying a presidency. William Gienapp (1987, 81, 37) noted, "The Kansas-Nebraska Act was one of the most fateful measures ever approved by Congress. It weakened the Democratic party throughout the North, disrupted the sectional balance within the parties, gave additional momentum to the ongoing process of party disintegration, and fundamentally altered the nature of the anti-Democratic opposition." As Carl Schurz (1907, 2:19) opined, "The seeming apathy of the public conscience concerning the slavery question was at last broken by the introduction of Senator Douglas's Nebraska bill, which was to overrule the Missouri Compromise and to open to all the National Territories to the ingress of the 'peculiar institution.' A sudden tremor shook the political atmosphere." Meanwhile, John Sherman (1895, 117–18) wrote,

> Before the proposition to repeal the Missouri Compromise was introduced to the Congress, the people of western Missouri were indifferent to the prohibition of slavery in the territory, and neither asked nor desired its repeal. When, however, the prohibition was removed by the action of Congress, the aspect of affairs entirely changed. The whole country was agitated by the reopening of a controversy which conservative men in different sections believed had been settled in every state and territory by some law beyond the danger of repeal. The excitement which always accompanied the discussion of the slavery question was greatly increased by the hope, on the one hand, of extending slavery into a region from which it had been excluded by law; and, on the other, by a sense of wrong done by what was regarded as a breach of public faith.

And James G. Blaine (1884, 1:115) related, "No previous anti-slavery excitement bore any comparison with that which spread over the North as the discussion progressed, and especially after the bill became law. It did not merely call forth opposition: it produced almost a frenzy of wrath on the part of thousands and tens of thousands in both the old parties, who had never before taken any part whatever in anti-slavery agitation." The Kansas-Nebraska Act, and the repeal of the Missouri Compromise, destroyed Franklin Pierce's presidency. As Blaine continued, "Pierce's policies produced sharp partisan conflict and unprecedented party turmoil." Hence, in *Proclamation 66: Law and Order in the Territory of Kansas* (February 11, 1856) Pierce stated, "If, in any part of the Union, the fury of faction or fanaticism, inflamed into disregard of the great principles of popular sovereignty which, under the Constitution, are fundamental in the whole structure of our institutions is to bring the country the dire calamity of an arbitrament of arms in that Territory, it shall be between lawless violence on the one side and conservative force on the other, wielded by legal authority of the General Government." As Bennett Rich (1941, 66) later advised, "The extraordinary caution exercised by the makers of the Constitution in the wording of Article IV, section 4, operated to the advantage of President Franklin Pierce just as it had previously aided Presidents Van Buren and Tyler to avoid interference with the affairs of state." The article reads, "The United States shall guarantee to every State in the Union a Republican Form of Government, and shall protect each of them against Invasion and on Application of the Legislature or the Executive (when the Legislature cannot be convened) against domestic violence."
Denied renomination, Pierce was repudiated by both his party and public opinion. As Blaine (1884, 1:115) wrote, "With his influence at an end, a casualty of the political realignment of the mid-decade." George Templeton Strong (1952a, 277) wrote in his diary on June 6, 1856,

> Buchanan nominated at Cincinnati. It might have been much worse. Northern divisions will make him the next President. Pierce is served right. The South has used him sufficiently and thrown him away, enjoyed the fruits of his treason and kicked him out of doors. He'll find cold comfort at home when he goes there; his neighbors have just been hanging him and Brooks in effigy. . . . So may he yet secure a few friends who will be willing to associate with him and recognize him in his approaching days of insignificance, and he cannot make

himself more infamous than he is already by any new exhibition of baseness.

Franklin Pierce was not the only one to blame for this monumental failure. As Hyman (1973, 20) concluded, "The fabric . . . appeared to be completely ripped apart again. The occasion was Senator [Stephen A.] Douglas's ultimately successful drive to push through Congress what became the 1854 Kansas-Nebraska law."

In response to the Kansas-Nebraska Act, Abraham Lincoln delivered his famous "house divided" speech on June 16, 1858. In this speech, Lincoln (Basler 1953, 2:462, 466) identified yet another form of sovereignty:

> The new year of 1854, found slavery excluded from more than half the States by State Constitutions, and from most of the national territory by Congressional prohibition. Four days later, commenced the struggle, which ended in repealing that Constitutional prohibition. This opened up all the national territory to slavery; and was the first point gained. This necessity has not been overlooked; but has provided for, as well as might be, in the notable argument of "squatter sovereignty," otherwise called "scared right of self government," which latter phrase, though expressively of the only rightful basis of any government, was so perverted in this attempted use of it as to amount to just this: That if any one man, choose to enslave another, no third man shall be allowed to object. That argument was incorporated into the Nebraska bill itself, in the language that follows: "It being the true intent and meaning of this act not to legislate slavery into any Territory or state, not exclude it therefrom; but to leave the people thereof perfectly free to form and regulate their domestic institutions in their own way, subject only to the Constitution of the United States." Then opened the roar of loose declamation in favor of "Squatter Sovereignty," and the "Sacred right of self government."

Lincoln continued, "Why mention a State? They were legislating for territories, and not for or about States. Certainly the people of a State are and ought to be subject to the Constitution of the United States; but why is mention of this lugged into this merely territorial law? Why are the people of a territory and the people of a state therein lumped together, and their relation to the Constitution therein treated as being precisely the same." Lincoln raised serious constitutional issues, yet following passage of the 1854 act, the ultimate decision as to the existence of slavery was decided not by the Constitution but by often violent pro- and anti-slavery advocates who sent supporters to Kansas and Nebraska to settle the land, and more importantly, to make them either free or slave states. When the controversial Lecompton Constitution was subsequently adopted in Kansas, James Hammond (1858, 4) of South Carolina urged the admission of the state to the Union, disagreeing vehemently with the logic of Lincoln's argument. He based his support for Lecompton on the sovereignty of the people, as well as the states: "The convention was an assembly of the people in their highest sovereign capacity, about to perform then highest possible act of sovereignty. . . . Congress is not sovereign. Congress has sovereign powers, but no sovereignty. Congress has no power to act outside of the limitations of the Constitution; no right to carry into effect the Supreme Will of any people, and, therefore, Congress is not sovereign. Nor does Congress hold the sovereignty of Kansas. The sovereignty of Kansas resides, if it resides anywhere, with the sovereign States of this Union."

Who, then, held sovereignty, the national government, Congress, the people, or the states? The answer was a matter of dueling constitutional interpretations. Given its genesis, it is perhaps ironic that the Kansas-Nebraska Act had two significant political implications. First, it divided the ruling Democratic Party. For example, Stephen Douglas, who had developed the idea of popular sovereignty in the Kansas-Nebraska Act, suddenly found himself in opposition of the Lecompton Constitution. Hence, as William Lowndes Yancey (1860, 11) remarked:

> But where has been Mr. Douglas for two years past? Warring on the Democracy that he now pretends to be the best exponent of. No sooner had the South procured an advantage under the Kansas-Nebraska bill, and sent the Territory of Kansas to the door of Congress with a slave Constitution, than he commenced a war upon the Democracy. . . . If his principle was right, that the people of a territory should form and regulate their own domestic institutions, in their own way, subject only to the Constitution of the United States—I want to know if he was not wrong when he said, "You have made this Constitution in my way, and I will send it back."

The second impact was the establishment of the new Republican Party. In 1856, in its first presidential platform, the Republican Party insisted that "the Constitution confers upon Congress sovereign powers over the Territories of the United States for their government; and that the exercise of this power, it is both the right and the imperative duty of Congress to prohibit in the Territories those twin relics of barbarism—Polygamy, and Slavery." This was in stark contrast to the Democratic platform: "That Congress has no power under the Constitution, to interfere with or control the domestic institutions of the several States . . . that all efforts of the abolitionists, or others, made to induce Congress to interfere with questions of slavery, or to take incipient steps in relation thereto, are calculated to lead to the most alarming and dangerous consequences" (Johnson and Porter 1973, 27, 25).

Popular sovereignty then emerged as a central topic in the famous Lincoln-Douglas debates. In the first debate, held in Ottawa, Illinois, on August 21, 1858, Senator Stephen Douglas declared (Basler 1953, 3:2–3, 11, 19, 51),

> In order that there might be no misunderstanding in relation to the principle involved in the Kansas and Nebraska bill, I put forth the true intent and meaning of the act in these words, "It is the true intent and meaning of this act not to legislate slavery into any State or Territory, or to exclude it therefrom, but to leave the people thereof perfectly free to form and regulate their domestic institutions in their own way, subject only to the federal constitution." Thus, you see, that up to 1854, when the Kansas and Nebraska bill was brought into Congress for the purpose of carrying out the principles that both parties [Democrats and Whigs] had up to that time endorsed and approved, there had been no division in this country in regard to that principle except the opposition of the abolitionists.

As to the Dred Scott decision, Douglas noted, "Now, I hold that Illinois had a right to prohibit slavery as she did, and I hold that Kentucky has the same right to continue and protect slavery that Illinois had to abolish it. I hold that New York had as much right to abolish slavery as Virginia to continue it, and that each and every state of this Union, is a sovereign power, with the right to do as it pleases upon this question of slavery, and upon all its domestic institutions." Douglas now cited the rights of the states, that is, states' rights and not territorial rights. Lincoln responded, "I will state—and I have an able man to watch me—my understanding is that Popular Sovereignty, as now applied to the question of Slavery, does allow the people of a Territory to have Slavery if they want to, but does not allow them *not* to have it if they *do not* want it." Douglas responded, "In my opinion the people of a territory can, by lawful means, exclude slavery from their limits prior to the formation of a State Constitution." In a speech delivered in Paris, Illinois, on September 7, 1858, Lincoln then endorsed the notion that the people were sovereign.

Beyond the Lincoln-Douglas debates, the search for constitutional meaning continued, and as it did, Southern Democrats found new sources of national power in their defense of slavery. They argued that the fifth amendment established "a requirement for Congress actively to protect slaves in regions under national jurisdiction." But as Hyman (1973, 20–21) continued, "It is less remarkable that the Fifth Amendment's meaning like beauty, should depend upon the beholder, than that opposite conclusions should rise from America's political parties." Everyone was searching for and finding new meanings in the Constitution, meanings that justified their viewpoints, not intrinsic meanings based on precedent or sound constitutional arguments. It was in this incendiary political environment that James Buchanan's *Message to Congress Transmitting the [Lecompton] Constitution of Kansas* on February 2, 1858 added the proverbial fuel to the fire:

> The sacred principle of popular sovereignty has been invoked in favor of the enemies of law and order in Kansas. But in what manner is popular sovereignty to be exercised in this country if not through the instrumentality of established law? . . . Popular sovereignty can be exercised here only through the ballot box; and if the people will refuse to exercise it in this manner, as they have done in Kansas at the election of delegates, it is not for them to complain that their rights have been violated. The Kansas convention, thus lawfully constituted, proceeded to frame a constitution, and, having completed their work, finally adjourned on the 7th day of November last. They did not think proper to submit the whole of this constitution to a popular vote, but they did submit the question whether Kansas should be a free or a slave State to the people.

The supporters of the Lecompton Constitution "did not think proper to submit the whole of this constitution to a popular vote," Buchanan continued. "It was never, however, my opinion that, independently of this act, they would have been bound to submit any portion of the constitution to a popular vote in order to give it validity." Obviously, consistency with the central idea of popular sovereignty was not a paramount consideration for President Buchanan. As officialdom debated popular sovereignty, the deliberation also played out in various books and pamphlets, particularly as the issue of the Fugitive Slave Law compounded the already combustible political world. For instance, George Fitzhugh (1854, 26) wrote, "Government is the creature of society, and may be said to derive its powers from the consent of the governed; but society does not owe its sovereign power to the separate consent, volition or agreement of its members. Like the hive, it is as much the work of nature as the individuals who compose it." Four years later, John Hurd (1858a, vi–vii; see also Hurd 1858b) noted, "Where popular sovereignty is recognized and visibly operative in the form of government; where law is seen to have its ultimate source in the collective judgment of the community, the individual member of society may the more easily confound law with matter of conscience, and legal inquiry with that investigation by which political or moral ends are to be attained." Hurd therefore recommended that sovereignty reside with the states united and not with the individual states—yet another form of state sovereignty. Meanwhile, Stephen Douglas was reelected as a senator from Illinois and became a likely presidential candidate for 1860. In one of many pamphlets on the issue, Jeremiah Black (e.g., Jeremiah Sullivan) (1859, 1) wrote,

> Mr. Douglas states that differences of opinion in respect to slavery in the Territories exist in the Democratic party, and describes those differences of opinion under the following classes: "First, Those who believe that the Constitution of the United States neither establishes nor prohibits slavery in the States or Territories beyond the power of the people legally to control it, but leaves the people thereof perfectly free to form and regulate their domestic institutions in their own way, subject only to the Constitution of the United States. Second. Those who believe that the Constitution establishes slavery in the Territories and withholds from Congress and the Territorial Legislature the power to control it, and who

insist that, in the event the Territorial Legislature fails to enact the requisite laws for its protection, it becomes the imperative duty of Congress to interpose its authority and furnish such protection. Third. Those who, while professing to believe that the Constitution establishes slavery in the territories beyond the power of Congress or the Territorial Legislature to control it, at, the same time protest against the duty of Congress to interfere for its protection; but insist that it is the duty of the judiciary to protect and maintain slavery in the Territories without; any law upon the subject."

Black/Sullivan then charged,

He did not dare to meet the issue squarely, and so, as other great men have done before him, taking discretion to be the better part of valor, he avoids it and discusses but one branch of the subject. The interventionist who insists on the dogma of Congressional protection to slavery in the Territories, and those who hold that the slave owner is entitled to protection, but resolutely oppose intervention under the specious plea that it is unnecessary because the judiciary can give it, are thus banded together in a common cause. These opposing forces, between whom there is no harmony whatever, inasmuch as each considers the other heretical, are the power, by which Senator Douglas is to be excommunicated from the Democratic party.

George Tickner Curtis (1859), who served as a co-counsel for Dred Scott before the US Supreme Court, argued for the "just supremacy of Congress over the territories," while a pamphlet containing a speech by Amos Phelps Granger (1859, 1), representative of New York, referenced Thomas Jefferson and the Southern viewpoint:

The States are supreme—are sovereign—within their geo-graphical limits, in reference to all powers not delegated to the General Government, nor prohibited by the Constitution. Thus far, they are sovereign against the world, and they are as much so against the Government at Washington, as against that at Paris, at London, or at St. Petersburgh; and of the extent of that sovereignty, they, the States, have a right to judge. The States have the same right to judge of the extent of their sovereignty, as the General Government has to judge of the extent of its sovereignty. Thus far they are equals.

In a speech before the House of Representatives on January 25, 1859, William Kellogg (1859, 1) of Illinois maintained, "From the discussion of the last few days, it is apparent that the political parties are preparing for the conflict of 1860." By 1860, slavery's designation in the Constitution and the laws was as irreconcilable as the nation itself. To promote his presidential aspirations, Stephen Douglas (1860) published a speech he delivered in the Senate, from May 15 and 16, 1860, again defending popular sovereignty. And in an 1859 speech in Wisconsin, Carl Schurz (1913, 80), later secretary of the interior under President Rutherford Hayes, professed,

> Mr. Douglas's doctrine of popular sovereignty proposed to bring the two antagonistic elements into immediate contact and to let them struggle hand to hand for the supremacy on the same ground. In this manner, he predicted, the slavery question would settle itself in the smooth way of ordinary business. He seemed to be confident of success; but hardly is his doctrine, in the shape of a law for the organization of territories, put upon the statute book, when the struggle grows fiercer than ever, and the difficulties ripen into a crisis.

It appeared that as he ran for president, Douglas now found support for national sovereignty. William Dennison Porter (1860, 3–4) commented on Douglas:

> To THE Men of the South:
>
> The recent speech of Mr. Douglas at Norfolk, in which he threatened the Southern States with military coercion in the event of secession, ought to startle and arouse the people of those States, like the blast of a hostile trumpet at midnight! The time, the place, and the circumstances under which this threat was uttered, give the last finish to its audacity and sanguinary significance! . . . *The powers and agencies of government!* Consider it for a moment in this point of view. If there be any virtue in government, it consists in justice, equality and the duty of

protection. Its proper functions, in reference to its own citizens or subjects, are those of peace and security. It is intended as a shield, not as a sword; as a dispenser of blessings, not as a scatterer of curses. What do you, what can you, think of that government which, forgetting its own nature, abandoning its proper duty, and perverting to the purposes of annoyance and destruction what was intended for the most kindly and beneficent action, shall deliberately and avowedly employ its resources and its powers to promote discord, to stir up sedition, to rend the country asunder, and array one part of it in mortal hatred against another—to proclaim and inaugurate between the institutions of one section and those of the other an irrepressible conflict, which must inevitably lead to issues of life and death, and can terminate only in subjugation on one hand or disruption on the other! And what are those powers and resources? The purse and the sword.

Regarding the issues of slavery, popular sovereignty, national sovereignty, the Fugitive Slave Law, the Lecompton Constitution, and the Constitution as a compact, arguments were based on practical political considerations, not on any close reading of the Constitution. In fact, some who cited the Constitution had never even read it. In this contentious political environment, the South favored state sovereignty, that is unless the Fugitive Slave Law was at issue, in which case national control was preferred or popular sovereignty if Kansas could be added to the union as a slave state. Those who opposed slavery were no more consistent in their approach. They favored national sovereignty, except in the case of the enforcement of the Fugitive Slave Law. At times state sovereignty surrender to territorial rights. As for popular sovereignty, even belief in a free and fair election in Kansas was not required. Consequently, dueling interpretations of the Constitution's meaning were at the heart of the impending crisis. Such views were deeply embedded by the different cultures in the North and South. In his memoir, General George McClellan (1887, 31), the Democratic candidate for president in 1864, argued that sovereignty was based on the educational training of Northerners and Southerners:

In judging the motives of men at this great crisis it must be remembered that the vast majority of Southern men had been educated in the doctrine of secession and of extreme State-rights which is, that allegiance was due first to the State, next to the general government, and that the State when it entered the Union retained the right to withdraw at will; while in the North the doctrine was generally held that allegiance to the general government was paramount and the Union indissoluble. The masses on each side were honest in their belief as to the justice of their cause. Their honesty and sincerity were proved by the sacrifices they made, by the earnestness with which so many devout Christians on both sides confidently relied upon the aid of God in their hour of trial, and by the readiness with which so many brave men laid down their lives on the field of battle.

And yet, different interpretations of sovereignty could be dispensed with when convenience required it. As John Burgess (1901, 1:46–47) noted,

President Buchanan had, after the Dred Scott decision, given up the doctrine of "Popular Sovereignty" in the Territories entirely, and for this reason, together with the defeat of his Lecompton plan for Kansas, effected chiefly by the opposition of Mr. Douglas, he and the wing of the Democratic party which he represented had developed a bitter hostility to Mr. Douglas, which was manifested first in the senatorial contest in Illinois in 1858, and then upon the larger field of the presidential contest in 1860. . . . During the year 1859, the contradiction between the "Popular Sovereignty" doctrine and the Dred Scott opinion became more and more clear and more and more generally appreciated, until by the opening of the spring of the year 1860 it was evident that the Democratic party would, in the coming campaign, probably split upon this issue, the Northern Democrats holding to the former doctrine, and the Southern Democrats to the latter.

And James Fitzjames Stephen (1874, 183) mentioned, "Who, looking at the matter dispassionately, can fail to perceive the vanity and folly of the attempt to decide the question between the North and the South by lawyers' metaphysics about the true nature of sovereignty or by conveyancing subtleties about the meaning of the Constitution and the principles on which written documents ought to be interpreted? You might as well try to infer the fortunes of a battle from the shape of the firearms." The creative use of language fostered confusion and with it the opportunity to promote different interpretations of the Constitution during a time of considerable turbulence and unrest.

Consequently, sovereignty was defined by the pressing realities of the unfolding political situation, rather than through a legalistic analysis of the text of the Constitution or the Framers' intent. This point was no more apparent than when a key member of the House of Representatives, Benjamin Wade, flip-flopped from a strong supporter of national sovereignty to state sovereignty (Hyman 1973, 23): "I shall plant myself upon 'State Rights' and shall invoke the [Virginia and Kentucky] Resolutions of 98–9 as containing the proper remedy for cases like the present . . . to [oppose] the execution of the 'Fugitive Slave Law' as they were [the proper remedy to oppose] . . . the old 'Alien and Sedition Law.' " The hypocrisy of sovereignty was further exposed by Chief Justice Roger Taney's decision in *Ableman v. Booth*, 62 U.S. (21 How.) 506 (1859), which "underscored the need in a federal system for national laws and courts to operate without harassment by state courts' writs" (Hyman 1973, 26). As Hyman remarked, "For what decent man could tolerate constitutional interpretations of the Scott and Abelman sorts? The former denied Congress power to keep the nation's territories free of slaves; the latter sustained the nation's power and duty to thrust deep into northern states in pursuit of runaway slaves. So interpreted, the Constitution was out of balance" (27). As the nation approached the whirlwind of the Civil War, such interpretations of the Constitution became ever more chaotic. As a means of preventing disunion, legislation was proposed that would have prolonged slavery while "promising to upend the federal system. . . . In this Orwellian Union the slave states were more sovereign than others. Even if Congress wished them to, free states' law codes could not gain export to national territories" (31).

The Civil War

The Constitution, ratified by the people of all the States, establishes a government of sovereign powers, supreme over the whole land, and the people of no State can rightly pass from under its authority except by the consent of the people of all the States, with whom it is bound by the most solemn and binding of contracts. The Rebel States broke, in *fact*, the contract they could not break in *right*.

—E. P. Whipple, "The President and His Accomplices"

As president, "Lincoln learned quickly how fearful state sovereignty constitutional thinking had diffused the energy in national government" (Hyman 1973, 55). Lincoln cited Daniel Webster's view of the union and national sovereignty as associated with the Declaration of Independence (inaugural address, March 4, 1861):

> The Union is perpetual confirmed by the history of the Union itself. The Union is much older than the Constitution. It was formed, in fact, by the Articles of Association in 1774. It was matured and continued by the Declaration of Independence in 1776. It was further matured, and the faith of all the then thirteen States expressly plighted and engaged that it should be perpetual, by the Articles of Confederation in 1778. And finally, in 1787, one of the declared objects for ordaining and establishing the Constitution was "to form a more perfect Union."

In his July 4, 1861, special message to Congress, Lincoln explicitly discussed the issue of national versus states' rights:

> Unquestionably the States have the powers and rights reserved to them in and by the National Constitution; but among these surely are not included all conceivable powers, however mischievous or destructive, but at most such only as were known in the world at the time as governmental powers; and certainly a power to destroy the Government itself had never been known as a governmental—as a merely administrative power. This relative matter of national power and State rights, as a principle, is no other than the principle of *generality* and *locality*. Whatever concerns the whole should be confided to the whole—to the General Government—while whatever concerns *only* the State should be left exclusively to the State. This is all there is of original principle about it. Whether the National Constitution in defining boundaries between the two has applied the principle with exact accuracy is not to be questioned. We are all bound by that defining without question.

Many agreed with Lincoln, such as clergyman Henry Ward Beecher (1863, 160–61): "By our Constitution, States are shorn of absolute sovereignty, and are limited in jurisdiction to their own local interests. Beyond that, in the sphere of interests common to all, the authority of All, represented by the Federal Government, takes precedence, and is sovereign, and forms the only absolute sovereignty known to our system of government." This sentiment was shared in 1863 by Durbin Ward (2010), an Ohio politician and lawyer: "If your rulers are restrained by the limits of constitutional power, they are also obligated by the grants of power which the Constitution confers. That instrument is not merely a network of negatives. It clothes the Government in the panoply of national power." The same year, J. H. Estcourt (1863, 6) stated,

> The election of Mr. Lincoln to the presidency in November, 1860, had not changed any part or altered one tittle of the constitution of the nation; it had violated no one right held in common by the people of the nation; it had not nullified one privilege which was enjoyed before his election; it had not altered the principle of the executive, the legislative, or the judicial powers of the nation. All were after, as they were before, the election. How then by possibility could the election have impaired any vested right held under the constitution? Where could the wrong be after that did not exist before, the election; and if before, why did not the wronged ones seek redress under their own rule and in their time of domination? No civil injustice had been done by Abraham Lincoln, therefore no justice needed to be sought.

In his two-hour-plus Gettysburg's speech preceding Lincoln's more famous two-minute address, Edward Everett (1864, 67–68) declared,

> Certainly I do not deny that the separate States are clothed with sovereign powers for the administration of local affairs. It is one of the most beautiful features of our mixed system of government; but it is equally true, that, in adopting the Federal Constitution, the States abdicated, by express renunciation, all the most important functions of national sovereignty, and, by one comprehensive, self-denying clause, gave up all right to contravene the Constitution of the United States . . . but to speak of the right of an individual State to secede, as a power that could have been, though it was not delegated to the United States, is simple nonsense.

Theophilus Parson (1861, 21, 23–25, 29) delivered a lecture before the Law School of Harvard University that raised several other relevant points. Was America a nation? He answered in the affirmative. But what of the public's role? If sovereignty ultimately rested with the people, did it encourage ambitious and unprincipled politicians? Was the public a responsible entity? If so, the people must "learn their danger and their duty." Questions about sovereignty continued to be at the forefront of American constitutional and political discourse. As Parsons remarked,

> Indeed, what year has passed since the adoption of our Constitution, which has not, by the whole character of our legislation and of the relations we have assumed with other States, declared and proved that we considered ourselves a nation, and that we were a nation? . . . And if we are a nation, how is it possible for a right of session to exist, excepting as a right of revolution? . . . This great peril is, that as all power is the gift of the people, and the people give this power, there grows up among us, by an inevitable necessity, the profession of politics.

For Parsons, the answer was a "government of law, and its strength is the Constitution. . . . But over us all the Constitution bends like the universal sky, holding us all within its embrace, but lifted up too high for any one to reach it with a sacrilegious hand." And as the war commenced, some former supporters of state sovereignty changed their minds. Writing in 1865, Orestes Brownson (2003, cxi–cxii, 5) declared,

> I reject the doctrine of State sovereignty, which I held and defended from 1828–1861, but still maintain that the sovereignty of the American Republic vests in the States, though in the States collectively, or united, not severally, and thus escape alike consolidation and disintegration. . . . I maintain, after Mr. Senator Sumner, one of the most philosophic and accomplished living American statesmen, that "State secession is State suicide . . . and accept the doctrine that the laws in force at the time of secession remain in force till superseded or abrogated by competent authority, and also that, till the State is revived and restored to the Union, the only authority, under the American system, competent to supersede or abrogate them is the United States, not Congress, far less the Executive."

Brownson continued, "It will hardly be questioned that either the constitution of the United States is very defective or it has been very grossly misinterpreted by all parties." Hence, the debate continued well after the war ended. At the turn of a new century, Samuel Peter Orth (1906, 297–98) wrote,

> POLITICAL philosophy does not make a nation until it is written in living letters and recorded in the book of experience. The theory of a union of independent states bound by an indissoluble bond to a national government was unquestionably the thought of a majority of the constitutional fathers. Had economic and social conditions been uniform in every portion of our domain there would probably have been no necessity for a severe struggle in working out the practical realization of this theory. But, unfortunately, this uniformity did not exist. . . . The real issue was, Are we a confederation or a nation? Does an eternal and necessary gravitation unite these states into a galaxy of stars, or does chance decree that we are only a temporary group of comets, thrown into company by coincidence? One hundred years were necessary to solve the question.

The Civil War was indeed about slavery. The debate over sovereignty was a justification for different constitutional rationales to maintain or eliminate that despicable institution. As Arthur Bestor (1964, 329) advised, "It was constitutional theorizing, carried on from the very birth of the Republic, which made secession the ultimate recourse to any group that considered its vital interests threatened." Similarly, the choice of state sovereignty was based on the South's need to protect slavery.

Conclusion

> The supremacy of the nation and its laws should be no longer a subject of debate. That discussion, which for half a century threatened the existence of the Union, was closed at last in the high court of war, by a decree from which there is no appeal: that the Constitution and the laws made in pursuance thereof are and shall continue to be the supreme law of the land, binding alike, upon the States and the people.
>
> —James Garfield, inaugural address, March 4, 1881

What was the war's impact on the state versus national sovereignty debate? Samuel Fuller stated, in his October 1865 *North American Review* article, "The Civil war which has changed the current of our ideas, and crowded into a few years the emotions of a lifetime, has in measure given to the preceding period in history the character of a remote state of political existence." Fuller referred to a triumph of nationalism, serving a coup de grâce to Jefferson's philosophy of decentralization and local government. An anonymous writer from 1871 then noted that this "'shifting power [was] the first revolution effected by the late Civil War and the legislation of reconstruction . . . [it] established more definite and better understood relations—whether better or worse is not here the question—between the general and state governments" (Hyman 1973, 172). Likewise, William Cullen Bryant and Sydney Howard Gay (1876, xix) noted, "Before the [civil] war the boundaries of the powers assigned to the National Government, and those which remained with the several States, were pretty sharply defined by usage, and attempts were but rarely made to go beyond them." But would these boundaries become more nebulous even after the Civil War seemingly settled the issue? In the penultimate year of the Civil War, Samuel Cox (1864, 13) remarked,

> If the States are obliterated and the source of power is centralized at the Federal capital, wherein does such a government differ from the rankest oriental despotism? What will be our fate, with such despotism? History is like Merlin's magic mirror, in which we may read our own future. The seeming strength of such a system as conquered provinces, or oligarchical States, to take the place of the Constitution and local State governments, is its weakness. Such a system is not to be commended for the imitation of Anglo Saxon people. Be assured, Representatives, that the people of America will never accept such a system in lieu of their old, any more than they will accept presidential edicts for legislation, State suicide for State resuscitation, or an abolition tithe suffrage for the sovereignty of the people!

But not all support for states' rights vanished as the war ended. As Hyman (1973, 300) noted, as lawmakers gathered in December 1865, they "were happily rid of the prewar fixation on state sovereignty, but they abandoned none of their reverence for all states' rights. Further, their assumption was that Congress—not the President—embodied the nation's invigorated will on all matters including the disposition of the defeated rebel states." At the same time, the federal courts secured greater authority over the state institutions. National court jurisdiction expanded, with several laws passed in the Reconstruction era providing the basis for individuals to take their cases from the state to the federal courts. As Hyman (256) wrote, "The enlargement of national court jurisdiction was more than a duration-only step. It was the beginning of the end to some of federalism's twilight zones which had helped to bring on the Civil War." Still, after the Civil War and Reconstruction, ambiguities remained. As Bray Hammond (1970, 363) wrote, "The parceling of authority among an increasing number of 'sovereign' states varying in population and resources had to give way, irregularly, confusedly, and haltingly, to centralization. For the Civil War had fixed no sharp line dividing authority but left a recondite, meandering watershed marked by ambiguities at every step."

One can argue that the pre–Civil War interpretations of the Constitution tell us more about who we were, the times in which we lived, and the era's momentous events than it did about the Constitution's actual words. Prior to the Civil War, for example, abolitionists and supporters of slavery found support in the Constitution, except when it was not in their personal interest to do so. When the Fugitive Slave Law was enacted in 1850, many of those who supported a states' rights suddenly found a justification for greater power in the national government. Various individuals on both sides of the slavery issue changed their viewpoints as political circumstances transformed, during a period when authoritative constitutional documents were not widely available, a law school education was not required to be a lawyer, and only one state, California, required the teaching of the Constitution.

The Constitution's ambiguity was therefore present in one of the most momentous debates of our nation's history and ambiguity provided the discretion necessary for individuals, politicians, and even judges to interpret the Constitution in different and not necessarily consistent ways. As I will examine in the next three chapters, there are many different interpretative frameworks available for discovering the Constitution's fundamental meaning. Some, such as a strict constructionist approach, limit presidential power, while others—the idea of a living constitution and the unitary executive—provide the basis for a more powerful presidential office. Because of constitutional ambiguity, people may choose the interpretative framework that works best for them. To better understand this point, I turn in chapter 6 to an examination of a strict constructionist constitutional interpretation and its implications for presidential power.

Chapter 6

A Strict Interpretation of the Constitution

The president of the United States has such powers as are strictly and properly executive; and, by his qualified negative on the legislature, is furnished with a guard to protect his powers against their encroachments. Such powers and such a guard he ought to possess: but a just distribution of the powers of government requires that he should possess no more. In this important aspect, the constitution of the United States has much more regular, more correct, and better proportioned features, than are those of the constitution of Great Britain.

—James Wilson, *Collected Works of James Wilson*, 1:730

Scores of volumes of prose have been dedicated to the explication, analysis, and interpretation of presidential power. Here, I limit the analysis to three basic types of interpretative frameworks, each reflecting different eras of presidential power. There is a precedent in the work of William Anderson (1947, 230–31), who examined three theories of the presidency. The first, "the 'Whig' theory was that the President should stay scrupulously within his legal powers, not attempt to be a leader in legislation, use his veto power only to prevent encroachments on his office and other unconstitutional acts, and simply enforce the law as Congress passed them. He was to be firm, dignified, safe—a protector of property, not a tribune of the people or a proposer of innovations in government and business." In this chapter I examine the Whig theory and the era of strict constructionism.

I begin with a seemingly simple question: Given the Constitution's demonstrated ambiguity, can it be interpreted literally, or must it be interpreted as a general document that leaves each successive generation to fill in the missing pieces? As I demonstrated in chapter 3, various observers throughout American history identified constitutional ambiguity. Furthermore, Nicholas Quinn Rosenkranz (2002, 2086) adjudged, "The hard truth of the matter is that American courts have no intelligible, generally accepted, and consistently applied theory of statutory interpretation." Likewise, Supreme Court Justice Antonin Scalia (1997, 14) wrote, "We American judges have no intelligible theory of what we do most. Even sadder, however, is the fact that the American bar and American legal education, by and large, are unconcerned with the fact that we have no intelligible theory. Whereas legal scholarship has been at pains to rationalize the common law . . . it has been seemingly agnostic as to whether there is even any such thing as good or bad rules of statutory interpretation." Does the same logic apply to the Constitution? On this point Thomas Dillon O'Brien (1922, 1–2) commented,

> Many people are debating the propriety of changes, more or less radical, in our form of Government. We have those who hold the Constitution of the United States, even to its utmost detail, to be an immutable declaration of great principles, incapable of improvement or change. Others regard it as an archaic jumble of ancient laws serving only to retard progress and constituting an impregnable barrier to enlightened social and remedial legislation. There are also those, happily less numerous, whose disposition or chagrin at individual failure leads them to snap and snarl at all existing conditions; government, politics, religion and business all come beneath their carping criticism. Finally we have the conscious traitor and corrupt agitator who may be dismissed with the couplet: No thief e'er felt the halter draw with good opinion of the Law. An honest discussion of our government and its fundamental laws is not only legitimate but highly desirable.

Consequently, James Beck (1926, 13) remarked, "The struggle to maintain the Constitution of the United States is an unending one. The battle is always on, although the fact be little appreciated. The old saying, 'eternal vigilance is the price of liberty' is more than a meaningless platitude." Interpretation, therefore, is far from an easy task and Donald McCoy (1991, 107–8) identified one reason why: "The Constitution of the United

States has stood on high ground of American life from the beginning. Its words have shaped our government, our politics, and much of our everyday life. Yet its meaning has never been static, subject as the Constitution has been to amendment and especially interpretation. The document has been explicit enough never to have been radically changed in its meaning, but it has been adaptable enough to satisfy the nation's contestants for power." Adaptability, however, requires interpretation. Hence, as Ronald Dworkin (1986, 50) commented, "People interpret in many different contexts, and we should begin by seeking some sense of how these contexts differ."

One method is to examine the Constitution in a historical context. Yet, as Philip Bobbitt (1982 edition, 9) noted,

> Historical arguments depend on a determination of the original understanding of the constitutional provision to be construed. At first, one must notice how odd it is that the original understanding in any field of study should govern present behavior. Certainly no one proposes an historical argument in physics: for example, that we should try to discover what Democritus had in mind when he used the word *atom* so that we could use the term properly when confronted with, say, problems associated with electron spin. . . . The very decision to produce a Constitution in writing supposes a different path.

Another method is to interpret the Constitution's actual words. Yet, Okyeon Yi (2011, 231) acknowledged,

> The court initially had two options in interpreting national power, either by reading the Constitution as a unitary document, or by reading the Constitution differently in breach of the traditional interpretation. By choosing the first interpretation, the court often found authority for a strong government both in foreign and domestic affairs by contending that an expansive foreign affairs power should provide for an expansive domestic affairs power. The court could alternatively have found authority for a weak and decentralized government both in foreign and domestic affairs. However, this alternative perspective never gained any serious support mainly because the Articles of Confederation was abandoned precisely for the sake of a

better and more effective national policy, both in the domestic and foreign realm.

Cass Sunstein (2009, 19) identified another complicating factor: "Many people claim that the Constitution must be interpreted in their preferred way. They insist that the very idea of interpretation requires judges to adopt their own method of construing the founding document. These claims are wrong. No approach to constitutional interpretation is mandatory. Any approach must be defended by reference to its consequences, not asserted as part of what interpretation requires." Or as Daniel Farber (2021, 2) opined, "Our tendency to tailor our view of presidential power to the current political situation makes the constitutional issues even harder to understand."

Along with these confounding factors, differences of interpretation are not value-free. As Laurence Tribe and Michael Dorf (1991, 66) noted, "Constitutional value choices cannot be made . . . without recourse to a system of values that is at least partly external to the constitutional text." As a result, various interpreters, especially presidents, have their own incentives in mind. As Irving Brant (1936, 32) noted, "All constitutional arguments germinating in self-interest are suspect. And if it be found that this relationship between opinion and self-interest runs back, in any form, through the history of the nation, then legal precedent becomes suspect and constitutional history is in need of re-examination." Or as Maury Maverick (1939, 5) conjectured, "I hope that America's renewed interest in constitutionalism will not fall into a vulgar Battle of Symbols. . . . For as a whole, American 'Constitutional Law' has purposely been made technical and obscure. Our people have been tricked by symbols, magic words, strange taboos. Many are the tricks played on the American people to make them stand for practices which are unfair indeed." Ambiguity provides a basis for the establishment of such "symbols, magic words, [and] strange taboos."

Fueling this process are the personal incentives of those who interpret the Constitution. In an article entitled "A Century of Constitutional Interpretation," *Century Magazine* (1882, 867, 869) advised, "The history of the past hundred years goes far to show that the constitutional opinions held by any set of men, at any particular time, and in any particular place, have been very largely determined by expediency." As motives change, expediency can drive interpretation in different directions. If so, can a strict interpretation return us to the Framers' original intent, and if so, would it establish the presidency that we need today? After all, if we are interested in an original understanding of the Framers, shouldn't our nineteenth-century presidents be our guide since they presumably were closer and therefore more familiar with original intent? But even as the nation experienced its first challenges in the last decades of the eighteenth century, two political parties, each with vastly different interpretations of the Constitution, were established, a factor that was not anticipated by the Framers or the Constitution. Additionally, while presidential power was largely constrained, would a strict constructionist approach be appropriate for our present world? By the dawn of the twentieth century, as Nelson Case (1904, 1–2) found,

> The fact is historically indisputable that our Constitution has been a subject of growth. What was placed in the written document by the constitutional fathers, who assembled in Philadelphia in 1787, was the condensed wisdom of a century and a half of colonial experience in Constitution forming and in contending for constitutional principles, in addition to all the knowledge they could gather from the study of the history of other nations. But the fathers who drew the Constitution in 1787 had little conception of what that instrument would become through a century's growth, because they could not at that time comprehend what a marvellous expansion there would be of the national germ which they saw sprout and commence to grow, and which the succeeding generations have seen come to a fuller perfection.

Hence, to employ Edward Corwin's (1957) famous aphorism in a different context, constitutional interpretation represents yet another "invitation to struggle." And constitutional interpretation is not risk-free. It can create a presidency that is too strong or too weak (Sunstein 1995; Laing 2012; Milkis, Tichenor, and Blessing 2013). Speaking in New York in 1907, at a dinner provided by the Kentuckians of New York, Supreme Court Justice John Marshall Harlan declared, "Let us not give our approval to any interpretation of the Constitution that will either cripple the Nation's authority or prostate the Nation at the feet of the States, or that will deprive the States of their just powers. Let us hold fast to the broad and liberal, and yet safe, rule of constitutional construction approved by the fathers and established by judicial decisions" (Kammen 1987, 187). A decade later, David Hill (1916a, 50–51; see also Hill 1913; 1916b) opined, "The dangers to the American conception of constitutional government do not arise from the open opposition of its enemies, for in the field of free debate it is abundantly able to defend itself. Its real foes—and they are not a few—are those who do not avowedly attack or resist it; but who, while professing to be its friends, and even its advocates, secretly repudiate or intentionally pervert its fundamental principles."

Despite its brevity, or perhaps because of it, most of our nineteenth-century presidents adopted a strict constructionist reading of the Constitution, following the letter of the law as they understood it. Yet as Samuel Tyler (1872, 153) noted, even the strict constructionist presidents expanded federal authority over the states. To understand this point, I examine the opinions and actual words of our eighteenth- and nineteenth-century presidents.

Washington to J. Adams

Never will I consent to straining the Constitution, nor never will I consent to the exercise of doubtful power. We come here the servants, not of the lords, of our constituents. The new Government, instead of being a powerful machine whose authority would support any measure, needs helps and props on all sides, and must be supported by the ablest names and the most shining characters which we can select.

—William Maclay, The Journal of William Maclay, April 29, 1789

If I have one general criticism of books on the presidency and the Constitution it is that they often fail to adequately cite the actual words of our presidents, and when they do, they tend to concentrate on only a few extraordinary presidents. Therefore, most of the nineteenth-century presidents are left in the dustbin of history. And yet, our earliest presidents had much to say about the Constitution and the powers that it confers. In their rhetoric most presidents adopted an originalist or strict constructionist viewpoint, which narrowly defines the exercise of presidential power, though they sometimes violated the basic constructs of strict constructionism when necessity intervened. I therefore examine these early presidents and their sentiments in some detail.

Writing in the 1830s, Justice Joseph Story (1858 1:283) stated, "The first and fundamental rule in the interpretation of all instruments is, to construe them according to the sense of the terms, and intention of the parties." A century later Guy Despard Goff (1931, 35) argued, "The Constitution is a written instrument. As such its meaning does not alter, and what it meant when adopted, it means now." Likewise, according to Harrison Tweed (1953, 493), "It was fundamental throughout the deliberations of the Convention that the government to be established was to be one limited by a written constitution. No one had any such reverence for the government of the mother country as to incline him towards an unwritten constitution as a framework for government." Given that they were the first presidents to govern under the new written Constitution, it is unsurprising that our early presidents paid significant attention to the Constitution's words. As such, most can be described as originalists. What then is *originalism*?

According to Walter Murphy, James Fleming, and Sotirios Barber (1995, 389–90), "In the United States . . . most thoughtful, responsible interpreters do not envision 'The Constitution' as completely enveloped within the text. Nevertheless, many interpreters stoutly argue that it is almost entirely so contained. These people insist that the appropriate dictionaries, grammars, and other linguistic tools to discover meaning are those used by the founding generation or the generation that adopted the amendment whose message is at issue." But as I noted in chapter 4, there was little published documentation to guide our earliest presidents. While they could follow their predecessors, they lacked much information of a critical nature, such as James Madison's *Notes* or the Anti-Federalist critiques of the Constitution.

Consequently, most of our first presidents were outspoken in their praise of the new Constitution and affirmatively dedicated to its purposes. David Stewart (2021, 319) noted, "As the first president under the Constitution, Washington would play a major role in defining the presidency and constitutional government. Because, as one scholar recently observed, the Constitution was 'deeply indeterminate,' creating a government according to its terms required not only legal interpretation, but also imagination." Stanley Elkins and Eric McKitrick (1995, 59) added, "Washington, ever sensitive to the possibility that he might be accused of overstepping his powers (such as presuming to initiate legislation), forbode in his inaugural address from telling Congress what measures he thought it ought to take." In his special message of August 11, 1790, George Washington promised, "I shall conceive myself bound to exert the powers intrusted to me by the Constitution in order to carry into faithful execution the treaty of Hopewell." In the case of the Whiskey Rebellion, Washington,

September 24, 1794, cited, "Obedience to that high and irresistible duty consigned to me by the Constitution to take care that the laws be faithfully executed." In his sixth annual address to Congress on November 11, 1794, Washington referred to the presidential oath of office: "Having thus fulfilled the engagement which I took when I entered into office, 'to the best of my ability to preserve, protect, and defend the Constitution of the United States,' on you, gentlemen, and the people by whom you are deputed, I rely for support." And in his farewell address on September 19, 1796 Washington spoke extensively and eloquently about the Constitution's separation of powers. He concluded,

> If in the opinion of the people the distribution or modification of the constitutional powers be in any particular wrong, let it be corrected by an amendment in the way which the Constitution designates. But let there be no change by usurpation; for though this in one instance may be the instrument of good, it is the customary weapon by which free governments are destroyed. The precedent must always greatly overbalance in permanent evil any partial or transient benefit which the use can at any time yield.

Regarding such statements, Glenn Phelps (1989, 263) observed, "What is remarkable about Washington's commitment to the rule of law was his willingness to subordinate other firmly held political sentiments to that standard. He had confided that 'there are some things in the new form [Constitution], I will readily acknowledge, I never did, and I am persuaded never will, obtain my cordial approbation.'" On certain issues Washington was adamant, however. He believed that the president should play the primary role in foreign affairs and therefore adopted a vigorous interpretation of the Constitution's provisions as they related to America's foreign policy. According to historian James Flexner (1970, 215), when the French king notified Washington of the death of the Dauphin, Washington responded that "the honour of receiving and answering" such communications no longer involved the Congress but was the president's duty alone. By this act Washington protected his right to receive information from foreign dignitaries and provided a precedent for the later claim that the president was the "sole organ" of the nation in its communications with foreign nations. Still, in his decorum, his actions, and his public statements, Washington was exceedingly careful to carve out what he considered the proper authority of the new presidential office, even to the extent of determining how many horses were required to lead his carriage. Was six too many? Was two enough? Four seemed like the right answer.

Washington developed yet another precedent. Despite his rhetoric, he did not always govern as a strict constructionist in domestic affairs. For instance, even though he initially thought the proposal was unconstitutional, he eventually adopted Alexander Hamilton's reasoning for the establishment of the First National Bank of the United States. He also accepted a broad interpretation of the vesting clause to justify his Neutrality Proclamation. Washington interpreted the Constitution as he understood it, but even during this first presidency his secretary of state, Thomas Jefferson, and Representative James Madison vehemently disagreed with the president's constitutional reasoning. Henceforth, during the two terms of our first president different interpretations of the Constitution emerged, differences that in time defined our first political parties.

Our second president, John Adams, made comments about executive power that differed from those of his predecessor. For example, in *Proclamation 9: Law and Order in the Counties of Northampton, Montgomery, and Bucks, in the State of Pennsylvania* on February 12, 1799, Adams made only a general reference to his constitutionally enumerated authority:

> Whereas by the Constitution and laws of the United States I am authorized, whenever the laws of the United States shall be opposed or the execution thereof obstructed in any State by combinations too powerful to be suppressed by the ordinary course of judicial proceedings or by the powers vested in the marshals, to call forth military force to suppress such combinations and to cause the laws to be duly executed; and Whereas it is in my judgment necessary to call forth military force in order to suppress the combinations aforesaid and to cause the laws aforesaid to be duly executed, and I have accordingly determined so to do, under the solemn conviction that the essential interests of the United States demand it.

Adams again relied on a general claim of executive authority in his third annual address to Congress on December 3, 1799, referencing "my duty." In his *Message in Reply to the House of Representatives* on December 27, 1800, Adams also asserted broad constitutional authority in negotiating treaties with other nations, this time explicitly referencing "executive power."

In sum, rather than specific citations for his use of presidential power, Adams relied on general claims, a practice not followed by his successor.

The Age of Jefferson

> There exists some reason to believe, that the original construction of the Presidential office was not perfectly acceptable to the mind of Mr. Jefferson. When the federal Constitution was formed, both Mr. Adams and Mr. Jefferson were absent from the United States, and neither of them had a direct participation in its edification.
>
> —Augustus Woodward, *The Presidency of the United States*

As Stanley Milkis and Michael Nelson (1994, 104) noted, "Jefferson's presidency marked an important change in the relationship between the president and the people. His predecessors, Washington and Adams, had believed that the power of the presidency derived from its constitutional authority. Jefferson, although not rejecting this view, maintained that the strength of the presidential office depended on the 'affections of the people.'" His presidency also represented a temporary revolution in the executive's relationship with Congress. As James MacGregor Burns (1963, 36) commented,

> Considering himself the national head of the party, he gave close leadership to the forces in Congress; he personally drafted bills and had them introduced in Congress; saw to it that the men he favored took leadership posts in Congress; induced men to run for Congress by holding out promises of advancement; made the Speaker the floor leader of the House his personal lieutenant; changed the leadership as he saw fit; used Ways and Means and other committees as instruments of presidential control; dominated the Republican caucus in the House. In short, he took the machinery that the congressional Republicans had built up against Federalist Presidents and turned it to his own use.

Despite such violations of a strict separation of powers, Jefferson praised the Constitution in his inaugural address on March 4, 1801:

"These principles form the bright constellation which has gone before us and guided our steps through an age of revolution and reformation. The wisdom of our sages and blood of our heroes have been devoted to their attainment." Jefferson also referred to the fear of power:

> I know, indeed, that some honest men fear that a republican government can not be strong, that this Government is not strong enough; but would the honest patriot, in the full tide of successful experiment, abandon a government which has so far kept us free and firm on the theoretic and visionary fear that this Government, the world's best hope, may by possibility want energy to preserve itself? I trust not. I believe this, on the contrary, the strongest Government on earth.

It was a remarkable statement for a president who is often referenced for his opinions on limited government. To allay fears of executive aggrandizement, however, Jefferson was particularly deferential in his congressional communications, as was the case with the Barbary pirates. While on December 8, 1801 he reported that a state of war already existed and that a confrontation had occurred, he also noted, "I communicate all material information on this subject, that in the exercise of this important function confided by the Constitution to the Legislature exclusively." Jefferson also expressed deference to the legislative branch regarding Spain's unwillingness to set borders related to Louisiana in his special message of December 6, 1805.

We can understand Jefferson's ideas about presidential power with reference to his linguistic choices. For example, Jefferson was the first president to refer to "my power" rather than the power of the presidency, such as in a special message to Congress on April 8, 1802 (Waterman et al., 2024). And while Jefferson espoused the limits of presidential power, he often exceeded such authority in practice. Jefferson's first prominent constitutional controversy involved the case of William Marbury—whether he was entitled to his commission, which had not been properly filed by John Marshall, who was now to decide Marbury's fate on the Supreme Court. As John Garraty (1987, 15) wrote, "The Jeffersonians, eager to block any investigation of executive affairs, used every conceivable mode of obstruction to prevent the case [*Marbury v. Madison*] from being decided." Along with the impeachment of one federal justice, and a failed attempt to impeach a Supreme Court justice, Jefferson's assault on the integrity of the court system represents his most ardent violation of constitutional norms. Consequently, despite his expressed desire to honor the Constitution, Jefferson often strayed from a strict constructionist approach.

The most prominent example is the Louisiana Purchase. Distinguished constitutional scholar Christopher Tiedeman (1890, 133; see also Spencer and Lossing 1874, 3:41; Pratt 1955, 97) wrote,

> In the case of the Louisiana purchase, the exercise of the questionable power was so plainly beneficial to the whole country that it was generally acquiesced in. But the claim of an express or implied power to make the purchase was so palpably untenable that the transaction has been tacitly admitted to have been an actual but necessary violation of the Constitution. Even Mr. Jefferson, to whom the credit of effecting the purchase of Louisiana was justly and chiefly due, was of the opinion that there was no warrant in the Constitution, for the exercise of such a power, and recommended the adoption of an amendment to the Constitution ratifying that purchase.

Thomas Bailey ([1940] 1950, 103) therefore noted, "With much anguish of spirit Jefferson turned over the problem in his mind." The only alternative seemed to be a constitutional amendment. Jefferson thus wrote to John Breckinrige (Meacham 2012, 389–90),

> This treaty must of course be laid before both houses because both have important functions to exercise respecting it. They I presume will see their duty to their country in ratifying and paying for it so as to secure a good which would otherwise probably never be again in their person. But I suppose they must then appeal to *the nation* for an article to the Constitution, approving and confirming an act which the nation had not previously authorized.

But months, if not years, of precious time would be wasted, and the opportunity to acquire the land, lost. Hence, on August 28, 1803, Jefferson wrote to secretary of the treasury Albert Gallatin (1879, 1:144):

> You will find that the French government, dissatisfied perhaps with their late bargain with us, will be glad to declare it void. It will be necessary, therefore, that we execute it with punctuality

and without delay. I have desired the Secretary of the Navy so to make his arrangement as that an armed vessel shall be ready to sail on the 31st of October with the ratification, and, if possible, with the stock to France; if the latter can be got through both Houses in that time it will be desirable.

Jefferson moved decisively. Expediency, not a critical reading of the Constitution, guided his decisions. As Jon Meacham (2012, 391) advised,

The philosophical Jefferson had believed an amendment was necessary. The political Jefferson, however, was not going to allow theory to get in the way of reality. "I confess . . . I think it important in the present case to set an example against broad construction by appealing for new power to the people," he wrote Wilson Cary Nicholas. "If however our friends shall think differently, certainly I shall acquiesce with satisfaction, confiding that the good sense of our country will correct the evil of construction when it shall produce ill effects."

Jefferson was trying to have it both ways. He now favored moving ahead without a constitutional amendment but still indicated support for it if "our friends shall think differently." By adopting this language, Jefferson provided a rationale should he face congressional opposition to the treaty or a call for a constitutional amendment. Still, Jefferson offered a warning in his letter: "Our peculiar security is in possession of a written Constitution. Let us not make it a blank paper by construction" (Bruff 2015, 70).

The constitutional debate within the Jefferson administration also was of critical value, as Henry Adams (1889–91, 2:78–79) documented: "When the President and Cabinet decided early in January, 1803, to send Monroe with two million dollars to buy New Orleans and Florida, a question was instantly raised as to the form in which such a purchase could be constitutionally made. Attorney-General Lincoln wished to frame the treaty or convention in such language as to make France appear not as adding new territory to the United States, but as extending already existing territory by an alteration of its boundary." Treasury Secretary Albert Gallatin (Gallatin 1879, 1:144) responded to the letter, "If the acquisition of territory is not warranted by the Constitution . . . it is not more legal to acquire for one State than for the United States. . . . To me it would appear, (1) that the United States, as a nation, have an inherent right to acquire territory; (2) that whenever that acquisition is by treaty, the same constituted authorities in whom the treaty-making power is vested have a constitutional right to sanction the acquisition." Henry Adams (1889–91, 2:79–80), who was hardly an adherent of Jefferson, concluded,

> Gallatin not only advanced Federal doctrine, but used also what the Virginians always denounced as Federalist play on words. "The United States as a nation" had an inherent right to do whatever the States in union cared to do; but the Republican party, with Jefferson, Madison, and Gallatin at their head, had again and again maintained that the United States government had the inherent right to do no act whatever, but was the crea-ture of the States in union; and its acts, if not resulting from an expressly granted power, were no acts at all, but void, and not to be obeyed or regarded by the States.

Hence, issues of national versus state sovereignty were involved in this decision.

As Meacham (2012, 392) concluded, "Things were neat only in the-ory and despite his love of ideas and image of himself, Thomas Jefferson was as much a man of action as he was of theory." Or as Willard Randall (1993, 567) noted,

> Jefferson's greatest diplomatic triumph created his trickiest constitutional dilemma. As the strict-constructionist president read the Constitution, "The general government has no pow-ers but such as the constitution has given it; and it has not given it a power of holding foreign territory, and still less of incorporating it into the Union." . . . He decided to seize "the fugitive occurrence which so much advances the good of their country," urge Congress to put behind them "metaphysical subtleties," buy Louisiana, and *then* go to the public to seek a constitutional amendment.

Consequently, as Rexford Tugwell (1977, 61) advised,

> When it came to deciding on the Louisiana Purchase, the commitment to strict construction might have proved fatal; Jefferson might have insisted on being guided by his principles,

either because of stubborn faith in their validity or because he feared their too conspicuous abandonment. But he must be supposed to have been aware, as all good politicians are, that inconsistency is an unimportant sin. It is soon forgotten, and the sooner if the action involved is concluded rapidly and successfully.

Hence, Andrew Shankman (2018, 5), wrote of Jefferson and Madison, "Above all else, they emphasized vast landmass that could belong to republican citizens if they were willing to seize it from the native peoples who already lived on it, and from the European empires that claimed large portions of it. For Jefferson and Madison, land was destiny." The importance of land therefore had to be weighed against the president's constitutional responsibilities. In sum, expediency outweighed Jefferson's interpretation of the Constitution. Though in July 1803 Jefferson and his secretary of state, James Madison, crafted a draft proposal for a Constitutional amendment to add Louisiana and its territory to the Union (Smith 1995, 2:1269–70), it was never consummated. Jefferson therefore strayed from a strict constructionist approach and expanded the power of the presidency. But as William MacDonald (1913, 17) opined, "Political consistency . . . has never been rigorously exacted from statesmen, and Jefferson is entitled to as great latitude of judgment as has commonly been accorded to other popular leaders."

In the view of history, Jefferson's willingness to stray from the strict constructionist approach was one of his strongest political assets. Yet, while Jefferson exerted considerable and often controversial presidential power, the succeeding presidents of the Jeffersonian era were more strictly devout followers of the Constitution. For instance, in his inaugural address on March 4, 1809, James Madison referred to the Constitution as "the cement of the union." On December 12, 1815, Madison stated,

> I can indulge the proud reflection that the American people have reached in safety and success their 40th year as an independent nation; that for nearly an entire generation they have had experience of their present Constitution, the off-spring of their undisturbed deliberations and of their free choice; that they have found it to bear the trials of adverse as well as prosperous circumstances; to contain in its combination of the federate

and elective principles a reconcilement of public strength with individual liberty, of national power for the defense of national rights with a security against wars of injustice, of ambition, and vain-glory in the fundamental provision which subjects all questions of war to the will of the nation itself, which is to pay its costs and feel its calamities. Nor is it less a peculiar felicity of this Constitution, so dear to us all, that it is found to be capable, without losing its vital energies, of expanding itself over a spacious territory with the increase and expansion of the community for whose benefit it was established.

But a strict interpretation had consequences. For example, in his March 3, 1817, veto message, Madison wrote,

I am not unaware of the great importance of roads and canals and the improved navigation of water courses, and that a power in the National Legislature to provide for them might be exercised with signal advantage to the general prosperity. But seeing that such a power is not expressly given by the Constitution, and believing that it can not be deduced from any part of it without an inadmissible latitude of construction and a reliance on insufficient precedents; believing also that the permanent success of the Constitution depends on a definite partition of powers between the General and the State Governments, and that no adequate landmarks would be left by the constructive extension of the powers of Congress as proposed in the bill, I have no option but to withhold my signature from it.

Expedience could have led to a different interpretation, but according to Madison's message, the "safe and practicable mode" would have required a series of constitutional amendments to deal with the development of everything from roads and canals to railroads. But such a constitution would have become a prolix of amendments.

James Monroe continued to espouse a strict constructionist framework announcing in his inaugural address on March 4, 1817:

Such, then, is the happy Government under which we live—a Government adequate to every purpose for which the social compact is formed; a Government elective in all its branches, under which every citizen may by his merit obtain the highest trust recognized by the Constitution; which contains within it no cause of discord, none to put at variance one portion of the community with another; a Government which protects every citizen in the full enjoyment of his rights, and is able to protect the nation against injustice from foreign powers.

Monroe further elaborated his views on the powers of the federal and state governments in his special message to the House of Representatives *Containing the Views of the President of the United States on the Subject of Internal Improvements* on May 4, 1822. He likewise vetoed a bill on internal improvements that he personally supported (Brown 1966, 65–79). In so doing, Monroe discussed the definitional problems associated with the constitutional divisions of power:

If there was a perfect accord in every instance as to the precise extent of the powers granted to the General Government, we should then know with equal certainty what were the powers which remained to the State governments, since it would follow that those which were not granted to the one would remain to the other. But it is on this point, and particularly respecting the construction of these powers and their incidents, that a difference of opinion exists, and hence it is necessary to trace distinctly the origin of each government, the purposes intended by it, and the means adopted to accomplish them. By having the interior of both governments fully before us we shall have all the means which can be afforded to enable us to form a correct opinion of the endowments of each.

Again, state versus national sovereignty was an issue, as was Monroe's deference to Congress. When he did employ executive power, Monroe, in his special message on January 17, 1822, was careful to refer to the executive's specific legislative authority. In Monroe's February 17, 1825, special message, he again deferred to Congress when a dangerous disease struck Washington, DC:

I invite the attention of Congress to the peculiar situation of this District in regard to the exposure of its inhabitants to contagious diseases from abroad, against which it is thought that adequate provision should now be made. The exposure being common to the whole District, the regulation should apply to the whole, to make which Congress alone possesses the adequate power. That the regulation should be made by Congress is the more necessary from the consideration that this being the seat of the Government, its protection against such diseases must form one of its principal objects.

Like Madison and Monroe, our sixth president, John Quincy Adams, followed the tradition of strict constructionism. In his inaugural address on March 4, 1825 Adams affirmed,

In unfolding to my countrymen the principles by which I shall be governed in the fulfillment of those duties my first resort will be to that Constitution which I shall swear to the best of my ability to preserve, protect, and defend. That revered instrument enumerates the powers and prescribes the duties of the Executive Magistrate, and in its first words declares the purposes to which these and the whole action of the Government instituted by it should be invariably and sacredly devoted—to form a more perfect union, establish justice, insure domestic tranquillity, provide for the common defense, promote the general welfare, and secure the blessings of liberty to the people of this Union in their successive generations.

In his inaugural address, Adams also referred to how the inherent ambiguity in the language of the Constitution had been quelled:

In the compass of thirty-six years since this great national covenant was instituted a body of laws enacted under its authority and in conformity with its provisions has unfolded its powers and carried into practical operation its effective energies. Subordinate departments have distributed the executive functions in their various relations to foreign affairs, to the revenue and expenditures, and to the military force of the Union by land and sea. A coordinate department of the judiciary has expounded the Constitution and the laws, settling in harmonious coincidence with the legislative will numerous weighty questions of construction which the imperfection of human language had rendered unavoidable. The year of jubilee since the first formation of our Union has just elapsed; that of the declaration of our independence is at hand. The consummation of both was effected by this Constitution.

While Madison, Monroe, and J. Q. Adams returned to a strict constructionist interpretation of the Constitution, the next president broke new ground in both presidential power and constitutional interpretation.

The Age of Jackson

Jackson drew his general political views from Thomas Jefferson. His Republican antecedents led him to a strict construction of federal powers, to reliance on the states, and to a guarded use of authority found in the Constitution.

—Leonard White, *The Jacksonians*

Each of the first six presidents had direct connections to the Founding. Washington and Madison attended the Constitutional Convention. Jefferson, though in Paris at the time, to the best our knowledge, read Madison's notes on the Constitutional Convention. James Monroe was an active participant in the Virginia Ratifying Convention. John Quincy Adams served in Washington's administration, as ambassador to the Netherlands, and in subsequent administrations, including as secretary of state under Monroe. William Cooper (2017) refers to Adams as the "Lost Founding Father." It therefore is unsurprising that these presidents expressed fealty to the Constitution. But what of the presidents in the next generation? The age of Jackson incorporated the concerns of a more mature nation. The size and scope of the nation had expanded, as had its population and commercial trade. As such, presidents were responsible for a new set of issues, with slavery and disunion dividing the nation. The second generation of presidents, from Jackson through Buchanan, correspondingly raised new issues directly related to the executive powers of the presidency. The age of Jackson therefore represents a revolution in political thought.

While he likewise noted his deference to the Constitution in his inaugural address, in his second annual message on December 6,1830, Andrew Jackson expressed reservations about the Electoral College, which had denied him the presidency in 1824. The most striking feature of Jackson's rhetoric, however, are his references to power. In his second annual message to Congress on February 3,1831, he discussed the limits of executive power:

> I can not discover that the President is invested with any power under the Constitution or laws to withhold a patent from a purchaser who has given a fair and valuable consideration for land, and thereby acquired a vested right to the same; nor do I perceive that the sole legislative resolution of the Senate can confer such a power, or suspend the right of the citizens to enter the lands that have been offered for sale in said district and remain unsold, so long as the law authorizing the same remains unrepealed. I beg leave, therefore, to present the subject to the reconsideration of the Senate.

Though he was deferential to Congress in this instance, Jackson greatly expanded presidential power. Jackson's predecessors had on occasion referenced "my power," but Jackson did so in a different context. Rather than discussing the limits of his power, he often cited the term as a justification for its use. Hence, Jackson's use of "my power" was more than just a mere rhetorical choice. It reflected a fundamental change in perception of presidential power. In his inaugural address on March 4, 1829, he stated, "To any just system, therefore, calculated to strengthen this natural safeguard of the country I shall cheerfully lend all the aid in my power." On February 10, 1831, Jackson explicitly declared his own authority when invoking military action in his *Proclamation 42: Ordering Persons to Remove From Public Lands in Arkansas*, though he also referenced authority provided by Congress: "Now, therefore, be it known that I, Andrew Jackson, President of the United States, by virtue of the power and authority vested in me in and by the said act of Congress, do issue this my proclamation."

Jackson broke tradition when he criticized Congress's power. While other presidents had done so diplomatically, in his veto message of July 10, 1832, Jackson drew attention to his claims for executive power, while challenging the power of Congress. First, Jackson noted that the Second Bank of the United States abused its power. Even Albert Gallatin, who disapproved of the course of Jackson's relation to currency, "was always very severe against the abuses of its management, and strong in denouncing the overaction into which the system ran."[1] What was particularly controversial then was Jackson's interpretation that the law establishing the bank violated the "necessary and proper" clause, a basic constitutional power of the legislative branch: "It will be found that many of the powers and privileges conferred on it can not be supposed necessary for the purpose for which it is proposed to be created, and are not, therefore, means necessary to attain the end in view, and consequently not justified by the Constitution." While his predecessors argued that it was unconstitutional for Congress to pass legislation establishing roads and canals, what was most striking was the aggressive tone of Jackson's remarks. But that was not the end of Jackson's assumption of presidential power. He also expressed his power over the states. In his *Proclamation 43: Regarding the Nullifying Laws of South Carolina* (December 10, 1832), Jackson proclaimed,

> I consider . . . the power to annul a law of the United States, assumed by one State, incompatible with the existence of the Union, contradicted expressly by the letter of the Constitution, unauthorized by its spirit, inconsistent with every principle on which it was founded, and destructive of the great object for which it was formed . . . nothing can be more dangerous than to admit the position that an unconstitutional purpose entertained by the members who assent to a law enacted under a constitutional power shall make that law void. . . . Our Constitution does not contain the absurdity of giving power to make laws and another to resist them. . . . The States have no control over the exercise of this right other than that which results from the power of changing the representatives who abuse it, and thus procure redress. Congress may undoubtedly abuse this discretionary power; but the same may be said of others with which they are vested. Yet the discretion must exist somewhere. The Constitution has given it to the representatives of all the people, checked by the representatives of the States and by the Executive power.

Regarding the claim that South Carolina could secede from the Union, Jackson argued, in words Abraham Lincoln would later study,

> The Constitution of the United States, then, forms a government, not a league; and whether it be formed by compact between

the States or in any other manner, its character is the same. It is a Government in which all the people are represented, which operates directly on the people individually, not upon the States; they retained all the power they did not grant. . . . And it is the intent of this instrument to proclaim, not only that the duty imposed on me by the Constitution "to take care that the laws be faithfully executed" shall be performed to the extent of the powers already vested in me by law, or of such others as the wisdom of Congress shall devise and intrust to me for that purpose, but to warn the citizens of South Carolina who have been deluded into an opposition to the laws of the danger they will incur by obedience to the illegal and disorganizing ordinance of the convention; to exhort those who have refused to support it to persevere in their determination to uphold the Constitution and laws of their country; and to point out to all the perilous situation into which the good people of that State have been led, and that the course they are urged to pursue is one of ruin and disgrace to the very State whose rights they affect to support. . . . the dictates of a high duty oblige me solemnly to announce that you can not succeed. The laws of the United States must be executed. I have no discretionary power on the subject; my duty is emphatically pronounced in the Constitution.

Though Jackson did not declare or identify any additional authority, rather than citing "my duty," his statement expressed the will of the president of the United States. James Buchanan's later lamentations, that he did not possess the power to act when secession occurred, pale in comparison. It was a strong declaration of presidential power, and according to Whig politician Philip Hone (1889, 1:68–69), writing in his diary on December 12, 1832, the proclamation was well received:

Very much to the surprise of some, and to the satisfaction of all our citizens, we have a long proclamation of President Jackson, which was published in Washington on the 12th inst., and is in all our papers this day. It is a document addressed to the nullifiers of South Carolina, occasioned by the late treasonable proceedings of their convention. . . . And I think Jackson's election may save the Union. If he is sincere in this proclamation he will put down this rebellion. Mr. Clay, pursuing the same measures, would not have been equally successful.

In his special message of January 16, 1833, Jackson defended his action on South Carolina's challenge to the Constitution: "If these measures can not be defeated and overcome by the power conferred by the Constitution on the Federal Government, the Constitution must be considered as incompetent to its own defense, the supremacy of the laws is at an end, and the rights and liberties of the citizens can no longer receive protection from the Government of the Union." Jackson thus suggested a change in the existing laws, giving the president greater authority to deal with similar situations in the future:

> No more will be necessary than a few modifications of its terms to adapt the [militia] act of 1795 to the present emergency, as by that act the provisions of the law of 1792 were accommodated to the crisis then existing, and by conferring authority upon the President to give it operation during the session of Congress, and without the ceremony of a proclamation, whenever it shall be officially made known to him by the authority of any State, or by the courts of the United States, that within the limits of such State the laws of the United States will be openly opposed and their execution obstructed by the actual employment of military force, or by any unlawful means whatsoever too great to be otherwise overcome.

Despite his rhetorical references to the need for greater congressionally delegated authority, Jackson's penchant was to expand presidential power. Jackson's actions therefore worried Philip Hone (1889, 1:112). In his diary for October 3, Hone wrote,

> Party-spirit runs exceedingly high in every part of the country. Timid people begin to be afraid of the consequences of the struggle which is soon to take place, by which the question will be determined whether General Jackson, by the aid of his interested advisers, can sustain himself in his unconstitutional assumption of power, and perpetuate it in the election of his favourite, the heir presumptive, Mr. Van Buren, or whether the people by a great and simultaneous effort, shall burst their

shackles, rescue the Constitution, and stand once more erect
in their majesty, free and disenthralled.

On November 21, 1834, Hone (1889, 1:120) referred to Jackson in the most
treacherous terminology: "Tyrants are fickle in their choice of servants."
On December 3, Hone (1:123) wrote of Jackson's request for the power to
issue letters of marque and reprisal in a brooding crisis with France: "I am
not one of those who wish to place power in the hands of the President,
and I almost wonder that he should have thought it necessary to ask for
it, after some of his late experiments, which must have satisfied him that
he may take what power he pleases and the people will bear him out in
it. The Constitution and the laws may stand in his way, to be sure, but
those are trifles." And as slavery became a dominant issue, in his August
13, 1835 entry, Hone (1:156) warned that the anti-slavery movement may
lead "civil war into the bosom of our hitherto happy country."

Jackson's most prominent statement on presidential power occurred
after the Senate censored him. It is here that Jackson reiterated Hamilton's
broad constitutional defense of executive power. He responded with a
lengthy and detailed constitutional argument, which because of its remarkable detail and relationship to presidential power, I cite at length. In his
defense, Jackson began by citing the presidential oath of office:

> In the present case . . . there is even a stronger necessity for
> such a vindication. By an express provision of the Constitu-
> tion, before the President of the United States can enter on
> the execution of his office he is required to take an oath or
> affirmation in the following words: I do solemnly swear (or
> affirm) that I will faithfully execute the office of President of
> the United States and will to the best of my ability preserve,
> protect, and defend the Constitution of the United States. The
> duty of defending so far as in him lies the integrity of the
> Constitution would indeed have resulted from the very nature
> of his office, but by thus expressing it in the official oath or
> affirmation, which in this respect differs from that of any other
> functionary, the founders of our Republic have attested their
> sense of its importance and have given to it a peculiar solem-
> nity and force. Bound to the performance of this duty by the
> oath I have taken, by the strongest obligations of gratitude to
> the American people, and by the ties which unite my every

earthly interest with the welfare and glory of my country, and perfectly convinced that the discussion and passage of the above-mentioned resolution were not only unauthorized by the Constitution, but in many respects repugnant to its provisions and subversive of the rights secured by it to other coordinate departments, I deem it an imperative duty to maintain the supremacy of that sacred instrument and the immunities of the department intrusted to my care by all means consistent with my own lawful powers, with the rights of others, and with the genius of our civil institutions.

Jackson next discussed the powers of the three branches of government. Of significant importance, he invoked the idea that the vesting clause created a shield of exclusive executive power. I have added italics to emphasize certain points:

The executive power is vested *exclusively* in the President, except that in the conclusion of treaties and in certain appointments to office he is to act with the advice and consent of the Senate. . . . But although for the special purposes which have been mentioned there is an occasional intermixture of the powers of the different departments, yet with these exceptions each of the three great departments is independent of the others in its sphere of action, and when it deviates from that sphere is not responsible to the others further than it is expressly made so in the Constitution. In every other respect each of them is the coequal of the other two, and all are the servants of the American people, without power or right to control or censure each other in the service of their common superior, save only in the manner and to the degree which that superior has prescribed.

Jackson held the Senate responsible for violating the intent of the Constitution, a clever twist, since it was the Senate that accused him of exceeding his constitutional authority: "The President of the United States, therefore, has been by a majority of his constitutional triers accused and found guilty of an impeachable offense, but in no part of this proceeding have the directions of the Constitution been observed." Jackson now shifted toward a defense of his actions under the vesting and take care clauses:

By the Constitution "the executive power is vested in a President of the United States." Among the duties imposed upon him, and which he is sworn to perform, is that of "taking care that the laws be faithfully executed." Being thus made responsible for the entire action of the executive department, it was but reasonable that the power of appointing, overseeing, and controlling those who execute the laws—a power in its nature executive—should remain in his hands. It is therefore not only his right, but the Constitution makes it his duty, to "nominate and, by and with the advice and consent of the Senate, appoint" all "officers of the United States whose appointments are not in the Constitution otherwise provided for," with a proviso that the appointment of inferior officers may be vested in the President alone, in the courts of justice, or in the heads of Departments.

Jackson then returned to his principal defense: the executive vesting clause.

The *whole executive power* being vested in the President, who is responsible for its exercise, it is a necessary consequence that he should have a right to employ agents of his own choice to aid him in the performance of his duties, and to discharge them when he is no longer willing to be responsible for their acts. In strict accordance with this principle, the power of removal, which, like that of appointment, is an original executive power, is left *unchecked by the Constitution* in relation to all executive officers, for whose conduct the President is responsible, while it is taken from him in relation to judicial officers, for whose acts he is not responsible.

Jackson also claimed coordinate authority, by which each branch of government has the power to interpret the Constitution's meaning: "Here, then, we have the *concurrent authority* of President Washington, of the Senate, and the House of Representatives, numbers of whom had taken an active part in the convention which framed the Constitution and in the State conventions which adopted it, that the President derived *an unqualified power of removal* from that instrument itself, which is 'beyond the reach of legislative authority.'" Again, Jackson claimed that he was clothed with full executive power:

Might he not be asked whether there was any such limitation to his obligations prescribed in the Constitution? Whether he is not equally bound to take care that the laws be faithfully executed, whether they impose duties on the highest officer of State or the lowest subordinate in any of the Departments? Might he not be told that it was for the sole purpose of causing all executive officers, from the highest to the lowest, faithfully to perform the services required of them by law that the people of the United States have made him their Chief Magistrate and the Constitution has clothed him with *the entire executive power* of this Government? The principles implied in these questions appear too plain to need elucidation.

Jackson next described the deleterious effect that would result from the Senate's resolution in violation of the separation of powers:

The resolution of the Senate as originally framed and as passed, if it refers to these acts, presupposes a right in that body to interfere with this exercise of Executive power. If the principle be once admitted, it is not difficult to perceive where it may end. . . . But if the Senate have a right to interfere with the Executive powers, they have also the right to make that interference effective, and if the assertion of the power implied in the resolution be silently acquiesced in we may reasonably apprehend that it will be followed at some future day by an attempt at actual enforcement. . . . Followed to its consequences, this principle will be found effectually to destroy one coordinate department of the Government, to concentrate in the hands of the Senate the whole executive power, and to leave the President as powerless as he would be useless—*the shadow of authority after the substance had departed.*

Jackson warned of the dangerous tendency of the Senate's arrogation of presidential power. In so doing, he interpreted his powers as president as deriving from the people, as the only official other than the vice president who is elected directly by a national constituency:

The dangerous tendency of the doctrine which denies to the President the power of the supervising, directing, and

removing the Secretary of the Treasury, in like manner with
other Executive offices, would soon be manifest in practice,
were the doctrine to be established. The President is the *direct
representative of the American People*, but the Secretaries are
not. . . . But if the course recently adopted by the Senate shall
hereafter be frequently pursued, it is not only obvious that
the harmony of the relations between the President and the
Senate will be destroyed, but that other and graver effects will
ultimately ensue.

It was a remarkable defense of presidential power, consistent with the
unitary executive theory, which I discuss in chapter 8. It raised issues
that have dominated the discussion of presidential power ever since,
including references to the oath of office, as well as the vesting, take
care, and appointment clauses. Though he compromised his language
with reference to duties and powers, Jackson defended the integrity of
the chief magistrate, a quaint nineteenth-century term of reference to
the presidency that suggests limited authority, while also deriving direct
authority from the people. While radical in its time, Jackson's argument
would set precedents for future presidents and become a standard justification for presidential power.

Given the conflictual nature of Jackson's presidency, it is unsurprising that his immediate handpicked successor (second annual message,
December 3, 1838), Martin Van Buren, returned to rather bland statements
regarding fealty to the Constitution:

The Constitution devised by our forefathers as the framework
and bond of that system, then untried, has become a settled
form of government; not only preserving and protecting the
great principles upon which it was rounded, but wonderfully
promoting individual happiness and private interests. Though
subject to change and entire revocation whenever deemed
inadequate to all these purposes, yet such is the wisdom of its
construction and so stable has been the public sentiment that
it remains unaltered except in matters of detail comparatively
unimportant. It has proved amply sufficient for the various
emergencies incident to our condition as a nation.

It was up to William Henry Harrison to respond to Jackson's dissertation on the accretion of presidential power, when he promised to return

the presidency to its strict constructionist foundations. In his inaugural address on March 4, 1841, he noted that the powers of the government were strictly demarcated: "The Constitution of the United States is the instrument containing this grant of power to the several departments composing the Government. On an examination of that instrument it will be found to contain declarations of power granted and of power withheld." Harrison's subsequent death, however, left the nation in the hands of his vice president, a former Jacksonian Democrat. In his fourth annual message of December 3, 1844, John Tyler declared, "A rigid and close adherence to the terms of our political compact and, above all, a sacred observance of the guaranties of the Constitution will preserve union on a foundation which can not be shaken, while personal liberty is placed beyond hazard or jeopardy." And yet Tyler adopted a Jacksonian interpretation of the president's veto power. He further strayed from strict constructionism when, after a treaty annexing Texas failed in the Senate, he employed a new technique—the joint resolution—to accomplish the same goal. Again, expediency, rather than constitutional fealty, was an issue.

An even greater deviation from strict constructionism occurred in the case of James Polk. In his inaugural address of March 4, 1845, Polk declared,

> The Constitution itself, plainly written as it is, the safeguard of our federative compact, the offspring of concession and compromise, binding together in the bonds of peace and union this great and increasing family of free and independent States, will be the chart by which I shall be directed. It will be my first care to administer the Government in the true spirit of that instrument, and to assume no powers not expressly granted or clearly implied in its terms.

Yet Polk, like Jackson, did not follow his own directive, particularly in relation to his initiation of the war against Mexico.

Polk's successor, however, returned to the language of strict constructionism. The Whig Platform of 1848 noted (Johnson and Porter 1973, 15),

> *Resolved*: The standing, as the Whig Party does, on the broad and firm platform of the Constitution, braced up by all its inviolable and sacred guarantees and compromises, and cherished in the affections because the protective interests of the people, we are proud to have, as the exponent of our opinions, one

who is pledged to construe it by wise and generous rules which Washington applied to it, and who has said, (and no Whig desires any other assurance) that he will make Washington's Administration the model of his own.

In his inaugural address on March 4, 1849, Zachary Taylor declared, "In the discharge of these duties my guide will be the Constitution, which I this day swear to 'preserve, protect, and defend.' For the interpretation of that instrument I shall look to the decisions of the judicial tribunals established by its authority and to the practice of the Government under the earlier Presidents, who had so large a share in its formation." Yet, after denouncing the veto power, Taylor wandered from the strict constructionist path when he threatened to veto the omnibus Compromise of 1850.

Upon Taylor's demise, Millard Fillmore confronted the same political dilemma and decided to sign the legislation as one of his principal presidential duties (Griffis 1915). While the death of William Henry Harrison induced panic among Whigs, with John Tyler, formerly a Democrat as the vice president, Fillmore was seen by Whig politicians as a more dependable replacement. In his diary on Wednesday, July 10, 1850, Orville Hickman Browning (1925, 1:7) wrote,

On the afternoon of today intelligence reached us that President Taylor died this morning at 4 Oclock. The nation may congratulate itself in having in the line of succession a patriot & statesman eminently qualified for the duties of the high & important station. Millard Fillmore is a man of native energy & vigor of intellect, of fine attainments and valuable experience in Civil affairs. American in all his feelings, and of unquestioned devotion to the interests of his Country and a true Whig. With him at the helm the Country will have nothing to fear—the Whigs will have nothing to fear. The duplicity of a Tyler will not again distract us. Firm, honest, manly and patriotic and better versed in civil affairs than his lamented predecessor the Country will lose nothing by the exchange.

Fillmore held firm to his Whig principles in his first annual message on December 2, 1850: "In our domestic policy the Constitution will be my guide, and in questions of doubt I shall look for its interpretation to the judicial decisions of that tribunal which was established to expound it and to the usage of the Government, sanctioned by the acquiescence of the country." Fillmore then signed the Fugitive Slave Act, even though he opposed it, because it was constitutionally satisfactory. This in turn proved to be the death knell of Fillmore's aspiration for a full term as president.

After Fillmore's short term of office, Franklin Pierce continued the tradition of strict constructionist fealty in his first annual message to Congress on December 5, 1853: "Our Government exists under a written compact between sovereign States, uniting for specific objects and with specific grants to their general agent. If, then, in the progress of its administration there have been departures from the terms and intent of the compact, it is and will ever be proper to refer back to the fixed standard which our fathers left us and to make a stern effort to conform our action to it." As noted in chapter 5, Pierce by supporting the Kansas-Nebraska Act moved the country on a steady path toward civil war.

Pierce's successor, James Buchanan, also was elected on a strict constructionist promise. The Cincinnati Democratic platform included the following passage: "That the Federal Government is one of limited power, derived solely from the Constitution, and the grants of power made therein ought to be strictly construed by all the departments and agents of the government, and that it is inexpedient and dangerous to exercise doubtful constitutional powers" (YA Pamphlet Collection 1856, 8). And in his inaugural address on March 4, 1857, Buchanan declared, "I desire to state at the commencement of my Administration that long experience and observation have convinced me that a strict construction of the powers of the Government is the only true, as well as the only safe, theory of the Constitution."

Yet Buchanan violated his constitutional role when it suited him, both in urging the Supreme Court to rule the Missouri Compromise unconstitutional in the Dred Scott decision and in his attempt to foist the undemocratic Lecompton Constitution on the nation. Fatal to his historical reputation, however, Buchanan held firm to his strict constitutional beliefs as several Southern states seceded from the union. While action was required, he decided that the president had no constitutional authority to intervene. Writing in his memoir, Buchanan (1866, iii–iv) determined, "To the Constitution, as interpreted by its framers, he has ever been devoted, believing that the specific powers which it confers on the Federal Government, notwithstanding the experience of the last dreary years, are sufficient for almost every possible emergency, whether in peace or in war. He, therefore, claims the merit—if merit it be simply to do one's duty—that whilst in the exercise of Executive functions, he never violated any of its provisions." Buchanan (9) also expressed his ideas regarding the Constitution and the issue of slavery:

> That the Constitution does not confer upon Congress power to interfere with slavery in the States, has been admitted by all parties and confirmed by all judicial decisions ever since the origin of the Federal Government. This doctrine was emphatically recognized by the House of Representatives in the days of Washington, during the first session of the first Congress, and has never since been seriously called in question. Hence, it became necessary for the abolitionists, in order to furnish a pretext for their assaults on Southern slavery, to appeal to a law higher than the Constitution.

As such, Buchanan (296) expressly affirmed a strict constructionist approach concluding, "I feel that my duty has been faithfully, though it may be imperfectly, performed; and whatever the result may be, I shall carry to my grave the consciousness that I at least meant well for my country." As William Dunning (1898, 3) stated,

> After reaching the conclusion that there was no constitutional right in a state to secede, he next examined the position of the executive under the circumstances. Following an opinion of Attorney-General Black, he concluded that existing laws did not empower him to bring force to bear to suppress insurrection in a state "where no judicial authority exists to issue process, and where there is no marshal to execute it, and where, even if there were such an officer, the entire population would constitute one solid combination to resist him." His conclusion itself was reached by an exceedingly strict construction of the law of 1795, in reference to calling out the militia.

Was Buchanan mistaken that he had no constitutional authority to intervene? A future president, Ulysses S. Grant, thought so, referring to Buchanan as "the present granny of an executive" (Chernow 2012, 121). Was there not a wellspring of power that presidents could employ in emergency situations? Apparently, Buchanan did not believe that such undefined power existed, nor did he concur with Andrew Jackson's constitutional sentiments. Consequently, history judges Buchanan's presidency as a failure—he has consistently been the lowest ranked president in the CSPAN historical surveys. Some contemporary newspapers also found fault with his leadership, as demonstrated by this item in the *New York Herald* on April 16, 1861 (Greeley 1865, 457–58): "The measures that have been adopted within the last few days, by the Government of Mr. Lincoln, entirely changed the aspect of public affairs. Had a similar course been pursued five months ago [by Buchanan], the last would have been heard from Secession before now. Not the firing of a gun would have been needed." And George Templeton Strong (1952b, 105) adjudged, "Old James Buchanan, the 'O.P.F.' stands lowest, I think, in the dirty catalog of treasonable mischief-makers. For without the excuse of bad Southern blood, without passion, without local prejudices, and in a great degree by mere want of moral force to resist his confessedly treasonable advisers, he has somehow slid into the position of boss-traitor and master-devil. He seems to me the basest specimen of the human race ever raised on this continent." Following Buchanan, the constitutional rationale for presidential power therefore changed once again. In one of the many ironies of American history, this transformation was led by a former Whig who also had been an avid opponent of presidential power.

Abraham Lincoln and the Post–Civil War Presidents

> I repeat sir, that whatever is necessary to be done for the common defense and the maintenance of the nation's life, may be done, and is required to be done by the very terms of the Constitution. And yet, sir, with a "sickly sentimentality," we have been admonished upon this floor and elsewhere that *necessity* is the plea of tyrants. Do not gentlemen know that it is only wrongfully arrogating and assuming the rightful powers of good government, that tyrants rule. Tyrants enforce their assumed authority and unrighteous decrees by arms.
>
> —Representative John Armor Bingham,
> House floor speech, 1862

Abraham Lincoln has been rewarded by historians as our greatest president. He earned this title by finding new powers in the Constitution. As Clinton Rossiter ([1948] 2011, 223) stated, "The one major institutional readjustment effected in the course of the war was the astounding expansion of the powers of the Presidency, the enforced disclosure of the hitherto well-hidden potentialities of this great office. A story of crisis government in the Civil War is the story of Abraham Lincoln." Or as Lincoln explained in his famous August 4, 1864, letter to Albert Hodges,

> I did understand . . . that my oath to preserve the constitution to the best of my ability imposed upon me the duty of pre-serving, by every indispensable means, that government—that nation—of which that constitution was the organic law. Was it possible to lose the nation, and yet preserve the constitution? By general law life and limb must be protected; yet often a limb must be amputated to save a life; but a life is never wisely given to save a limb. I felt that measures, otherwise unconsti-tutional, might become lawful, by becoming indispensable to the preservation of the constitution, through the preservation of the nation. Right or wrong, I assumed this ground, and now avow it. I had even tried to preserve the constitution, if, to save slavery, or any minor matter, I should permit the wreck of government, country, and Constitution all together.

These were remarkable sentiments from Lincoln, who repeatedly described himself as an "Old Whig." As such, he had opposed James Polk's rationale for the Mexican War. Now he realized that in times of emergency, the strict constructionist approach severely, perhaps even fatally, limited presidential power and the future of the Union. Consequently, how one interpreted the Constitution in a time of fundamental crisis was signifi-cant, as Elias Peissner (1861, 163–64) wrote at the war's commencement:

> But until it is decided whether the original Constitution or the amended one shall henceforth be the Supreme Law of the land, the proper policy of the United States Government is as clear and distinct as its right and duty.
>
> Whatever the future may bring, peace or war, the United States must—
>
> 1. Keep, defend, and in case of treason or defeat, retake, at any cost, all *national* fortifications necessary for the protection of all her old boundaries, and for common national safety.

2. She must keep, defend, and, in case of necessity, retake, at any cost, the Mississippi from its source to its mouth.

3. She must, in all other respects, leave the States undisturbed in their *internal* process of secession, unless they attack national property.

4. She must give the secessionary States time to recover from their excitement, and leave to them the same *initiatory* step in returning to the Union that they assumed in seceding from it. This must be the present course of action on the part of the United States. It follows from the constitutional principle of *Protection to National Interest and Noninterference with Local Matters* and will probably cover all future contingencies.

Rather than follow Buchanan's example, many later presidents followed the paradigms of Washington, Jefferson, Jackson, Tyler, Polk, and Lincoln, each of whom unearthed new powers from creative readings of the Constitution, such as Lincoln's remarkable discovery of the president's "war powers." As a concept, this power was not original. As Henry Ward (1962, 188) noted, "The war powers of the President were rapidly broadened. Washington realized that matters of war were primarily a responsibility of the Executive, that in time of emergency it was his duty to act swiftly and to secure the approval of Congress afterwards. The course of the Executive going its own way separate from that of the Legislature was itself a strengthening of the war powers of the national government." Lincoln, however, elevated the phrase "war powers" to a new and heightened status. As Michel Les Benedict (1991, 55) noted, "In his claims of inherent executive authority, powers implied by his obligation to execute the laws and defend the Constitution, and war powers as commander in chief, Lincoln set precedents for presidential power that remain potent today." He also expanded the powers of the federal government, as an official in Lincoln's War Department, William Whiting (1862, 13–14), noted,

If the ground-plan of our government was intended to be more than a temporary expediency,—if it was designed, according to its authors, for a *perpetual* Union,—then it will doubtless be found, upon fair examination, to contain whatever is essential to carry that design into effect. Accordingly, in addition to the

provisions for adapting it to great changes by *amendments*, we
find that powers essential to its own perpetuity are vested in the
executive and legislative departments, to be exercised *according
to their discretion*, for the good of the country—powers which,
however dangerous, must be intrusted to every government,
to enable it to maintain its own existence, and to protect the
rights of the people. . . . Therefore they gave to the President,
and to the Congress, the means essential to the preservation
of the republic, but none for its dissolution. . . . The question
whether the republican constitutional government shall now
cease in America, must depend upon the construction given
to these *hitherto unused powers.*

Because he adopted these innovations, Lincoln was referred to by his
opponents as a dictator. On this point, in his first annual message to Congress on December 3, 1861, Lincoln stated, "Monarchy itself is sometimes
hinted at as a possible refuge from the power of the people. In my present
position I could scarcely be justified were I to omit raising a warning
voice against this approach of returning despotism." And in an interview
with the *New York Times*, historian Henry Steele Commager on March 2,
1941 noted, "The Constitution, according to contemporary critics, reeled
under the blows which Lincoln administered. Here was dictatorship, here
was despotism, here was the end of American liberties. Lincoln himself
admitted he had gone pretty far and the courts later agreed with him, but
he excused his acts on the ground that it was better to save the Union
without the Constitution than the Constitution without the Union. Posterity has endorsed this view."[2]

In 2021, Noah Feldman wrote,

Who created the Constitution we have today? As a law professor, I've always thought the best answer was the framers:
James Madison, Alexander Hamilton and the other delegates
who attended the Philadelphia convention in the summer of
1787. The Constitution they drafted has since been amended
many times, of course, sometimes in profound ways. But the
document, I've long reasoned, has also exhibited a fundamental
continuity. We've always had one Constitution. I no longer
think this conventional understanding is correct. Over the
course of several years of research and writing, I've come to

the conclusion that the true maker of the Constitution we have today is not one of the founders at all. It's Abraham Lincoln.[3]

And Philip Paludan (2007, 12) wrote,

> Implicit in the discussion of Lincoln's dictatorship is the question of his constitutional philosophy. If Lincoln was a dictator then clearly he had either no respect for the Constitution or he interpreted the document in a way which made it so flexible, that it became whatever he wished it to be. Lincoln clearly had enough respect for the Constitution that he cited it often and claimed to be following it. His success in saving the union and freeing four million slaves provided an endorsement for a flexible Constitution, a "living" Constitution responsive to the needs of the people as they faced crises beyond the ken of the founding fathers. Lincoln thus could be injected into the constitutional arguments of modern times over how free judges and presidents might be to interpret the Constitution flexibly.

With the end of the Civil War, new precedents had been set for presidents to interpret their war power beyond the narrow scope of a strict constitutional construction. Yet, in a speech delivered in the Senate on December 18 and 19, 1860, future president Andrew Johnson (1860, 2) defiantly declared,

> I think that, this battle ought to be fought not outside, but inside of the Union, and upon the battlements of the Constitution itself. I am unwilling voluntarily to walk out of the Union which has been the result of a Constitution made by the patriots of the Revolution. They formed the Constitution; and this Union that is so much spoken of, and which all of us are so desirous to preserve, grows out of the Constitution. . . . It is our Constitution; it is our Union, growing out of the Constitution; and we do not intend to be driven from it or out of the Union.

It was a courageous speech. Five years later, in his first annual message (December 4, 1865) as president, Johnson's praise for the Constitution and the Framers was once again effusive: "The Constitution to which life was thus imparted contains within itself ample resources for its own preservation. . . . The parting advice of the Father of his Country, while yet President, to the people of the United States was that the free Constitution, which was the work of their hands, might be sacredly maintained." Yet Johnson's presidency evoked a strong congressional backlash against presidential power, leading to his impeachment. While his impeachment involved the president's removal power, Johnson also used the pardon and veto powers in unprecedented ways, establishing additional precedents for future presidents. Thus, even during the era of strict construction, precedents were established that would benefit presidents who sought to permanently expand the presidency's powers.

Rhetorically, the next president, Ulysses S. Grant, returned to the linguistics of strict constructionist thought. In his first inaugural address (March 4, 1869) Grant declared,

> Your suffrages having elected me to the office of President of the United States, I have, in conformity to the Constitution of our country, taken the oath of office prescribed therein. I have taken this oath without mental reservation and with the determination to do to the best of my ability all that is required of me. The responsibilities of the position I feel, but accept them without fear. The office has come to me unsought; I commence its duties untrammeled. I bring to it a conscious desire and determination to fill it to the best of my ability to the satisfaction of the people.

In his veto message on April 10, 1872, Grant referred to his constitutional *duty* rather than his *power*. Yet Grant too established new precedents. He defended the president's removal authority and made active use of the military to protect the rights of the freedmen and women of the South.

Each president, Lincoln, Andrew Johnson, and Grant, then, contributed in different ways to advancement of presidential power. With presidential power in retreat, the next presidents merely sought to restore constitutional balance, particularly regarding the appointment and removal authority. In his first annual message to Congress on December 3, 1877, President Rutherford Hayes declared, "My experience in the executive duties has strongly confirmed the belief in the great advantage the country would find in observing strictly the plan of the Constitution." And in his inaugural address (March 4, 1881), James Garfield proclaimed, "And now, at the close of this first century of growth, with the inspirations of its history in their hearts, our people have lately reviewed the condition of the nation, passed judgment upon the conduct and opinions of political parties, and have registered their will concerning the future administration of the Government. To interpret and to execute that will in accordance with the Constitution is the paramount duty of the Executive." And yet both Hayes and Garfield confronted issues related to legislative infringement on the presidential appointment power. Consequently, the struggle to define the president's authority under the Constitution was a continuing issue.

Meanwhile, Chester Arthur offered a different approach in his *Address upon Assuming the Office of President of the United States* (September 22, 1881): "The Constitution defines the functions and powers of the executive as clearly as those of either of the other two departments of the Government, and he must answer for the just exercise of the discretion it permits and the performance of the duties it imposes. Summoned to these high duties and responsibilities and profoundly conscious of their magnitude and gravity, I assume the trust imposed by the Constitution." Arthur's specific mention of "the just exercise of discretion" the Constitution "permits" at least suggested that executive power requires interpretation. Though his overall viewpoint emphasized constitutional fealty, another sliver of light appeared between the strict constructionist viewpoint and the idea that presidents can exert some undefined and additional extra-constitutional authority.

Though he issued far more vetoes than any president in history, Grover Cleveland returned to a more traditional viewpoint in his inaugural address (March, 4, 1885): "In the discharge of my official duty I shall endeavor to be guided by a just and unstrained construction of the Constitution, a careful observance of the distinction between the powers granted to the Federal Government and those reserved to the States or to the people, and by a cautious appreciation of those functions which by the Constitution and laws have been especially assigned to the executive branch of the Government." And in his inaugural address (March 4, 1889), Benjamin Harrison likewise affirmed, "My promise is spoken; yours unspoken, but not the less real and solemn. The people of every State have here their representatives. Surely I do not misinterpret the spirit of the occasion when I assume that the whole body of the people covenant with me and with each other to-day to support and defend the Constitution and the Union of the States, to yield willing obedience to all the laws and each to every other citizen his equal civil and political rights." In his *Remarks at an Afternoon Banquet at the Bennington Monument of Bennington, Vermont*, on the occasion of the centennial of the US Constitution, Harrison avowed,

> I think these centennial observances which have crowded one upon another from Concord to the centennial of the adoption of the Constitution and the organization of the Supreme Court have turned the thought of our people to the most inspiring incident in our history, and have greatly intensified and developed our love of the flag and our Constitution. I do not believe there has been a time in our history when there has been a deeper, fonder love for the unity of the States, for the flag that emblematizes this unity, and for the Constitution which cements it.

Finally, the last president to serve in the nineteenth century, William McKinley, also pledged fealty to the Constitution in his March 4, 1897 inaugural address, though unlike his predecessors, he based his commitment to the Constitution in religious terms:

> In obedience to the will of the people, and in their presence, by the authority vested in me by this oath, I assume the arduous and responsible duties of President of the United States, relying upon the support of my countrymen and invoking the guidance of Almighty God. Our faith teaches that there is no safer reliance than upon the God of our fathers, who has so singularly favored the American people in every national trial, and who will not forsake us so long as we obey His commandments and walk humbly in His footsteps.

In his fourth annual message (December 3, 1900), McKinley noted, "The Constitution, with few amendments, exists as it left the hands of its authors. The additions which have been made to it proclaim larger freedom and more extended citizenship. Popular government has demonstrated in its one hundred and twenty-four years of trial here its stability and security, and its efficiency as the best instrument of national development and the best safeguard to human rights." While McKinley rhetorically followed his immediate predecessors in exalting the Constitution, he broke with them in another, more fundamental regard. While Grover Cleveland had governed as a strict constructionist, often arguing that as president his powers were limited, particularly in relationship to the president's leadership of Congress, McKinley dismissed the idea of "a strict construction of the Constitution of the United States, that stood in opposition to internal improvements" (Taylor 2024, 329). As such, McKinley opened the door for a more active presidential role, one that relaxed the assumptions of strict constructionism. As such, he paved the way for a more active presidency for his twentieth-century successors, particularly Theodore Roosevelt, who would turn strongly toward an entirely new relationship between the president and the Constitution.

In sum, all the nineteenth-century presidents paid homage to the Constitution. William Howard Taft (1916, 139–40), in his analysis of the powers and duties of the chief magistrate, followed the nineteenth-century tradition by proposing a literal theory of the presidency: "The President can exercise no power which cannot be fairly and reasonably traced to some specific grant of power or justly implied and included within such express grant as proper and necessary to its exercise." Taft, however, was a far more activist president than his nineteenth-century predecessors. In fact, Taft was even more active than Theodore Roosevelt regarding trust-busting (Arnold 2009). By the dawn of the twentieth century, a new era in presidential power commenced. The century would see the emergence of the presidency as the central organ of the US government, but that would require a new understanding of the relationship between the presidency and the Constitution and a new interpretive framework.

Conclusion

While a strict constructionist approach constrained the power of the presidency during the nineteenth century, not all strict constructionist presidents followed the dictates of original intent. When practical politics or *expediency* dictated, Washington, Jefferson, Jackson, Tyler, Polk, Lincoln, and Andrew Johnson acted aggressively. Why then were so many of our earliest presidents committed to a strict interpretation of the Constitution? One obvious reason is that they were in the process of creating the presidency and therefore looked to the Constitution as the only available guidance. Another reason is that most of our earliest presidents were lawyers. As the former Speaker of the House Champ Clark (1920, 2:132) wrote,

> Twenty-eight men have held the presidential office, twenty-four
> of whom were lawyers and twenty-two of whom were country
> lawyers, though, truth to tell, several of them were not very
> busy with their professional duties. . . . Not only were the
> Presidents lawyers in proportion of more than five to one, but
> so were the men whom they defeated for the nominations and
> the elections. The two greatest men that ever aspired to the
> Presidency, without being able to secure even a nomination,
> were both lawyers—Daniel Webster and John C. Calhoun.

And while the inaugural addresses of fourteen of the first nineteen presidents noted a promise to defend the Constitution and/or the Union, only one out of eighteen of the most recent presidents (through Bill Clinton) did so (Lim 2002). Other qualities would be required beyond a legal degree as the country expanded and the complexity of the issues it confronted were amplified.

Chapter 7

A Living Constitution

Government is not a thing; it is not a mere matter of charters, constitutions and laws. It is a living organism. It is made up of men.

—Lincoln Steffens, *The Letters of Lincoln Steffens*

Most of the strict constructionist presidents of the eighteenth and nineteenth
centuries held firm to the Constitution's words and ideals, at least in their
rhetoric, and yet the presidents from that era who are best remembered
today are those who, through expediency or other motivations, expanded
the power of the American presidency. Historians and political scientists
generally reward presidents who expanded the powers of their office. In
contrast, it is one lesson of history that a strict constructionist approach
established a presidency that was too weak and especially ill-equipped to
deal with the realities of a nation emerging, by the dawn of the twentieth
century, as a world foreign and economic power. After the Civil War,
America experienced a rapid growth in population, the development
of an intercontinental railroad system, and the development of large
corporations that often defied the people's will. Added to these issues
were demographic changes: a quickly expanding immigrant population,
congested and crime-ridden cities, and industrialization.

The question therefore arose, Could the Constitution as it was
written in 1787 deal with the fundamental transformation occurring in
America by the late nineteenth and early twentieth centuries? If not, was
it necessary to develop an alternative to a strict constructionist approach,
one that opened the possibility of a stronger presidency? In response, a

new theory of constitutional interpretation was developed: the idea of a living constitution.

Flexible, Elastic, and Organic

> We are dealing with words that also are a constituent act, like the Constitution of the United States, we must realize that they have called into life a being the development of which could not have been foreseen completely by the most gifted of begetters. It was enough for them to realize or to hope that they had created an organism; it has taken a century and has cost their successors much sweat and blood to prove they created a nation. The case before us must be considered in the light of our whole experience and not merely in that of what was said a hundred years ago.

> —Justice Oliver Wendell Holmes,
> qtd. in *The Nature of Our Freedom*

Strict construction is but one method of constitutional interpretation. Its major limitation is that it created a series of weak presidents who were incapable of dealing with the changing realities of American life and government. Consequently, as Erwin Chemerinsky (2018, 24) later observed, "The Constitution must be adapted to the problems of each generation; we are not living in the world of 1787 and should not pretend that the choices for that time can guide ours today." Hence, as US congressman Maury Maverick (1939, 7) declared, "*We* are the people—a part of a *living constitution.*" And yet, as Supreme Court Justice Antonin Scalia (2020, 19) remarked, "So don't love the living Constitution because it will bring you flexibility and choice: it will bring you rigidity, which is precisely what it is designed for." Or as Jack Balkin (2009, 11) asked, "Is our Constitution a living document that adapts to changing circumstances, or must we interpret it according to its original meaning? For years now, people have debated constitutional interpretation in these terms. But the choice is a false one. Constitutional interpretation requires fidelity to the original meaning of the Constitution and to the principles stated by the text or that underlie the text."

America was entering a new period of constitutional interpretation, and with it there were different viewpoints regarding how to interpret the Constitution. Fueling this change in constitutional interpretation, by the late nineteenth century, America was a nation in transition, as Jonathan Baxter Harrison (1880, 2–3) explained,

> Since the civil war we have had new elements and conditions in our national life, and there have been important changes in the relative strength of certain of the old forces. We have been confronted by problems and dangers which we had thought could never arise in the path of a nation with institutions like ours. . . . We had little practical knowledge of pauperism or the labor question. Our politicians had but slight knowledge of political economy, and generally thought the study of such subjects unnecessary in our country. They knew little of financial theories or methods, or of the principles which the long experience of the civilized world had established in connection with the relation of government to the money and industries of the people. Indeed, the politicians of those days cannot be said to have studied anything very deeply besides party politics, except the slavery question; and they were fond of repeating that history had no lessons for us, and that the experience of other nations was not in any way valuable for our guidance. We rejoiced in our exemption from the ills and dangers of European society.

And historian Frederick Jackson Turner (1993, 59) noted,

> Behind institutions, behind constitutional forms and modifications, lie the vital forces that call these organs into life, and shape them to meet changing conditions. Now, the peculiarity of American institutions is the fact that they have been compelled to adapt themselves to the changes of an expanding people—to the changes involved in crossing a continent in a winning a wilderness, and in developing at each area of this progress out of the primitive economic and political conditions of the frontier into the complexity of city life.

It therefore was argued that a strict constructionist approach was incapable of adapting to these rapidly changing conditions. A new interpretive method therefore had to be capable of responding to America's newly evolving social, economic, and political conditions. This new constitutional framework also provided a rationale for an expanded presidential role.

Still, despite the allure of a more flexible, elastic and organic living constitution, adherence to strict construction did not vanish. Rather the to interpretive frameworks now did battle with each other. As Alfred Kelly, Winfred Harbison, and Herman Belz (1983, 454) identified, "In the first third of the twentieth century two separate streams of constitutional precedent and public policy existed. One [a living constitution] pointed to increasing government regulation of social and economic life, principally under federal but also involving state authority. The other [strict construction] promised to maintain traditional limitations on government in the interest of personal liberty and entrepreneurial freedom." Consequently, as Carl Swisher (1953a, 234) noted, "During the course of our constitutional history we have witnessed a running battle between the advocates of increased power in the federal government and those who would restrain the exercise of that power. The two groups alternate in ascendancy. Neither has ever been completely victorious."

While a living constitution was better able to respond to changing conditions than a strict constructionist approach, which favors stability, it also created a new problem. How can we find new meanings in the Constitution when it still contained the same words? This was an issue that troubled many constitutional scholars. Hence, Thomas Shelton (1918, xix) commented,

> A Rip Van Winkle, awakened during the second decade of the twentieth century, would be amazed by the magnificent railroads that have taken the place of the road cart, by the swift steamships that now tower above the little sailing schooner, by the splendid glow of electric lights that have made useless the humble tallow candle. . . . Bewildered at all things else standing awestruck before the portals of the temples of justice, at the bar, he would feel at home. . . . He need only become familiar with certain "statutory amendments," the crutches upon which decrepitude has hobbled these fifty years or more.

The world was changing, but the Constitution was not. Ralph Gabriel (1938, 247–48) described this evolution:

> When Americans of the new generation met to celebrate the fiftieth anniversary of their constitution, they remarked that the

experimental period had passed . . . Americans in the middle
period lived in a climate of opinion different from that of the
Founding Fathers. . . . The popular symbol of social stability
for this generation was not, as in our day, the Constitution of
the United States or the Supreme Court, but rather the village
church, whose spire pointed significantly heavenward.

In contrast, toward the end of the nineteenth century, John Alexander
Jameson (1886, 12–13) noted,

The form of our government in 1885 is widely different from
its form in 1789; the brief document called the constitution
of the United States remains the same. The executive departments have doubled in number. Their heads have decreased in
power. The spoils system has risen and declined. . . . Yet of all
these momentous changes, every one of which is an important
alteration in our constitution, the few pages of print called by
that name bear no trace.

More recently, Daniel Stid (1998, 47) noted one consequential president
of this era:

[Woodrow] Wilson focused his dispute with the Founders
and the defenders of their Constitution on this point. He
believed that the Founders' attempt to establish a permanent
constitutional order was ultimately mistaken because that order
had naturally and inevitably evolved over time. Government,
Wilson argued, "is accountable to Darwin, not to Newton. It is
modified by its environment, necessitated by its tasks, shaped
to its functions by the sheer pressure of life." Wilson was not
arguing against the idea of constitutionalism. He only wanted
to expand it to encompass what he held to be the fact as well
as the promise of the living constitution.

While the Constitution is the foundation of our governmental system,
through historical practice and new methods of constitutional interpretation, presidential power expanded beyond the Framers' original intent.
It is therefore as if we have two different constitutions: one with words

that must be strictly interpreted according to their original meaning, and a second that provides only general guidance and hence greater flexibility. Each has dramatic implications for presidential power.

What then is the fundamental logic of a living constitution, and is it so open-ended that it provides limited checks on the power of the federal government? Certainly, as noted, the Framers could not have been aware of the many changes—technological, social, political, economic, moral, demographic, international, and geographical—that transformed the basic issues confronting Americans. If so, how could a constitution that was written for a nation of thirteen states cradling the Atlantic, with a rural economy and a population of less than four million, including slaves, deal with the many evolving issues of a later century? On this point, Timothy Farrar (1867, viii–ix) mused,

> The difference between a community of three millions of people, scattered along a narrow belt of sea-coast, inclosed by impenetrable forests; and thirty or forty millions, occupying half a continent, and pursuing all the objects, and by all the arts and means, which the reason or passions, the interest or ambition, the virtues or vices, of men could invent,—must soon make itself apparent in the inevitable development of those powers of regulation which were expressly designed and intended to provide for just such increasing claims for their exercise. At no period of our history has the trial of our institutions, and their adaptation to expand with the augmented demands of a great and increasing nation, been so thoroughly tested, and so cautiously and intelligently accepted, as during the late civil war, which can hardly yet be considered at an end.

According to proponents of a living constitution, the answer was that a strict construction of the Constitution could not address these many new issues. How then could a new theory be introduced? Once again, constitutional ambiguity provided a basis for reinterpreting the essential meaning of the Constitution. As Victoria Nourse (2018, 12–13) explained, "The most obvious and basic feature of our Constitution is that its text is sparse. Economy of expression distinguishes a constitution from a legal code. No linguist denies that, faced with skimpy texts, interpreters are likely to interpolate or add to the meaning of raw text when seeking to apply the text to a particular context." And if we accept a strict constructionist interpretation of the Constitution, how do we account for the expansion of presidential power over time? Future Supreme Court justice George Sutherland (1910, 373) offered the following enigmatic interpretation: "At one extreme of the controversy have been those who asserted that the government possessed only such powers as were expressly conferred by the Constitution strictly construed. . . . Between those who, upon the one extreme, would put the government of the United States in a constitutional strait-jacket, and those who, on the other hand, would turn it adrift upon a boundless sea of unrestricted power, all varieties and shades of opinion are to be found." If original intent placed the Constitution in a straitjacket, were the Framers' words the only method for understanding presidential power?

Is the Constitution Still Relevant?

This does mean that the powers of the government are not fixed, but it does mean that they are not fixed within any narrow or rigid bounds.

—George Sutherland, *Constitutional Power and World Affairs*

With the beginning of the Civil War, scholars asked an even more fundamental question: Is the Constitution relevant anymore? Timothy Farrar (1862) asked this question, as did many later observers who believed the Civil War was evidence of the Constitution's failure (see also Godkin 1898). Civil War historian James Garfield Randall (1929, 7–8) advised, "Is there, after all, anything 'sacred' about the Constitution? Time has amply tested the wisdom and even the remarkable power of divination of the statesmen of 1787, but that is not to say that the product of their labor has a right to outlive its practical usefulness." If the Constitution as written in 1787 was no longer relevant, then a new theory was required to justify governmental action. But could this new theory ignore the Constitution from which it derived? These indeed were complex questions.

To understand its derivation, the idea of a living constitution can be traced back to at least the decade before the American Civil War. On page 2 of its October 16, 1851, edition, the *New York Times* maintained that the US Constitution should be flexible. The idea then gained broader expression during the Civil War. Theophilus Parsons (1861, 6) referred to the "organic powers and functions of the State," while Sidney Fisher in 1861 wrote in his diary, "No organic law can be framed with a provision specifically applicable to every case that may occur in its practical administrations" (Paludan 1975, 182). An official in Lincoln's War Department, William Whiting (1862, 11) wrote,

> Some treat that frame of government as though it were a cast-iron mould, incapable of adaptation or alteration—as one which a blow would break in pieces. Others think it a hoop placed around the trunk of a living tree, whose growth must girdle the tree, or burst the hoop. But sounder judges believe that it more resembles the tree itself,—native to the soil that bore it,—waxing strong in sunshine and in storm, putting forth branches, leaves, and roots, according to the laws of its own growth, and flourishing with eternal verdure.

In 1865, Orestes Brownson (2003, 94, 109, 143–44, 157–58) noted, "The constitution drawn up, ordained, and established by a nation for itself is a law—the organic or fundamental law, if you will, but a law, and is and must be the act of the sovereign power." Still, Brownson added a caveat:

> Though the constitution of the people is congenital, like the constitution of an individual, and cannot be radically changed, without the destruction of the state, it must not be supposed that it is wholly withdrawn from the action of the reason and free-will of the nation, nor from that of individual statesmen. All created things are subject to the law of development, and may be developed either in a good sense of in a bad; that is, may be either completed or corrupted.

After the Civil War, Joel Parker (1869, 103) stated, "I am no partisan of President [Andrew] Johnson, but I honor him with all my heart for his firmness in endeavoring to sustain and vindicate the organic law of the republic." Two decades later, James Bryce (1888, 1:25) wrote, "Yet, after all deductions, it ranks above every other written constitution for the intrinsic excellence of its scheme, its adaptation to the circumstances of the people, the simplicity, brevity, and precision of its language, its judicious mixture of definiteness in principle with elasticity in details." The following year, J. L. Clark Hare (1889, 1:v) explained the political implications of an elastic Constitution:

> If an apology is needed for the publication of a book on a subject which has been treated by many able pens, it may

perhaps be found in the growth of the Constitution of the United States which, though confined by its character as a written instrument to certain bounds, was yet intended "to live and take effect in all successions of ages." The delegates who sat in the federal convention wisely, therefore, limited themselves to enumerating the powers conferred on the government and the objects for which they were to be exercised, and left the task of devising the means to those who were to administer the system which they had framed. The government of the United States, consequently, has a capacity for adaptation "to the various crises of human affairs," which is rarely found in written constitutions. Although it is the same government which went into operation a century ago, it has undergone the development incident to maturity, and can act with an assured strength which was necessarily wanting at the commencement.

In a lecture delivered in 1898, Albert Beveridge (1968, 4) noted,

As the necessities . . . for all time could not possibly have been foreseen by the men who wrote the Constitution, it follows that they could not have intended to confine the purposes of the Constitution and the powers it confers to the necessities of the people of 1789; that they so wrote it that it might meet the requirements of the people for all time. If that is so, it follows that the Constitution must steadily grow, because the requirements of the people steadily grow.

In an *Atlantic Monthly* article, Alfred Dennis (1905, 535) concluded, "The old conflict between the unyielding law and the living organism has resulted, as it must always result in any expanding life, in a victory for the organism." And Theodore Burton (1908, 212) wrote, "Our constitution was framed in the days of the spinning wheel, the stage coach and the sail boat. Times have changed, and there have been world-wide revolutions in the relations between governments and the people. Laws and constitutions must change with the times. Prime ministers, legislators and presidents must change their views to meet the changing conditions, else they fail of their duty."

While scholars discussed this new interpretive framework, the Supreme Court entered the fray in the case of *South Carolina v. U.S.*, 199

U.S. 437 (1905), where it attempted to deal with the contradiction between a written constitution and changing circumstances:

> The Constitution is a written instrument. As such its meaning does not alter. That which it meant when adopted it means now. Being a grant of powers to a government its language is general, and as changes come in social and political life it embraces in its grasp all new conditions which are within the scope of the powers in terms conferred. In other words, while the powers granted do not change, they apply from generation to generation to all things to which they are in their nature applicable. This in no manner abridges the fact of its changeless nature and meaning. Those things which are within its grants of power, as those grants were understood when made, are still within them, and those things not within them remain still excluded.

The court's decision was an attempt to balance the needs of a changing nation with the Constitution's original words. Hence, while the powers were specified, the actions of the three branches could respond to change, but only if the power to do so existed. However, the court identified that the "language is general." These words suggest some room for ambiguity and therefore for different possible interpretations of those powers. As such, *South Carolina v. U.S.* did not definitively settle the question. Later, in a dissenting opinion in the case of *Gompers v. U.S.*, 233 U.S. 604 (1914), Oliver Wendell Holmes wrote, "Provisions of the Constitution of the United States are not mathematical formulas having their essence in their form, but are organic living institutions transplanted from English soil. Their significance is not to be gathered simply from the words and a dictionary, but by considering their origin and the line of their growth." But these decisions raised as many questions as they settled. Among them was the power of the presidency.

The Perils of a Living Constitution

From Founding Fathers to modern scholars, the study of the Presidency has been "greased" with doubt and ambiguity. . . . Indeed, the Founding Fathers "could not have foreseen" the structure of the twentieth-century Presidency.

—Emmet John Hughes, *The Living Presidency*

One explanation for the growth of presidential power is that, as with the need for an adaptable living constitution, the office transformed in response to changes in the nation's political and economic conditions. Societal factors created the need for a new method of constitutional interpretation and increased presidential power. Meawhile, constitutional ambiguity provided the opportunity for both of these developments. Regarding the transformation in constitutional law, Christopher Tiedeman (1890, 79–80, 155, 156) declared,

> In the early days of our national life, the discussions in constitutional law were chiefly confined to a consideration of the more formal provisions, which determined the methods of governmental procedure, and defined the limits of each branch of the government, the all-important question being the relative superiority of the National and State governments. . . . But a change has since then come over the political thought of the country. Under the stress of economical relations, the clashing of private interests, the conflicts of labor and capital, the old superstition that government has the power to banish evil from the earth, if it could only be induced to declare the supposed causes illegal, has been revived; and all these so-called natural rights, which the framers of our constitutions declared to be inalienable, and the violation of which they pronounced to be a just cause for rebellion, are in imminent danger of serious infringement.

But while flexibility provided the basis to deal with changing circumstances, it also raised questions: How can presidential power be constrained within *accountable* barriers if the president's powers are flexible? Saikrishna Prakash (2020) argued that while a strict interpretation may indeed have made the government "a rope of sand," the theory of a flexible Constitution provided the basis for a vast and potentially dangerous expansion of presidential power. Bruce Ackerman (2016, 483) likewise granted, "Even in today's degraded environment, the Progressive vision of the president has provided Americans with a certain focus for their political concerns. . . . Yet this progressive victory has come at a heavy price. Now that presidents have transformed themselves into voices of the People, they have increasingly used this authority to act unilaterally to execute the national will—especially when the House or Senate is controlled by the opposing party."

If the Constitution is living, then the presidency is as well. Thus, we can extrapolate Prakash's and Ackerman's concerns by placing the word president before any of these terms: flexible, elastic, organic, or living, as in a flexible presidency, an elastic presidency, an organic presidency, or a living presidency. The danger here is that if something is flexible, it can stretch into a form that lacks any strictly definable limits by adding new powers as well as responsibilities. Similarly, if there is an elastic presidency, it too can stretch. But if you stretch it too far, will it snap when a president exerts too much power, or in the case of Donald Trump and the insurrection of January 6, 2020, as well as his autocratic campaign promises in his 2024 presidential run, when the very ideals of democracy are undermined? And if presidents have virtually complete immunity for all "official acts," are there any barriers to abuses of power? Certainly, some of the Framers and Anti-Federalists thought so, as they warned of executive tyranny. And if there is an organic presidency, is it likely to grow and replicate, and perhaps even mutate its very form over time, as do the cells in our bodies? Will it evolve into an autocratic or strongman presidency? Likewise, if the presidency is an organism, does it rigidify as it ages and can it be corrupted by illness? If there is a living presidency, can it die, that is, can it become a presidency in name only? And finally, is there a point where we either no longer require a presidency or, more likely, it morphs into an institution that is autocratic and a veritable danger to the Constitution?

The answers to these questions are not self-evident. And yet, as James Woodburn and Thomas Moran (1919, 183, 185) stated, "Any constitution that will not bend must break. It must change and expand with the expansion and growth of the country for which it was made. It must accommodate itself to changed conditions or it will be laid aside. If a constitution is too rigid, its provisions will be violated or it will be treated with such loose construction as to be equivalent to evasion." As judges employ a textual analysis of the Constitution, are they creating a governmental system that is too rigid, based as it is on the understanding of words written more than two centuries ago? And if a strict constructionist presidency can break if it is too rigid, could a living constitution alternatively develop a presidency that is too powerful? What do the words of the Constitution mean if they can be continually redefined? Finally, is there any room between these two extremes: a rigid constitution and a flexible one, a Constitution that can establish an accountable presidency that can meet the changing needs of the nation?

If we step away from the theoretical issues for a moment and simply examine history, we find that since its creation, the presidency has indeed been flexible. It has been elastic, it has evolved and changed forms (e.g., the development of the institutional presidency or the modern and imperial presidencies) like an organism, and perhaps it is becoming too powerful, leading to its decay, death, or rebirth as an entirely different and potentially autocratic institution. For Prakash, then, the living constitution begets a living presidency, which begets the potential for a greater and more dangerous threat of presidential abuses of power, including dictatorship and tyranny. Or as Jackson Main (1987, 59) warned when he cited James Burgh (a Whig politician and the author of a popular 1775 book, *Political Disquisitions*), "Power is of an elastic nature, ever extending itself and encroaching on the liberties of the subjects."

There are observable consequences of the living presidency. Over time, new presidential responsibilities and greater public expectations have been added to president's agenda. These expectations in turn have led to a gap between what the public expects from its leaders and what those leaders can accomplish, resulting in lower presidential approval ratings and an increased probability that an incumbent will not be reelected (Stimson 1976–1977; Waterman, Silva, and Jenkins-Smith 2014). Concomitantly, it has encouraged an accretion of presidential command and unilateral authority, as presidents search for new means to extend their influence (Moe 1985; Moe and Howell 1999; Howell 2003). As presidents demand more power to satisfy public expectations, this trend, at times, has threatened democracy. As demonstrated by the Nixon and Trump presidencies, or by Lyndon Johnson's mistruths that led our nation into a terrible war in Vietnam, democracy also is elastic, and it can be stretched even to the breaking point. We therefore need to consider these sentiments from Walter Lippman (1913, 12–13, 21, 104, 184): "This is no slack philosophy, for the chance is denied by which we can lie back upon the perfection of some mechanical contrivance. Yet in the light of it government becomes alert to a process of continual creation, an unceasing invention of forms to meet constantly changing needs." Lippman added this caveat:

> The invisible government is malign. But the evil does not come from the fact that it plays horse with the Newtonian theory of the constitution. What is dangerous about it is that we do not see it, cannot use it, and are compelled to submit to it. The nature of political power we shall not change. If that is

the way human societies organize sovereignty, the sooner we face that fact the better. For the object of democracy is not to imitate the rhythm of the stars but to harness political power to the nation's need.

Lippman also noted, "In the face of clotted intricacy in the subject-matter of politics, improvements in knowledge seem meager indeed. The distance between what we know and what we need to know appears to be greater than ever. . . . The worship of the constitution amounts, of course, to saying that men exist for the sake of the constitution. The person who holds fast to that idea is forever incapable of understanding either men or constitutions."

In 1927, the former US solicitor general James Beck (1927, 6, 13, 18) added,

> The proof that ours is a changing Constitution can be attested by a fact, which few intelligent students of our history would deny, that, if the framers of the Constitution were to revisit the "glimpses of the moon," and now study their handiwork as it has been developed since 1787, they would in many respects fail to recognize the product of their labors. . . . Is there, then, nothing in the Constitution that remains unaltered? Have we built our government upon shifting sands?

The answer, apparently, is yes. Beck then raised serious concerns regarding the powers of the three branches. Furthermore, is the Constitution even recognizable? On this point, Randall (1929, 6) wrote,

> Where a constitution has this quality of adaptability, it becomes especially important to distinguish between the constitution on paper and the construction in reality. The practical application of any document prescribing a fundamental law necessarily proceeds by a sort of "trial and error" system, and while certain clauses of the constitution are enormously expanded in their application, others are not put into practical effect. A stranger to our institutions would, in fact, obtain only an incorrect and artificial conception of our government if he confided his attention to the Constitution itself.

If there is constitutional ambiguity and if interpretation becomes a matter of trial and error, who decides what is or is not necessary?

And if times change, as they always do, must the power of our governmental institutions also change? Is that an inevitability? According to Charles Merriam (1931, 12) the answer is yes: "Each generation has produced a new constitution of government with fundamental changes in spirit and form." Hence, the very concept of presidential power was transformed during the Great Depression and World War II, two crises where Franklin Roosevelt invoked broad executive power. Once again, as during the Civil War, the nation's survival was at stake. In such circumstances, then, should the power of the presidency be constrained within a nineteenth-century straitjacket, or are FDR and George W. Bush following the 9/11 terrorist attacks justified in broadening the scope of presidential power? If so, should these precedents only relate to periods of extraordinary danger? Can presidential power in so-called normal times be separated from precedents set during crises? Unfortunately, there are no easy answers to these fundamental questions.

As Supreme Court Justice William Brennan (Prakash 2020, 99) noted in a speech delivered in 1985, "The ultimate question must be: What do the words of the text mean in *our time*? For the genius of the Constitution rests not in any static meaning it might have had in a world that is dead and gone, but in the adaptability of its great principles to cope with current needs. What the constitutional fundamentals meant to the wisdom of the other times cannot be the measure to the vision of our time." Hence, presidential power has expanded to "cope with current needs." But in turn, can we ignore the Framers' intent? As Bruce Ackerman (2007, 1754) wrote, "While the effort to make the Constitution into something truly wonderful is an ever-present temptation, the problem with this high-sounding aspiration is obvious: there are lots of competing visions of liberal democratic constitutionalism, and the Constitution shouldn't be hijacked by any one of them. The aim of interpretation is to understand the constitutional commitments that have actually been made by the American people in history, not the commitments that one or another philosopher thinks they should have made."

The clear and continuing problem is that constitutional interpretation would be facilitated if the document's meaning was clear. However, given the Constitution's ambiguity, the words written in 1787 are open to reinterpretation, while a living constitution leaves wide open the question of precisely which powers should be assigned to a flexible, elastic, organic, and living presidency. If our Constitution is indeed flexible, we need some reasonable method of defining the acceptable parameters of presidential power. And yet, at the present time, no such boundaries exist. Therefore, if we rely on the idea of a living constitution, we must accept that it comes with both the benefits and dangers.

Chapter 8

The Unitary Executive Theory

Since the executive is an independent branch of the government, it follows that in the performance of his duties the President is subject to the control of no other department or body. The grand theory of the constitution makes him a co-equal in the tri-partite organization. He draws his power from the same source as the national legislature and the judiciary; he is answerable to neither; his discretion is absolute as that of any legislator, and more so than that of any judge; no other branch of the government may rightfully interfere with him in the exercise of that discretion. Hence it follows that the President is privileged from the jurisdiction and process of any court. He cannot be arrested for any reason whatsoever, and is answerable for misconduct only before one tribunal—the Senate of the United States as a court of impeachment.

—William Backus Guitteau, *Government and Politics in the United States*

In his postpresidential autobiography, Theodore Roosevelt (1913, 357) famously proposed an entirely new interpretation of presidential power:

I declined to adopt the view that what was imperatively necessary for the nation could not be done by the President unless he could find some specific authorization to do it. My belief was that it was not only his right but his duty to do anything that the needs of the Nation demanded unless such action was forbidden by the Constitution or by the laws . . . I did not usurp power, but I did greatly broaden the use of executive power.

Or as Roosevelt said, "The new Nationalism regards the executive power as the steward of the public welfare" (Arnold 2009, 1). Roosevelt's stewardship theory "asserted that the chief executive possessed both the power and the duty to take whatever action would best serve the nation, without need for constitutional or statutory authorization" (Calabresi and Yoo 2008, 24–25). And yet, "the Constitution says very little about what powers might be available to a stewardship presidency" (Rudalevige 2013, 4).

The voices opposing Roosevelt's legal reasoning were loud and proximate. In the case of *Kansas v. Colorado*, 206 U.S. 46, 89–90 (1907) the Supreme Court decided, "We have no officers in this government, from the President down to the most subordinate agent, who does not hold office under the law, with prescribed duties and limited authority." In a response to the *Kansas* decision, the *Yale Law Journal* ("Powers of the Federal Government" 1907, 49) commented, "The soundness of the doctrine reiterated by this case has long been apparent; and the enunciation of such views at this time is opportune as serving to bring vividly before the country the temper and conservatism of the Supreme Court. The forcible emphasis laid by the court upon the fact that ours is a government of delegated powers may serve as a significant hint to the numerous advocates of a further extension of Federal power." Roosevelt's handpicked successor, William Howard Taft (1916, 139–40), similarly rejected the stewardship theory:

> The true view of the Executive functions is, as I conceive it, that the President can exercise no power which cannot be fairly and reasonably traced to some specific grant of power or justly implied and included within such express grant as proper and necessary to its exercise. Such specific grant must be either in the Federal Constitution or in an act of Congress passed in pursuance thereof. There is no undefined residuum of power which he can exercise because it seems to him to be in the public interest. . . . The grants of Executive power are necessarily in general terms in order not to embarrass the Executive within the field of action plainly marked for him, but his jurisdiction must be justified and vindicated by affirmative constitutional or statutory provision, or it does not exist.

Still, Taft (1916, 157) did not view the presidency as a weak office:

The Constitution does give the President wide discretion and great power, and it ought to do so. It calls from him activity and energy to see that within his proper sphere he does what his great responsibilities and opportunities require. He is no figurehead, and it is entirely proper that an energetic and active clearsighted people, who, when they have work to do, wish it done well, should be willing to rely upon their judgment in selecting their Chief Agent, and having selected him, should entrust to him all the power needed to carry out their governmental purpose, great as it may be.

In his autobiography, Calvin Coolidge (1984, 94–95) adopted a middle ground between these two interpretations:

The President exercises his authority in accordance with the Constitution and the law. He is truly the agent of the people, performing such functions as they have entrusted to him. The Constitution specifically vests him with the executive power. Some Presidents have seemed to interpret that as an authorization to take any action which the Constitution, or perhaps the law, does not specifically prohibit. Others have considered that their powers extended only to such acts as were specifically authorized by the Constitution and the statutes. This has always seemed to me to be a hypothetical question, which it would be idle to attempt to determine in advance. It would appear to be the better practice to wait to decide each question on its merits as it arises. Jefferson is said to have entertained the opinion that there was no constitutional warrant for enlarging the territory of the United States, but when the actual facts confronted him he did not hesitate to negotiate the Louisiana Purchase. For all ordinary occasions the specific powers assigned to the President will be found sufficient to provide for the welfare of the country. That is all he needs.

Regarding these different views of presidential power, Clarence Berdahl (1921, 14) agreed that Taft "reflected the better opinion when he stated the true view of executive power." Yet Berdahl also noted, "Altho the weight of authority upholds the contention that executive power in the United States is limited definitely to the powers enumerated in the Constitution, or clearly implied there from, the interpretation of those enumerated powers is frequently such as to give to the President an extraordinary and practically undefined range of authority." Again, ambiguity was a key issue in providing the parameters of presidential power.

The Supreme Court entered the fray when it ruled in *Trump v. United States* (603 U.S. 2024)—reversed the precedent set in *Kansas v. Colorado* and created the potential for an even more powerful presidency, one virtually protected from prosecution for "official acts," principally those involving the president's constitutional authority. As Chief Justice John Roberts wrote, "Under our constitutional structure of separated powers, the nature of Presidential power entitles a former President to absolute immunity from criminal prosecution for actions within his conclusive and preclusive constitutional authority." No constitutional justification was offered for this ruling. Given the vast ambiguity involved in each of the Article II presidential powers and duties (Waterman, forthcoming), presidents therefore can greatly redefine their powers, such as by claiming vast authority under the vesting clause. As such, presidential power may be virtually unlimited!

History provides us with insights into this possible future presidency. By the turn of the twentieth century, the presidency was becoming a more powerful office, and in time, the dominant branch of government. That power has expanded ever since. How and why did this fundamental transformation occur? What change took place in the text of the Constitution? Other than the twelfth amendment, which impacted the presidential election process; the twenty-second amendment, which limited presidents to two terms in office; and the twenty-fifth amendment, which dealt with presidential disability and succession, not a word in that document related to presidential power had changed. No revolution had taken place, although one can refer to the change in constitutional interpretation toward a living constitution as a constitutional coup d'état. And while the 1920s witnessed a return to a more restrained presidency, particularly during Calvin Coolidge's tenure, following the advent of the Great Depression even Herbert Hoover became a more activist president than his nineteenth-century predecessors (Stein 1969).

Franklin Roosevelt's inaugural address (March 4, 1933) then represented a full-throated endorsement of a wide-ranging vision of executive power: "In the event that the Congress shall fail to take one of these two courses, and in the event that the national emergency is still critical, I shall not evade the clear course of duty that will then confront me. I shall ask the Congress for the one remaining instrument to meet the crisis—broad Executive power to wage a war against the emergency, as great as the power that would be given to me if we were in fact invaded by a foreign foe." Like his eponymous predecessor, Franklin Roosevelt was not shy about assuming a range of new presidential powers. *The President's Committee on Administrative Management: The Brownlow Committee 1937* (Mosher 1976, 131–32) later advised, "The preservation of the principle of full accountability of the Executive to the Congress is an essential part of our republican system. In actual practice the effectiveness of this accountability is often obstructed and obscured, and sometimes is defeated by the processes of diffusion, processes which are at work not only in the Executive Branch but in the Congress itself."

Presidents were gaining greater control over the executive branch even before the *Hoover Commission Report: Commission on Organization of the Executive Branch of the Government* (Hoover 1949, 3–4) advised,

> If disorder in the administrative machinery makes the executive branch of the Government work at cross purposes within itself, the Nation as a whole must suffer. It must suffer—if its several programs conflict with each other and executive authority becomes confused—from waste in the expenditure of public funds, and from the lack of national unity that results from useless friction. An energetic and unified executive is not a threat to free and responsible government, as Alexander Hamilton pointed out in "The Federalist" (no. 70).

There was indeed a practical need for presidents to exert greater control over the executive branch, especially as the administrative state expanded after the turn of the century and especially during the presidencies of Franklin Roosevelt and Lyndon Johnson. And Congress, through both delegations of its power to the executive and inactivity in response to executive initiatives, actively encouraged this expansion of presidential power, which induced Justice Felix Frankfurter to declare in his concurring opinion in *Youngstown Sheet & Tube Company v. Sawyer* (1952):

> Deeply embedded traditional ways of conducting government cannot supplant the Constitution or legislation, but they give meaning to the words of a text or supply them. It is an

inadmissibly narrow conception of American constitutional law to confine it to the words of the Constitution and to disregard the gloss which life has written upon them. In short, a systematic, unbroken, executive practice, long pursued to the knowledge of Congress and never before questioned, engaged in by Presidents who have also sworn to uphold the Constitution, making as it were such exercise of power part of the structure of our government, may be treated as a gloss on "executive power" vesting in the president by [Section] 1 of Art. II.

Yet the broad power that Theodore Roosevelt and Franklin Roosevelt invoked is but a whisper of that office's great power today. In the twentieth and twenty-first centuries, if there is a bias in our constitutional interpretation, it favors the expansion of presidential power. The question for many scholars then is, Has presidential power expanded too much, and if so, is it now such a danger that it threatens to create the very tyranny many in the Founding generation feared? As Peter Shane (2022, 5, 6) warned in the wake of the Trump presidency, "What we are facing . . . is an accelerating threat of dangerous claims for presidential power based on poor legal arguments that, in turn, reflect an approach to constitutional interpretation that itself is not justified. . . . If you think it likely that presidential unilateralism is your surest path to political success, you will find the legal arguments on behalf of presidential unilateralism appealing." And Shane was writing before the Supreme Court's ruling in *Trump v. US*.

Consequently, another theory of presidential power has important implications, especially as presidents rely on unilateral and command authority to a far greater extent than at any time in our nation's history. While the idea of a living constitution provided fodder for the growth of presidential power, as Saikrishna Prakash (2020) noted, it was not specifically designed for that purpose and it also opened the door for other institutions, such as the administrative state, to acquire additional authority that could thwart presidential initiatives. As the need for increased presidential power became apparent in the post–World War II era, a theory exclusively dedicated to presidential power awaited a later day. What then is this new theory? According to Christopher Yoo, Steven Calabresi, and Anthony Colangelo (2004–2005, 601) the *unitary executive theory* (UET) is based on three basic concepts:

The president's power to remove subordinate policy-making officials at will, the president's power to direct the manner in which subordinate officials exercise the discretionary executive power, and the president's power to veto or nullify such officials' exercises of discretionary power. We do not claim that there is consensus among all three branches of government as to the president's control of the removal power and the powers to direct and nullify. Rather, we claim only that there is no consistent, three-branch custom, tradition, or practice to which presidents have acquiesced permitting congressionally-imposed limits on the president's sole power to execute the law.

While the Framers used the term "unitary" at the Constitutional Convention, and they created a unitary executive, the Framers made no explicit argument in support of a powerful presidency. As an opponent of the UET, Laurence Tribe (2008, 19) stated, "If the Constitution is a nearly sacred text, there is an unbridgeable gap between the one set of *Words* that constitutes it and the mere collection of *words* of those who interpret and apply it." We therefore need to examine more than just the Constitution's words to determine its meaning. Historical practice is also a guide, and Steven Calabresi and Christopher Yoo (2008) provide an extensive historical record of the president's removal power to control the cabinet and other administrative agencies. Still, as John MacKenzie (2008, 5–6) wrote,

> The case for the unitary executive consumes hundreds of heavily footnoted books and law review pages. Among the complex arguments, two themes recur among many. One is "energy in the executive," comprising strong general and enumerated, and sometimes "inherent," powers. The other is a defense to any control by Congress based on constitutional checks and balances. Both arguments claim attention, but each fails on examination. The term *unitary* does not surface in and around the 1787 constitutional convention. Some framers, Hamilton especially, spoke of "unity"—not to broaden the sweep of executive power but rather to describe the framers' early choice of a single-person executive as opposed to some multi-headed committee or counsel.

For additional support, unitarians turn to Alexander Hamilton. And yet, as James Madison wrote, "No man's ideas were more remote from the plan than his were known to be" (MacKenzie 2008, 6). Rather than a monarch for life, the establishment of a unitary or single executive did not prevent the Framers from establishing various checks and balances designed to constrain presidential power, such as placing many of the king's prerogative powers with the legislative branch. And finally, regarding the original intent of the Framers, while the final vote to have a single executive was 7 states to 2, various members vehemently disagreed. The Framers' intent was far from unified. Consequently, a much stronger defense of the unitary executive can be found in Hamilton's later essays related to the Neutrality Proclamation and, as I noted in chapter 6, Andrew Jackson's defense of the president's powers after he was censured by the Senate. It is in these exchanges that we find early evidence for the UET.

Furthermore, basic concepts of the UET have long been discussed by scholars. As John Fairlie (1905, 16) delineated,

> Not only does the President exercise much influence over the personnel of the administration through his powers of nomination and removal, but he can also control and direct in large degree, the actions of the administrative officials. The constitutional provisions which authorize this power are those vesting the executive power in the President, and requiring him to take care that the laws are faithfully executed. But the principal means by which the President can make his control effective is the power of removal, the possibility of which will usually secure obedience to his orders, while if any official persists in disobedience his removal permits the appointment of some one who will carry out the President's wishes.

One also can find support for the unitary executive in the Decision of 1789, wherein Representative James Madison took a leading role in promoting the president's removal authority under the Article II vesting clause. Furthermore, as Steven Calibresi, Christopher Yoo, and Laurence Nee (2004) and Calibresi and Yoo (1997) argued, broad removal authority can be found among virtually every single president, including the nineteenth-century strict constructionists. They do not, however, note that presidents beginning with Ulysses S. Grant favored civil service reform, which effectively reduced their removal authority over tens of thousands of federal employees.

Calibresi and Yoo's (2008) version of the UET is limited to the president's removal authority and the president's authority to interpret the law through *coordinate construction,* a concept I discuss later in this chapter. Presidents thus should have the ability to control the bureaucracy, including civil servants and bureaucrats serving in agencies that are presently isolated from presidential control, such as the Federal Reserve Board and the independent regulatory commissions. No president, unitarians contend, can manage the executive branch unless they have unfettered control over the entire branch. Dividing authority undercuts both presidential responsibility and accountability. While this version of the unitary executive is controversial, there is yet another, even more expansive iteration of the theory. Its principal proponent is John Yoo (2009b, 1937):

> Calabresi and [Christopher] Yoo . . . define the unitary executive in a much narrower way than the current controversy over presidential power would demand. They define the unitary executive as founded on the president's constitutional authority to command or remove all subordinate officials. As to whether the president possesses any other inherent or implied powers, the authors proclaim themselves to be 'agnostic.' Focusing on the procedure, rather than the substance, of executive power may make sense as a matter of lawyerly argument. . . . But it is unclear as a matter of theory that we can separate the independence of the executive branch from its substance.

John Yoo's theoretical approach confers vastly greater power on the presidency, but there are similarities between the two models. Yoo (2020, 34) believed, "The president alone bears the constitutional duty to execute federal law. That responsibility requires presidential control over all federal offices who assist him in carrying out the law. Condemning presidential interference in law enforcement is akin to criticizing justices for interfering in Supreme Court cases." As a defense, Yoo cited chief justice and former president William Howard Taft's decision in *Myers v. U.S.,* 272 U.S. 52 (1926). Yoo (2020, 48) also agreed with Steven Calibresi and Christopher Yoo when he noted that the Constitution "concentrates all of the executive power in one person: the president. All other officials are subordinates who exist only to assist the president in carrying out his constitutional responsibilities."

Thus far, the two schools of unitary thought remained on the same page. However, John Yoo's further defense of presidential power included a claim that presidents can move first by initiating war without a congressional declaration, thus invalidating an important constitutional power. John Yoo (1996, 172) wrote that the separation of powers doctrine did not provide a basis for including Congress as the sole initiator of war:

> Historical practice . . . has contrasted starkly with these constitutional arguments. Congress has issued a declaration of war only five times in its history. The post-1945 era has borne witness to a litany of undeclared wars and an even longer list of less significant uses of the military. The President has initiated conflict, often without any formal signs of congressional approval, and certainly without a declaration of war. With few exceptions, the federal courts either have refused to hear constitutional challenges to these wars, or have upheld the propriety of the executive action.

To determine the just application of the declaration clause, we must again determine what the word *declare* meant to the Framers. John Yoo (2020, 183, 185–86; see also Yoo 2004, 796; 2006b, 23) stated, "First, the Constitution does not treat 'declare war' as synonymous with the power to begin military hostilities. . . . Nowhere does the constitutional text provide that the commander-in-chief power must wait for a declaration of war before its use. . . . Placement of the power to declare war," along with the grant of letters of marque and reprisal and rules concerning captures on land and water, "is significant, because they clearly involved the power of Congress to recognize or declare the legal status and consequences of certain wartime actions and not the power to authorize those actions. . . . When the Framers employed 'declare,' they usually used it in a juridical manner, in the sense that the courts 'declare' the state of the law or the legal status of a certain event or situation." John Yoo (2020, 190–91, 193–94) continued, "Eighteenth-century Americans could use the phrase 'declare war' to mean beginning military hostilities. But 'declare war' also held the narrower legal meaning of setting international legal relations. . . . As with the Constitution, 'engage' in war contained the broadest grant of power to begin hostilities; 'declare' refers to a narrower subset of the war power that does not even make an appearance in our nation's first constitution [the Articles of Confederation]. . . . [Moreover] Hamilton never defined the power to declare war [in *The Federalist no. 69*], nor did he raise it as a legislative check on the executive. . . . By granting Congress the power to declare war, the Framers enabled it to serve notice to American citizens, neutral nations, and intended or actual foreign enemies of the existence of a state of war."

Yoo (2002, 1640) based his interpretation on the idea that "the Constitution creates a flexible system of war of powers." Therefore, he seemed to invoke the flexible, living constitution as a justification, though in fact he disavowed that approach. He noted that "pro-Congress scholars have not advanced a convincing textual defense of their views, and that they have been unable to explain the historical evidence that favors presidential control over the initiation of military hostilities." In response to the charge that he promoted an unreasonable aggrandizement of presidential power, Yoo (2020, 175, 180) replied, "Congress has an arsenal of authorities to block presidential war-making, such as control over the size and shape of the military. . . . The president's power is not unilateral, but the check on it does not arise from the Declare War Clause. Instead, the legislature's main restraint on presidential power comes from the power of the purse."

As John Yoo noted, the United States has committed the military more than 130 times since the ratification of the Constitution. And of course, the number of military involvements continues to grow year by year. Yoo was not finished, however. He also argued that presidents have vast emergency power. The subject of the president's emergency and war powers was described by Donald McCoy (1991, 122) as "a murky area, one in which the courts have been reluctant to act." Yoo had no such reservations. And Yoo asserted that presidents as the chief executive even have the authority to violate the law with impunity, unless Congress decides to impeach the president, a position now upheld by the Supreme Court's ruling in *Trump v. US*. And regarding the faithful execution of the law, W. Trickett (1907, 848–49) advised, "Is there any indication that the makers of the Constitution intended that the Executive, in any of its branches, administrative or judicial, should have the right to abort a law by refusing to it the effects whose sequence only gives it the quality of law? The debates in the Federal Convention are equivocal." Hence, combined with constitutional ambiguity, John Yoo's approach vastly expanded presidential power beyond the idea that presidents have broad removal or supervisory authority over the executive branch. It can and has been characterized as establishing more than an imperial presidency: an autocratic presidency, a point that was a concern in the final months of Donald Trump's presidency as the embattled president was urged to declare martial law to seize voting machines throughout the nation. John Yoo (2020) explicitly did not endorse such actions, though his defense of the Trump presidency certainly raised eyebrows among those concerned with the possibility of an autocratic presidency.

Not surprisingly, many notable scholars disagreed with John Yoo's legal reasoning, as well as that of Steven Calabresi and Christopher Yoo. Lawrence Lessig and Cass Sunstein (1994) referred to the theory as an ahistorical myth. Meanwhile, Andrew Coan and Nicholas Bullard (2016, 794) wondered why the court fixated on this removal power as a basis for the UET: "The removal power has no special textual significance. That is not to say that the removal power has no plausible constitutional foundation. But the removal power has no greater constitutional foundation than a more general freedom to execute the laws free from congressional interference. The Court, however, has refused to scrutinize Congress' other levers of influence over presidential administration." In fact, the removal power is one of the Constitution's silences; it is never recognized explicitly in that document.

Consequently, Jeffrey Crouch, Mark J. Rozell, and Mitchel A. Sollenberger (2020, 150) opined, "The unitary executive theory is largely about power. Whether Democrat or Republican, any president wants to have as much flexibility as possible to address the many concerns that find their way to the Oval Office. At the same time, the president is just one actor in a system of separated powers and checks and balances that the framers designed to frustrate the ability of any single branch of the federal government to unilaterally impose its will on the other two." And Stephen Skowronek, John Dearborn, and Desmond King (2021, 24, 27) offered, "The unitary executive is another provocative proposition with political currency in contemporary discourse. It too is a plausible conjecture, and it too is casting a long shadow over modern American government. As with the concept of the Deep State, a great deal can be pulled under the umbrella of a unitary executive, so long as the rubric is not scrutinized too closely." As the authors continued,

> The claim is not that there is too much power in the executive branch but rather that not enough of it is under the president's direct control. The idea is that presidents should be able to deploy the executive power for their own purposes, with accountability only to the people who put them in the office. By denying administrative integrity of its own, the assertion of the unitary executive magnifies the personal, populist, charismatic character of presidential power. It converts

the widely recognized authority of the president to supervise the executive branch into a power of command and control. Under its auspices, the transfer of "executive power" from one incumbent to another—long associated with the creation of a "new administration"—swells into a warrant for remaking the executive branch wholesale, in the new incumbent's image.

Responding to their critics, Steven Calabresi and Christopher Yoo (1997, 1472, 1457, 1462–63, 1469) wrote, "We start with the premise . . . that the Framers set up a strongly unitary executive and that this is normatively appealing." They added, "over the past 208 years a powerful tradition has grown up whereby Presidents have consistently defended the prerogatives the text of the Constitution originally gave them and that public choice theory suggests they should have. . . . We claim only that there is no consistent three branch anti-unitarian custom, tradition, or practice that Presidents have acquiesced in that trumps the constitutional text and the original design." But the authors made a remarkable admission when they discussed their methodology:

> We do not claim to be historians, and we do not claim here to have produced original, ground-breaking research. Although we have canvassed many original sources, we have relied heavily on the famous and principle secondary works that discuss each of the presidencies or historical epochs. . . . We thus approach this historical research project as constitutional lawyers and not as legal historians. We are interested in history in this project, but only in the way that lawyers are interested in history.

In other words, they are lawyers representing their case before the jury of the American public, without reference to any counterarguments that may undercut their defense. Henceforth, it was acceptable for the authors to ignore the Constitutional Convention's debates: "Although the Framers chose to create an independent, co-equal, and strongly unitary executive branch of government, many of the issues surrounding the distribution of powers among the three branches of the federal government were not directly addressed in the Constitution." How then can a theory be based on sound constitutional principles if its concerns were not directly addressed at the Constitutional Convention?

The authors likewise admitted that they found inconsistent evidence for their theory during the period between Andrew Jackson and Abraham Lincoln, an era of strict constructionist presidents (Calabresi and Yoo 2003). And the material I cite in chapter 6 demonstrates that many nineteenth-century presidents had a firm commitment to a strict constructionist approach, even if they did maintain the right to remove officials from office or initiate action based on expediency. Hence, if the UET is not founded on constitutional principles, but rather on a selective reading of history, what are the limits of presidential power, and can the Constitution be read in any manner that justifies any limits to such power? As I will discuss, if under the idea of coordinate construction presidents have the same right to interpret laws as the courts or Congress, is there any dividing line between the authority of the three branches of government or does it represent yet another invitation to struggle? And are presidents magnifying their authority in contravention of the Constitution's checks and balances by separating power in their own favor? To address some of these issues, Calabresi and Yoo (1997, 1469) provided a caveat:

> Not every presidential claim of executive power deserves to be given weight by all who believe in the legitimacy of three-branch construction of the constitution. Some presidential assertions of power are extraordinary and are associated with unusual Presidents or unusual national crises that seemed to require an extraordinary response. We deal here with a claim of presidential power that is as old as the Republic and that has been asserted to one degree or another by virtually every occupant of the presidential office. That kind of defensive claim about the scope of presidential power does deserve the attention of those who believe in three-branch constitutional review.

What then are the extraordinary responses and where can they be found in the Constitution? The Constitutional Convention debated only one issue related to the UET: the decision to adopt a unitary versus a plural executive. Other than that, there is little evidence from the convention itself regarding the Framers' intent, and even this decision was merely the choice between having one president and a council of presidents. Since we cannot find support for the UET at the 1787 convention, what then is the constitutional basis for the UET? Presidential expert Richard Pious (2010, 164) answered,

In brief, the theory consisted of several propositions: there is an "executive branch" that the president controls through "the executive power"; all executive functions are to be exercised by the president and subordinates; Congress may not infringe on the "core functions" of the presidency (war, foreign affairs, intelligence, national security); and the president's powers are anterior and superior to those of Congress, which should play a perfecting role in executive initiatives. Under this theory Congress could not, through framework legislation such as the War Powers Act, the Intelligence Oversight Act, or the Foreign Intelligence Surveillance Act, regulate or limit presidential executive power in these areas.

Much of the UET therefore depends on how far the president's authority extends to interpret the Constitution. What then have various observers of the US Constitution had to say about this matter?

Who Interprets the Constitution?

Mr. Jefferson announced the principle that each department of the government was the sole judge of the extent and character of its powers under the Constitution,—or, in other words, was an independent interpreter of that instrument. In his private and public political writings he advocated this view with great earnestness, and acted upon it, in some instances, while President. After him President Jackson reiterated the same dogma, brought it into bold relief, and based much of his official action upon it. . . . In our own times the dogma under consideration has been asserted by some public men and political writers who are warm partisans of the intrinsic and absolute nationality and sovereignty of the United States. . . . What ruinous, destructive consequences would immediately result, if it should be practically admitted that the several departments might independently judge and decide as to the extent and character of the powers conferred by the Constitution! The collisions would as readily and as often arise between the Executive and the legislature as between either and the Judiciary.

—John Norton Pomeroy, *An Introduction to the Constitutional Law of the United States*, 88, 90

Of paramount importance to the parameters of presidential power is the issue of who interprets the Constitution. Charles and William Beard (1930, 23) offered this viewpoint:

> Who . . . makes the Constitution an instrument of control, by answering the thousands of questions which it leaves unanswered? According to the formula of the child's book in civics, it is the Supreme Court of the United States, or at least a majority of the judges, that "interprets" the Constitution. But even a superficial examination of the instrument itself reveals a fatal weakness in this contention. . . . Moreover, the Court has repeatedly ruled that some cases are political in character and lie outside its jurisdiction. If for the sake of argument, however, it be admitted that the Supreme Court in the final analysis answers all questions arising under the Constitution, then it is proper to ask, What Supreme Court? Judges die. Times change. New Presidents are elected and nominate new judges to fill vacancies on the bench. . . . Sometimes new judges reverse the opinions of their predecessors, give an opposite meaning to the Constitution. Since this is so, it follows that nothing is settled definitely by saying that the Constitution is the document as expounded by the Supreme Court.

Justices are appointed by the president, with the advice and consent of the Senate. Hence, as Alpheus Mason and William Beaney (1978, xiii) wrote, "The Supreme Court has always consisted largely of politicians, appointed by politicians, confirmed by politicians, all in the furtherance of controversial political objectives. From John Marshall to Warren Burger, the Court has been the guardian of some particular interest and the promoter of preferred values." As political questions swirl around the current Supreme Court, we can extend Mason and Beaney's comment to the John Roberts court.

Thomas Mason (1959, iii) even referred to the Supreme Court "as a *participant* in the political process." Hence, is there a justification for other institutions to interpret the law, as well as the Supreme Court? Regarding this question, Supreme Court Justice Arthur Sutherland (1965, vii) counseled,

> The Supreme Court is by no means the only source of our constitutional theory. Lower federal courts decide important

questions that never go above the Courts of Appeal. Analysis of many issues requires study of State cases: constitutional doctrines which would seem, from federal opinions, to have died a generation ago may still have a flourishing life in State Supreme Courts, often sheltered by "adequate state grounds" which preclude review in the Supreme Court of the United States. And non-judicial writings are much relied on by courts in deciding such mingled questions of policy and law as those of due process, or equal protection, or the validity of State action in the presence of the Commerce Clause. For a book undertaking to marshal all this material, a corps of indexers would be needed more than an author.

Henceforth, the Supreme Court is not the only interpreter of the Constitution. Even if it was, all courts do not share the same constitutional theories when deciding cases. For example, Richard Posner (2008, chap. 1) identified nine different theories that justices employ when they interpret the Constitution. Meanwhile, James Garfield Randall (1929, 2) wrote, "Constitutional history is no subject for the legalists. It is no subject for one whose interest in the forms of law blinds him to the essential forces that work through law." In his battles with President Andrew Johnson, Senator Charles Sumner declared in 1872, "I take it that each branch of the government can interpret the Constitution for itself. I think that Congress is as good an authority in its interpretation as the Supreme Court, and I hope that Congress, in its legislation, will proceed absolutely without any respect to a decision [Dred Scott] which has already disgraced the country, and which ought to be expelled from its jurisprudence" (Wilson 1902, 3:430).

In his extraordinary analysis of American politics, James Bryce (1917, 1:262) opined,

It is . . . an error to suppose that the judiciary is the only interpreter of the Constitution, for a certain field remains open to the other authorities of the government, whose views need not coincide, so that a dispute between those authorities, although turning on the meaning of the Constitution, may be incapable of being settled by any legal proceeding. This causes no great confusion, because the decision, whether of the political or the judicial authority, is conclusive so far as regards the particular controversy or matter passed upon.

Furthermore, as Felix Frankfurter and James Landis (1928, 299) added, Congress can alter the authority of the court and has done so several times. Carl Swisher (1943, 4–5; also see Swisher 1958) likewise advised, "Judicial decisions alone provide an inadequate basis for an understanding of constitutional development. . . . The executive branch of the government, like Congress and the judiciary, plays an important part, both positively and negatively, in the development of the Constitution." Hence as Cass Sunstein (2006, 2583) wrote, presidents play a key role in constitutional interpretation. Cornelia Pillard (2004, 677), a judge on the DC Court of Appeals, had a different view: "The executive, in my view, has failed fully to meet the challenges of interpreting and applying the Constitution on its own. . . . As the Office of Legal Counsel's 'torture memos' illustrate, there are substantial risks associated with executive decisionmaking on fundamental questions of executive power and individual rights."

In sum, the question of who interprets the Constitution is a far more complex issue than we normally teach in American Government PS 101 classes. And as Walter Murphy, James Fleming, and Sotirios Barber (1995, 18) noted, "Questions of *who* shall interpret have had and will continue to have obvious and critical implications for the country. . . . And differences in institutional competence, and procedure may make important differences in the values and policies various branches of government accept as more or less fundamental and the capacity of one branch to persuade and the others to agree to that ranking."

Further complicating matters is the issue at hand. As Thomas Cooley (1891, 37–38) wrote, "It is not in the nature of institutions to remain stationary, however they may be formulated and declared, especially when the government has within itself the power to determine its own jurisdiction, and to solve in its own favor at discretion all questions of disputed authority. . . . The gradual energizing of federal authority has been accomplished quite as much by the course of public events as by the new amendments to the Constitution." Three decades later, the dean of Harvard Law School, Roscoe Pound (1923, 1), wrote, "Law must be stable and yet it cannot stand still. Hence all thinking about law has struggled to reconcile the conflicting demands of the need of stability and of the need of change." As a result, speaking about the Constitution in 1948, Owen Roberts (1953, 411–12), a former Supreme Court justice, remarked, "I think it clear . . . that we live today under a very different system from that contemplated by those who drafted our Constitution."

Varying interpretations by different political actors have contributed to constitutional ambiguity and as our country developed, this has led to different interpretations of the Constitution. As Carl Swisher (1953b, 311) stated in his 1947 Gaspar G. Bacon Lecture at Boston University, "A constitution is like a garment on the body politic. However well the garment may initially fit, it may become a misfit if it is made to stretch or shrink without corresponding changes in the body, or if the body expands or loses bulk beyond the range of the easy adjustment of cloth. While the pattern of our constitution has changed hardly at all, the body upon which it is worn has expanded and changed beyond recognition. It is as if a boy of four had changed into a man of forty."

Consequently, multiple dimensions are involved in the simple question, Who interprets the Constitution? Is it the courts? If so, what are the consequences for precedent if new justices are added who offer a different interpretation or if Congress alters the Supreme Court's size or jurisdiction? Can the state courts advance their own legal reasonings, even if they conflict with those of the Supreme Court? Do presidents, Congress, and even the public have a say in constitutional interpretation? What impact does time have on the nature of constitutional interpretation, or should it have any impact at all? And how do different modes of interpretation impact the power of the presidency? Once again, while the US Constitution was written in 1787, debated and ratified throughout 1788, implemented in 1789, and amended eleven times during the 1790s, as Akhil Amar (2021, 529–30) noted,

> The task after 1800 was no longer to ponder what the text *should* say and should mean, but rather to discern what the terse text, including amendments, truly did *say* and mean. . . . The key questions for the truly faithful constitutional interpreters in the early nineteenth century were questions such as these: What words did the document in fact use and not use? Why had the document used certain words and rejected other words? What were the overarching purposes that animated the document? What had the American people in fact agreed to, and why had they done so when they said "yes, We do," in the pivotal year of 1788? How should the words of 1788 be read in light of the amendments of the 1790s and vice versa? To the extent that the document contained ambiguities, should the early

precedents and practices that emerged in the First Congress and the Washington administration carry any weight, and if so, how much weight and what kind of weight?

The issue of interpretation therefore is fundamental to the UET and to the expansion of presidential power.

Coordinate Construction

The unitary executive is all alone in the spotlight. But is this a sufficient guarantee of his government's responsibilities? Might we not object to [Alexander] Hamilton that a unitary executive might attempt all sorts of things that run contrary to the wishes and interests of many people, perhaps a majority, so long as he might reasonably gamble that his misdeeds would not be deemed sufficient grounds for removing him from office? This is a natural question, but the person who asks it does not see how remarkably far-reaching Hamilton's argument is. In its fullest implications, Hamilton's argument for executive unity implies that unity is not only the necessary condition for responsible government, but the sufficient condition, as well.

> —John Koritansky, "Alexander Hamilton's
> Philosophy of Government and Administration"

It is interesting to note that political science and history were late to the debate over the unitary executive. A vast and interesting literature in legal journals predates their concerns. Almost immediately, legal scholars directed their attention to an October 21, 1986, Tulane University speech delivered by Ronald Reagan's second attorney general, Edwin Meese, entitled "The Law and the Constitution."[1] In his speech, Meese drew a distinction between the Constitution and constitutional law:

Once we understand the distinction between constitutional law and the Constitution, once we see that constitutional decisions need not be seen as the last words in constitutional construction, once we comprehend that these decisions do not necessarily determine future public policy—once we see all of this, we can grasp a correlative point: that constitutional interpretation is not the business of the Court only, but also, and properly, the business of all branches of government. The Supreme Court, then, is not the only interpreter of the Constitution. Each of the three coordinate branches of government created and empowered by the Constitution—the executive and legislative no less than the judicial—has a duty to interpret the Constitution in the performance of its official functions. In fact, every official takes an oath precisely to that effect.

As such, the attorney general introduced the controversial idea of *coordinate construction*: the idea that presidents have the power to interpret the law, no matter that Article III can be interpreted as granting that authority to the judicial branch. Certainly, presidents had done so through their use of the veto power. In various veto messages, James Madison, James Monroe, Andrew Jackson, John Tyler, and James Polk argued that various legislative actions, particularly those designed to provide federal funding for roads and canals, were unconstitutional. But such interpretations were limited to the veto power and based on a strict constructionist interpretation of the Constitution. Could, by inference, presidents extend coordinate construction to other matters? George Washington did so when he issued the Neutrality Proclamation. Even though only Congress has the right to declare war, Washington warned Americans that the nation was at peace and therefore must act under the applicable international laws. And as the administrative state expanded, presidents redefined their own authority, expanding control over executive branch activities, such as via a more aggressive use of the appointment and removal powers. They also ignored any legislation designed to limit presidential power, such as any constraints placed by Congress on the president's removal power, or the limitations imposed by the War Powers Act.

What then is the textual support for coordinate construction? One source is *The Federalist no. 49*: "The several departments being perfectly co-ordinate by the terms of their common commission, neither of them, it is evident can pretend to an exclusive or superior right of settling the boundaries between their respective powers." It also can be found in *Federalist no. 72*: "The persons therefore, to whose immediate management these different matters are committed, ought to be considered as the assistants or deputies of the chief magistrate; and on this account, they ought to derive their offices from his appointment, at least from his nomination, and ought to be subject to his superintendence." Likewise, Hamilton's essays on the presidency noted the need for "energy in the executive," which is not possible if presidents cannot control the executive branch. Furthermore, the written opinions clause of Article II, Section 2, can be read as providing presidents with superordinate authority over their department heads, and by inference, other members of the executive branch.

Still, as Ron Chernow (2004, 259) wrote, "Notwithstanding his preference for a strong president, Hamilton applauded many checks on presidential power. . . . In the *Federalist Papers*, Hamilton was quick to applaud checks and balances as those powers themselves, as he continued his lifelong effort to balance freedom and order." Donald Brand (2006, 160) also believed that Hamilton did "not intend to preclude congressional supervision of administration through the lawmaking (and budgetary) process." And as Jeremy Bailey (2008, 454, 456) wrote, "Because the defenders of the unitary executive rely on originalist arguments to make their case, it is no surprise that a common characteristic is that they rely on Alexander Hamilton. Hamilton, after all, is perhaps the most famous American defender of executive power." And yet, Hamilton's views conflict with those of James Madison and Thomas Jefferson. So which Founders should we trust? If we desire a stronger presidency, then Hamilton is the obvious model.

As Garry Wills (2011, 212) noted, "The unitary theory was originally created for a narrow purpose—to let the President get rid of those pesky regulations. To the horror of its first inventors, they found in time that they had been Frankensteins birthing a monster." Consequently, Steven Calibresi and Christopher Yoo (2008, 19–20, 21) commented,

> Despite the [Bush] administration's attempt to tie claims of emergency powers to the theory of the unitary executive, the inherent executive power that it asserts has little to do with the framers' decision to vest the executive power in a single person rather than a plural body or with ensuring that the president possesses sufficient power to exercise supervisory authority over the entire executive branch. As a result, the Bush administration's claims of broad, inherent executive power standing on a footing in terms of the Constitution's text and ratification history that is very different from the basis of the theory of the unitary executive that grew out of the frustrations spawned by the ineffective plural executives of the early state constitutions as well as the "executive by committee" established under the Articles of Confederation.

Steven Calibresi and Christopher Yoo therefore disagreed with John Yoo's more expansive UET, though they did not repudiate the idea of coordinate construction. To many legal scholars, political scientists, and historians, coordinate construction is legal dynamite. If a president and their legal team can decide what the Constitution means, can they also have the authority to state, as John Yoo did, that Congress solely has a technical right to declare war but presidents are free to initiate it? Could this expanded authority provide the president with the right to recommend torture, in violation of the Geneva Conventions? And as John Yoo claimed, can presidents violate the law with impunity, except for the threat of impeachment? As Lionel McPherson (2011, 146–47) opined,

> I am skeptical that the president has distinctive authority to engage in illegal activities, even when the stakes are highest. . . . Positive duties are not necessarily accompanied by special authority to violate the law in order to satisfy them . . . the very notion of "executive discretion"—namely as a function of distinctive authority to justify illegal activities on grounds of national security—is conceptually unstable. If and when there is a morally extraordinary rationale for violating the law, no special authority to violate the law would appear to be required.

As noted, the Supreme Court decided this matter in the case of *Trump v. US*. Hence, presidents do have a legal right to violate the law. As such, the court validated one of John Yoo's arguments in favor of the UET.

Meanwhile, the Tulane speech was not the first time Meese introduced his new theory of coordinate construction. In a speech delivered on November 15, 1983, before the Federalist Society Lawyers Division, Meese (1988, 158–59) stated, "The Constitution is not a legislative code bound to the time in which it was written. Neither, however, is it a mirror that simply reflects the thoughts and ideas of those who stand before it." Meese then noted,

> We know that those who framed the Constitution chose their words carefully. They debated at great length the most minute points. The language they chose meant something. Their words were studied with equal care by the state ratifying conventions. This is not to suggest that there was unanimity among the framers and ratifiers on all points. . . . Nobody got

everything he wanted. What is more, the framers were not clairvoyants—they could not foresee every issue that would be submitted for judicial review. Nor could they predict how all foreseeable disputes would be resolved under the Constitution. The point is, however, that the meaning of the Constitution can be known.

In fact, as was noted in chapter 2, the Framers spent but a few days discussing the president's constitutional powers, and they did not debate every word or clause in detail. Furthermore, most of the state ratifying conventions spent little time debating Article II (see Waterman, forthcoming, chapter 2). And as noted in chapter 3, constitutional scholars, historians, political scientists, and political practitioners throughout American history have noted the ambiguity of both the Constitution and Article II. Ambiguity combined with coordinate construction therefore provides the basis for presidents to entirely redefine their authority. Consequently, compelling evidence and arguments refute Meese's main point. Yet Meese (1988, 160–61) continued,

> The Constitution remains a document of powers and principles. . . . The approach of this Administration is rooted in the text of the Constitution as illuminated by those who drafted, proposed, and ratified it. . . . Our approach understands the significance of a written document and seeks to discern the particular and general principles it expresses. It recognizes that there may be debate at times over the application of these principles, but it does not mean these principles can not be identified. . . . In the main, a jurisprudence that seeks to be faithful to our Constitution—a jurisprudence of original intention, as I have called it—is not difficult to describe. Where the language of the Constitution is specific, it must be obeyed. Where there is demonstrable consensus among the framers and ratifiers as to the principle stated or implied by the Constitution, it should be followed. Where there is ambiguity as to the precise meaning or reach of a constitutional provision, it should be interpreted and applied in a manner so as to at least not contradict the text of the Constitution itself.

Again, what Meese did not acknowledge is that Article II is replete with ambiguous language. Therefore, under the idea of coordinate construction, since most presidents prefer more power than less, they are likely to interpret their authority in the broadest terms possible. With regard to coordinate construction, the Office of Legal Counsel (OLC) plays a critical role (Saltzman 2010). Jack Goldsmith (2007, 9) described, "Though little known outside the government, OLC holds an exalted status within it as the chief advisor to the President and the Attorney General about the legality of presidential actions. This small office of twenty-two lawyers determines whether the government's most important and sensitive plans are lawful, and thus whether they can be implemented." Billy Monroe (2021) referred to the OLC as the "President's Law Firm." Adoree Kim (2018, 791–92) concluded, "The OLC does not offer 'detached, apolitical legal advice' in practice. Rather, the OLC is deeply and systematically deferential to the President." Moreover, the OLC "is frequently asked to opine on issues of first impression that are unlikely to be resolved by the courts a circumstance in which OLC's advice may effectively be the final word on the controlling law."

As a result, the OLC provides presidents with legal cover and, when necessary, a rationale for acts that otherwise would be illegal. As such, the UET and Meese's speeches in defense of coordinate construction drew immediate criticism from the legal community, particularly his comments about the need to follow original intent. In an October 15, 1985, address at Georgetown University, Supreme Court Justice William Brennan (1988, 168–69) responded,

> There are those who find legitimacy in fidelity to what they call "the intentions of the Framers." In its most doctrinaire incarnation, this view demands that Justices discern exactly what the Framers thought about the question under consideration and simply follow that intention in resolving the case before them. It is a view that feigns self-effacing deference to the specific judgments of those who forged our original social compact. But in truth it is little more than arrogance cloaked as humility. It is arrogant to pretend that from our vantage we can gauge accurately the intent of the Framers on application of principle to specific, contemporary questions. All too often, sources of potential enlightenment such as records of the ratifying debates provide sparse or ambiguous evidence of the original intention. Typically, all that can be gleaned is that the Framers themselves did not agree about the application or meaning of particular constitutional provisions, and

hid their differences in cloaks of generality. Indeed, it is far from clear whose intention is relevant—that of the drafters, the congressional disputants, or the ratifiers in the States—or even whether the idea of an original intention is a coherent way of thinking about a jointly drafted document drawing its authority from a general assent of the states.

In a reply to Justice Brennan, Lino Graglia (1988, 180) wrote, "To state that judges should interpret the Constitution as intended by those who wrote and ratified it ('the Framers') is only to state the basic premise of our political-legal system that the function of judges is to apply, not to make, the law. Indeed, it would be difficult to say what interpretation of a law means if not to determine the intent of the lawmaker." Henry Steele Commager (1988, 199) then commented,

> Original intention means the intention of those who were living in 1787. Concealed in Mr. Meese's seductive and extraordinary phrase is also the question that Justice Oliver Wendell Holmes raised when he assured us that "the life of the law has not been logic, it has been experience." The felt necessities of the time, the prevalent moral and political theories, institutions of public policy, even the prejudices that judges share with their fellow men, all have had a good deal more to do than syllogisms in determining the rules by which men should be governed.

And Leonard Levy (1988, 1) reminded us,

> James Madison, Father of the Constitution and the Bill of Rights, rejected the doctrine that the original intent of those who framed the Constitution should be accepted as an authoritative guide to its meaning. "As a guide in expounding and applying the provisions of the Constitution," he wrote in a well-considered and consistent judgment, "the debates and incidental decisions of the Convention can have no authoritative character." The fact that Madison, the quintessential Founder, discredited original intent is probably the main reason that he refused throughout this life to publish his "Notes of Debates in the Federal Convention," incomparably our foremost source for the secret discussions of that hot summer in Philadelphia in 1787.

The Framers were not alone in this regard. Saul Cornell (1999, 24) advised, "Many of the key terms associated with the Anti-Federalists critique of the Constitution, such as 'aristocracy,' 'democracy,' or 'virtue,' were interpreted in radically different ways by various groups within the Anti-Federalist coalition." In other words, constitutional ambiguity is a factor that should be considered when interpreting the Constitution's meaning. It also challenges understandings, not only of the UET and the living constitution but of original intent. As Donald Drakeman (2020, 10–11) noted, through the publication of the *OLP Sourcebook* in 1987, the "rationale" was switched "from the Framers' intentions to the original public meaning" of the Constitution's words. As such, originalism took a back seat to a textual analysis, based largely on dictionary definitions of the words as they were used in 1787. But do dictionary definitions adequately express the meaning of the words the Framers used? Were they merely parroting phrases used in various state constitutions? And did the public interpret these words in the same manner as the Framers? Such difficulties arise when we examine the meaning of the vesting clause and its reference to "executive power," a fundamental constitutional provision expounded by UET advocates.

Further complicating matters has been the inaction of the courts. They often avoid ruling in cases involving so-called political questions, such as issues of national security (Fisher 2017). As Cecil Crabb Jr. and Pat Holt (1989, 1) wrote, "Throughout American history, the judiciary has largely been content to play a passive role in the foreign policy process. When the Supreme Court has concerned itself with foreign policy questions (which it does rarely), it has nearly always taken one of two positions: Either it has declared foreign policy issues to be political questions that are not susceptible of resolution by the judicial system, or it has forcefully upheld the exercise of executive power." While J. Peter Mulhern (1988) defended the political question doctrine, if the courts recuse themselves, can the president then decide the facts of the case? Under the UET's theory of coordinate construction, the answer is yes, and presidents do, in practice, when the courts do not act. Still, as Rachel Barkow (2002, 240) wrote, "That notion—that some constitutional questions ultimately must be decided by the political branches and not through judicial review—is beginning to seem antiquated. Yet the demise of the political question doctrine is of recent vintage, and it correlates with the ascendency of a novel theory of judicial supremacy."

Consequently, the argument in favor of executive power, as Edward Corwin (1953, 54) commented, "Has shifted somewhat since the early nineteenth century." When Corwin wrote, it no longer relied "exclusively, or even chiefly, on the opening clause of Article II." Rather, as Corwin continued,

> To the terminology of political disputation in the Jacksonian period it is indebted for such concepts as "residual," "resultant," and "inherent" powers. Thanks to Lincoln, it is able to invoke the president's duty to "take care that the laws," i.e., all the laws, "be faithfully executed," and his power as commander-in-chief of the armed forces. Of more recent origin is the quite baffling formula of an "aggregate of powers vesting in the President by the Constitution and the laws." The chief constitutional value which overextension of presidential power threatens is, of course, the concept of a "government of laws and not of men"—the "Rule of Law" principle.

And while unitarians claim broad power derived from the executive vesting clause, Calabresi (1994, 1394) argued that the Article II and III vesting clauses "gain most of their content from the specifications that follow." The clauses derive "almost the whole of their discernable meaning either from (1) the subsequent language of the Articles which appear or from (2) the other Vesting Clauses and the language that follows." A. Michael Froomkin (1994, 1426) responded, "This reads like a retreat from the suggestion that the Vesting Clause of Article II is a broad grant of unenumerated powers (among which we find the removal power) to the view that the Vesting Clause is 'limited and unusual' grant of unenumerated powers."

A key question then is whether the original intent of the Framers is consistent with the UET. Prakash (1993, 1015) argued,

> The Framers had an extremely sophisticated understanding of how federal law would be administered. . . . No one else but the unitary executive had been given "the executive power" or the authority and responsibility "to take Care that the Laws are faithfully executed." It should come as no surprise that the Framers considered the President the Chief Administrator and all other administration officials as merely his assistants. Any other arrangement would detract from the unitary, responsible executive the Framers sought to construct.

And yet, if that were the case, why did the Framers place the appointment of "inferior officers" in hands other than the president's? That decision contradicts the notion of a unitary executive with power over the entire executive branch.

Many legal experts cite originalism, but their expansive view of presidential power is inconsistent with the strict constructionist approach I described in chapter 6. As such, this new form represents a different form of originalism, or what Eric Segal (2018, 82; see also Lessig 2019) referred to as the *new originalists*, while Sotirios Barber and James Fleming (2007) refer to *broad originalism*. It also raises another issue. Again, is it possible to apply an originalist perspective to the presidency given the constitution's inherent ambiguity?

On one point there is clear constitutional support. The Framers, in devising a scheme of checks and balances, were intent on ensuring that none of the three branches could infringe upon the powers of the other. Hence, the president was provided with the veto power. As Justice Antonin Scalia wrote in *Freytag v. Commissioner*, 501 U.S. 868 (1991), "It was not enough to repose the power to execute the laws (or to appoint) in the President; it also was necessary to provide him with the means to resist legislative encroachment upon that power. The means selected were various, including a separate political constituency, to which he alone was responsible, and the power to veto encroaching laws . . . or even to disregard them when they are unconstitutional." The full court was not willing to go as far as Scalia, however, and in the case of *Hamdan v. Rumsfeld*, 548 U.S. 557 (2006), Scalia filed a fiery dissent. Of this opinion, Steven Calabresi and Gary Lawson (2007, 1047) wrote,

> Justice Scalia's (and the Bush Administration's) views of Article II, which emphasize that Congress cannot derogate from the constitutional grants of authority to the President, are in considerable tension with their views on Article III, which seem to contemplate a wide congressional power to derogate from the constitutional grants of authority to the Supreme Court. Justice Scalia's position on Article II is correct, and it applies as well to Article III. Congress can determine whether the Supreme Court will have original or appellate jurisdiction over federal cases, but it cannot determine whether the Supreme Court will have jurisdiction at all. The Constitution has already done that.

What then was the intent of the UET? Was it merely a theory to describe the Framers' original intent or was it another tool promoting the accretion of presidential power? According to Crouch, Rozell, and Sollenberger (2020, 2–4), the UET is "a normative view of the presidency used not to describe presidential behavior but to justify it." As to its constitutional underpinnings, they continued,

> The fundamental tenets of the unitary executive theory are not supported by core, constitutional principles of separation of powers and checks and balances. Nor is it a theory for which supporters can marshal empirical evidence that the American government currently, or ever, has adopted it as a working model that advances republican principles. Despite these realities, the unitary executive theory has increasingly become an influential tool for shaping presidential behavior and has paved the way for presidents such as Donald Trump to take aggressive unilateral actions.

Stephen Skowronek (2009, 2103) offered another constitutional point of view:

> There may be good reasons to alter the terms and conditions under which presidential power extended its reach in the twentieth century and American government as a whole reoriented its operations. But the time has long passed when doing so in the name of reclaiming the wisdom of the Framers was a straightforward proposition. The more sober option for twenty-first-century governance may be the one that reckons with political development more directly and follows the example of the institution builders who transformed American government in the nineteenth and twentieth centuries. They did not resist new claims of presidential power, but neither did they accept them before staking out fresh claims of their own.

An Autocratic Presidency?

A new construction of the presidency gains currency when it legitimizes the release of governmental power for new political purposes. . . .

The power of ideas is registered, first and foremost, in ideas about power. . . . The phalanx of legal scholars currently debating the claims of the unitary executive is indicative not only of the high political stakes at issue in the moment at hand, but also of the high premium to be paid in the twenty-first century for a coherent theory of American government.

—Stephen Skowronek, "The Conservative Insurgency and Presidential Power"

William Howell (2023, 25) noted, there are two "competing imperatives" of presidential power: "Deep distrust of concentrated power and recognition of the need for effective, energetic governance." These competing imperatives are likewise at the heart of attempts to understand how much power the presidency has and how much power it *should* have. Steven Calabresi and James Lindgren (2006, 2611–18, 2622) offered one viewpoint: "We suggest that when political power is examined more broadly, Presidents and their parties generally have less power in the United States than commentators realize. We believe the President today is less a king than a lightning rod. Indeed, the constitutional and practical weakness of the presidency is, if not a threat to American democracy, at least a worrisome limitation on it." They argued, in this pre-Trump essay, "No American President has ever seriously threatened our democratic system of government, but democracy may be undermined when people regularly mobilize for and participate in a presidential election that is likely to produce on balance the exact opposite policy consequences from those for which the people have voted. Rather than worry about imaginary threats of dictatorship, we ought to be worried today about an electoral system that may regularly be frustrating the popular will."

Alternatively, the word *authoritarianism* is now widely applied to presidents. The Bush-Cheney administration, as well as that of Barack Obama, was accused of authoritarian tendencies. And yet, as Henry Giroux (2011, 436) wrote, "If it is true that a new form of authoritarianism is developing in the United States, undercutting any vestige of a democratic society, then it is equally true that there is nothing inevitable about this growing threat. The long and tightening grip of authoritarianism in American political culture can be resisted and transformed." The Trump presidency, however, and his attempts to overthrow the result of the 2020 presidential election via a fake elector scheme and the January 6,

2021 insurrection, did represent a direct threat to the most fundamental element of a democracy: free and fair elections. Kathryn Kovacs (2018, 516) therefore introduced a more foreboding interpretation of the UET:

> The Theory of the unitary executive is a theory no longer. The President now operates on the premise that, because the Constitution vests all executive power in him, his appointees merely assist him in performing his constitutional duty to take care that the laws are faithfully executed. Even statutory delegations to a particular office are read as within the President's authority. The rise of the unitary executive is not a new phenomenon. Each president exceeds his predecessor's control of the Fourth Branch. "Presidential administration" is morphing into autocracy.

After January 6, 2021, the so-called imaginary threat to democracy was real. One of the primary advocates of the UET, Steven Calabresi, "called January 6 an 'insurrection' and blasted Trump as an oathbreaking insurrectionist who lied to the American people for years that the election had been stolen and continues to repeat those lies even to the present day." He then urged the Supreme Court to "open the dictionary and tell us what we all already know—that Trump incited an insurrection and is disqualified from being on any primary or general election ballots." But as the 2024 election approached, with Trump the clear favorite to win the Republican nomination, Calabresi charged that the 2020 election resulted in a "fundamentally illegitimate Biden victory." He then concurred that the election was "probably stolen." Once again, expediency trumped fealty to an interpretive theory. If Donald Trump indeed was a threat to democracy, that fact could not stand in the way of his reelection or the triumph of a more powerful presidency.

The idea that the president is not powerful enough remains a key assumption of the unitary theory. On this point, Robert Spitzer (2011, 64–65) responded,

> Key to the unitary theory is the contrarian and counterfactual assumption that presidential power has declined, not increased, since the enactment of the Constitution in 1787. In an essay published in 1989, Theodore Olson (who also served as assistant attorney general in the Reagan administration and as

solicitor general in the second Bush administration) asserted that the presidency had endured "two centuries of unrelenting encroachments by Congress," during which time Congress had "adeptly and persistently eroded and disassembled executive power." The capstones of the congressional erosion of presidential power, by this view, were the War Powers Act of 1973 and congressional actions related to the Iran-Contra scandal of the Reagan administration. In order to rectify this alleged imbalance and recapture presumably latent or dormant constitutional presidential powers, the unitary theory strikes out two sets of aggressive claims. The first is that presidents have sole and complete control over the executive branch. . . . In addition, Bush's unitary approach asserted that the other branches of government could not interfere with presidential actions arising from these executive powers.

Indeed, presidential power has expanded since the Founding and as Andrew Rudalevige (2005) argued, the Watergate era legislation was followed by a renewed *imperial presidency* (see also Wolfensberger 2002). As a result, Robert Spitzer asked, "Is the constitutional presidency obsolete?" Spitzer (2011, 73–74) then provided the following propositions as an answer to his own question:

Proposition 1: The Constitution simply does not have all the answers to the riddle of executive power. This fact alone points to the flaws of certitude and generality that typify originalism as constitutional doctrine.

Proposition 2: The arc of presidential power from past to present is rooted in, but cannot adequately be explained by, Article II powers alone.

Proposition 3: Like the Constitution itself, Article II is not a Rorschach ink blot, the meaning of which is to be interpreted in any manner by whoever happens to be viewing it. All theories are not equally tenable; not every constitutional debate consists of two equally valid and legitimate points of view. Text and historical evidence provide some answers. On the other hand, some questions simply cannot be answered.

Proposition 4: An originalist reading of the Constitution leads to legislative supremacy, not to the unitary executive.

Proposition 5: The unitary theory fails on the merits in its attempts to bridge its grandiose power claims with an originalist reading of the Constitution. It is faux originalism. Despite its pretensions to seriousness, it is the product of a pseudoscholarly enterprise that, at bottom, suffers from a fatal flaw: it rejects the essence of the separation of powers/checks-and-balances system (while falsely claiming obedience to it) precisely because it deems to vest in the president a constitutional power to reject or ignore statutory law if the president decides solely for him—or herself that such law trammels executive prerogatives. The unitary theory further denies to the courts the right to adjudicate matters that the executive deems, by any self-made standard, beyond the court's reach. The unitary theory is not just against the Constitution; it's bad law, bad governance, and bad politics.

And as to justifying the UET on another prominent interpretive theory, Spitzer (2011, 75) added, "The unitarians do not rest their arguments on any such 'Living Constitution' view, because their ideological restraints them to justify their actions and theory on originalism, which leads us back to the faux 'scholarship' of a few lawyers that is the fountainhead of the theory." Hence, as Christine Reed (2008, 356) remarked, "Current trends suggest a troubling disregard by federal officials for the rule of law." Michael Fitts (1996, 835) also provided a functional basis to criticize the theory:

I argue that the structural changes that appear to enhance the power of the president under public choice approaches and the unitary executive principles can, at the same time, actually undermine the president's reputation, his ability to resolve conflicts, and ultimately, his political strength. As a result, formal attempts to strengthen the presidency may have "diminishing marginal returns" and perhaps even negative effects, at least in some contexts. The reasons are complicated but straightforward: the individuality, centrality, and visibility of the "personal unitary presidency," which is seen as an advantage in terms of collective choice and public debate, can be a disadvantage when it comes to conflict resolution and public assessment.

And yet, as Ryan Barilleaux and Christopher Kelley (2020, 224) noted, "*Assertive presidential unilateralism is here to stay.* Presidential candidates get elected promising to do things with the office, and presidents in office want to put their stamp on national policy. The prevailing theme of the presidency since World War II has been assertiveness, and at least since the Ford presidency unilateralism has been an important element in that assertiveness." Furthermore, as Christopher Kelley (2005, 53–55), who was among the first political scientists to address the UET, stated,

> The unitary executive argues that the president has aggressively pushed the boundaries of constitutional power in order to protect the prerogatives of the Office and to control the executive branch agencies. It has developed over the course of three presidencies—Reagan, Bush I, and Clinton. It has only been in the Bush II administration that the unitary executive has fully developed. . . . And the danger in this is that unilateral actions taken by a president that go unchecked establish a precedent for the benefit of future presidents. And when a precedent is established, the courts are reluctant to find the action unconstitutional if it has gone unanswered by the Congress.

George W. Bush therefore set precedents for Trump, who in turn set precedents for a future president. Like a snowball gaining both mass and momentum, precedent ensures an ever stronger presidency.

Consequently, as Saikrishna Prakash (2013, 1364–65) surmised, "Going forward, what is certain is that chief executives (and their acolytes) will claim extraordinary authority in extraordinary times, reading the supposed ambiguities of Article II as an invitation to act." Meanwhile, Prakash viewed the president's authority as limited:

> Despite all that can be said in favor of an energetic emergency executive—the arguments from policy, text, structure, and practice—*the Founders rendered the Chief Executive almost entirely impotent in crises.* The original Constitution did not vest the President with legal authority to act *contra legem* or to do whatever he judged necessary to save the nation or

the Constitution. The President even lacked authority to take temporary measures to preserve the status quo until Congress could address an incipient crisis. In a nutshell, the Constitution fashioned something of an imbecilic emergency executive, one lacking constitutional authority to take property, suspend habeas corpus, or impose military rule.

Prakash's statement is consistent with a strict constructionist interpretation. The presidential conundrum is that the strict constructionist approach provides for a presidency that is too weak and therefore unable to meet the needs of the twenty-first century. But the living constitution and the UET, while providing a basis for increased presidential power, do not provide a basis for holding the presidency accountable, other than impeachment, elections, or in the case of war, Congress' power of the purse. Given the shortcomings of the three theories, is it possible to apply any one theory? Neal Katyal (2006, 2314) offered an alternative:

> Instead of doing away with the unitary executive, this Essay proposes designs that force internal checks but permit temporary departures when the need is great. Of course, the risk of incorporating a presidential override is that its great formal power will eclipse everything else, leading agency officials to fear that the President will overrule or fire them. But just as a filibuster does not tremendously constrain presidential action, modest internal checks, buoyed by reporting requirements, can create sufficient deterrent costs.

What then is the appropriate dividing line between the powers of the presidency and the other branches? Is there a Goldilocks zone regarding the power of the American presidency, where power is not too strong or too weak, but just right?

Alexander Hamilton provided a rationale for a strong executive when he opined, "The ingredients which constitute energy in the Executive are, first, unity; secondly, duration; thirdly, an adequate provision for its support; fourthly, competent powers." James Kent (1826, 253–54) penned,

> The characteristical required in the executive department, are promptitude, decision and force; and these qualities are most likely to exist when the executive authority is limited to a

single person, moving by the unity of a single will. Division, indecision, and delay, are exceedingly unfavorable to that steady and vigorous administration of the law, which is necessary to secure tranquility at home, and command the confidence of foreign nations. . . . Unity increases not only the efficacy, but the responsibility of the executive power. Every act can be immediately traced and brought home to the proper agent. There can be no concealment of the real author, and, generally, none of the motives of public measures, when there are no associates to divide, or to mask responsibility.

Even as energy in the executive is required, and dispatch and secrecy are necessary to the nation's foreign policy, we are still left with the key question: What are the limits of presidential power? Without accountability, the answer may very well be tyranny and dictatorship. The task of our present generation is to discover a path toward an accountable and workable presidency.

Conclusion

In sum, there are at least three major theories of presidential power: (1) a strict constructionist reading of the Constitution that severely limits presidential power; (2) the idea that the Constitution is flexible, elastic, and organic, which provides a basis for the development of presidential power but is not normatively committed to such an expansion of presidential power; and (3) the unitary executive, which is specifically dedicated to increasing presidential power. The basic problem in choosing between these three theories is the Constitution's inherently ambiguous language. And Article II's ambiguity is rampant; virtually every provision is undefined. Hence, we are left to question what power the commander-in-chief clause provides. Is the executive vesting clause a mere introduction to Article II or does it confer *all* executive power on the president? Are the take care clause and other provisions of Article II, Section 3 merely duties and not powers? And where in the Constitution can we find guidance on such questions as whether presidents have coordinate construction authority?

When we add the Constitution's many silences, what does that tell us about the UET? The UET is based primarily on the president's removal authority, and yet there is no provision for removal in the Constitution, other than the impeachment clause. While the use of unilateral power is widespread by today's presidents, there is no mention of executive orders, proclamations, memoranda, or other unilateral techniques. On all such questions, the Constitution provides no guidance. Therefore, our government has existed in the land of extra constitutionalism since the Constitution left the Framers' pens, beginning with the Decision of 1789. Are we therefore to determine that the Framers, who greatly feared monarchy, intentionally designed just such an office? The arguments in favor of a strong, practically unaccountable presidency cannot be justified by the Constitution. Perhaps, then, it is best that we all read that document again!

It is therefore difficult, and I would argue impossible, to identify one true method of interpretation, or to paraphrase *The Lord of the Rings*, there is no one theory to rule them all. Each theory offers its own values, and each has its own strengths and limitations. So which theory should we adopt? The answer is far from certain. In crises we favor greater presidential power. In normal times, such power can represent a movement toward autocracy. And despite our theoretical musings, it is often presidents who choose between these interpretive frameworks. Unless "We the People" offer a compelling rebuttal, the incentive of presidents is to always increase their power at the expense of the other Constitutional actors and in contravention of the Constitution itself.

Chapter 9

The Constitution and the
Supreme Practical Test

My historical approach should persuade the reader that three recently
fashionable approaches to constitutional law are flawed. First, those
who advocate an "original intent" approach to constitutional interpretation would strip away the rich accretions of meaningful precedent
that has occurred since the founding. Second, those who advocate
a "unitary executive," a president who possesses plenary power to
dismiss and supervise all the officers who execute the law, slight the
important and accepted role of Congress in controlling executive
officers by both statutes and informal practices. Third, those who
advocate broad and exclusive executive power in the national security
realm envision a presidency shorn of controls that our history has
shown to be indispensable.

—Harold Bruff, Untrodden Ground, 5

Constitutional ambiguity raises a key question: Can constitutional constraints, including the separation of powers and checks and balances,
prevent such an accumulation of power that would lead to an autocratic
presidency? As I noted in chapters 6, 7, and 8, there are widely different
methods of interpreting the Constitution. Again, interpreting the Constitution would be easy if the powers of the presidency were clearly defined.
But concerns with constitutional ambiguity have been a common theme
throughout American history, from George Washington's time forward. As
a result, as the power of the presidency expands, can its powers be contained and the office be made accountable? If not, then we may confront

not a brave new world but the frightening prospect of a presidency out of control, a veritable threat to the existence of our republic.

America has never been so close to the precipice of autocracy as we are today. As we face a growing threat of political violence, and in some quarters even a call for a new civil war, it is important to remember what John Jay (1861, 4) wrote during the Civil War:

> Eighty-five years of almost uninterrupted prosperity and unex-ampled growth! eighty-five years of culture and experience in a century of progress such as the world has never seen before! Eighty-five years of thoughtful reflection on the character of the men who laid the foundation of our national glory and of the broad principles of right on which they based the edifice or American freedom! Those years have passed; their results are written on the map of America, on the page of history, and to-day, the 4th of July 1861, the American congress convenes again at the call of the president at the capital bearing the name of Washington, to meet the question, whether the republic is to be maintained in its integrity with the constitution proclaimed by Washington based on the will of the majority, or whether it is to be sundered and shattered by a defeated faction that sets at defiance the will of the people and would trample the constitution in the dust.

We are now approaching 240 years since our Constitution was written. Should we cast aside almost two and a half centuries of prosperity, as well as a democracy that has endured wars, depressions, and other challenges, or will our Constitution endure? As to this question, we can learn from history. A February 26, 1862, letter to Oliver Wendell Holmes (1892, 413) from historian John Lothrop Motley noted the key contentious constitutional issue of that day: "The question is distinctly proposed to us, Shall Slavery die, or the great Republic? It is most astounding to me that there can be two opinions in the free States as to the answer. If we do fall, we deserve our fate." Can one make the same statement about our democracy today? If we fall, it will be our own fault, or as Benjamin Franklin noted at the conclusion of the Constitutional Convention, we have given you "a Republic, if you can keep it."

As the nation faced an existential crisis, then as now, such practical concerns provide a potent incentive for a better understanding of our

Constitution. As Joel Parker (1862, 29) remarked, "Constitutional and unconstitutional propositions press upon us with such rapidity at the present day, that, before we have time to dispose of one set of them, another claims our attention." And in another statement that relates to our own time, A. J. Cline (1861, 5) appealed to the nation to step back "from the madness of disunion to the sobriety of the Constitution and common sense." That statement from 1861 could (and should) be written today. We therefore should heed Harold Hyman's (1973, 100, 101) warning: "Disagreement in high places about the Constitution hurt, because for more than seventy years Americans had believed that it was a perfect, finished work that since initiation had required only technical adjustments in the form of two amendments." Quoting Edwin Lawrence Godkin, Hyman continued, "No longer could reasonable men think of the Constitution as 'a final rule of right, behind which there was nothing to which good citizens were called for guidance.' " Hyman added, "Thereafter the Constitution deserved respect, not adoration; employment, not adulation. In short, in 1861, [as Godwin concluded] 'criticism has been let loose even upon the Constitution of the United States.' " Or as Samuel Nicholas (1865, 15, 21) declared, "We are in the midst of two perilous wars—the war against the Union and the war against the Constitution. All supersedure of the Constitution by an alleged higher law, law of necessity or of war, are mere pretexts for unnecessary usurpation by would-be tyrants."

Is Our Constitution Adequate?

As the Southern states seceded from the Union, and as the nation entered a war for its very survival, scholars and practitioners such as Timothy Farrar (1862) asked another fundamental question that is relevant to our own time: Was the Constitution adequate or had it failed? Farrar's answer was that it was indeed adequate. Alfred Kelly, Winfred Harbison, and Herman Belz (1983, 299–300) later advised, "The first constitutional issue presented at the outbreak of hostilities was the adequacy of the Constitution in time of war." Although this was an academic question, it had serious practical applications. If the Constitution was not perfect, then as Hyman (1973, 186) wrote, "the appeal to perfection was irrelevant. Few Republican voices—certainly not Lincoln's—demanded it. In Congress as in the White House the goals were adequacy, effectiveness, and promptness." One should add to that list accountability.

Others agreed with Farrar. Henry Ward Beecher (1863, 156, 181), a congregational clergyman and devout opponent of slavery, noted that the Constitution, "For three quarters of a century . . . [had] been in operation with a success which has made the world marvel." He reminded his audience,

> There are men yet living who saw the period of the Revolutionary War. . . . And yet, within the lifetime of a single man, this nation has, under the benign protection of this government, sprung to a position second to that of no nation on the globe. Nor was there ever a government that, for a period of seventy-five years, or thereabouts, was administered with as much wisdom, and with so many benefits, as that government which now it is sought to overthrow.

Poet Walt Whitman pronounced, "Our national democratic experiment, principle, and machinery could weather such a shock, and that our Constitution could weather it, like a ship in a storm, and come out of it as sound and whole as before, is by far the most signal proof yet of the stability of that experiment—Democracy—and of those principles in the Constitution" (Hyman 1973, 133). Reverend Joseph Parrish Thompson (1864, 5) added, "To reassure ourselves that the Constitution, the Union, the Government will stand, we must go down and explore the foundations to see whether any accepted principle has been dislodged; any pillar shaken out of place; any arch or beam is cracked and ready to fall. The scrutiny may be anxious and severe; but the process is salutary and the result certain." The title of his work, *Revolution against Free Government Not a Right but a Crime*, provided a justification for presidential power as well as a continuing defense of the Constitution. Rejecting Thomas Jefferson's ideas about periodic revolutions, Thompson (1864, 18, 22, 24) advised, "The well-being of political society requires stability in government, no less than freedom of individual life and of social progress, under that government." He noted, "That society be organized in FREE INSTITUTIONS, which themselves are vital and permanent." Likewise,

> To insure stability in government, THE GOVERNING POWER MUST FAIRLY REPRESENT THE WELFARE OF THE WHOLE PEOPLE. . . . Yet it is needful that a free government be defined and regulated by a CONSTITUTION, itself amendable. The

community, whose good is the end of government, does not always at the first discern its own good; does not always consult that good simply, or in the best manner; is not always free from prejudice or passion, from ignorance or party bias, or the influence of base and artful men; and therefore a free popular government needs checks upon itself, in the interest of both justice and liberty.

Thompson (1864, 29–30) concluded,

Never before in the history of the world have these several elements of stability in government been combined as in the Government of these United States. Founded upon the broadest declaration of the essential equality and the inalienable rights of men; embosomed in organic institutions of justice and of freedom; fairly representing the whole people, and constituted for their equal benefit; and ordered by that grand Constitution, the elaborated, concentrated, and harmonious wisdom of the sages of the nation; accepted by the people, and by them ordained "to establish justice, promote the general welfare, and secure the blessings of liberty to themselves and their posterity": a Constitution that denies to the ablest general or statesman a title of nobility; that makes the President of the nation liable to impeachment for treason, bribery, or other high crimes and misdemeanors; that forbids Congress to assume any powers not expressly delegated; that watches and checks every tendency of government to encroach upon the people; and then says to the humblest citizen, in the name of the greatest of nations, "Your speech, your religion, your business, your locomotion shall be free; your person and your house shall be secure; you shall not be deprived of life, liberty, or property, without due process of law; if accused of crime, you shall have a speedy and public trial, by an impartial jury of your own district; you can compel your witnesses, and shall have counsel at our cost for your defence. You the individual man, down there in the most humble and obscure position in society in the eye of the Constitution, are greater than all its official executors: them it watches and restrains, that they do you no wrong; you it defends and secures in every right."

Such a government is made to stand; it ought to stand; IT WILL STAND.

Principal among the supporters of the Constitution was Daniel Agnew (1863, 5) in *Our National Constitution: Its Adaptation to a State of War or Insurrection*. On the book cover, Agnew wrote of the Constitution,

> And now the great question which we have to settle is, shall this mighty aggregate of prosperity perish, or shall it endure? Shall this imperial heritage of blessings descend unimpaired to our posterity, or shall it be ignominiously, profligately thrown away? Shall the territory of the Union, lately so happy under the control and adjustment of the national and State governments, be broken up into miserable fragments, sure to be engaged in constantly recurring border wars; and all lying at the mercy of foreign powers, or shall it preserve its noble integrity under the aegis of the National government?

The comments made by George Boutwell (1867, 97–98), in an address before the Phi Beta Kappa Society of Harvard University, have direct relevance to our own time:

> This, then, is not a rebellion of the people against tyrants; but, for the first time in the annals of mankind, we behold a rebellion of tyrants against the people, . . . a rebellion of tyrants against humanity, a rebellion of tyrants against justice, a rebellion of tyrants against law, a rebellion of tyrants against liberty, a rebellion of tyrants against the sovereignty of the American States, a rebellion of tyrants against the integrity of the American Union, a rebellion of tyrants against the hopes of the whole human race in the capacity of the people to govern themselves. Tyrants whose aims are so hostile to mankind could not be otherwise than false to every sentiment of truth, justice, and honor, as well as traitors to the country whose fostering care they had received. Being tyrants and traitors, they were prepared for the meanest acts and the vilest crimes.

Although the Constitution had its defenders, other such as Andrew Wilcox (1862, 5) argued that it was defective. Canadian scholar Thomas

McGee D'Arcy (1865, 34, 40) also wrote, "The Constitution of the United States was a compromise between state jealousy and the strong sentiment of self-preservation; Between the science and scholarship of such, men as the authors of the Federalist, and the wild theories of the demagogues of the day. It betrays, therefore, very naturally, both in its strength and its weakness, in its provisions and omissions, the unmistakable marks of this twofold parentage." In other words, constitutional ambiguity was the fulcrum of the debate over the Constitution's adequacy. D'Arcy added, "One lesson . . . has been already taught to every just-minded observer of the still waging war, namely, that those who formerly held the Constitution of 1789 to be perfect, were not farther from the truth, than those who have since spoken of it as a complete failure."

Following the January 6, 2021, insurrection at the US Capitol, and President Donald Trump's continuing efforts to subvert the will of the American people and prevent the duly elected president, Joseph Biden, from succeeding him on January 20, 2021, we confront many of these same issues today. Is our Constitution adequate? Can it protect us against tyrants? Can it prevent our union from dividing into warring camps or even a disunited states? Observations from the Civil War era, consequently, are still of immediate relevance.

The Power of the Presidency

William Howell and Terry Moe (2016) referred to the Constitution as a "relic," one designed for an agricultural nation with thirteen states straddled along the Atlantic Coast and with fewer than four million citizens. They also warned of a "strongman presidency" (Howell and Moe 2023). Other scholars, while defending the Constitution, provided fodder for a far more activist conceptualization of the presidential office, and they found support among past observers of the presidency. For instance, Agnew (1863, 16, 11) wrote that the war provided "express, unlimited, and unconditional authority [for the president] to use the whole physical force of the nation." He also noted the "sleeping powers of the Constitution," a reference to the presidency's silent power, that is powers that exist beyond the Constitution's mere written words. As Hyman (1973, 131–32) wrote, "It was becoming clear that the Constitution's silence on waging war was necessary and proper. Neither the framers of 1787 nor congressmen since could foresee history's hazards. The choice of means had to lie with Congress or the

President, or appropriate reaction to unanticipated events was impossible." But silence is not golden when it comes to the Constitution. It also raises the specter of tyranny.

To reconcile these complicated matters, the Lincoln administration hired some of the nation's best lawyers. Lincoln's second secretary of war, Edwin Stanton, was one "of the nation's most effective trial and corporation lawyers." Solicitor William Whiting was joined as "the War Department's legal secretariat by patent attorney Peter Watson, former cabinet officer Joseph Holt, Columbia University Professor Francis Lieber, and law-yers-become-generals Ethan Allen Hitchcock and Henry Halleck. From 1861–65, no university law faculty or private firm in the nation equaled this association of lawyers." Furthermore, on July 17, 1862, "as part of the statute which afforded the President [the right to] appeal jurisdiction from courts-martial and military commissions, Congress established within the War Department a new Judge Advocate General" (Hyman 1973, 190). The department's primary consideration was to devise "apparatuses and procedures more likely to achieve civilian control over generals and justice for soldiers and civilians than anything that existed before Sumter or until World War II" (189).

These developments did not by any means signify that all legal experts agreed on the significant issues of the day, but it did compel scholars to search for new meanings in the Constitution. As they did, they concen-trated far more attention on the role of the president and the Congress than they had prior to the Civil War. The era of strict construction began to give way to the idea of an organic, elastic, and flexible living consti-tution. Among "the sources of strength in the constitutional system was the flexibility and responsiveness of existing constitutional institutions. Of these none was more important than the executive power." Yet, as scholars examined these issues and increasingly referred to "Lincoln's Constitutional Dictatorship," they discovered that "neither the nature nor the location of the war power was established beyond debate by the Constitution." Consequently, constitutional scholars revisited existing ideas about the Constitution and its effectiveness, as well as addressing the many other gaps in military law. As Hyman (1973, 179) continued, "The literature of the law was silent, incomplete, or contradictory on many matters which the War dredged up." Hence, the Civil War was a period "when professionals in the law were heightening their influence on every level of government."

For a time, then, America's faith in the Constitution was challenged as never before. An English observer, Walter Bagehot ([1861] 2001) was critical of the US Constitution, just as many Americans wondered if the Constitution was fatally defective. Sidney Fisher (1862, 357) noted, in his *Trial of the Constitution*, one of the first Civil War texts on the Constitution, "This war is a test of the Constitution." And as the president of Yale College, Theodore Woolsey (Lieber 1877, 10), wrote,

> The tendency is plaining toward a more centralized government by a freer interpretation of the United States Constitution. The dangers which menace us from this tendency, and from what may be called democratic abstraction, are met by such a book as this, which teaches that there is no safe liberty but one under checks and guarantees, one which is articulated, one which by institutions of local self-government educates the whole people and moderates the force of administrations, one which sets up the check of state power within certain well-defined limits against United States power, one which draws a broad line between the unorganized masses of men calling themselves the people and the people formed into bodies, "joined together and compacted" by constitutions and institutions.

Once again, these words could be written today, for they have not lost their germaneness. And the central question, of course, continues: What are the "well-defined limits against" the United States' power? That question has proven to be as enduring and as mysterious as the Constitution itself.

A Continuing Debate

> After our Constitution got fairly into working order it really seemed as if we had invented a machine that would go of itself, and this begot a faith in our luck which even the civil war itself but momentarily disturbed. Circumstances continued favorable, and our prosperity went on increasing. I admire the splendid complacency of my countrymen, and find something exhilarating and inspiring in it. We are a nation which has struck oil, but we are also a nation that is sure the well will never run dry. And this confidence in our luck with the absorption in material interests, generated by unparalleled opportunity, has in some respects made us neglectful of our political duties.

> —James Russell Lowell, *The Independent in Politics*, 16–17

Once the nation was reconstructed and survived a violent Civil War, the Constitution remained a subject of continuing debate, though various constitutional interpretations often were driven by expediency as well as a careful reading of the document's text. As historian David Donald (2016, 59) wrote, "Every theory of reconstruction [proposed by the Radical Republicans] required the twisting of the words in the Constitution to purposes never envisaged by the framers of that document." As such, the Constitution became a highly controversial document. For example, in a scathing critique, a German professor at the University of Freiburg, Hermann von Holst (1876, 5–6), commented,

> It is possible for us to trace the earliest beginnings of the worship of the constitution. At first it was looked upon as the best possible constitution for the United States. By degrees it came to be universally considered as a masterpiece, applicable to every country. This was preached with so much unanimity and honest conviction, although internal quarrels were raging all the time, that the propagandism of the new faith reached even to Europe. In the United States this conviction grows steadily stronger, although parties not only differ concerning the advisability of certain practical provisions of the constitution, but have been from the first diametrically opposed to one another in their understanding of the principles on which it is founded. From the close of the century, that is, from the time when the opposing principles assumed a fixed form, the constitution has been the political Bible of the people. The child sucked in with his mother's milk the conviction that this was the light in which he should regard it.

Various observers also noted the changing nature of the Constitution. In one of the most popular books of the 1880s, a prominent socialist, Laurence Gronlund (1884, 164) opined, "Our present 'constitution' is a very different one from what it was in 1850. The point of change was the period when people prated about 'upholding the constitution.' Whenever a 'Constitution' needs being 'upheld,' it is going, or gone." Five years later, Jay Guggenheimer (1889, 116) wrote, "The prevalence of the notion that our Constitution, complete in all its parts, came into existence suddenly and spontaneously, by a marvelous inspiration of the Philadelphia Convention, has long had a depressing effect upon the historical study of American institutions. It has discouraged, or at least offered no incentive to, the thorough investigation of their sources, whether colonial, classical, British, or other. . . . The birth of American institutions, however, was far from being miraculous."

Religious figures also expressed their views of the Constitution. While most were positive, there was the occasional critic. Clergyman and abolitionist Moncure Conway wrote in 1887, "The investment in the Constitution was large enough to evolve a generation of believers that it came down from heaven. Since the overthrow of slavery the silver image has shown some signs of turning to clay" (Kammen 1986, 142). Writing at the end of the nineteenth century, George Wharton Pepper (1898, 6, 8, 14), Christian activist and a professor at the University of Pennsylvania School of Law, offered this warning:

> Our Constitution has stood unchanged throughout an era during which the unwritten constitution of England has been transformed. "How will it stand the strain?" You reply, "It will never feel the strain. It will stand unmoved and immovable as the everlasting hills." I trust that you are right. I believe that you are. At the same time I fancy that I can discern in our constitutional development tendencies that are fraught with danger to the Republic. Perhaps at such a time as this it is permissible to substitute for frantic boasts an earnest and dispassionate review of the situation in which we find ourselves.

One can argue that the time Pepper warned of has arrived. Importantly, then, according to Pepper, what kept the Constitution in balance and made it the "bulwark" protecting democracy was neither the president nor Congress—it was the courts: "The exercise of this vast power may be regarded as essential to the conception of a written constitution. The supremacy of the judiciary over the legislature has been our boast. It is a feature of our constitutional system which has excited the admiration of foreigners." And yet, as Michael Kammen noted, "A few radicals even called for outright abolition of the Constitution. As a philosophy professor at Swarthmore asserted late in 1931: 'I don't believe in one generation deciding what the others shall do. Our forefathers didn't know anything about a country of 120,000,000 people, with automobiles, trains, and radios.'" Interestingly, the era of the living constitution resulted in contradictory results: the expansion of democracy thus giving more power to the people, while concomitantly increasing the power of the federal government and the presidency.

Today, we face a crisis of governmental and constitutional legitimacy, with none of the three branches receiving anywhere near majority support in various opinion surveys. As we do so, we must once again ask, Is our Constitution adequate to the meet the dangers of our own time? If so, how are we to interpret it? The various observers of history I have cited throughout this book have identified vastly different interpretations of presidential power. Is any one of them the correct one, or must we find consensus among different interpretations? As textualists and today's new originalists do battle with strict constructionist originalists, as well as supporters of a living constitution and the UET, we must ask, Is one interpretive framework right while all the others are wrong? Can we rely on such certainty—or arrogance—to guide our nation's future? In this book I have noted the perils of each approach: strict constructionist created a weak presidency that would not be able to deal with the many emerging problems endemic to American politics; the idea of a living constitution provides the basis for an organic presidency that is capable of evolving, but it has no limits or methods of accountability other than to the public; and the unitary executive theory is specifically designed for one purpose only: to expand the power of the presidency over the executive branch again without definable limits. Each approach has potential benefits, but none alone provides the sort of presidency we need today.

To address issues of interpretation, we first must acknowledge that much has changed since 1787. The presidency is now a far more powerful institution than any of the Framers, other than Alexander Hamilton, would recognize. This transformation did not occur because of changes in the Constitution, however. The words in Article II remain precisely the same. Instead, historical practice had much to do with the accretion of presidential power. As Donald Trump promises to further expand presidential power if he is elected again in 2024, we therefore need to consider the possibility that the presidency will become such a dominant institution that it will overwhelm the other branches of government. Are we headed not toward an imperial presidency, but rather an autocratic presidency? If so, the Constitution provides only so much guidance. Its silences, and the nooks and crannies of constitutional ambiguity, provide the basis for the expansion of presidential power. Consequently, the question we should be asking is, How much power can we safely place in the hands of our presidents? And how can we make the office and its occupants accountable for their actions? The answers to these questions will determine if our nation and our Constitution can survive this latest supreme practical test.

Notes

Chapter 1

1. I have retained all of the original spelling, formatting, italics, and capitalization from the original texts throughout this book.

2. Elizabeth Goltein and Andrew Boyle, "Trump Has Emergency Powers We Aren't Allowed to Know About," *New York Times*, April 10, 2020, https://www.nytimes.com/2020/04/10/opinion/trump-coronavirus-emergency-powers.html.

3. Dominick Mastrangelo, "Two-Thirds of Republicans Think Biden's Victory Was Not Legitimate: Poll," May 26, 2021, https://thehill.com/homenews/administration/555584-two-thirds-or-republicans-think-bidens-victory-was-not-legitimate.

4. William G. Gale and Darrell M. West, "Is the US Headed for Another Civil War?," September 16, 2021, https://www.brookings.edu/blog/fixgov/2021/09/16/is-the-us-headed-for-another-civil-war/.

5. Stephen Collinson, "Attack on Trump Opens Chilling Chapter in American Politics," CNN, July 14, 2024.

Chapter 2

1. Technically, there was a position called the president, but it had no power, rotated annually and was not a model for the US Constitution's presidency.

2. For the actual state constitutions, see Poore 1878.

3. Published originally in 1828. Goodrich was a clergyman who famously declared, "A place for everything and everything in its place."

Chapter 4

1. An English executioner.

2. Valerie Strauss, "For Constitution Day, a Sobering New Finding on 2021 Survey on Americans' Civics Knowledge," *Washington Post*, https://www.washingtonpost.com/education/2021/09/17/americans-civics-survey-sobering-insurrection/.

3. Annenberg Public Policy Center, 2023, "Many Don't Know Key Facts about U.S. Constitution, Annenberg Civics Study Finds," *Penn Today*, https://penntoday.upenn.edu/news/many-dont-know-key-facts-about-us-constitution-annenberg-civics-study-finds.

Chapter 5

1. Both King's and Madison's quotes are from Roger Foster 1895, 67–68.

2. All references to presidential statements not otherwise identified are from the American Presidency Project.

3. Black Past, "(1860) Frederick Douglass, 'The Constitution of the United States: Is It Pro-Slavery or Anti-Slavery?,'" Black Past, March 15, 2012, https://www.blackpast.org/global-african-history/1860-frederick-douglass-constitution-united-states-it-pro-slavery-or-anti-slavery/.

Chapter 6

1. The quote is from an 1843 publication entitled *Biographical Memoir of Albert Gallatin* (p. 14). No author is listed. It was reprinted from *The Democratic Review*, June 1843.

2. Henry Steele Commager, "The War Powers of the President; A Historian Examines the Present Charge of Dictatorship," *New York Times*, Oct. 19, 1941, https://timesmachine.nytimes.com/timesmachine/1941/10/19/105405731.html?pageNumber=142.

3. Noah Feldman, "This Is the Story of How Lincoln Broke the Constitution," *New York Times*, Nov. 2, 2021, https://www.nytimes.com/2021/11/02/opinion/constitution-slavery-lincoln.html.

Chapter 8

1. The speech can be found at Tulane University, "The Law of the Constitution," October 21, 1986, https://www.justice.gov/sites/default/files/ag/legacy/2011/08/23/10-21-1986.pdf. It is interesting that the unitary executive theory (UET) was first postulated at about the same time as conservatives established the Federalist Society. Steven Calabresi, who played a central role in the development of the UET, also was one of the founders of the Federalist Society

at Yale Law School (Lynch 2022, 7). As Steven Teles (2008, 136) identified, the Federalist Society "engages in *recruitment* of law students and practicing attorneys who can identify with and participate in the movement. Second, it invests in *human capital* of members through frequent debates, which acquaint them with conservative legal ideas and heighten their intellectual self-confidence, and through their participation in its student, lawyer, and practice groups, which provide leadership experience. Third, the Society produced *cultural capital*, in that its activities facilitate the orderly development of conservative legal ideas and their injection into the mainstream, reducing the stigma associated with those ideas and their injection into the legal mainstream, reducing the stigma associated with those ideas in institutions that produce and transmit professional distinction. Fourth, and perhaps most importantly, the Society is a producer of *social capital* in the form of networks that develop as by-products of Society activities. In the absence of an organization like the Federalist Society, these movement public goods would be produced in a haphazard, uncoordinated, and redundant fashion, if produced at all." As such, the Federalist Society has been instrumental to the propagation and legitimation of the UET.

References

Ackerman, Bruce. 1998. *We the People: Transformations*. Cambridge, MA: Belknap Press of Harvard University Press.

———. 2005. *The Failure of the Founding Fathers: Jefferson, Marshall, and the Rise of Presidential Democracy*. Cambridge, MA: Belknap Press of Harvard University Press.

———. 2007. "The Living Constitution." *Harvard Law Review* 120 (7): 1737–1812.

———. 2010. *The Decline and Fall of the American Republic*. Cambridge: Belknap Press of Harvard University Press.

———. 2016. "What Is to Be Done? A New Progressivism for a New Century." In *The Progressives' Century: Political Reform, Constitutional Government, and the Modern State*, edited by Stephen Skowronek, Stephen M. Engel, and Bruce Ackerman, 478–94. New Haven, CT: Yale University Press.

Adams, Henry Brooks. 1889–1991. *History of the United States of America: During the Administration of Thomas Jefferson*. 2 vols. New York: Scribner's.

Adams, John. 2016. *Writings from the New Nation: 1784–1826*. New York: Literary Classics of the United States.

Agnew, Daniel. 1863. *Our National Constitution: Its Adaptation to a State of War or Insurrection*. Philadelphia: C. Sherman, Son, and Co.

Amar, Akhil Reed. 2006. *America's Constitution: A Biography*. New York: Random House Trade Paperbacks.

———. 2012. *America's Unwritten Constitution: The Precedents and Principles We Live By*. New York: Basic Books.

———. 2015. *The Law of the Land: A Grand Tour of Our Constitutional Republic*. New York: Basic Books.

———. 2021. *The Words That Made Us: America's Constitutional Conversation, 1760–1840*. New York: Basic Books.

Anderson, William. 1947. *The National Government of the United States*. New York: Henry Holt.

Andrews, Israel Ward. 1900. *Manual of the Constitution of the United States*. New York: American Book Company.

Anonymous. 1862. *Of the Birth and Death of Nations: A Thought for the Crisis.* New York: Putnam.

Arnold, Peri E. 2009. *Remaking the Presidency: Roosevelt, Taft, and Wilson, 1901–1915.* Lawrence: University Press of Kansas.

Arnold, Thurman Wesley. (1935) 1945. *The Symbols of Government.* New Haven, CT: Yale University Press.

Bagehot, Walter. (1861) 2001. *The English Constitution.* Oxford: Oxford University Press. Citations refer to the 2001 edition.

Bailey, Jeremy D. 2008. "The New Unitary Executive and Democratic Theory: The Problem of Alexander Hamilton." *American Political Science Review* 102 (4): 453–65.

———. 2019. *The Idea of Presidential Representation: An Intellectual and Political History.* Lawrence: University Press of Kansas.

Bailey, Thomas A. (1940) 1950. *A Diplomatic History of the American People.* New York: Appleton-Century-Crofts. Citations refer to the 1950 edition.

———. 1956. *The American Pageant: A History of the Republic.* Boston: D. C. Heath.

Bailyn, Bernard. 1993. *The Debate on the Constitution: Federalist and Antifederalist Speeches, Articles and Letters During the Struggle over Ratification.* Vols. 1 and 2. New York: Literary Classic of America.

Baker, Newton Diehl. 1925. *Progress and the Constitution.* New York: Scribner's.

———. 1934. *The Making and Keeping of the Constitution.* James Goold Cutler Lecture. Seventh Lecture Under the James Goold Cutler Trust. College of William and Mary.

Balkin, Jack M. 2009. "Fidelity to Text and Principle." In *The Constitution in 2020*, edited by Jack M. Balkin and Reva B. Siegel, 11–24. New York: Oxford University Press.

———. 2020. *The Cycles of Constitutional Time.* New York: Oxford University Press.

Bamzai, Aditya. 2017. "The Origins of Judicial Deference to Executive Interpretation." *Yale Law Journal* 126 (4): 908–1101.

Bancroft, Aaron. 1807. *An Essay on the Life of George Washington: Commander in Chief of the American Army, Through the Revolutionary War, and the First President of the United States.* Worchester, MA: Thomas and Sturtevant.

Bancroft, George. 1826. *An Oration Delivered on the Fourth of July, 1826, at Northampton, Massachusetts.* Northampton, MA: T. W. Shepard.

———. 1889. *History of the Formation of the Constitution of the United States of America.* Vols. 1 and 2. New York: D. Appleton.

———. 1891. *History of the United States, From the Discovery of the Continent.* Vol. 6. New York: D. Appleton.

Barber, Sotirios A. 1984. *On What the Constitution Means.* Baltimore: John Hopkins University Press.

Barber, Sotirios A., and James E. Fleming. 2007. *Constitutional Interpretation: The Basic Questions.* New York: Oxford University Press.

Bardeen, C. W. 1903. *The Regents Questions in Civics 1891-1900*. Syracuse, NY: C. W. Bardeen.

Barilleaux, Ryan J., and Christopher S. Kelley. 2010. "Going Forward." In *The Unitary Executive and the Modern Presidency*, edited by Ryan J. Barilleaux and Christoper S. Kelley, 219-30. College Station: Texas A&M University Press.

Barkow, Rachel E. 2002. "More Supreme than Court? The Fall of the Political Question Doctrine and the Rise of Judicial Supremacy." *Columbia Law Journal* 102 (2): 237-336.

Basler, Roy P., ed. 1953. *The Collected Works of Abraham Lincoln*. New Brunswick, NJ: Rutgers University Press. Mulitple volumes.

Bates, Edward. 1933. *The Diary of Edward Bates 1859-1966*. Edited by Howard K. Beale. Washington, DC: Government Printing Office.

Bauer, Bob, and Jack Goldsmith. 2020. *After Trump: Reconstructing the Presidency*. Washington, DC: Lawfare Press.

Beard, Charles Austin. (1910) 1914. *American Government and Politics*. New York: Macmillan. Reprinted in 1920.

Beard, Charles Austin, and William C. Bagley. 1920. *A First Look in American History*. New York: Macmillan.

Beard, Charles Austin, and Mary Ritter Beard. 1918. *American Citizenship*. New York: Macmillan.

———. 1921. *History of the United States*. New York: Macmillan.

Beard, Charles Austin, and William Beard. 1930. *The American Leviathan: The Republic in the Machine Age*. New York: Macmillan.

Beard, Charles Austin, and George H. E. Smith. 1940. *The Old and the New Deal*. New York: Macmillan.

Beck, James Montgomery. 1922. *The Constitution of the United States: A Brief Study of the Genesis, Formulation, and Political Philosophy of the Constitution of the United States*. London: Published for *The Daily Telegraph* by Hodder and Stoughton.

———. 1926. *The Vanishing Rights of the States: A Discussion of the Right of the Senate to Nullify the Action of a Sovereign State in the Selection of its Representatives in the Senate*. New York: George H. Doran.

———. 1927. *Our Changing Constitution*. First Lecture Under the James Goold Cutler Trust. College of William and Mary.

———. 1939. "The Future of the Constitution." In *The Bacon Lectures on the Constitution of the United States Given at Boston University*, 363-74. Worchester, MA: Heffernan Press.

Becker, Carl. 1920. *The United States: An Experiment in Democracy*. New York: Harper and Brothers.

Beecher, Henry Ward. 1863. *Freedom and War: Discourses on Topics Suggested By The Times*. Boston: Ticknor and Fields.Belz, Herman. 1969. *Reconstructing the Union: Theory and Policy During the Civil War*. Ithaca, NY: Cornell University Press.

———. 1984. *Lincoln and the Constitution: The Dictatorship Question Reconsidered*. Fort Wayne, IN: Louis A. Warren Lincoln Library Museum.

———. 1988. "Abraham Lincoln and American Constitutionalism." *Review of Politics* 50 (2): 169–97.

Benedict, Michael Les. 1991. "The Constitution of the Lincoln Presidency and the Republican Era." In *The Constitution and the American Presidency*, edited by Martin L. Fausold and Alan Shank, 45–61. Albany: State University of New York Press.

Berdahl, Clarence A. 1921. *War Powers of the Executive in the United States*. Urbana: University of Illinois.

Berman, Emily. 2021. "Weaponizing the Office of Legal Counsel." *Boston College Law Review* 62:515–70.

Bestor, Arthur. 1964. "The American Civil War as a Constitutional Crisis." *American Historical Review* 69:327–52.

Beveridge, Albert J. 1902. *Republicanism: The Spirit of Conservative Progress*. Washington, DC: Library of Congress.

———. 1916. *The Life of John Marshall*. 4 vols. Boston: Houghton Mifflin.

———. 1968. *The Meaning of the Times, and Other Speeches*. Indianapolis, IN: Bobbs-Merrill.

Bickel, Alexander M. 1962. *The Least Dangerous Branch: The Supreme Court at the Bar of Politics*. New Haven, CT: Yale University Press.

Bilder, Mary Sarah. 2015. *Madison's Hand: Revising the Constitutional Convention*. Cambridge, MA: Harvard University Press.

Bimbilovsky, Ivan. 2009. *Constitutional War Powers: A Perceptual Ambiguity in VII Acts*. New York: Lambert Academic Publishing.

Binkley, Wilfred E. 1937. *The Powers of the President: Problems of American Democracy*. Garden City, NJ: Doubleday, Doran.

———. 1947. *President and Congress*. New York: Alfred A. Knopf.

Biskupic, Joan, and Elder Witt. 1997. *The Supreme Court & the Powers of the American Government*. Washington, DC: Congressional Quarterly.

Bissette, Joseph M., and Jeffrey K. Tulis. 1981. *The Presidency in The Constitutional Order*. Baton Rouge: Louisiana State University Press.

———. 2009. *The Constitutional Presidency*, 1–27. Baltimore: John Hopkins University Press.

Black, Jeremiah (Jeremiah Sullivan). 1859. *Observations on Senator Douglas's Views of Popular Sovereignty, as expressed in Harper's Magazine for September, 1859*. Washington, DC: Thomas McGill.

Blackburn, John S., and William Naylor McDonald. 1871. *A Grammar-School History of the United States: From the Discovery of America to the Present Time*. Baltimore: W. J. C. Dulany.

————. 1880. *New School History of the United States from the Earliest Discoveries to the Present Time.* Baltimore: W. J. C. Dulany.

Blackstone, William. 1979. *Commentaries on the Laws of England.* Chicago: University of Chicago Press.

Blaine, James G. 1884. *Twenty Years of Congress.* 2 vols. Norwich, CT: Henry Bill Publishing.

Bobbitt, Philip. (1982) 1984. *Constitutional Fate: A Theory of the Constitution.* New York: Oxford University Press.

————. 1991. *Constitutional Interpretation.* Cambridge, MA: Blackwell.

Boorstin, Daniel J. 1989. *The Americans: The Democratic Experience.* New York: Vintage Press.

Bordewich, Fergus M. 2016. *The First Congress: How James Madison, George Washington, and a Group of Extraordinary Men Invented the Government.* New York: Simon and Schuster.

Borgeaud, Charles. 1892. "The Origin and Development of Written Constitutions." *Political Science Quarterly* 7 (Dec.): 613–32.

————. 1895. *Adoption and Amendment of Constitutions in Europe and America.* New York: MacMillan.

Boutwell, George S. 1867. *Speeches and Papers Relating to the Rebellion and the Overthrow of Slavery.* Boston: Little, Brown.

Bowen, Catherine Drinker. 1966. *Miracle at Philadelphia.* Boston: Little, Brown.

Bacon, Gaspar G. 1928. *The Constitution of the United States: In Some of Its Fundamental Aspects.* Cambridge, MA: Harvard University Press.

Bacon's Guide. 1863. *Bacon's Guide to American Politics; or, a Complete View of the Fundamental Principals of the National and State Government, with the Respective Powers of Each.* Patterson's Row, EC: Sampson, Low, Son, and Co.

Bradley, Curtis A., and Trevor W. Morrison. 2013. "Presidential Power, Historical Practice, and Legal Constraint." *Columbia Law Review* 113 (4): 1097–1161.

Brand, Donald R. 2006. "Progressivism, the Brownlow Commission, and the Rise of the Administrative State." In *Modern America and the Legacy of the Founding*, edited by Ronald J. Pestritto and Thomas G. West. Lanham, MD: Lexington Books.

Brand, H. R. 2023. *Founding Partisans: Hamilton, Madison, Jefferson, Adams and the Brawling Birth of American Politics.* New York: Doubleday.

Brant, Irving. 1936. *Storm Over the Constitution.* New York: Bobbs-Merrill.

————. 1954. "Mr. Crosskey and Madison." *Columbia Law Review* 54 (Mar.): 443–50.

Brennan, William J. 1988. "The Constitution of the United States: Contemporary Ratification." In *The U.S. Constitution and the Supreme Court*, edited by Steven Anzovin and Janet Podell, 166–79. New York: H. H. Wilson.

Brest, Paul, Sanford Levinson, Jack M. Balkin, Akhil Reed Amar, and Reva B. Siegel. 2015. *Processes of Constitutional Decisionmaking: Cases and Materials.* New York: Wolters Kluwer Law and Business.

Brinkley, Alan, and Davis Dyer. 2004. *The American Presidency.* New York: Houghton Mifflin.

Brogan, D. W. 1933. Government of the People: A Study in the American Political System. New York: Harper and Brothers.

Brookhiser, Richard. 2018. *John Marshall: The Man Who Made the Supreme Court.* New York: Basic Books.

Brown, James Scott. 1918. *James Madison's Notes of the Debates of the Federal Convention of 1787 and Their Relation to a More Perfect Society of Nations.* New York: Oxford University Press.

Brown, Ralph Adams. 1975. *The Presidency of John Adams.* Lawrence: University Press of Kansas.

Brown, Stuart Gerry. 1966. *The American Presidency: Leadership, Partisanship, and Popularity.* New York: Macmillan.

Browning, Orville Hickman. 1925. *The Diary of Orville Hickman Browning 1850–1864.* Springfield: Illinois State Historical Library.

Brownlow, Louis. 1949. *The President and the Presidency.* Chicago: University of Chicago Press.

Brownson, Orestes A. 1865. *The American Republic: Its Constitution, Tendencies, and Destiny.* New York: P. O'Shea.

———. 2003. *The American Republic: Its Constitution, Tendencies and Destiny.* Wilmington, DE: ISI Books.

Bruff, Harold H. 2015. Untrodden Ground: How Presidents Interpret the Constitution. Chicago: University of Chicago Press.

Bryant, William Cullen, and Sydney Gay Howard. 1876. *A Popular History of the United States: From First Discovery of the Western Hemisphere by the Northmen to the End of the First Century of the Union of the States; Preceded by a Sketch of the Pre-Historic Period and the Age of Mound Builders.* New York: Scribner's.

Bryce, James. 1888 (1893). *The American Commonwealth.* 2 vols. London: Macmillan.

———. 1917. *The American Commonwealth Volume 1.* New York: Macmillan.

———. 1995. *The American Commonwealth Volume 2.* Indianapolis, IN: Liberty Fund.

Buchanan, James. 1868. *Mr. Buchanan's Administration on the Eve of the Rebellion.* New York: D. Appleton.

Burgess, John W. 1901. *The Civil War and the Constitution.* 2 vols. New York: Scribner's.

Burns, James MacGregor. 1963. *Deadlock on Democracy.* Englewood Cliffs, NJ: Prentice Hall.

———. 1965. *Presidential Government: The Crucible of Leadership.* Boston: Houghton Mifflin.

Burton, Theodore E. 1908. "The Development of the Federal Government." *Annals of the American Academy of Political and Social Science* 32 (July 1): 212–17.

Butler, Charles Henry. 1902. *The Treaty Making Power of the United States.* Vols. 1 and 2. New York: Banks Law Publishing.

Butler, Nicholas Murray. 1917. *Why Should We Change Our Form of Government? Studies in Practical Politics.* New York: Scribner's.

Calabresi, Steven G. 1994. "The Vesting Clauses as Power Grants." *Northwestern University Law Review* 88 (4): 1377–94.

Calabresi, Steven G., and Gary Lawson. 2007. "The Unitary Executive, Jurisdiction Stripping, and the *Hamdan* Opinions: A Textualist Response to Justice Scalia." *Columbia Law Review* 107 (4): 1003–47.

Calabresi, Steven G., and James Lindgren. 2006. "The President: Lighting Rod or King?" *Yale Law Journal* 115 (9): 2611–22.

Calabresi, Steven G., and Kevin H. Rhodes. 1992. "The Structural Constitution: Unitary Executive, Plural Judiciary." *Harvard Law Review* 105 (April): 1153–1216.

Calabresi, Steven G., and Christopher S. Yoo. 1997. "The Unitary Executive During the First Half-Century." *Case Western Reserve Law Review* 47:1451–1561.

———. 2003. "The Unitary Executive During the Second Half-Century." *Harvard Journal of Law Public Policy* 26:668–801.

———. 2008. *The Unitary Executive: Presidential Power from Washington to Bush.* New Haven, CT: Yale University Press.

Calhoun, John Caldwell. 1992. *Union and Liberty: The Political Philosophy of John C. Calhoun.* Edited by Ross Lence. Indianapolis, IN: Liberty Fund.

Cappon, Lester J., editor. 1987. *The Adams-Jefferson Letters: The Complete Correspondence Between Thomas Jefferson and Abagail and John Adams.* Chapel Hill: University of North Carolina Press.

Carr, Robert Kenneth. 1951. *American Democracy in Theory and Practice: The National Government.* New York: Rinehart.

Carson, Hampton L. 1889. *History of the Celebration of the One Hundredth Anniversary of the Formulation of the Constitution of the United States.* 2 vols. Philadelphia: J. B. Lippincott.

Case, Nelson. 1904. *Constitutional History of the United States.* New York: Trow Press.

Century Magazine. 1882. "A Century of Constitutional Interpretation." *Century Magazine* 39. New York: Century: 866–78.

Chambrun, Adolphe de. 1874. *The Executive Power in the United States: A Study of Constitutional Law.* Lancaster, PA: Inquirer Printing and Publishing.

Chase, Anthony. 1979. "The Birth of the Modern Law School." *American Journal of Legal History* 23 (4): 329–48.

Chemerinsky, Erwin. 2018. *We the People: A Progressive Reading of the Constitution for the Twenty-First Century*. New York: Picador.

Chernow, Ron. 2004. *Alexander Hamilton*. New York: Penguin.

———. 2010. *Washington: A Life*. New York: Penguin.

———. 2012. *Grant*. New York: Penguin.

Chipman, Nathaniel. 1833. *Principles of Government: A Treatise on Free Institutions, Including the Constitution of the United States*. Burlington, VT: Edward Smith.

Clark, Champ. 1920. *My Quarter Century of American Politics*. 2 vols. New York: Harper and Brothers.

Clark, Eleanor Jane. 1910. *Outlines of Civil Government with Suggestions for Civic Training by Original Work*. Boston: Palmer.

Cline, A. J. 1861. *Secession Unmasked or An Appeal from the Madness of Disunion to the Sobriety of the Constitution and Common Sense*. Washington, DC: Henry Polkinhorn.

Cloyd, David Excelmons. 1916. *Civics and Citizenship*. Des Moines: Published by the author.

Coan, Andrew, and Nicholas Bullard. 2016. "Judicial Capacity and Executive Power." *Virginia Law Review* 102 (3): 765–831.

Commager, Henry Steele. 1988. "The Constitution and Original Intent." In Anzovin and Podell, *The U.S. Constitution and the Supreme Court*, 199–205.

Committee for Immigrants in America. 1916. *Citizenship Syllabus: A Course of Study and Syllabus in Civic Training and Naturalization for Adult Immigrants in Evening Schools*. Albany: State University of New York Press.

Congressional Research Service. (2017) 2020. *The Constitution of the United States of America: Analysis and Interpretation*. Washington, DC: Government Printing Office.

Conkling, Alfred. 1866. *The Powers of the Executive Department of the Government of the United States*. Albany, NY: Weare C. Little.

Cooley, Thomas McIntyre. 1889. *Constitutional History of the United States as Seen in the Development of American Law*. New York: Putnam.

———. 1891. *General Principles of Constitutional Law in the United States of America*. Boston: Little, Brown.

Coolidge, Calvin. 1984. *The Autobiography of Calvin Coolidge*. Walking Through the World.

Cooper, Carl E. Jr. 2005. *Constitutional War Powers: The Fundamental Relevance of the War*. Submitted in Partial Fulfillment of Master of Military Studies. U.S. Marine Corps.

Cooper, William J. 2017. *The Lost Founding Father: John Quincy Adams and the Transformation of American Politics*. New York: Liverlight.

Cornell, Saul. 1999. *The Other Founders: Anti-Federalism & Dissenting Tradition in America, 1788–1828*. Chapel Hill: University of North Carolina Press.

Cornman, Oliver P., and Oscar Gerson. 1907. *A Brief Topical Survey of United States History*. Boston: D. C. Heath.

Corwin, Edward Samuel. 1911. "The Doctrine of Due Process of Law Before the Civil War. IV." *Harvard Law Review* 24:460–79.

———. 1914. "The Treaty-Making Power: A Rejoinder." *North American Review* 199:893–901.

———. 1925. "Constitution v. Constitutional Theory." *American Political Science Review* 19 (2): 290–304.

———. (1940) 1957. *The President: Office and Powers: 1787–1957*. New York: New York University Press. Multiple volumes.

———. 1941. "Some Aspects of the Presidency." *Annals of the American Academy of Political and Social Science* 281 (Nov.): 122–31.

———. 1953. "The Steel Seizure Case: A Judicial Case Without Straw." *Columbia Law Review* 53 (1): 53–66.

Corwin, Edward S., and Louis W. Koenig. 1956. *The Presidency Today*. New York: New York University Press.

Cox, Henry Bartholomew. 1984. *War, Foreign Affairs, and Constitutional Power: 1829–1901*. Cambridge, MA: Ballinger Publishing.

Cox, Samuel Sullivan. 1864. *The Nation's Hope in the Democracy: Historic Lessons for Civil War: Speech of Hon. S.S. Cox, of Ohio, on the Bill of H. Winter Davis, "To Guarantee to Certain States, Whose Governments Are Usurped or Overthrown, a Republican for of Government"; Delivered in the House of Representatives, May 1864*. Washington, DC: L. Towers, Printers.

Crabbe, Cecil V. Jr., and Pat M. Holt. 1989. *Invitation to Struggle: Congress, the President, and Foreign Policy*. Washington, DC: Congressional Quarterly Press.

Creel, George. 1920. *The War, The World, and Wilson*. New York: Harper and Brothers.

Cronin, Thomas E. 1989. "The President's Executive Power." In *Inventing the Presidency*, 180–208. Lawrence: University Press of Kansas.

Cronin, Thomas E., Michael A. Genovese, and Meena Bose. 2018. *Paradoxes of the Presidency*. New York: Oxford University Press.

Crosskey, William W. 1953. *Politics and the Constitution in the History of the United States*. Vols. 1 and 2. Chicago: University of Chicago Press.

Crosskey, William W., and William Jeffrey Jr. 1980. *Politics and the Constitution in the History of the United States: The Political Background of the Federal Convention*. Chicago: University of Chicago Press.

Crouch, Jeffrey P., Mark J. Rozell, and Mitchel A. Sollenberger. 2020. *The Unitary Executive Theory: A Danger to Constitutional Government*. Lawrence: University Press of Kansas.

Crovitz, L. Gordon, and Jeremy A. Rabkin. 1989. *The Fettered Presidency: Legal Constrains on the Executive Branch*. New York: AEI Press.

Currie, David P. 1965. *The Constitution in the Supreme Court: The Second Century 1888–1986*. Chicago: University of Chicago Press.

———. 1997. *The Constitution in Congress: The Federalist Period 1789–1801*. Chicago: University of Chicago Press.

Curry, Jabez Lamar. 1889. *Causes of the Power and Prosperity of the United States: An Address Delivered at the Annual Commencement of the University of Michigan, Thursday, June 27, 1889*. Ann Arbor, MI: Board of Regents.

———. 1901. *Civil History of the Government of the Confederate States with Some Personal Reminiscences*. Richmond, VA: B. F. Johnson Publishing.

Curtis, George Tickner. 1859. *The Just Supremacy of Congress Over the Territories*. Boston: A. Williams.

———.1884. "The Constitution of the United States, and Its History." In *Narrative and Critical History of America*, edited by Justin Winsor, vol. 7, 237–55. Boston: Houghton Mifflin.

———. (1858) 1889. *Constitutional History of the United States: From Their Declaration of Independence to the Close of the Civil War*. 2 vols. New York: Harper and Brothers.

Curtis, Thomas, and Donald Westerfield. 1992. *Congressional Intent*. Westport, CT: Praeger Press.

Cushman, Robert E. 1940. *The Supreme Court and the Constitution*. New York: Public Affairs Pamphlets.

Dahl, Robert A. 1956. *A Preface to Democratic Theory*. Chicago: University of Chicago Press.

Dane, Nathan. 1823–29. *A General Abridgment and Digest of American Law, with Occasional Notes and Comments*. 9 vols. Boston: Cumming, Hillard.

D'Arcy, Thomas McGee. 1865. *Notes on Federal Governments Past and Present*. Montreal: Dawson.

Davidson, Roger H. 2011. "Presidential Relations with Congress." In *Understanding the Presidency*, edited by James P. Piffner and Roger H. Davidson, 253–72. New York: Pearson.

Davidson, Roger H., Walter J. Oleszek, Frances E. Lee, and Eric Schickler. 2018. *Congress and Its Members*. Washington, DC: Sage/Congressional Quarterly.

Davis, Horace Andrew. 1884. *American Constitutions: The Relations of the Three Departments as Adjusted by A Century*. San Francisco: Read Before the Chit-Chat Club of San Francisco.

Davis, Jefferson. 1881. *The Rise and Fall of the Confederate Government*. Pantianos Classics.

Dearborn, John A. 2021. *Power Shifts: Congress and Presidential Representation*. Chicago: University of Chicago Press.

Deering, Christopher J. 1988. "Congress, the President, and Military Policy." *Annals of the American Academy of Political and Social Science* 499 (Sept.): 136–47.

Dennis, Alfred Pearce. 1905. "Our Changing Constitution." *Atlantic Monthly* 96 (Oct.): 525–35.

DiPaolo, Amanda. 2010. *Zones of Twilight: Wartime Presidential Powers and Federal Court Decision Making.* Lanham, MD: Lexington Books.

Diplomatic Correspondence. 1833. *The Diplomatic Correspondence of the United States of America, From the Signing of the Definitive Treaty of Peace, 10th September, 1783, to the Adoption of the Constitution, March 4, 1789.* 5 vols. Washington, DC: Francis Preston Blair.

Doctorow, E. L. 2014. "A Citizen Reads the Constitution." In *Citizen Doctorow: Art & Politics; The Nation Essays 1978–2015,* edited by Richard Lingeman. New York: National.

Donald, David Herbert. 2016. *Charles Sumner and the Rights of Man.* New York: Open Road Media.

Douglass, Frederick. 1960. Speech before the Scottish Anti-Slavery Society in Glasgow, Scotland, March 26, 1860.

Drakeman, Donald L. 2020. *The Hollow Core of Constitutional Theory: Why We Need the Framers.* New York: Cambridge University Press.

Driesen, David M. 2021. *The Specter of Dictatorship: Judicial Enabling of Presidential Power.* Stanford, CA: Stanford University Press.

Duer, William Alexander. 1858. *A Course of Lectures on the Constitutional Jurisprudence of the United States: Delivered Annually in Columbia College, New York.* New York: Harper and Brothers.

Dulles, John Foster. 1939. *War, Peace, and Change.* New York: Harper and Brothers.

Dunning, William Archibald. 1898. *Essays on the Civil War and Reconstruction and Related Topics.* New York: Macmillan.

Dwight, Theodore William. 1867. "Trial by Impeachment." *American Law Register.* Philadelphia: E. C. Markley and Sons.

Dworkin, Ronald. 1986. *Law's Empire.* Cambridge, MA: Belknap Press of Harvard University Press.

Earle, Edward Mead. 1937. *Federalist: A Commentary on the Constitution of the United States.* New York: Modern Library.

Eggers, Rowland. 1963. *The President of the United States.* New York: McGraw-Hill.

Elkins, Stanley, and Eric McKitrick. 1995. *The Age of Federalism: The Early American Republic, 1788–1800.* New York: Oxford University Press.

Eliot, Charles William. 1910. *American Historical Documents.* Vol. 43. New York: P. F. Collier and Sons.

Eliot, Charles William, Moorfield Storey, Louis D. Brandeis, Adolph J. Rodenbeck, and Roscoe Pound. 1915. "Preliminary Report on Efficiency in the Administration of Justice." *International Journal of Ethics* 25 (2): 252–54.

Elliot, Jonathan. 1836 (1888–1907). *The Debates in the Several State Conventions, of the Adoption of the Federal Constitution at Philadelphia in 1787 [. . .].* 5

vols. Washington: Printed for the editor. Originally published in 1836, then again in several volumes over several years from 1888 to 1907.

Elliott, William Y. 1938. *The Crisis of the American Constitution*. Tenth Lecture Under the James Goold Cutler Trust. College of William and Mary.

Ellis, Richard J. 1999. *Founding the American Presidency*. Boulder, CO: Rowman and Littlefield.

————. 2012. *The Development of the American Presidency*. New York: Routledge.

————. 2015. *The Quartet: Orchestrating the Second American Revolution, 1783–1789*. New York: Alfred A. Knopf.

Emerson, William. 1958–1959. "Franklin Roosevelt as Commander in Chief in World War II." *Military Affairs* 22 (4): 181–207.

Estcourt, J. H. 1863. *Rebellion and Recognition: Slavery, Sovereignty, Secession, and Recognition Considered*. Manchester, UK: Union and Emancipation Society.

Everett, Edward. 1861. *An Oration Delivered at the New York Academy of Music, July 4, 1861*. New York: James G. Gregory.

————. 1864. *Address of Hon. Edward Everett at the Consecration of the National Cemetery at Gettysburg, 19th November, 1863 [. . .]*. Boston: Little, Brown.

Ewald, William. 2012. "The Committee of Detail." *Constitutional Commentary* 28 (2): 197–285.

Fallon, Richard. H. (2004) 2014. *The Dynamic Constitution: An Introduction to American Constitutional Law*. New York: Cambridge University Press.

Fairlie, John Archibald. 1905. *The National Administration of the United States of America*. New York: Macmillan.

Farber, Daniel A. 2003. *Lincoln's Constitution*. Chicago: University of Chicago Press.

————. 2021. *Contested Ground: How to Understand the Limits of Presidential Power*. Oakland: University of California Press.

Farrand, Max. 1904. "Compromises of the Constitution." *American Historical Review* 9 (1): 479–89.

————. 1913. *The Framing of the Constitution of the United States*. New Haven, CT: Yale University Press.

————. 1921. *The Fathers of the Constitution: A Chronicle of the Establishment of the Union*. New Haven, CT: Yale University Press.

————, ed. 1966. *The Records of the Federal Convention of 1787*. 4 vols. New Haven, CT: Yale University Press.

Farrar, Timothy. 1862. "Adequacy of the Constitution." *New Englander* 21 (Jan.): 51–73.

————. 1867. *Manual of the Constitution of the United States of America*. Boston: Little, Brown.

Farrier, Jasmine. 2019. *Constitutional Dysfunction on Trial: Congressional Lawsuits and the Separation of Power*. Ithaca, NY: Cornell University Press.

Faulkner, Walter S. 1936. *A Child's History and Interpretation of the Constitution of the United States: The Constitution and Amendments Together with an Analytical Index*. 2nd vol. Lebanon, TN: Published by the author.

Fausold, Martin L. 1991. "An Historians Last Word." In Fausold and Shank, *The Constitution and the American Presidency*, 245–46.

Field, David Dudley. 1855. *Law Reform: An Address to the Graduating Class of the Law School of the University of Albany, Delivered March 23, 1855*. Albany, NY: W. C. Little.

Field, Jessie, and Scott Nearing. 1917. *Community Civics*. New York: Macmillan.

Finch, Charles Edgar. 1921. *Everyday Civics: Community, State, and Nation*. American Book Company.

Fisher, Louis. 1974. "Delegating Power to the President." In *Resolved: That the Powers of the Presidency Should Be Curtailed; A Collection of Excerpts and Bibliography Relating to the Intercollegiate Debate Topic, 1974–1975*, 258–82. Washington, DC: Congressional Research Service.

———. 2014. *The Law of the Executive Branch: Presidential Power*. New York: Oxford University Press.

———. 2017. *The Supreme Court Expansion of Presidential Power: Unconstitutional Leanings*. Lawrence: University Press of Kansas.

Fisher, Sidney George. 1860. *The Laws of Race as Connected with Slavery*. Philadelphia: Willis P. Hazard.

———. 1862. *Trial of the Constitution*. Philadelphia: J. B. Lippincott.

Fisher, Sidney George, and Charles Edward. 1856. *Kansas and the Constitution*. By "Cecil." Boston: Printed by Damrell and Moore.

Fiske, John. 1898. *The Critical Period of American History 1783–1789*. Boston: Houghton Mifflin.

Fitts, Michael A. 1996. "The Paradox of Power in the Modern State: Why a Unitary, Centralized Presidency May Not Exhibit Effective or Legitimate Leadership." *University of Pennsylvania Law Review* 144 (3): 827–902.

Fitzhugh, George. 1854. *Sociology for the South: Or, the Failure to Free Society*. Richmond, VA: A. Morris Publisher.

Flexner, James Thomas. 1970. *George Washington and the New Nation: (1783–1793)*. Boston: Little, Brown.

Foley, Michael. 1989. *The Silence of Constitutions: Gaps, "Abeyances," and Political Temperament in the Maintenance of Government*. New York: Routledge.

Ford, George. 1888. *Pamphlets on the Constitution of the United States: Published During Its Discussion by the People 1787–1788*. Brooklyn, NY: Burt Franklin Publisher.

Ford, Henry Jones. 1898. *The Rise and Growth of American Politics, a Sketch of Constitutional Development*. New York: Macmillan.

———. 1910. *The Cost of Our National Government: A Study in Political Pathology*. New York: Columbia University Press.

Ford, Paul. 1892. *Essays on the Constitution of the United States: Published during Its Discussion by the People, 1787–1788*. Brooklyn, NY: Historical Printing Club.

———. 1896. *George Washington*. Philadelphia: J. B. Lippincott.

Foster, Roger. 1895. *Commentaries on the Constitution of the United States, Historical and Juridical, with Observations upon the Ordinary Provisions of State Constitutions and a Comparison with the Constitutions of Other Countries.* Boston: Boston Book.

Frank, Jeffrey. 2022. *The Trials of Harry S. Truman: The Extraordinary Presidency of an Ordinary Man, 1945–1953.* New York: Simon and Schuster.

Frank, John P. 1966. "Edward Bates, Lincoln's Attorney General." *American Journal of Legal History* 10 (1): 34–50.

Frankfurter, Felix, and James M. Landis. 1928. *The Business of the Supreme Court: A Study in the Federal Judicial System.* New York: Macmillan.

Franklin, Daniel P. 1991. *Extraordinary Measures: The Exercise of Prerogative Powers in the United States.* Pittsburgh: University of Pittsburgh Press.

Freeman, Douglas Southall. 1954. *George Washington: A Biography.* Vol. 6, *Patriot and President.* New York: Scribner's.

Friedman, Lawrence M. 2019. *The History of American Law.* New York: Oxford University Press.

Friedrich, Carl J. 1967. *The Impact of American Constitutionalism Abroad.* Boston: Boston University Press.

Froomkin, A. Michael. 1994. "Still Naked After All These Years." *Northwestern University Law Review* 88 (4): 1420–35.

Frothingham, Richard. 1872. *The Rise of the Republic of the United States.* Boston: Little, Brown.

Gabriel, Ralph Henry. 1938. "Constitutional Democracy: A Nineteenth Century Faith." In *The Constitution Reconsidered*, edited for the American Historical Association by Conyers Reed, 247–58. New York: Columbia University Press.

Gallatin, Albert. 1879. *The Writings of Albert Gallatin.* 3 vols. Edited by Henry Adams. Philadelphia: J. B. Lippincott.

Garraty, John A. 1987. *Quarrels That Have Shaped the Constitution.* New York: Harper Perennial.

Garrison, William Lloyd. 1862. *The Abolitionists, and Their Relations to the War: An Address by William Lloyd Garrison, Delivered Tuesday Evening, January 14, 1862, at the Cooper Institute, New York.* Revised by the author.

Garvey, Todd. 2014. *The Take Care Clause and Executive Discretion in the Enforcement of the Law.* Washington, DC: Congressional Research Service.

Genovese, Michael A. 2011. *The Presidential Dilemma: Revisiting Democratic Leadership in the American System.* New Brunswick, NJ: Transaction Publishers.

Giffin, William Milford. 1888. *Civics for Young Americans; or, First Lessons in Government.* New York: A. Lovell and Co.

Gienapp, William E. 1987. *The Origins of the Republican Party 1852–1856.* New York: Oxford University Press.

Giroux, Henry A. 2011. "Barack Obama and the Resurgent Specter of Authoritarianism." *JAC* 31 (3/4): 415–40.

Glennon, Michael J. 1990. *Constitutional Diplomacy*. Princeton, NJ: Princeton University Press.

Godkin, Edwin Lawrence. 1864. "The Constitution, and Its Defects." *North American Review* 94:136–45.

———. 1898. *Unforeseen Tendencies of Democracy*. Boston, MA: Houghton Mifflin.

Goff, Guy Despard. 1931. The Appointing and Removal Powers of the President Under the Constitution of the United States. Fourth Lecture of the Cutler Foundation. https://scholarship.;aw.wm.edu/cutler/17.

Goldsmith, Jack. 2007. *The Terror Presidency: Law and Judgment Inside the Bush Administration*. New York: W. W. Norton.

Goldsmith, Jack, and John F. Manning. 2016. "The Protean Take Care Clause." *University of Pennsylvania Law Review* 164 (June): 1835–67.

Goldsmith, William M., ed. 1980. *The Growth of Presidential Power: A Documented History*. New York: Confucian Press.

———. 1984. "Separation of Powers and the Intent of the Founding Fathers." In *Congress, the President, and Foreign Policy*. Washington, DC: American Bar Association Committee on Law and National Security.

Goodnow, Frank J. 1904. *The Work of the American Political Science Association*. Proceedings of the American Political Science Association.

Goodrich, Charles Augustus. 1843. *A History of the United States of America, on a Plan Adapted to the Capacity of Youth, and Designed to Aid the Memory by Systematic Arrangement and Interesting Associations*. Boston: Jenks and Palmer.

Gormley, Ken. 2020. *The Presidents and the Constitution*. Vol. 1, *From the Founding Fathers to the Progressive Era*. New York: New York University Press.

Graglia, Lino A. 1988. "How the Constitution Disappeared." In Anzovin and Podell, *The U.S. Constitution and the Supreme Court*, 180–98.

Granger, Amos Phelps. 1859. *State Sovereignty—the Constitution—Slavery*. Remarks in the House of Representatives, Feb. 17, 1859.

Graubard, Stephen. 2004. *Command of Office: How War, Secrecy, and Deception Transformed the Presidency from Theodore Roosevelt to George W. Bush*. New York: Perseus Books.

Greeley, Horace. 1865. *The American Conflict: A History of the Great Civil War in the United States of America 1860-64*. Hartford, CT: O. D. Case & Company.

Greenstein, Fred I. 1994. *The Hidden-Hand Presidency: Eisenhower as Leader*. Baltimore: John Hopkins University Press.

———. 2009. *Inventing the Job of President: Leadership Style from George Washington to Andrew Jackson*. Princeton, NJ: Princeton University Press.

Griffis, William Elliot. 1915. *Millard Fillmore, Constructive Statesman, Defender of the Constitution, President of the United States*. Ithaca, NY: Andrus and Church.

Gronlund, Lawrence. 1884. *The Cooperative Commonwealth in Its Outlines: An Exposition of Modern Socialism*. New York: Lee and Shepard Publishers.

Guggenheimer, Jay Caesar. 1889. "The Development of the Executive Depart-ments." In *Essays in the Constitutional History of the United States in the Formative Period, 1775–1789*, edited by John Franklin Jameson, 116–85. Boston: Houghton Mifflin.

Guitteau, William Backus. 1911. *Government and Politics in the United States: A Textbook for Secondary Students*. Boston: Houghton Mifflin.

Haight, David E., and Larry D. Johnston. 1965. *The President: Roles and Powers*. Chicago: Rand McNally.

Hall, Ford P., Pressly S. Sikes, John E. Stoner, and Francis D. Wormuth. 1949. *American National Government: Law and Practice*. New York: Harper and Brothers.

Hall, Kermit, and Mark Hall. 2007. *Collected Works of James Wilson*. 2 vols. Indianapolis, IN: Liberty Fund.

Hallowell. 1826. *The Federalist, on The New Constitution, Written in the Year 1788, by Mr. Hamilton, Mr. Madison and Mr. Jay*. Glazier.

Hamilton, Alexander. 2001. *Alexander Hamilton: Writings*. New York: Literary Classics of the United States.

Hammond, Bray. 1970. *Sovereignty and an Empty Purse: Banks and Politics in the Civil War*. Princeton, NJ: Princeton University Press.

Hammond, James Henry. 1858. *Speech of Hon. James H. Hammond of South Carolina, on the Admission of Kansas under the Lecompton Constitution*. Washington, DC: Lemuel Towers.

Han, Lori Cox, and Diane J. Heith. 2018. *Presidents and the American Presidency*. New York: Oxford University Press.

Hardin, Charles M. 1974. *Presidential Power & Accountability: Toward a New Constitution*. Chicago: University of Chicago Press.

Hare, J. I. Clark. 1889. *American Constitutional Law*. 2 vols. Boston: Little, Brown.

Hargrove, Erwin C., and Roy Hoopes. 1975. *The Presidency: A Question of Power*. Boston: Educations Associates.

Harrison, Benjamin. 1897. *This Country of Ours*. New York: Scribner's.

Harrison, Benjamin, and Mary Lord Harrison. 1901. *View of an Ex-President, Benjamin Harrison: Being His Addresses and Writings Since the Close of His Administration as President of the United States*. Indianapolis, IN: Bowen-Merrill.

Harrison, Jonathan Baxter. 1880. *Certain Dangerous Tendencies in American Life: And Other Papers*. Boston: Houghton, Osgood.

Hart, Albert Bushnell. 1893. *Epochs of American History Formation of the Union 1750–1829*. New York: Longmans, Green.

———. 1898. *American History Told by Contemporaries*. Vol. 3, *National Expansion 1783–1845*. New York: Macmillan.

———. 1901. *American History Told by Contemporaries*. Vol. 4, *Welding of the Nation*. New York: Macmillan.

Hartz, Louis. 1955. *A Liberal Tradition in America: An Interpretation of American Political Thought Since the Revolution.* New York: Harcourt, Brace.

Haynes, Richard F. 1973. *The Awesome Power: Harry S. Truman as Commander in Chief.* Baton Rouge: Louisiana State University Press.

Heclo, Hugh. 1977. *Studying the Presidency.* A report to the Ford Foundation.

Heike, Paul. 2014. *The Myths That Made America: An Introduction to American Studies.* Transcript Publishing.

Henderson, Phillip G. 2000. *The Presidency: Then and Now.* Boulder, CO: Rowman and Littlefield.

Henkin, Louis. 1996. *Foreign Affairs and the Constitution.* New York: Oxford University Press.

Hennessey, Susan, and Benjamin Wittes. 2020. *Unmaking the Presidency: Donald Trump's War on the World's Most Powerful Office.* New York: Farrar, Straus and Giroux.

Henriques, Peter R. 2006. *Realistic Visionary: A Portrait of George Washington.* Charlottesville: University of Virginia Press.

Herring, E. Pendleton. 1940. *Presidential Leadership: The Political Relations of Congress and the Chief Executive.* New York: Rinehart.

Herring, George C. 2008. *Years of Peril and Ambition: U.S. Foreign Relations, 1776-1921.* New York: Oxford University Press.

Herz, Michael. 1993. "Imposing Unified Executive Branch Statutory Interpretation." *Cardozo Law Review* 15 (Oct.): 219-71.

Hetherington, Marc J., and Jonathan D. Weiler. 2009. *Authoritarianism & Polarization in American Politics.* New York: Cambridge University Press.

Hickey, William L. 1853. *The Constitution of the United States.* Philadelphia: T. K. and P. G. Collins.

Hill, David Jayne. 1913. "The Crisis in Constitutionalism." *North American Review.* Presented by Hon. Frank B. Brandegee of Connecticut in the Senate of the United States, Dec. 22, 1913, Washington, DC.

———. 1916a. *Americanism: What It Is.* New York: D. Appleton.

———. 1916b. "A Defense of the Constitution." *North American Review* 205 (736): 389-97.

Hill, John Philip. 1916. *The Federal Executive.* Boston: Houghton Mifflin.

Hill, Mabel, and Philip Davis. 1922. *Civics for New Americans.* Boston: Houghton Mifflin.

Hillard, George Stillman. 1868. *Memoir of Joseph Story, LL.D.* Boston: John Wilson.

Hinsdale, B. A. 1895. *The American Government: National and State.* Chicago: Werner School Book Company.

Hirschfield, Robert S. 1976. "The Scope and Limits of Presidential Power." In *Power and the Presidency,* edited by Philip C. Dolce and George H. Skau, 292-303. New York: Scribner's.

Hoar, George Frisbie. 1903. *Autobiography of Seventy Years.* Vols. 1 and 2. New York: Scribner's.

Hodder-Williams, Richard. 1987. "The President and the Constitution." In *The Modern Presidency: From Roosevelt to Reagan,* edited by Malcolm Shaw. New York: Harper and Row.

Holcombe, Arthur N. 1958. *Our More Perfect Union: From Eighteenth-Century to Twentieth-Century Practice.* Cambridge, MA: Harvard University Press.

Holmes, Oliver Wendell. 1892. *Ralph Waldo Emerson John Lothrop Motley Two Memoirs.* Boston: Houghton Mifflin.

———. 1896. *The Life and Letters of Oliver Wendell Holmes.* London: S. Low, Morston.

———. 1991. *The Common Law.* New York: Dover.

Holst, Hermann von. 1876. *The Constitutional and Political History of the United States.* Chicago: Callaghan.

———. 1887. *The Constitutional Law of the United States of America.* Chicago: Callaghan.

Holt, Henry. 1901. *Talks on Civics.* New York: Macmillan.

Hone, Philip. 1889. *The Diary of Philip Hone, 1821–1851.* 2 vols. New York: Dodd, Mead.

Hoover, Herbert. 1949. *The Hoover Commission Report: U.S. Commission on Organization of the Executive Branch of the Government.* 2nd edition. New York: McGraw-Hill.

———. 1952. *The Memoirs of Herbert Hoover: 1829–1941; The Great Depression.* New York: Macmillan.

Hopkins, John Henry. 1857. *American Citizen: His Rights and Duties, According to the Spirit of the Constitution of the United States.* New York: Pudney and Russell.

Horwill, Hervbert W. 1925. *The Usages of the American Constitution.* New York: Oxford University Press.

Horwitz, Morton J. 1992. *The Transformation of American Law 1870–1960: The Crisis of Legal Orthodoxy.* New York: Oxford University Press.

Howell, William G. 2003. *Power Without Persuasion: The Politics of Direct Presidential Action.* Princeton, NJ: Princeton University Press.

———. 2023. *An American Presidency: Institutional Foundations of Executive Politics.* Princeton, NJ: Princeton University Press.

Howell, William G., and David Milton Brent. 2013. *Thinking About the Presidency: The Primacy of Power.* Princeton, NJ: Princeton University Press.

Howell, William G., and Terry M. Moe. 2016. *Relic: How Our Constitution Undermines Effective Government and Why We Need a More Powerful Presidency.* New York: Basic Books.

———. 2023. "The Strongman Presidency and the Logic of Presidential Power." *Presidential Studies Quarterly* 53 (2): 145–68.

Hughes, Emmet John. 1972. *The Living Presidency*. New York: Coward, McCann, and Geoghegan.

Hunt, Gaillard, and James Brown Scott, eds. 1920. *The Debates in the Federal Convention of 1787 Which Framed the Constitution of the United States of America*. New York: Oxford University Press.

Hunt, Samuel Furman. 1908. *Orations and Historical Addresses*. Cincinnati, OH: R. Clarke.

Huntington, Samuel P. (1957) 1985. *The Soldier and the State: The Theory and Politics of Civil-Military Relations*. Cambridge, MA: Belknap Press of Harvard University Press.

Hurd, John Codman. 1858a. *The Law of Freedom and Bondage in the United States*. Boston, MA: Little, Brown.

———. 1858b. *A Treatise on the Right of Personal Liberty, and on the Writ of Habeas Corpus and the Practice Connected with It: With a View of the Law of the Extradition of Fugitives*. Albany, NY: W. C. Little, Law Booksellers.

Hutson, John H. 1983. "The Creation of the Constitution: The Integrity of the Documentary Record." *Texas Law Journal* 65:1–39.

———. 1986. "The Creation of the Constitution: The Integrity of the Documentary Record." *Texas Law Journal* 65:1–39.

———. 1987. "Riddles of the Federal Constitutional Convention." *William and Mary Quarterly* 44 (3): 411–23.

Hyman, Harold M. 1973. *A More Perfect Union: The Impact of the Civil War and Reconstruction on the Constitution*. New York: Alfred A. Knopf.

Jackson, Robert H. 1939. "Back to the Constitution." *American Bar Association Journal* 25 (9): 745–49.

———. 1941. *The Struggle for Judicial Supremacy: As Study of a Crisis in American Power Politics*. New York: Alfred A. Knopf.

Jameson, John Alexander. 1867. *The Constitutional Convention: Its History, Powers, and Modes of Proceeding*. Chicago: S. C. Groggs.

———. 1886. *An Introduction to the Study of the Constitutional and Political History of the States*. Baltimore: John Hopkins University Press.

———. 1890. "National Sovereignty." *Political Science Quarterly* 5 (2): 193–213.

———. 1902. *The United States: Its History and Constitution*. New York: Scribner's.

Jay, John. 1861. *The Great Conspiracy: An Address Delivered at Mt. Kisco, Westchester County, New York*. New York: James G. Gregory.

Jefferson, Thomas. 1984. *Thomas Jefferson: Writings*. New York: Literary Classic of America.

Jenkins, Gerald L. 1974. "The War Powers Resolution: Statutory Limitation on the Commander in Chief." In *Resolved: That the Powers of the Presidency Should Be Curtailed; A Collection of Excerpts and Bibliography Relating to the Intercollegiate Debate Topic, 1974–1975*, 142–57. Washington, DC: Congressional Research Service.

Jennings, Louis John. 1868. *Eighty Years of Republican Government*. London: John Murray.

Johnson, Allen. 1912. *Readings in American Constitutional History, 1776–1876*. Boston: Houghton Mifflin.

———. 1915. *Union and Democracy*. Boston: Houghton Mifflin.

Johnson, Andrew. 1860. *The Constitutionality and Rightfulness of Secession: Speech of Hon. Andrew Johnson of the United States, December 18 and 19, 1860*.

Johnson, Claudius, Daniel Ogden Jr., H. Paul Castleberry, and Thor Swanson. 1970. *American National Government*. New York: Thomas Y. Crowell.

Johnson, Donald Bruce, and Kirk H. Porter. 1973. *National Party Platforms: 1840–1972*. Urbana: University of Illinois Press.

Johnson, Reverdy. 1859. *Remarks on Popular Sovereignty: As Maintained and Denied Respectively by Judge Douglas, and Attorney-General Black*. Baltimore: Murphy.

Johnson, Rossiter. 1910. *The Story of the Constitution of the United States*. New York: Wessels and Bissel.

Johnson, Samuel. 1818. *Johnson's Dictionary of the English Language in Miniature*. London: C. Whittingham.

———. 1836. *Johnson's Dictionary Improved by Todd Abridged for the Use of Schools*. Boston: Charles J. Hendee.

———. 1855. *Johnson's Dictionary of the English Language, for the Use of Schools*. London: G. Routledge.

Johnston, Alexander. (1880) 1890. *History of American Politics*. New York: Henry Holt.

Kammen, Michael. 1987. *A Machine That Would Go of Itself: The Constitution in American Culture*. New York: Alfred A. Knopf.

Kasson, John A. 1904. *The Evolution of the Constitution of the United States of America and History of the Monroe Doctrine*. Boston: Houghton Mifflin.

Katyal, Neal Kumar. 2006. "Internal Separation of Powers: Checking Today's Most Dangerous Branch from Within." *Yale Law Journal* 115 (9): 2314–49.

Keller, Charles Roy, and George Wilson Pierson. 1930. "A New Madison Manuscript Relating to the Federal Convention of 1787." *American Historical Review* 36 (Oct.): 17–30.

Kelley, Christopher S. 2005. "Rethinking Presidential Power: The Unitary Executive and the George W. Bush Presidency." Paper presented at the Midwest Political Science Association, Chicago.

Kellogg, William. 1859. *Speech of Hon. W. Kellogg, of Illinois, on the Government of the Territories, and Donation of Land to Actual Settlers: Delivered in the House of Representatives, January 25, 1859*. Printed by Lemuel Towers.

Kelly, Alfred H., and Winfred A. Harbison. 1970. *The American Constitution: Its Origins and Development*. New York: W. W. Norton.

Kelly, Alfred H., Winfred A. Harbison, and Herman Belz. 1983. *The American Constitution: Its Origins and Development*. New York: W. W. Norton.

Kent, James. 1826. *Commentaries on American Law*. Vol. 1. New York: O. Halstead.

———. 1872. "Autobiographical Sketch of Charles Kent." *Southern Law Review* 2 (3): 381–91.

Ketcham, Ralph. 1986. *The Anti-Federalist Papers and the Constitutional Convention Debates*. New York: New American Library.

Kim, Adoree. 2018. "The Partiality Norm: Systematic Deference in the Office of Legal Counsel." *Cornell Law Review* 103 (3): 757–816.

Kimball, Everett. 1920. *The National Government of the United States*. Boston: Ginn.

Koenig, Louis William. 1944. *The Presidency in Crisis: Powers of the Office from the Invasion of Poland to Pearl Harbor*. New York: King's Crown Press.

———. 1975. *The Chief Executive*. New York: Harcourt Brace Jovanovich.

———. 1981. "Historical Perspective: The Swings and Roundabouts of Presidential Power." In *The Tethered Presidency: Congressional Restraints on Executive Power*, edited by Thomas M. Franck, 38–63. New York: New York University Press.

Koritansky, John C. 1979. "Alexander Hamilton's Philosophy of Government and Administration." *Publius* 9 (2): 99–122.

Kovacs, Kathryn E. 2018. "Rules about Rulemaking and the Rise of the Unitary Executive." *Administrative Law Review* 70 (3): 515–67.

Knott, Stephen F. 2019. *The Lost Soul of the American Presidency: The Decline into Demagoguery and the Prospects for Renewal*. Lawrence: University Press of Kansas.

Krent, Harold J. 2005. *Presidential Powers*. New York: New York University Press.

Laing, Matthew. 2012. "Towards a Pragmatic Presidency? Exploring the Waning of Political Time." *Polity* 44, no. 2 (April): 234–59.

Landon, Judson Stuart. 1889. *The Constitutional History and Government of the United States: A Series of Lectures*. Boston: Houghton Mifflin.

Langbein, John. 2004. *The History of the Yale Law School: Provenance and Perspective*. Edited by Anthony T. Kronman. New Haven, CT: Yale Law School.

Lawson, Gary. 2008. "What Lurks Beneath: NSA Surveillance and the Executive Power." *Boston University Law Review* 88 (2): 375–94.

Leighton, Ella V. 1920. *Making Americans: Responsive Readings for Teaching Citizenship*. Dansville, NY: F. A. Owen Publishing.

Lessig, Lawrence. 2019. *Fidelity & Constraint: How the Supreme Court Has Read the American Constitution*. New York: Oxford University Press.

Lessig, Lawrence, and Cas R. Sunstein. 1994. "The President and the Administration." *Columbia Law Review* 94 (1): 1–123.

Levitsky, Steven, and Daniel Ziblatt. 2018. *How Democracies Die: What History Reveals About Our Future*. New York: Viking.

Levy, Leonard W. 1988. *Original Intent and the Framers' Constitution*. Chicago: Ivan R. Dee.

Lewis, William Draper. 1909. "Treaty Powers: Protection of Treaty Rights by Federal Government." *Annals of the American Academy of Political and Social Science* 34 (2): 93–108.

Lieber, Francis. 1853. *On Civil Liberty and Self Government.* London: Richard Bentley.

———. 1861. *What Is Our Constitution, League, Pact, or Government? Two Lectures on the Constitution of the United States Concluding a Course on the Modern State, Delivered in the Law School of Columbia College, During the Winter of 1860 and 1861 to Which is Appended an Address on Secession Written in the Year 1851.* New York: Printed by direction of the board of trustees.

———. 1877. *On Civil Liberty and Self Government.* Philadelphia: J. B. Lippincott.

Lim, Elvin T. 2002. "Five Trends in Presidential Rhetoric: An Analysis of Rhetoric from George Washington to Bill Clinton." *Presidential Studies Quarterly* 32 (June): 328–48.

Lippman, Walter. 1913. *A Preface to Politics.* New York: Mitchell Kennerley.

Lodge, Henry Cabot. 1888. *The Federalist: A Commentary on the Constitution of the United States, Being a Collection of Essays Written in Support of the Constitution Agreed Upon September 17, 1787, by the Federal Convention.* New York: Putnam.

Lossing, Benson. 1868. *The Pictorial Field-Book of the War of 1812; or, Illustrations, by Pen and Pencil, of the History, Biography, Scenery, Relics and Traditions of the Last War for American independence.* New York: Harper and Brothers.

Lowell, James Russell. 1888. *The Independent in Politics: An Address Delivered Before the Reform Club of New York, April 13, 1888.* New York: Putnam.

Lowrey, Grosvenor Porter. 1863. *The Commander-in-Chief: A Defense Upon Legal Grounds of the Proclamation of Emancipation; and an Answer to ex-Judge Curtis' Pamphlet, entitled "Executive Power."* New York: Putnam.

Lynch, Peter. 2022. *The Influence of the Federalist Society on Judicial Politics and Law in the United States.* PhD diss., University of Kentucky, Department of Political Science.

MacDonald, William. 1906. *The American Nation: A History.* Vol. 15, *Jacksonian Democracy 1829–1837.* New York: Harper and Brothers.

———. 1913. *From Jefferson to Lincoln.* New York: Henry Holt.

———. 1921. *A New Constitution for a New Nation.* New York: B. W. Huebsc.

MacKenzie, John P. 2008. Absolute Power: How the Unitary Executive Theory Is Undermining the Constitution. New York: Century Foundation Press.

Maclay, Charles. 1890. The Journal of William Maclay: United States Senator from Pennsylvania 1789–1791. Boston: Little, Brown.

Mader, George. 2022. "Taking Care with Text: 'The Laws' of the Take Care Clause Do Not Include the Constitution, and There is No Autonomous Presidential Power of Constitutional Interpretation." *Denver Law Review* 99:1–44.

Madison, James. 1865. *Letters and Other Writings of James Madison.* Washington, DC: Government Printing Office.

————. 1999. *The Papers of James Madison: Presidential Series*. Vol. 4. Charlottesville: University Press of Virginia.

————. 2004. *The Papers of James Madison: Presidential Series*. Vol. 5. Charlottesville: University Press of Virginia.

Magruder, Allan B. 1890. *American Statesmen John Marshall*. Boston: Houghton Mifflin.

Maier, Pauline. 2010. *Ratification: The People Debate the Constitution 1787-1788*. New York: Simon and Schuster Paperbacks.

Main, Jackson Turner. 1987. "The Antifederalists: Critics of the Constitution." In *The Case Against the Constitution: From the Antifederalists to the Present*, edited by John F. Manley and Kenneth M. Dolbeare, 53-71. Amonk, NY: M. E. Sharpe.

Malone, Dumas. 1974. *Jefferson the President: First Second Term, 1805-1809*. Boston: Little, Brown.

Manheim, Lisa and Kathryn Watts. 2018. *The Limits of Presidential Power: A Citizen's Guide to the Law*. Published by the authors.

Manning, John F. 2004. "Foreword: The Means of Constitutional Power." *Harvard Law Review* 128 (1): 1-84.

Marshall, John. 2000. *The Life of George Washington*. Indianapolis, IN: Liberty Fund.

Mason, Thomas Alpheus. 1959. *The Supreme Court in a Free Society*. Englewood Cliffs, NJ: Prentice Hall.

Mason, Thomas Alpheus, and William M. Beaney. 1978. *American Constitutional Law: Introductory Essays and Selected Cases*. Englewood Cliffs, NJ: Prentice Hall.

Matheson, Scott M. Jr. 2009. *Presidential Constitutionalism in Perilous Times*. Cambridge, MA: Harvard University Press.

Maverick, Maury. 1939. *In Blood and Ink: The Life and Documents of American History*. Book 2, *Documents Tell the Tale*. New York: Morgan Age Books.

May, Samuel Joseph. 1869. *Some Recollections of Our Antislavery Conflict*. Boston: Fields, Osgood.

McAdam, David, Henry Bischoff Jr., Richard H. Clarke, Jackson O. Dykman, Joshua M. Van Cott, and George G. Reynolds. 1897. *History of the Bench and Bar of New York*. New York: New York History Company. Multiple volumes.

McBain, Howard Lee. 1928. *The Living Constitution: A Consideration of the Realities and Legends of Our Fundamental Law*. New York: Macmillan.

McCabe, James D. 1874. *The Centennial History of the United States: From the Discovery of the Continent to the Close of the First Century of American Independence*. Philadelphia: National Publishing.

McCarthy, Charles. 1916. *A Manual for Teachers of Civics in the Upper Grammar Grades, Junior High Schools, and Continuing Schools*. New York: Thompson, Brown.

McClain, Emlin. 1910. *Constitutional Law in the United States*. New York: Longmans, Green.

McCleary, James Thompson. 1908. *Studies in Civics*. New York: American Book Company.

McClellan, George Brinton. 1887. *McClellan's Own Story: The War for the Union, The Soldiers Who Fought It, The Civilians Who Directed It and His Relations to It and to Them*. New York: Charles L. Webster and Co.

McConnell, Michael W. 2020. *The President Who Would Not Be King: Executive Power Under the Constitution*. Princeton, NJ: Princeton University Press.

McCoy, Donald R. 1991. "The Constitution and the Truman Presidency and the Post-World War II Era." In *The Constitution and the American Presidency*, edited by Martin L. Fausold and Alan Shank, 107–28. Albany: State University of New York Press.

McDonald, Forrest. 1994. *The American Presidency: An Intellectual History*. Lawrence: University Press of Kansas.

———. 2017. "Foreword to the Liberty Fund Edition." In *The Creation of the Presidency, 1775–1789*, by Charles C. Thach Jr. Indianapolis, IN: Liberty Fund.

McGee, Thomas D'Arcy. 1865. *Notes on Federal Governments, Past and Present*. Montreal: Dawson Brothers.

McIlwain, Charles Howard. 1932. The American Political System. London: Hamish Hamilton.

McLaughlin, Andrew C., editor, and Albert Bushnell Hart. 1914. Cyclopedia of American Government. Vol. 3. New York: D. Appleton.

McLaughlin, Andrew Cunningham. 1905. The Confederation and the Constitution, 1783–1789. New York: Harper and Brothers.

———. 1935. *A Constitutional History of the United States*. New York: D. Appleton.

McMaster, John Bach. 1885. *A History of the People of the United States, From the Revolution to the Civil War*. 5 vols. New York: D. Appleton.

———. 1890. *Political History of the United States: Outline of the Lectures Delivered before the Junior Class, Wharton School*. Philadelphia: Department of American History, University of Pennsylvania.

McPherson, Edward. 1864. *The Political History of the United States During the Great Rebellion from November 6, 1860, to July 4, 1864*. Washington, DC: Philip and Solomons.

McPherson, Lionel K. 2011. "The Instability of 'Executive Discretion.'" *Nomos* 50:144–55.

Meacham, Jon. 2012. *Thomas Jefferson: The Art of Power*. New York: Random House.

Meese, Edwin. 1988. "Interpreting the Constitution." In Anzovin and Podell, *The U.S. Constitution and the Supreme Court*, 156–65.

Merriam, Charles Edward. 1931. *The Written Constitution and the Unwritten Attitude*. Chicago: R. R. Smith.

Mezey, Michael L. 1989. *Congress, the President and Public Policy*. Boulder: Westview Press.

Milkis, Stanley M., and Michael Nelson. 1994. *The American Presidency: Origins and Development*. Washington, DC: Congressional Quarterly.

Milkis, Sidney M., Daniel J. Tichenor, and Laura Blessing. 2013. "The Historical Presidency: 'Rallying Force': The Modern Presidency, Social Movements, and the Transformation of American Politics." *Presidential Studies Quarterly* 43, no. 3 (Sept.): 641–70.

Miller, Merle. 1974. *Plain Speaking: An Oral Biography of Harry S. Truman.* New York: Berkeley Books.

Milton, George Fort. 1945. *The Use of Presidential Power, 1789–1943.* Boston: Little, Brown.

Minnigerode, Meade. 1924. *The Fabulous Forties: 1840–1950.* New York: Garden City Publishing.

Moe, Terry M. 1985. "The Politicized Presidency." In *New Directions in American Politics*, edited by John E. Chubb and Paul E. Peterson. Washington, DC: Brookings Institution.

Moe, Terry M., and William Howell. 1999. "The Presidential Power of Unilateral Action." *Journal of Law, Economics, and Organization* 15 (1): 132–79.

Monaghan, Henry P. 1993. "The Protective Power of the Presidency." *Columbia Law Review* 93 (1): 1–74.

Monroe, Billy W. 2021. *The President's Law Firm: The Office of Legal Counsel from Roosevelt to Trump.* New York: Peter Lang.

Moore, John Bassett. 1912. *Four Phases of American Development: Federalism, Democracy, Imperialism, Expansion.* Baltimore: John Hopkins University Press.

Moran, Thomas Francis. 1895. *The Rise and Development of the Bicameral System in America.* Baltimore: John Hopkins University Press.

———. 1904. *The History of North America: The Formation and Development of the Constitution.* Vol. 7. Philadelphia: Printed for subscribers by G. Barrie and Sons.

———. 1917. *American Presidents: Their Individualities and Their Contributions to American Progress.* New York: Thomas Y. Crowell.

Morey, William C. 1891. "The Genesis of a Written Constitution." *Annals of the American Academy of Political and Social Science*, April.

Morison, Samuel Eliot, and Henry Steele Commager. 1962. *The Growth of the American Republic.* New York: Oxford University Press.

Morrill, Donald. 1903. *Federal and State Government: An Elementary Treatise on the Civil Government of the United States and the State of Michigan.* Chicago: Scott, Foresman.

Morris, Charles. 1900. *The Child's History of the United States from the Earliest Times to the Present Day.* Washington: W. E. Scull.

Morris, Irwin L. 2010. *The American Presidency: An Analytical Approach.* Boston, MA: Cambridge University Press.

Mortenson, Julian Davis. 2019. "Article II Vests the Executive Power, Not the Royal Prerogative." *Columbia Law Review* 119 (5): 1169–1272.

———. 2020. "The Executive Power Clause." *University of Pennsylvania Law Review* 168 (5): 1269–1367.

Mosher, Frederick C., ed. 1976. *Basic Documents of American Public Administration 1776–1950*. New York: Holmes and Meier Publishers.

Motley, John Lothrop. 1889. *The Correspondence of John Lothrop Motley*. London: J. Murray.

Mounk, Yascha. 2018. *The People vs. Democracy: Why Our Freedom Is in Danger & How to Save It*. Cambridge, MA: Harvard University Press.

Mulford, Elisha. 1877. *The Nation: The Foundations of Civil Order and Political Life in the United States*. New York: Hurd and Houghton.

Mulhern, J. Peter. 1988. "In Defense of the Political Question Doctrine." *University of Pennsylvania Law Review* 137 (1): 97–176.

Munro, William Bennett. 1930. *The Makers of the Unwritten Constitution: The Fred Morgan Kirby Lectures, Delivered at Lafayette College, 1929*. New York: Macmillan.

———. 1946. *The Government of the United States*. New York: Macmillan.

Munro, William Bennett, Lawrence B. Evans, and Roger Sherman Hoar. 1917. *A Manual for the Constitutional Convention*. Boston: Wright and Potter Printing.

Murphy, Walter F., James E. Fleming, and Sotirios A. Barber. 1995. *American Constitutional Interpretation*. Westbury, NY: Foundation Press.

Natelson, Robert G. 2009. "The Original Meaning of the Constitution's 'Executive Vesting Clause'—Evidence from Eighteenth Century Drafting Practice." *Whittier Law Review* 31 (1): 1–46.

Nathan, Richard P. 1991. "The Presidency after Reagan: Don't Change It—Make It Work." In *Looking Back on the Reagan Presidency*, edited by Larry Berman, 195–206. Baltimore: John Hopkins University Press.

National Education of the United States. 1915. *The Teaching of Community Civics*. Washington, DC: Government Printing Office.

Neustadt, Richard E. 1960 (1990). *Presidential Power and the Modern Presidents: The Politics of Leadership from Roosevelt to Reagan*. New York: Free Press.

Nevins, Allan. 1953. "The Constitution, Slavery, and the Territories." In *The Gaspar G. Bacon Lectures on the Constitution of the United States 1940–1950*, 97–141. Boston: Boston University Press.

New England History Teacher's Association. 1904. *Outline of American History, Reprinted from "A History Syllabus for Secondar Schools."* Boston: D. C. Heath.

———. 1910. *An Outline for the Study of American Civil Government, with Special Reference to Training for Citizenship*. New York: Macmillan.

Nichols, David K. 1994. *The Myth of the Modern Presidency*. University Park: Pennsylvania State University Press.

Nourse, Victoria. 2018. "Reclaiming the Constitutional Text from Originalism: The Case of Executive Power." *California Law Review* 106 (1): 1–44.

O'Brien, Thomas Dillon. 1922. *The Great Experiment*. New York: Encyclopedia Press.

Odell, Talbot. 1942. *War Powers of the President: War Powers of the American Presidency Derived from the Constitution and Statutes of Their Historical Background*. Booklet 220. Washington Service Bureau.

Orth, Samuel P. 1906. *Five American Politicians: A Study in the Evolution of American Politics.* Cleveland, OH: Burrows Brothers.

Paludan, Philip Shaw. 1975. *A Covenant with Death: The Constitution, Law, and Equity in the Civil War Era.* Urbana: University of Illinois Press.

Parker, Alton B. 1922. "Teaching 'Back the Constitution.'" *Virginia Law Register* 7:732–35.

Parker, Joel. 1862. *Constitutional Law: With Reference to the Present Condition of the United States.* Cambridge, MA: Welch, Bigelow.

———. 1869. *The Three Powers of Government. The Origin of the United States; and the Status of the Southern States, on the Suppression of the Rebellion. The Three Dangers of the Republic. Lectures Delivered in the Law School of Harvard College, and in Dartmouth College, 1867–68, and '69.* New York: Hurd and Houghton.

Parsons, Theophilus. 1861. *The Constitution, Its Origin, Function and Authority.* A lecture introductory to the subject of constitutional law, delivered before the law school of Harvard University. Boston: Little, Brown.

Paschal, George Washington. 1868. *The Constitution of the United States: Defined and Carefully Annotated.* Washington, DC: W. H. and O. H. Morrison, Law Booksellers.

———. 1870. *Lecture Delivered to the American Union Academy of Literary, Science, and Art, at the Special Meeting Called for the Purpose, March 7, 1870.* Washington, DC: W. H. and O. H. Morrison, Law Booksellers.

Patrick, John J. 1987. *Teaching and Learning about the Constitution in Secondary School Courses on American History: Persistent Problems and Promising Practices.* Bloomington: Indiana University Press.

———. 1991. *The Constitution and Bill of Rights in the Curricula of Our Schools: Coverage, Materials, and Methods.* Bloomington: Indiana University Press.

Patrick, John J., Richard C. Remy, and Mary Jane Turner. 1986. *Education on the Constitution in Secondary Schools: Teaching Strategies and Materials for the Bicentennial and Beyond.* Bloomington: Indiana University Press.

Patterson, Caleb Perry. 1929. *American Government.* New York: D. C. Heath.

———. 1947. *Presidential Government in the United States: The Unwritten Constitution.* Chapel Hill: University of North Carolina Press.

Paludan, Phillip Shaw. 2007. "'Dictator Lincoln': Surveying Lincoln and the Constitution." *OAH Magazine of History* (Jan.): 8–13.

Peffer, W. A. 1900. "Imperialism America's Historic Policy." *North American Review* 171:246–58.

Peissner, Elias. 1861. *The American Question in Its National Aspect.* New York: H. H. Lloyd.

Pennsylvania Minority. 1987. "The Address and Reasons of Dissent of the Minority of the Convention of Pennsylvania to Their Constituents." Published originally in the *Pennsylvania Packet and Daily Advertiser,* Dec. 18, 1787, as "The Case Against the Constitution: From the Antifederalists to the Present," edited by John F. Manley and Kenneth M. Dolbeare, 72–91. Amonk, NY: M. E. Sharpe.

Pepper, George Wharton. 1898. *Our National Constitution as Related to National Growth: A Consideration of Certain Aspects of the War with Spain.* Philadelphia: G. H. Buchanan.

Peterson, Mark A. 2007. "The Three Branches of Government: Powers, Relationships, and Checks." In *A Republic Divided*, by the Annenberg Democracy Project, 91–120. New York: Oxford University Press:

Phelps, F. W. 1920. *The United States Constitution Simplified: Don't Quarrel with Your Government Read Your Constitution.* Seattle: F. W. Phelps.

Phelps, Glenn A. 1989. "George Washington and the Founding of the Presidency." *Presidential Studies Quarterly* 17 (2): 345–63.

Pickens, Francis Wilkinson. 1851. *Speech of Hon. F. W. Pickens, Delivered before a Public Meeting of the People of the District, Held at Edgefield C. H., S. C., July 7, 1851.* Edgefield, SC: Printed at the Advertiser Office.

Pillard, Cornelia, T. L. 2004. "The Unfulfilled Promise of the Constitution in Executive Hands." *Michigan Law Review* 103 (4): 676–758.

Pious, Richard M. 1991. "Presidential War Powers, the War Powers Resolution, and the Persian Gulf." In Fausold and Shank, *The Constitution and the American Presidency*, 195–210.

———. 2010. *Why President's Fail: White House Decision Making from Eisenhower to Bush II.* Boulder, CO: Rowman and Littlefield.

Plass, Anna Alida. 1912. *Civics for Americans in the Making.* Boston: D. C. Heath.

Pollard, Edward Alfred. 1866. *The Lost Cause: A New Southern History of the War of the Confederates.* New York: E. B. Treat Publishers.

Polsby, Nelson W. 1986. *Congress and the President.* Englewood Cliffs, NJ: Prentice Hall.

Pomeroy, John Norton. 1868. *An Introduction to the Constitutional Law of the United States: Especially Designed for Students, General and Professional.* New York: Hurd and Houghton.

Porter, William Dennison. 1860. *State Sovereignty and the Doctrine of Coercion, by the Hon. W. M. D. Porter; Together with a Letter from Hon. J. K. Paulding, Former Sec. of Navy. The Right to Secede by "States."* Charleston, SC: Evans and Cogwell's Steam-Power Presses.

Posner, Eric A. 2008. *How Judges Think.* Cambridge, MA: Harvard University Press.

———. 2016. "Presidential Leadership and the Separation of Powers." *Daedalus* 145 (3): 35–43.

Posner, Eric A., and Adrian Vermeule. 2007. "The Credible Executive." *University of Chicago Law Review* 74 (3): 865–913.

———. 2011. *The Executive Unbound: After the Madisonian Republic.* New York: Oxford University Press.

Pound, Roscoe. 1923. *Interpretations of Legal History.* New York: Macmillan.

Powell, Thomas Reed. 1912. "Separation of Powers Administrative Exercise of Legislative and Judicial Power: The Delegation of Power to Act." *Political Science Quarterly* 27 (2): 215–38.

———. 1913. *The Principle of Separation of Powers in Its Application to the Administrative Exercise of the Police Power.* Submitted in partial fulfillment of the requirements of the degree of doctor of philosophy in the faculty of political science, Columbia University.

"Powers of the Federal Government." 1907. *Yale Law Journal* 17 (1): 47–49.

Prakash, Saikrishna Bangalore. 1993. "Hail to the Chief Administrator: The Framers and the President's Administrative Power." *Yale Law Journal* 102 (4): 991–1017.

———. 2013. "The Imbecilic Executive." *Virginia Law Review* 99 (7): 1361–1433.

———. 2015. *Imperial from the Beginning: The Constitution of the Original Executive.* New Haven, CT: Yale University Press.

———. 2020. *The Living Presidency: An Originalist Argument Against Its Ever-Expanding Powers.* Cambridge, MA: Befknap Press of Harvard University.

Pratt, Julius W. 1955. *A History of United States Foreign Policy.* New York: Prentice Hall.

Pritchett, Charles Herman. 1959. *The American Constitution.* New York: McGraw-Hill.

Prolman, Marilyn. 1969. *The Story of the Constitution.* Chicago: Children's Press.

Rakove, Jack N. 1990. "Mr. Meese, Meet Mr. Madison." In *Interpreting the Constitution: The Debate over Original Intent,* 179–94. Boston: Northeastern University Press.

Randall, James Garfield. 1929. "The Interrelation of Social and Constitutional History. *American Historical Review* 35 (Oct.): 1–13.

Randall, William Sterne. 1993. *Thomas Jefferson: A Life.* New York: Henry Holt.

Rasmussen, Dennis C. 2021. *Fears of a Setting Sun: The Disillusionment of America's Founders.* Princeton, NJ: Princeton University Press.

Rawle, William. 1824. *Two Addresses to "The Associate Members of the Bar of Philadelphia."* State Library Pennsylvania.

———. 1825. *An Inaugural Discourse Delivered on the 5th of November, 1825, Before the Historical Society of Pennsylvania.*

———. 1829. *A View of the Constitution of the United States of America.* Philadelphia: P. H. Nicklin.

Rawles, William A. 1904. *Historical Sketch of the University.* Bloomington: Indiana University Press.

Rav, Orman. 1945. *Introduction to American Government: The National Government.* Century Political Science Series. Century.

Reed, Christine M. 2008. "Public Administration Theory and the 'Soft' State." *Administrative Theory & Praxis* 30 (3): 355–58.

Remini, Robert V. 2006. *The House: The History of the House of Representatives*. New York: Harper Collins.

Renan, Daphna. 2018. "Presidential Norms and Article II." *Harvard Law Review* 131 (8): 2186–2282.

Rhodes, James Ford. (1896) 1920. *History of the United States*. Vols. 1–9. New York: Macmillan.

Riccards, Michael P. 1987. *A Republic, If You Can Keep It: The Foundation of the American Presidency, 1700–1800*. New York: Greenwood Press.

Rich, Bennett Milton. 1941. *The Presidents and Civil Disorder*. Washington, DC: Brookings Institution.

Richardson, James D. 1897. *A Compilation of the Messages and Paper of the Presidents*. Washington, DC: Bureau of National Literature.

Roberts, Owen. 1953. "American Constitutional Government: The Blueprint and the Structure." In *The Gaspar G. Bacon Lectures on the Constitution of the United States 1940–1950*, 381–422.

Robinson, Donald. 1987. *"To the Best of My Ability": The Presidency and the Constitution*. New York: W. W. Norton.

Roche, John P., and Leonard W. Levy. 1964. *The Presidency*. New York: Harcourt, Brace, and World.

Rodell, Fred. 1939. *Woe unto You Lawyers*. Open Source Collection.

Rogowski, Jon C. 2015. "The Historical Presidency: Presidential Incentives, Bureaucratic Control, and Party Building in the Republican Era." *Presidential Studies Quarterly* 45 (4): 796–811.

Romaine, Benjamin. 1832. *State Sovereignty: And a Certain Dissolution of the Union*. New York: James Kennaday.

Roosevelt, Franklin. 1934. *On Our Way*. London: Faber and Faber.

Roosevelt, Theodore. 1913. *An Autobiography*. New York: Scribner's.

Rosen, S. McKee. 1935. *Political Process: A Functional Study in American Government*. New York: Harper and Brothers.

Rosenkranz, Nicholas Quinn. 2002. "Federal Rules of Statutory Interpretation." *Harvard Law Review* 115 (June): 2085–2157.

Rossiter, Clinton. (1948) 2011. *Constitutional Dictatorship: Crisis Government in the Modern Democracies*. New York: Routledge. Citations refer to the 2011 edition.

———. (1956) 1960. *The American Presidency*. New York: Harcourt, Brace, and World.

———. 1966. *1787 the Grand Convention*. New York: Macmillan.

Rudalevige, Andrew. 2005. *The New Imperial Presidency: Renewing Presidential Power After Watergate*. Ann Arbor: University of Michigan Press.

———. 2013. "Unilateral Powers of the Presidency." In *The Powers of the Presidency*, 1–34. Washington, DC: Congressional Quarterly Press.

Rush, Benjamin. 1886. "The Defects of the Confederation." In *American Patriotism: Speeches, Letters, and Other Papers Which Illustrate the Foundation, the Development, the Preservation of the United States of America*, edited by Selim H. Peabody. New York: John R. Alden.

Russell, Bertrand. (1938) 1996. *Power: A New Social Analysis*. London: George Allen and Unwin.

Saffell, David C. 1973. *The Politics of American National Government*. Cambridge, MA: Winthrop Publishers.

Saltzman, Rachel Ward. 2010. "Executive Power and the Office of Legal Counsel." *Yale Law & Policy Review* 28 (2): 439–80.

Scalia, Antonin. 1997. *A Matter of Interpretation: Federal Courts and the Law*. Princeton, NJ: Princeton University Press.

———. 2020. *The Essential Scalia: On the Constitution, the Courts, and the Rule of Law*. Edited by Jeffrey S. Sutton and Edward Whelan. New York: Crown Forum.

Schlesinger, Arthur M. Jr. 1986. *The Cycles of American History*. Boston: Houghton Mifflin.

———. (1973) 2004a. *The Imperial Presidency*. Washington, DC: Brookings Institution.

———. 2004b. *War and the American Presidency*. New York: W. W. Norton.

Schurz, Carl. 1907. *The Reminiscences of Carl Schurz*. 3 vols. New York: McClure.

———. 1913. *Speeches, Correspondence and Political Papers of Carl Schurz*. Selected and edited by Frederic Bancroft. Vol. 1. New York: Putnam.

Schwartz, Bernard. 1963. *The Power of Government*. Vol. 2, *The Powers of the President*. New York: Macmillan.

Scott, David B. 1878. *Scott's Manual of United States History: A Manual of History of the United States*. New York: Collins and Brother.

Scott, Eben Grenough. 1882. *The Development of Constitutional Liberty in the English Colonies of America*. New York: Putnam.

———. 1895. *Reconstructing During the Civil War in the United States of America*. Boston: Houghton.

Schouler, James. 1908. *Ideals of the Republic*. Boston: Little, Brown.

Segal, Eric J. 2018. *Originalism as Faith*. Cambridge, MA: Cambridge University Press.

Sergeant, Thomas. 1822. *Constitutional Law. Being A Collection of Points Arising Upon the Constitution and Jurisprudence of the United States Which Have Been Settled by Judicial Decision and Practice*. Philadelphia: Abraham Small.

Shane, Peter M. 2009. *Madison's Nightmare: How Executive Power Threatens American Democracy*. Chicago: University of Chicago Press.

———. 2022. *Democracy's Chief Executive: Interpreting the Constitution and Defining the Future of the Presidency*. Oakland: University of California Press.

Shane, Peter M., and Harold H. Bruff. 2011. *Separation of Powers: Cases and Materials*. Durham, NC: Carolina Academic Press.

Shank, Alan. 1991. "A Political Science Perspective." In Fausold and Shank, *The Constitution and the American Presidency*, 247–49.

Shankman, Andrew. 2018. *Original Intents: Hamilton, Jefferson, Madison and the American Founding*. New York: Oxford University Press.

Sheffer, Martin S. 1999. *The Judicial Development of Presidential War Powers*. Westport, CT: Praeger Publishers.

Shelton, Thomas W. 1918. *Spirit of the Courts*. Baltimore: John Murphy.

Sherman, John. 1895. *John Sherman's Recollections of Forty Years in the House, Senate, and Cabinet. An Autobiography*. Chicago: Werner.

Sims, Henry Upson. 1917. "The Problem of Reforming Judicial Administration in America: IV. The Problem of Reforming the Bar." *Virginia Law Review* 4:612–33.

Skowronek, Stephen. 1993. *The Politics Presidents Make: Leadership from John Adams to George Bush*. Cambridge, MA: Harvard University Press.

———. 2008. *Presidential Leadership in Political Time: Reprise and Reappraisal*. Lawrence: University Press of Kansas.

———. 2009. "The Conservative Insurgency and Presidential Power: A Developmental Perspective on the Unitary Executive." *Harvard Law Review* 122 (8): 2070–2103.

———. 2015. "The Unsettled State of Presidential History." In *Recapturing the Oval Office: New Historical Approaches to the American Presidency*, edited by Brian Balogh and Bruce J. Schulman, 13–33. Ithaca, NY: Cornell University Press.

———. 2021. *Phantoms of a Beleaguered Republic: The Deep State and the Unitary Executive*. New York: Oxford University Press.

Skowronek, Steven, John Dearborn, and Desmond King. 2021. *Phantoms of a Beleaguered Republic: The Deep State and the Unitary Executive*. New York: Oxford University Press.

Smith, James Morton, ed. 1995. *The Republic of Letters: The Correspondence between Thomas Jefferson and James Madison 1776–1826*. New York: W. W. North.

Sparks, Jared. 1839. *The Life of George Washington*. Boston: Ferdinand Andrews.

———. 1855. *The Writings of George Washington; Being His Correspondence, Addresses, Messages, and Other Papers, Official and Private, Selected and Published from the Original Manuscripts; with A Life of the Author, Notes, and Illustrations*. Boston: Little, Brown.

Spencer, Jesse Ames, and Benson John Lossing. 1874. *History of the United States of America*. 8 vols. New York: Johnson and Miles.

Spitzer, Robert J. 2011. "Is the Constitutional Presidency Obsolete?" In *The Presidency in the Twenty-First Century*, edited by Charles W. Dunn. Lexington: University Press of Kentucky.

Spooner, Lysander. 1870. *No Treason: The Constitution of No Authority.* Pantianos Classics.

Southworth, A. T. 1924. *The Common Sense of the Constitution of the United States.* New York: Allyn and Bacon.

Steffens, Lincoln. 1938. *The Letters of Lincoln Steffens.* New York: Harcourt, Brace.

Stein, Herbert. 1969. *The Fiscal Revolution in America.* Chicago: University of Chicago Press.

Stephens, Alexander H. 1868. *A Constitutional View of the Late War Between the States: Its Causes, Character, Conduct and Results.* Philadelphia: National Publishing.

Stephen, James Fitzjames. 1874. *Liberty, Equality, Fraternity.* London: Smith, Elder.

Stevens, C. Ellis. 1894. *Sources of the Constitution of the United States, Considered in Relation to Colonial and English History.* New York: Macmillan.

Stewart, David O. 2021. *George Washington: The Political Rise of America's Founding Father.* New York: Dutton.

Stickney, Albert. 1879. *A True Republic.* New York: Harper and Brothers.

Stid, Daniel D. 1998. *The President as Statesman: Woodrow Wilson and the Constitution.* Lawrence: University Press of Kansas.

Stimson, Frederic Jesup. 1907. "The Constitution and the People's Liberties." *North American Review* 184:508–12.

Stimson, James A. 1976. "Public Support for American Presidents: A Cyclical Model." *Public Opinion Quarterly* 40:1–21.

———. 1976–1977. "On Disillusionment with the Expectations/Disillusion Theory: A Rejoinder." *Public Opinion Quarterly* 40 (Winter): 541–43.

Storing, Herbert. 1981a. *The Complete Anti-Federalist.* 7 vols. Chicago: University of Chicago Press.

———. 1981b. *What the Anti-Federalists Were For: The Political Thought of the Opponents of the Constitution.* Chicago: University of Chicago Press.

Story, Joseph. 1829. "An Address Delivered before the Members of the Suffolk Bar, at Their Anniversary, on the Fourth of September, 1821, at Boston." *American Jurist and Law Magazine* 1 (1): 1–34.

———. 1833. *Commentaries on the Constitution of the United States.* Boston: R. Rotunda and J. Nowek.

———. 1840. *A Familiar Exposition of the Constitution of the United States: Containing a Brief Commentary on Every Clause, Explaining the True Nature, Reasons, and Objects Thereof; Designed for the Use of School and Libraries and General Readers.* Boston: Thomas H. Webb.

———. 1858. *Commentaries on the Constitution of the United States: With a Preliminary Review of the Constitutional History of the Colonies and States Before the Adoption of the Constitution.* Vols. 1 and 2. Clark, NJ: Lawbook Exchange.

———. 1873. *Commentaries on the Constitution of the United States*. Boston: Little, Brown.

Storey, Moorfield. 1911. *The Reform of Legal Procedure*. New Haven, CT: Yale University Press.

Strang, Lee J. 2019. *Originalism's Promise: A Natural Law Account of the American Constitution*. Cambridge, MA: Cambridge University Press.

Strong, George Templeton. 1952a. *The Diary of George Templeton Strong: The Turbulent Fifties 1850–1859*. Edited by Allan Nevins and Milton Halsey Thomas. New York: Macmillan.

———. 1952b. *The Diary of George Templeton Strong: The Civil War 1860–1865*. Edited by Allan Nevins and Milton Halsey Thomas. New York: Macmillan.

Strum, Albert L. 1974. "Emergencies and the Presidency." In *Resolved: That the Powers of the Presidency Should Be Curtailed: A Collection of Excerpts and Bibliography Relating to the Intercollegiate Debate Topic, 1974–1975*, 62–77. Washington, DC: Congressional Research Service.

Sunstein, Cass R. 1995. "An Eighteenth Century Presidency in a Twenty-First Century World." *Arkansas Law Review* 48 (1): 1–22.

———. 2006. "Beyond Marbury: The Executive Power to Say What the Law Is." *Yale Law Journal* 115 (9): 2580–2610.

———. 2009. *A Constitution of Many Minds: Why the Founding Document Doesn't Mean What I Did Before*. Princeton, NJ: Princeton University Press.

Sutherland, George. 1910. "The Internal and External Powers of the National Government." *North American Review* 191:373–89.

———. 1919. *Constitutional Power and World Affairs*. New York: Columbia University Press.

Swisher, Carl Brent. 1943. *American Constitutional Development*. New York: Houghton Mifflin.

———. 1951. *American National Government*. New York: Houghton Mifflin.

———. 1953a. *The Growth of Constitutional Power in the United States*. Chicago: University of Chicago Press.

———. 1953b. "The Post-War Constitution." In *The Gaspar G. Bacon Lectures on the Constitution of the United States 1940–1950*, 311–78.

———. 1958. *The Supreme Court in Modern Rule*. New York: New York University Press.

Taft, William Howard. 1907. *Four Aspects of Civic Duty*. New York: Scribner's.

———. 1916. *Our Chief Magistrate and His Powers*. New York: Columbia University Press.

Talkington, Henry. 1908. *Civics in the Grades*. Lewiston, ID: Lewiston State Normal School.

Tatalovich, Raymond, and Byron W. Daynes. 1979. "Towards a Paradigm to Explain Presidential Power." *Presidential Studies Quarterly* 9 (4): 428–41.

———. 1984. *Presidential Power in the United States*. Monterey, CA: Brooks/ Cole Publishing.

Taylor, Hannis. 1906. "Elasticity of Written Constitutions." *North American Review* 182 (Feb.): 204–14.

———. 1916. "A Review of President Wilson's Administration." Washington, DC: Library of Congress Collection.

Taylor, John. 1823. *New Views of the Constitution of the United States*. Washington, DC: Printed by the author, by Way and Gideon.

Taylor, Mark Zachary. 2024. *Presidential Leadership in Feeble Times: Explaining Executive Power in the Gilded Age*. New York: Oxford University Press.

Teles, Steven M. 2008. *The Rise of the Conservative Legal Movement: The Battle for Control of the Law*. Princeton, NJ: Princeton University Press.

Thach, Charles Coleman Jr. 1922. *The Creation of the Presidency 1775–1789: A Study in Constitutional History*. A dissertation submitted to the board of the University Studies of the John Hopkins University in conformity with the requirements for the degree of Doctor of Philosophy.

———. (1923) 1969. *The Creation of the Presidency 1775–1789: A Study in Constitutional History*. Baltimore: Johns Hopkins University Press. Citations are from the 1969 edition.

———. 2017. *The Creation of the Presidency 1775–1789: A Study in Constitutional History*. Carmel, IN: Liberty Fund.

Thayer, James Bradley. 1908. *Legal Essays*. Boston: Boston Book.

Thomas, George. 2000. "As Far as Republican Principles Will Admit: Presidential Prerogative and Constitutional Government." *Presidential Studies Quarterly* 30 (3): 534–52.

Thomas, Norman, Joseph Pika, and Thomas Watson. 1993. *The Politics of the Presidency*. Washington, DC: Congressional Quarterly Press.

Thompson, Joseph Parrish. 1864. *Free Government Not a Right But a Crime. An Address Delivered Before the Union League Club and Published at Their Request*. New York: Club-House, Union Square.

Thorndike, Rachel Sherman. 1894. *The Sherman Letters: Correspondence between General and Senator Sherman from 1837 to 1891*. New York: Scribner's.

Thorpe, Francis Newton. 1901. *A Constitutional History of the American People, 1776–1850*. 3 vols. Chicago: Callaghan.

Tiedeman, Christopher Gustavus. 1890. *The Unwritten Constitution of the United States: A Philosophical Inquiry into the Fundamentals of American Constitutional Law*. New York: Putnam.

Tocqueville, Alexis De. 2004. *Democracy in America*. New York: Literary Classic of America.

Travis, Walter Earl. 1967. *Congress and the President: Readings in Executive-Legislative Relations*. New York: Teachers College Press.

Tribe, Laurence H. 2008. *The Invisible Constitution*. New York: Oxford University Press.

Tribe, Laurence H., and Michael Dorf. 1991. *On Reading the Constitution*. Cambridge, MA: Harvard University Press.

Trickett, W. 1907. "Judicial Nullification of Acts of Congress." *North American Review* 185 (621): 848–56.

Truman, David B. 1955. *The Governmental Process: Political Interests and Public Opinion*. New York: Alfred A. Knopf.

Truman, Harry S. 1960. *Mr. Citizen*. New York: Popular Library.

———. 1989. *Where the Buck Stops: The Personal and Private Writings of Harry S. Truman*. Edited by Margaret Truman. New York: Warner Books.

Turner, Frederick Jackson. 1993. *History, Frontier and Section: Three Essays by Frederick Jackson Turner*. Albuquerque: University of New Mexico Press.

Tweed, Harrison. 1953. "Provisions of the Constitution Concerning the Supreme Court of the United States." In *The Gaspar G. Bacon Lectures on the Constitution of the United States 1940–1950*, 489–541.

Tugwell, Rexford G. 1969. *The Democratic Roosevelt*. Baltimore: Penguin.

———. 1977. *The Enlargement of Presidential Power*. New York: Octagon Books.

Tyler, Samuel. 1872. *Memoir of Roger Brooke Taney, LL.D. Chief Justice of the Supreme Court of the United States*. Baltimore: John Murphy and Co.

Ulrich, Marybeth P. 2012. "National Security Powers: Are the Checks in Balance?" *U.S. Army War College Guide to National Security Issues*. http://www.jstor.com/stable/resrep12027.7.

Upshur, Abel P. 1863. *The Federal Government: Its True Nature and Character Being a Review of Judge Story's Commentaries on the Constitution of the United States*. New York: Van Evrie, Horton.

US Congress. 1976. "Final Report of the Special Committee on National Emergencies and Delegated Emergency Powers." Government Printing Office, Washington, DC.

US Information Service. 1957. *President and Congress*. London: Mardon, Son, and Hall.

Upton, Ralph Richard. 1907. *American Civics Handbook*. Streator, IL: Free Press Print.

Vaughn, Justin S., and José D. Villalobos. 2015. *Czars in the White House: The Rise of Policy Czars as Presidential Management Tools*. Ann Arbor: University of Michigan Press.

Veeder, Van Vechten. 1903. *Legal Masterpieces: Specimens of Argumentation and Exposition by Eminent Lawyers*. 2 vols. St. Paul, MN: Keefe-Davidson.

Vile, M. J. C. 1998. *Constitutionalism and the Separation of Powers*. Indianapolis, IN: Liberty Fund.

Vile, John R. 2013. *The Men Who Made the Constitution: Lives of the Delegates to the Constitutional Convention*. Plymouth, UK: Scarecrow Press.

Walcott, Charles Doolittle. 1901. *Relations of the National Government to Higher Education and Research.* New York: Reprinted from *Science, N.S.* 13 (June 28): 1001–5.

Ward, Durbin. 2010. *Life, Speeches and Orations of Durban Ward of Ohio.* Kessinger Publishing.

Ward, Henry M. 1962. *The Department of War, 1781–1795.* Westport, CT: Greenwood Press.

Warren, Charles. 1908. *The History of the Harvard Law School and of Early Legal Conditions in America.* New York: Lewis Publishing.

Warren, Sidney. 1964. "The President in the Constitution." In *The Dynamics of the American Presidency,* edited by Jack L. Walker, 4–7. New York: Wiley.

Washington, George. 1858. *Diary of Washington: From the First Day of October, 1789, to the tenth day of March, 1790.* Edited by John Benson Lossing. Washington, DC: One hundred copies privately printed.

———. 1931. *The Writings of George Washington from the Original Manuscript Sources 1745–1799.* Washington, DC: Government Printing Office. Multiple volumes.

Waterman, Richard W. Forthcoming. *Through the Constitution's Eyes: An Historical Analysis of the President's Article II Powers and Duties.* Albany: State University of New York Press.

Waterman, Richard W., Sherelle Roberts, Yu Ouyang, and Seth Schockley. 2024. "How America's 18th and 19th Century Presidents Invoked Power." *Congress and the Presidency* 51 (2): 123–47.

Waterman, Richard W., Carol L. Silva, and Hank C. Jenkins-Smith. 2014. *The Presidential Expectations Gap: Public Attitudes Concerning the Presidency.* Ann Arbor: University of Michigan Press.

Wayne, Stephen J. 1978. *The Legislative Presidency.* New York: Harper and Row.

Webster, Noah. 1864. *Dr. Webster's Complete Dictionary of the English Language.* London: Bell and Daldy.

Weyl, Walter E. 1912. *The New Democracy: An Essay on Certain Political and Economic Tendencies in the United States.* New York: Macmillan.

Wharton, Francis. 1884. *Commentaries on Law: Embracing Chapters on the 643. Nature, the Source, and the History of Law; on International Law, Public and Private; and on Constitutional and Statutory Law.* Philadelphia: Kay and Brother.

Whipple, H. G. 1866. "The President and His Accomplices." *Atlantic,* Nov., 634–

White, G. Edward. 2012. *Law in American History.* Vol. 1, *From the Colonial Years Through the Civil War.* New York: Oxford University Press.

White, Leonard D. 1954. *The Jacksonians: A Study in Administrative History 1829–1861.* New York: Macmillan.

White, Theodore H. 1961. *The Making of the President 1960.* New York: Atheneum Publishers.

Whiting, William. 1862. *War Powers of the President, and the Legislative Powers of Congress in Relation to Rebellion, Treason, and Slavery.* Boston: John L. Shorey.

Wilcox, Andrew J. 1862. *A Remedy for the Defects of the Constitution.* Baltimore: Baltimore Bar.

Williams, George S. 1872. *The Constitution of the United States. For the Use of Schools and Academies.* Cambridge, MA: Welch, Bigelow.

Willoughby, Westel. 1917. *Government and Administration of the United States.* Wentworth Press.

Wills, Garry. 2011. *Bomb Power: The Modern Presidency and the National Security State.* New York: Penguin.

Wilson, Woodrow. (1885) 1981. *Congressional Government: A Study in American Politics.* Baltimore: John Hopkins University Press. Multiple volumes.

———. 1902. *A History of the American People.* 5 vols. Harper and Brothers.

———. 1908. *Constitutional Government in the United States.* New York: Columbia University Press.

Winchester, Elhanan. 1796. *A Plain Catechism. Intended for the Use of Schools, in the United States of America: Wherein the Great Principles of Liberty, and of the . . . and explained by Way of Question and Answer.* T. Dickman Press.

Wirt, William. 1849. *Memoirs of the Life of William Wirt, Attorney-General of the United States.* Edited by John P. Kennedy, 2 vols. Philadelphia: Blanchard and Lea.

Wolfensberger, Donald R. 2002. "The Return of the Imperial Presidency?" *Wilson Quarterly* 26, no. 2 (Spring): 36–41.

Wood, Gordon S. 2007. *Revolutionary Characters: What Made the Founders Different.* New York: Penguin.

———. 2017. *Friends Divided: John Adams and Thomas Jefferson.* New York: Penguin.

———. 2021. *Power and Liberty: Constitutionalism in the American Revolution.* New York: Oxford University Press.

Woodburn, James Albert, and Thomas Francis Moran. 1919. *The Citizen and the Republic; a Text-book in Government.* New York: Longmans, Green.

Woodward, Augustus B. 1809. *Considerations of the Executive Government of the United States.* Isaac Riley.

———. 1825. *The Presidency of the United States.* New York: Derick Van Veghen, for the proprietor. J and J. Harper, printers.

Woody, C. A. 1886. *Outlines of United States History: Exponential System.* Covington, IN: Teacher's Book Firm.

Wright, Benjamin Fletcher. 1958. *Consensus and Continuity, 1776–1787.* Boston: Boston University Press.

Wuerth, Ingrid Brunk. 2007. "International Law and Constitutional Interpretation: The Commander in Chief Clause Reconsidered." *Michigan Law Review* 106 (1): 61–100.

YA Pamphlet Collection. 1856. *James Buchanan, His Doctrines and Policy as Exhibited by Himself and Friends.* Champaign: University of Illinois.

Yankwich, Leon R. 1950. *The Nature of Our Freedom: An Interpretation of Our Constitutional Heritage; Its Source and Meaning.* Los Angeles: Research Publishing.

Yi, Okyeon. 2011. "Befuddling Executive Power with Executive Unilateralism in the Unitary Executive." *Korean Political Science Review* 45 (6): 223–51.

Yoo, Christopher S. 2016. "Presidential Signing Statements: A New Perspective." *University of Pennsylvania Law Review* 164 (7): 1801–34.

Yoo, Christopher S., Steven G. Calabresi, and Anthony J. Colangelo. 2004–2005. "The Unitary Executive in the Modern Era, 1945–2004." *Iowa Law Review* 90:601–825.

Yoo, Christopher S., Steven G. Calabresi, and Laurence D. Nee. 2004. "The Unitary Executive During the Third Half-Century, 1889–1945." *Notre Dame Law Review* 80:1–109.

Yoo, John Choon. 1996. "The Continuation of Politics by Other Means: The Original Understanding of War Powers." *California Law Review* 84 (2): 167–305.

———. 2004. "War, Responsibility, and the Age of Terrorism." *Stanford Law Review* 57 (3): 793–823.

———. 2006a. *War by Other Means: An Insider's Account of the War on Terror.* New York: Atlantic Monthly Press.

———. 2006b. "Exercising Wartime Powers: The Need for a Strong Executive." *Harvard International Review* 28 (1): 22–25.

———. 2009a. *Crisis and Command: The History of Executive Power from George Washington to George W. Bush.* New York: Kaplan.

———. 2009b. "Unitary, Executive, or Both?" *University of Chicago Law Review* 76 (4): 1935–2018.

———. 2020. *Defender in Chief: Donald Trump's Fight for Presidential Power.* New York: All Points Books.

Young, James Sterling. 1966. *The Washington Community.* New York: Columbia University Press.

Zelizer, Julian E. 2012. *Governing America: The Revival of Political History.* Princeton, NJ: Princeton University Press.

Index

Adams, John, 12, 15, 23–24, 26, 30, 54, 99, 129, 166, 169–70
Adams, John Quincy, 61, 132, 178–79
Adams, Samuel, 49
alien and sedition laws, 121, 129, 153
Anti-Federalist Papers, 2, 49, 53, 61, 96, 99, 167, 214, 245
appointment power, 33, 199
aristocracy, 15, 245
Arthur, Chester, 199
Article II, 6–7, 9, 40, 44, 47, 49–50, 58–61, 63, 66–70, 72, 74–75, 78–79, 222, 226, 239–40, 242, 246–47, 251, 253, 255, 268
Articles of Confederation, 27–29, 31, 36, 41, 50, 118, 120, 123, 135, 137, 154, 228, 240
authoritative documents, 83, 93, 97
autocracy, 1, 14, 250, 256, 258; autocratic presidency, 1, 14, 16, 214, 229–30, 248, 268

Biden, Joseph, 21, 71, 250, 263
Bill of Rights, 33, 88, 127, 244
Blackstone's Commentaries, 84, 86, 88, 121
Buchanan, James, 19, 63, 143, 147–48, 152, 179, 182, 191–93, 195
Bush, George Herbert Walker, 69

Bush, George Walker, 19, 70, 217, 240, 247, 249, 251, 253

Carter, Jimmy, 68
checks and balances, 11, 14, 46, 226, 230, 240, 247–48, 257
chief executive, 1, 19, 33, 36, 42, 60, 68, 70, 220, 229, 253
civil war, 6, 12–14, 21, 55, 63, 72, 75, 83, 88–89, 105, 116, 122, 127–29, 137–40, 153, 155, 157–59, 184–85, 191, 193, 197, 203, 205, 210, 217, 258, 263–66
Cleveland, Grover, 64, 199–200
Clinton, Bill, 69, 202, 253
colonial governors, 32, 58–59, 117
commander in chief, 8–9, 16, 33, 36, 52–53, 57, 68, 72, 79, 95, 117, 195, 228, 246, 255
Coolidge, Calvin, 92, 221–22
committee of detail, 45–46
committee on postponed matters (Committee of Eleven), 46
committee on style and arrangement, 46–47
congress, 2, 7, 8, 18, 20, 23–25, 28–31, 37, 40–43, 45–50, 53, 58, 61, 68–70, 72, 74–79, 81, 83, 89, 95–100, 104, 106, 108, 119–20, 123,

congress *(continued)*
137, 139, 142, 144–49, 153–54,
156, 158, 161, 167–71, 173–74,
176–78, 180–83, 191–92, 195,
198, 201, 204, 220, 222–23, 225,
227–30, 232–33, 235–41, 244, 247,
251, 253–54, 257–59, 261, 263–64,
267; congressional, 171, 179, 224;
congressmen, 64, 263; continental
congress, 33, 41, 51, 118, 126
Constitutional Centennial Committee,
89, 104
Constitutional Convention, 27, 31, 36,
39, 43–44, 47, 53, 59, 69, 94, 99,
108, 118, 133, 179, 225, 231–32,
258

Declaration of Independence, 15, 32,
109, 118, 123–24, 154, 179; Virginia
Declaration of Rights, 33
delicate, 40
demagogue, 11, 16, 19, 55, 263
despotism, 12, 18, 158, 196; despot,
17, 63
dictatorship, 13, 16, 18–19, 79,
196–97, 215, 249, 255, 264, 270
Douglas, Stephen, 145–46, 148, 150
Dred Scott decision, 97–98, 139, 146,
152, 191, 235

Eisenhower, Dwight, 67
emergency power, 19–20, 229, 240,
269
English Constitution, 15, 17, 36
executive power, 6–7, 10, 12–13, 15,
24–25, 28, 33–34, 39, 41, 44, 47,
52–54, 60, 63–64, 69–70, 73–74,
77–78, 169, 177, 179–81, 184–87,
199, 217, 219–21, 223, 225–27,
230–33, 240, 245–46, 250–51, 255,
257, 264

Federalist Papers, 2, 11, 36, 42, 52–53,
55, 61, 94, 121, 126, 228, 240, 263
Fillmore, Millard, 190–91
Ford, Gerald, 253
founders, 11, 16, 23, 31, 53, 70, 74,
109, 130, 184, 197, 207, 240, 253
framers, 2–3, 6–8, 10–11, 13, 16, 21,
23, 27, 31–32, 36, 38–39, 41–48,
53–55, 57–58, 61, 66, 68–71, 73–74,
77–78, 80, 93, 99–100, 104, 117–18,
123, 129, 135, 153, 164–65, 191,
196–97, 207–209, 213–14, 216–17,
225–26, 228, 230–32, 240–48, 256,
263, 266, 268
Franklin, Benjamin, 11, 43

Garfield, James, 157, 198–99
Grant, Ulysses, 198, 226
Great Depression, 12, 19, 66, 217, 222

Hamilton, Alexander, vi, 11, 26, 28,
37–38, 42, 95, 103, 169, 184, 196,
223, 225–26, 228, 238–40, 254, 268
Harrison, Benjamin, 33, 199, 200
Harrison, William Henry, 188–89
Hayes, Rutherford, 150, 196, 199
Hoover, Herbert, 12, 19, 66, 222–23
House of Representatives, 48, 103,
123–24, 150, 153, 169, 177, 186,
192

insurrection, 5, 10, 16, 21, 113, 192,
214, 250, 262–63, 270

Jackson, Andrew, 62, 70, 77–78, 132,
134–35, 179–89, 192, 195, 201, 226,
232–33, 239, 246
Jackson, Robert, 76
Jackson, William, 99
Jefferson, Thomas, 11, 14–15, 17–18,
23–26, 30–32, 87–88, 99, 121, 129,

130, 135, 149, 158, 169–75, 179, 195, 201, 221, 233, 240, 260
Johnson, Andrew, 17, 64, 197–98, 201, 210, 235
Johnson, Lyndon, 4, 13, 68, 215, 223
Johnson, Samuel, 40, 172

Kansas-Nebraska Act, 142–45, 191
Kennedy, John, 68
kings, 14, 17, 27; kingship, 116
Korean War, 78

law of nations, 8, 117
law schools, 80, 82–86, 89, 93
Lecompton Constitution, 145, 147–48, 151–52, 191
legislative power, 10, 17, 24, 60, 64, 67, 78
Lincoln, Abraham, 6, 17–19, 21, 72, 89, 136, 138, 144–47, 154–55, 173, 181, 193–98, 201, 210, 246, 259, 264
living constitution, 35, 60, 63, 159, 203–209, 211–15, 217–18, 222, 224, 229, 252, 264, 267–68
Louisiana Purchase, 172, 174

Madison, James, 11, 23–25, 31–32, 39, 47, 61, 70–71, 88, 99–103, 107, 119–23, 132, 167, 169, 171, 174–76, 178–79, 196, 225–26, 239–40, 244
magistrate, 25, 33, 38–40, 45, 178, 187–88, 201, 239
Marshall, John, 37, 82–83, 86–88, 131, 165, 171, 234
Meese, Edwin, 238, 241–44
militia, 33, 45, 49, 52, 183, 192
Missouri Compromise, 143–43, 191
monarchy, 11, 15, 27–28, 32, 39, 41, 43–44, 52, 63, 71, 74, 77, 116, 196
Monroe, James, 7, 109, 123–25, 132, 173, 176–79, 239

New Deal, 19
Nixon, Richard, 14, 20, 68–69, 215

oath of office, 16, 44, 168, 184, 188, 198
Obama, Barack, 70, 249
office of legal counsel, 19, 236, 243
originalist interpretation, 53, 73, 166–67, 240, 247, 252, 268

Patrick Henry, 41, 51
pardon, 33, 45, 49–50, 53
Pierce, Franklin, 17, 143–44, 191
plenary power, 9, 77, 257
Polk, James, 8, 189, 194, 195, 201, 239
presidential power, 1–21, 24, 26–28, 30, 32, 34, 36, 38, 40, 42, 44–48, 50, 52, 54–60, 62, 64, 66, 68, 70–80, 82–84, 86, 88, 90, 92, 94, 96, 98, 100, 102, 104, 106, 108, 110, 112, 115–18, 120, 122, 124, 128–32, 134–36, 140, 142, 144, 146, 148, 150, 154, 156, 158–59, 161–62, 164–66, 168, 170–72, 174–76, 178–82, 184, 186–88, 190, 192–96, 198, 200–202, 204, 206–10, 212–14, 216–24, 226–30, 232, 234, 236, 238–40, 242, 244, 246–52, 254–56, 258, 260, 262, 264, 266, 268, 270
privy council, 39
Project 2025, 57

ratifying conventions, 3, 11, 23, 42, 44, 48, 49, 51, 53, 57, 120, 127, 179, 241–43; ratifying, 133, 172
Reagan, Ronald, 68, 238, 250–51, 253
recess appointment, 7
reconstruction, 6, 63, 158–59, 266
Roosevelt, Franklin, 12–13, 18, 25, 57, 67, 75, 79, 217, 222–24
Roosevelt, Theodore, 17, 76, 201, 219–20, 224

rule of law, 168, 246

Senate, 12, 14–15, 24–25, 44–46,
    48–49, 51–52, 98, 135, 150, 180,
    184–89, 197, 213, 219, 234
separation of powers, 42, 51, 67, 168,
    170, 187, 228, 252, 257
Shays's Rebellion, 30
sovereignty (sovereign), 27, 30, 63, 76,
    106, 115–39, 141–59, 174, 177, 210,
    216, 233, 262
state constitutions, 28, 31–35, 144,
    245, 269
strict constructionist, 2, 73, 129, 159,
    161, 165–66, 169, 172, 174–76,
    178–79, 189–92, 194, 197, 199, 201,
    203–6, 208, 214, 226, 232, 239, 247,
    254–55, 264, 268
strongman, 1, 14, 16, 214, 263
Supreme Court, 50, 62, 65, 73, 79,
    82–83, 91, 98, 107, 111–12, 121,
    131, 140–41, 149, 162–63, 165,
    171–72, 191, 200, 204, 207, 209,
    211–12, 217, 220, 222, 224, 227,
    229–30, 235–37, 239, 241, 245, 247,
    250; court room, 97; courts, 7–9, 42,
    77, 78, 81, 84–85, 87–88, 109, 142,
    153, 157, 183, 186, 196, 200, 219,
    232, 238, 243, 250, 252, 253, 267;
    courts martial, 264, federal courts,
    159, 228, 234; state courts, 153;
    Supreme Court Justice, 236, 243

take care clause, 7, 16, 74, 168, 182,
    185, 187, 226, 246, 250, 255
Taft, William Howard, 65, 201,
    220–21, 227
Taney, Roger, 89, 141, 153
Taylor, Zachary, 190
treaty power, 8; treaty-making power,
    8, 95, 117
textualist interpretation, 40, 59, 73,
    268

Truman, Harry, 1, 15, 67, 76
Trump, Donald, 5, 14, 16, 20–21, 26,
    57, 70, 79, 214, 216, 222, 224, 220,
    230–31, 241, 248–50, 253, 263,
    268–69
Tyler, John, 143, 189–90, 195, 201, 239
tyranny, 11, 16, 18, 91, 95, 214–15,
    224, 255, 264; tyrannically, 11, 13,
    95

undefined power, vi, 6–8, 811, 192
unitary executive theory (UET), 2, 45,
    75, 159, 163, 188, 219, 221, 223–27,
    229–33, 235, 237–42, 245–55, 257,
    268, 270

Van Buren, Martin, 63, 100, 183, 188
vesting clause, 6–7, 169, 186, 222,
    245–46, 255
veto, 32–33, 45–46, 52, 161, 176–77,
    180, 189–90, 198–99, 225, 239, 247
Vietnam War, 8, 12, 215

war power, 6, 69, 79, 195, 197, 228,
    264; war powers act, 233, 239, 251
Washington, George, 13–14, 19,
    30–31, 36–39, 43–44, 53–54, 59, 64,
    96, 98, 102, 104–105, 121, 126–27,
    149, 166–70, 179, 182, 188, 190,
    192, 195, 201, 238–39, 257, 258
Watergate, 14, 251
We the People, 115, 135
Wilson, James, 44, 54, 161
Wilson, Woodrow, 18–19, 64–65, 72,
    75, 207, 235
World War I, 18
World War II, 9, 18, 57, 271, 224,
    253, 264
written constitution, 34–35, 42, 63,
    66, 126, 132, 167, 210–12, 267

Youngstown Sheet & Tube Co. v.
    Sawyer, 73, 76–77, 223

www.ingramcontent.com/pod-product-compliance
Lightning Source LLC
Chambersburg PA
CBHW021216270326
41929CB00010B/1155